LOVE, INT.
AFRICAN AMERICAN COUPLE

This exciting new text on counseling African American couples outlines critical components to providing culturally sensitive treatment. Built around a framework that examines African American couples' issues as well as the specific contextual factors that can negatively impact their relationships, it:

- Addresses threats to love and intimacy for Black couples
- Provides culturally relevant, strengths-based approaches and assessment practices
- Includes interesting case studies at the conclusion of each chapter that illustrate important concepts.

The chapters span the current state of couple relationships; readers will find information for working with lesbians and gays in relationships, pastoral counseling, and intercultural Black couples. There is also a chapter for non-Black therapists who work with Black clients. Dispersed throughout the book are interviews with prominent African American couples' experts: Dr. Chalandra M. Bryant, relationship expert Audrey B. Chapman, Dr. Daryl M. Rowe and Dr. Sandra Lyons-Rowe, and Dr. Thomas Parham. They provide personal insight on issues such as the strengths African Americans bring to relationships, their skills and struggles, and gender and class considerations. This must-read book will significantly help you and your clients.

Katherine M. Helm, PhD, is a Professor of Psychology and Director of Graduate Programs in Psychology at Lewis University, and is a practicing psychologist.

Jon Carlson, PsyD, EdD, ABPP, is a Distinguished Professor of Psychology and Counseling at Governors State University, and a psychologist at the Wellness Clinic in Lake Geneva, Wisconsin.

THE FAMILY THERAPY AND COUNSELING SERIES

SERIES EDITOR
JON CARLSON, Psy.D., Ed.D.

THE FAMILY THERAPY AND COUNSELING SERIES

SERIES EDITOR
JON CARLSON, Psy.D., Ed.D.

LOVE, INTIMACY, AND THE AFRICAN AMERICAN COUPLE

Edited by
Katherine M. Helm and Jon Carlson

Routledge
Taylor & Francis Group

NEW YORK AND LONDON

First published 2013
by Routledge
711 Third Avenue, New York, NY 10017

Simultaneously published in the UK
by Routledge
27 Church Road, Hove, East Sussex BN3 2FA

Routledge is an imprint of the Taylor & Francis Group, an informa business

© 2013 Taylor & Francis

Library of Congress Cataloging in Publication Data
Love, intimacy, and the African American couple / edited by
Katherine Helm, PhD & Jon Carlson, PsyD.
    pages cm. – (Family therapy and counseling)
   Includes bibliographical references and index.
   1. African Americans – Marriage. 2. Couples therapy.
   I. Helm, Katherine (Katherine M.) II. Carlson, Jon.
   E185.86.L68 2013
   616.89'156–dc23   2012038701

ISBN: 978-0-415-89262-9 (hbk)
ISBN: 978-0-415-65649-8 (pbk)
ISBN: 978-0-203-81771-1 (ebk)

Typeset in Baskerville
by HWA Text and Data Management, London

To: Anton Lewis—my husband, friend, and love
For: my daughter Abigail Lewis. May you use the wisdom of this
book in your relationships
Thanks to: Luke & Beverly Helm, Anton Lewis,
Edmund Kearney, Jon Carlson, Kevin Cokley, Gordon Pitz,
Jamie Kontos, and the Chicago Chapter of the Association of
Black Psychologists for your invaluable insights and support
Katherine M. Helm

To: my colleagues in the Division of Psychology & Counseling at
Governors State University for over forty years of support and caring
Jon Carlson

CONTENTS

CONTENTS

CONTRIBUTORS

Editor Biographies

Katherine M. Helm is a Professor of Psychology and Director of Graduate Programs in Psychology at Lewis University where she happily teaches a wide range of graduate and undergraduate counseling and psychology courses. Dr. Helm is also a licensed psychologist. She regularly sees individual clients and couples and supervises a clinical training program for masters and doctoral practicum students. She is an active member of the Association of Black Psychologists and the American Psychological Association. Dr. Helm's scholarly contributions and interests are in the areas of: individual and couples counseling, sexuality issues and education, training and supervision, multicultural issues in counseling, the treatment of trauma for sexual abuse, pedagogy of multicultural courses, and cultural sensitivity training. Dr. Helm has counseling and consultative experience in psychiatric hospitals, community mental health, college counseling centers, and agency settings.

Jon Carlson, PsyD, EdD, ABPP, is Distinguished Professor, Psychology and Counseling, at Governors State University and a psychologist at the Wellness Clinic in Lake Geneva, Wisconsin. Jon has served as editor of several periodicals including the *Journal of Individual Psychology* and *The Family Journal*. He holds Diplomates in both Family Psychology and Adlerian Psychology. He has authored 170 journal articles and 60 books, including *Time for a Better Marriage, Adlerian Therapy, Inclusive Cultural Empathy, The Mummy at the Dining Room Table, Bad Therapy, The Client Who Changed Me, Their Finest Hour, Creative Breakthroughs in Therapy, Moved by the Spirit, Duped: Lies and Deception in Psychotherapy*, and *Never Be Lonely Again*. He has created over 300 professional trade video and DVDs with leading professional therapists and educators. In 2004 the American Counseling Association named him a "Living Legend." In 2009 the Division of Psychotherapy of the American Psychological Association (APA) named him "Distinguished Psychologist" for his life contribution to psychotherapy and in 2011 he received the APA Distinguished Career Contribution to Education and Training Award. He has received similar awards from four other professional organizations. Recently he syndicated an advice cartoon, "On The Edge," with cartoonist Joe Martin. Jon and Laura have been married for 45 years and are the parents of five children.

Contributor Biographies

Tennille Allen is an Assistant Professor of Sociology at Lewis University, where she is also Program Director of both African American Studies and Applied Sociology and Political Science. She has a Bachelor of Arts from the University of Illinois at Urbana-Champaign and Master of Arts and Doctor of Philosophy degrees—both in Sociology—from Northwestern University. She is an urban sociologist, whose research explores social networks, capital, and support among low-income and working-class African American women, mixed-income public housing, boundary-making within African American communities, and intersectionality theory.

Sharon Bethea, PhD, is an Associate Professor in the Department of Counselor Education, Inner City Studies and African/African Studies at Northeastern Illinois University. Sharon Bethea's research interest includes: "Social Justice Counseling Paradigms," "The Resiliency of African American children," "Strengths of the African American community," "The impact of Oakland Freedom Schools on the wellbeing of African American children," and The Development of a Counselor's Identity." Sharon Bethea is the Leadership Development Chair of the Association of Black Psychologists and past President of the Chicago Chapter of the Association of Black Psychologists. Sharon Bethea has been providing psychological and educational services for inner city families and communities for over 25 years.

Nancy Boyd-Franklin, PhD, is an African American psychologist and a Distinguished Professor (Professor II) at Rutgers University in the Graduate School of Applied and Professional Psychology. She is the author of numerous professional articles and chapters and five books including: *Black Families in Therapy: A Multisystems Approach* (Guilford Press, 1989) and an editor of *Children, Families and HIV/AIDS* (Guilford Press, 1995). Her books include *Reaching Out in Family Therapy: Home-based, School and Community Interventions* with Dr. Brenna Bry (Guilford Press, 2000) and *Boys Into Men: Raising Our African American Teenage Sons* with Dr. A.J. Franklin (Plume, 2001). Guilford Press published the second edition of *Black Families in Therapy: Understanding the African American Experience* in 2003. She is currently writing a book entitled: *Therapy in the Real World: Intervention Strategies for Clinicians*. An internationally recognized lecturer and author, Dr. Boyd-Franklin has written articles on issues such as multicultural treatment approaches, cultural competency, ethnicity and family therapy, the treatment of African American families, extended family issues, spirituality and religion, home-based family therapy, group therapy for Black women, HIV and AIDS, parent and family support groups, community empowerment, and the Multisystems Model. Dr.

Boyd-Franklin has received numerous awards from professional organizations. These have included: an Honorary Doctorate from the Phillips Graduate Institute in 2006, the Ernest E. McMahon Award from Rutgers University in 2005 for the development of a creative, multilevel community intervention, and the Solomon Carter Fuller Award from the American Psychiatric Association in 2005 for outstanding contributions to the field through scholarship and programs related to the treatment of African Americans. The Graduate Student Association at Rutgers (GSAPP) in 2004 gave her the "Professor of the Year Award." In 2003, she received the "Ethnic and Racial Diversity Award" from the National Council of Schools of Professional Psychology. Division 43 of the American Psychological Association acknowledged her work with the "Family Psychologist of the Year Award" in 2003. In 2001, she received the Drs. Charles and Shirley Thomas Award from Division 45 of the American Psychological Association. She received the "Outstanding Contribution to the Field" award from the Association of Black Social Workers in 2001 and the "Distinguished Psychologist of the Year Award" from the Association of Black Psychologists in 1994. In 1995, she was invited by President Bill Clinton to present her community and family interventions at the first White House Conference on AIDS.

Chante' D. DeLoach is a licensed clinical psychologist; and founder and Executive Director of her private practice, luminesce psychological services, llc, where she provides clinical services to individuals, couples, and families from culturally diverse backgrounds. In addition, Dr. DeLoach is an Associate Professor of Clinical Psychology at the Chicago School of Professional Psychology, Chicago and serves as the Co-Chair for The Chicago School of Professional Psychology Center for African Psychology. She teaches courses in family systems, couples and family therapy, traumatilogy, and cultural and international psychologies.

Beverly Greene, PhD, ABPP, is a Professor of Psychology at St. John's University and a practicing psychologist in New York City. Dr. Greene is Board Certified in Clinical Psychology by the American Board of Professional Psychology; and is a Fellow of the Academy of Clinical Psychology, the American Psychological Association and seven of its divisions (9, 12, 29, 35, 42, 44, 45, 52). She is the author of over 100 publications in the psychological literature, including 10 books. She has received over 35 national awards for distinguished contributions to the profession and its scholarly literature, including 12 awards for publications deemed significant contributions to the psychological literature on marginalized populations. She is the 2009 recipient of the American Psychological Association's award for Distinguished Contributions to Psychology in the Public Interest, the APA Society for the Psychology of Women's prestigious 2008 Carolyn Wood Sherif Award, and the APA Society for Clinical Psychology's 2006 Florence Halpern Award for Distinguished Contributions to Clinical Psychology. She and co-author Dorith Brodbar are recipients of the Association for Women in Psychology's 2012

Jewish Women's Caucus Award for Scholarship for their edited book, *A Minyan of Women: Family Dynamics, Jewish Identity and Psychotherapy Practice* (Routledge, 2011). She is a co-editor of forthcoming *Psychologist's Desk Reference 3rd edition* (with Gerald Koocher and John Norcross, Oxford University Press), and *Psychological Health of Women of Color* (with Lillian Comas-Diaz, Praeger Press).

Anton M. Lewis, PhD, currently teaches as an Assistant Professor of Accounting at Saint Xavier University, in Chicago. His courses consist of teaching graduate Managerial Accounting, as well as undergraduate Business, Ethics and Society classes. His dissertation research utilized Critical Race Theory to investigate the experience of Black accountants in the UK through qualitative methods. His future research goals include expanding to develop critical models and conceptual frameworks of multicultural diversity of accountants in government bodies and accountancy organizations in the United States. He is currently studying a research sample of professional Black accountants in the US for a forthcoming pilot study. His publications include *A Critical Analysis of the Black Accounting Experience in the UK: Tales of Success and Failure in the British Professional Workplace* (Lambert Academic Publishing, 2012), *Frankenstein is Black: A Tale of Black Accountancy* that is currently under review, and a book chapter currently in progress, titled *No, I Don't Know How to Play Golf: Social Networking and Support*.

Marissa N. Petersen-Coleman, PsyD, is a postdoctoral fellow at Emory University School of Medicine. She recently graduated from the Clinical PsyD program at The Chicago School of Professional Psychology, where she specialized in International Psychology and Human Rights. Her research and clinical work center on post-traumatic adjustment, cultural and spiritual reflection, and privileging indigenous modes of healing. Her previous publications include: "A critical analysis of complex trauma: A Rwandan fight for liberation" (with S. Swaroop, *Journal of Pan African Studies*, 4 (2011), 3, 1–19); "African spiritual methods of healing: The use of Candomblé in traumatic response" (with C. Deloach, *Journal of Pan African Studies*, 3 (2010), 8, 40–65); and "Colonialism and trauma: Intersections of the past and present" (with S. Swaroop and A. Uttamchandani, *Traumatic Stresspoints*, 24 (2010), 2, 4–6). Dr. Petersen-Coleman will co-author a chapter focused on childhood depression within the *Handbook of Depression* (3rd ed.) for Guilford Press, with an anticipated publication date of 2013. Dr. Petersen-Coleman's field collaborations include: Candomblé temples in Salvador da Bahia, Brazil; Children's homes in Pretoria and Johannesburg, South Africa; resettlement communities in El Salvador; and non-profit development and programming in Accompong Town, Jamaica.

Khyana K. Pumphrey, PhD, LPC, is a faculty member at Waukesha County Technical College in the Department of Communication Skills/Social Science where she teaches Psychology of Human Relations, Abnormal Psychology,

Workplace Psychology, Race and Ethnicity, and Introduction to Ethics. She also provides clinical services at REACH, Inc. Comprehensive Mental Health Clinic in Glendale, Wisconsin. Dr. Pumphrey holds a Bachelor of Science Degree in English Education from the University of Wisconsin-Whitewater, MS in Curriculum and Instruction from the University of Wisconsin-Milwaukee, and PhD in Urban Education-Counseling Psychology from the University of Wisconsin-Milwaukee. Dr. Pumphrey completed clinical training at St. Luke's Medical Center in the Cancer Counseling Center, pre-doctoral internship at the University of Wisconsin-Madison's Counseling and Consultation Services and post-doctoral training with Wheaton Franciscan Behavioral Health. She is currently licensed as a professional counselor in the State of Wisconsin and served a brief stint on the State of Wisconsin Regulation and Licensing Board for Professional Counselors.

Feliesha Shelton-Wheeler, PsyD, is a staff therapist at the Counseling Center at Gannon University in Erie, Pennsylvania. She received her PsyD in Clinical Psychology at The Adler School of Professional Psychology in Chicago, Illinois in October 2012. Dr. Shelton-Wheeler's clinical interests include interpersonal relationships, academic achievement of college students, and women's issues with a special interest in issues related to African American females. Dr. Shelton-Wheeler also enjoys creative writing and journaling in her spare time.

Philip B. Spivey, PhD, is a clinical psychologist in independent practice in New York City. He has over 30 years of clinical experience with people from diverse ethnic and socio-economic backgrounds, including Black men, Black couples and same-gender-loving men and women. His areas of expertise and interest include treating chemical and psychological dependencies, identity conflicts, depression, life-stage issues, as well as fostering spiritual well-being. Dr. Spivey has taught at the City College of New York; supervised and taught at the Fifth Avenue Center for Mental Health, the Gay Men's Health Crisis, and at the Lesbian, Gay, Bisexual and Transgender Center—all in New York City. He has worked in a variety of outpatient hospital settings including positions as Director of Outpatient Services at the Smithers Center of Roosevelt Hospital; Senior Psychologist at Bellevue Hospital Center; and Program Coordinator for the Long Island College Hospital outpatient alcoholism treatment services.

Byron Waller is an Associate Professor of Counseling on the Clinical Mental Health Counseling sequence at Governors State University. Dr. Waller received his PhD in Counseling Psychology from Loyola University Chicago, Master's in Counseling from Chicago State University, Bachelor's degree from Grace College, and Associate's degree from Moody Bible Institute. Dr. Waller has specialties in areas of Christian, career development and counseling, multicultural and cross-cultural, and African American counseling. His research focuses on the experiences of African Americans in their cultural context, career development process and educational performance, forgiveness, financial honesty and infidelity, and multicultural and diversity issues. He has written and presented in areas of counselor training and supervision, Christian counseling, clinical training, crisis management, multicultural counseling, couples finances, forgiveness, clinical supervision, career development, and spirituality. He also enjoys and maintains a private practice.

Torrey Wilson, PhD (Loyola University, Chicago, 1997), has extensive academic, administrative and clinical experience. Dr. Wilson is President-elect of the National Council of Schools and Programs of Professional Psychology (NCSSP) and outgoing President of the Chicago Chapter of the Association of Black Psychologists. He is currently Associate Professor in the clinical psychology program at the Illinois School of Professional Psychology. He has served as the doctoral program director at the Adler School of Professional Psychology; Program Director at Gilda's Club Chicago, a cancer support community; and was the Director of GAPS (Guidelines for Adolescent Preventive Services) at the American Medical Association. Dr. Wilson serves on several professional and community boards. His interests include health psychology-behavioral medicine, public health, and diversity. His clinical work has focused on couples, families, and adolescents. Additionally, Dr. Wilson has worked in the substance abuse arena, along with dual diagnosis. Dr. Wilson also has extensive consulting experience, having provided management and diversity training to corporations and organizations.

Shena J. Young, MEd, MA, is a fourth year doctoral student at the Chicago School of Professional Psychology in Chicago, Illinois. She received her Master's of Education in Counseling from the University of Houston and earned a Bachelors of Science degree in Human Development and Family Sciences from the University of Texas at Austin. Her clinical interests and experience are in sexual trauma, women's issues, and performing art communities. She is passionate about addressing disparities in mental health care for marginalized communities, exposing the mental health effects of sex trafficking, and international psychology as a point of intervention abroad. As a clinician she offers therapy from an existential-relational framework and is exploring creative avenues for incorporating trauma sensitive yoga in the healing process.

SERIES EDITOR'S FOREWORD

It took a lot of blood, sweat and tears to get to where we are today, but we have just begun. Today we begin in earnest the work of making sure that the world we leave our children is just a little bit better than the one we inhabit today.

(Barack Obama, Victory Speech)

According to Stanford University Professor Richard Ralph Banks in his book *Is Marriage for White People? How the African-American Marriage Decline Affects Everyone*, 70 percent of African American woman are unmarried—single, widowed or divorced—compared to 45 percent of their white counterparts. African Americans have higher divorce rates than any other group. Fifty percent of black couples divorce within the first 10 years of marriage compared to about a third of whites. The title for the book came from a 2006 *Washington Post* article (http://www.washingtonpost.com/wp-dyn/content/article/2006/03/25/AR2006032500029.html) in which a writer quotes an African American sixth grader in a Washington, D.C. classroom who said: "Marriage is for white people." Despite President Obama's observation, is it possible for African-Americans to have functional marriages?

I have spent most of my professional career teaching graduate students in the counseling program at Governors State University. Many of our students are African Americans who talk openly about their personal struggles with marriage. Initially I believed that marriage was the same regardless of ethnicity and that maybe this relational challenge had more to do with some other variable such as being a graduate student. However, the more I listened and observed the more it became apparent that there were unique challenges to marriage in the African American community. The couples' therapy literature did not provide much help as few studies or professional articles specifically addressed creating successful marriage for African American couples.

Since that time I have heard stories of how educated Black men are in short supply and that Black women need to marry non-Black men or feel forced to stay in unsatisfying marriages or not have a marriage. Racism and economic hardships have impacted marital intimacy creating a Black marriage crisis. Explanations for the relationship problems are often that Black men are irresponsible and promiscuous while Black women are aggressive and unreasonable. This is certainly not accurate as many Black couples have close, intimate, long-term marriages. What are the real issues then? What can couples' therapists do to address these issues and others that are unique to this community? The authors of this volume are hopeful as they tailor treatment to Black couples and answer these questions as they show others how to provide meaningful service.

In *Love, Intimacy, and the African American Couple*, Dr. Katherine Helm and her colleagues address the present and future of African American marriage and the unique challenge this group presents to couples' therapists. The many talented contributors are practitioners in the field who have specialized in working with this underserved population. They present a realistic assessment of the situation and provide many creative strategies for changing the picture painted by Dr. Banks.

Jon Carlson, PsyD, EdD
Series Editor

Reference

Banks, R.R. (2011) *Is Marriage for White People? How the African-American Marriage Decline Affects Everyone*. New York: Dutton.

PREFACE

My wife and I were sitting on the couch the other day discussing the state of marriage in the Black community. Even though, in our ethnically diverse city, we are surrounded by a significant number of Black professionals, we simply do not know that many Black married couples. We find this both disappointing and frightening. So while discussing this very point with my wife, I began to think about why strong romantic partnerships in the Black community are important. Clearly, there is a structural fissure currently taking place in Black marriage. Black marriage is now a rarity, a situation much changed from the African American marriage experience of the 1960s. A lot of the data on the subject both within this text and elsewhere highlights the steady decline of Black marriage rates at a time when marriage in general is on the decline in the West as a whole. Yet this behooves the question of why are Black marriage rates declining so much faster?

I suggest that the incarceration of so many U.S. Black men has fractured the potential of Black women and Black men to enter into stable unions of marriage (Delgado, 1995). Quite simply Black women cannot marry Black men who are physically incarcerated in such large numbers. Black marriage becomes the victim. Tropes of the male Black buck as sexual predator (Pattons and Snyder-Yuly, 2007) often creates what Majors and Billson (1993) denote as the "cool pose". Here bell hooks suggests that this fosters "patriarchal masculinity" leading to familial family terrorism that erodes commitment and trust. Black unemployment and underemployment also undermine strong Black family structures. As is discussed in this book, African Americans in general and Black men in particular are far less likely to wed if they are not employed.

Threats to Black marriage are both internal and external. Sue et al. (2008) highlights the existence of "racial microaggressions" as those subtle as well as hidden racialized slights common in the workplace that often denigrate and invalidate the culture and experience of people of color. He goes further to produce a given taxonomy of microaggressions and outlines the existence of environmental microaggressions (Sue 2010). Such a microaggression is constituted by the absence of people of color within an organization that "Blacks are not welcome" within this workplace. I posit that in a similar fashion the dwindling number of Black married couples serves as a "marriage environmental microaggression". With so few Black couples that look similar, happy, and healthy to each other, the authenticity of Black marriage is subtly undermined. This lends credence to racialized tropes underlining the pathos of Black relationships. At a hidden level a tacit acceptance exists in society of maladjusted baby mamas and baby daddies. Black families, no longer headed by a two-parent majority, may struggle as a result as single parents frequently have fewer resources (economically, emotionally, and socially) than two. Thus, although single mothers and fathers work hard to raise strong children with less, the burden they face is often much more than society may realize. We ask much of these single parents. As such, society views fractured Black family relations as the authentic family structure and expect Black families to look this way. As a result, Black marriage has degenerated beneath acceptable (White) societal norms.

So given my rather pessimistic assessment of the state of Black marriage where does this leave us? As with any other attack I believe the Black community must resist hidden subtle assaults. Recognition of the detrimental existence and very real harm of the structural forces arrayed against Black marriage is paramount. Next, a full acceptance of the individual foibles of Black men and women must be addressed at the level of the personal. At the same time we must accept the exterior threats to Black unions given the structural context of trying to enter and maintain Black marriage in a systemically racist society (Bell 2005). That is to say that Black couples must unite and stay strong against the hidden forces within themselves and externally to maintain the Black family unit. An argument exists for the creation of a coalition of Black married couples to redress the notion of Black marriage as inauthentic or deviant, like the usual racialized expectations fostered by a dominant majority society expecting the worst from Black marriage. Long-term committed Black coupleships, married or not, serve as the backbone to strong Black families. Although the Black community holds marriage in high regard, room must be made for non-traditional coupleships as well (e.g. long-term cohabiting couples). The key, here, is the emotional health of the couple. The authors of this text have produced excellent contributions in illuminating the myriad contradictions, highs and lows that constitute Black marriage and coupleships in the United States as it stands today.

Anton Lewis, PhD
Saint Xavier University
Chicago, IL

References

Bell, D. (2005). *The Derrick Bell Reader*. New York, New York University Press.
Delgado, R. (1995). *The Rodrigo Chronicles: Conversations about America and Race*. New York, New York University Press.

Majors, R., & Billson, J.M. (1993). *Cool Pose: The Dilemmas Of Black Manhood In America*. New York, Touchstone.

Pattons, T. O., & Snyder-Yuly, J. (2007). "Any Four Black Men Will Do: Rape, Race, and the Ultimate Scapegoat." *Journal of Black Studies* 37(6): 859–895.

Sue, D.W. (2010). *Microaggressions in Everyday Life: Race, Gender and Sexual Orientation*. New Jersey, John Wiley & Sons.

Sue, D.W., & Capodilupo, C.M., et al. (2008). "Racial Microaggressions in the Life Experience of Black Americans." *Professional Psychology: Research and Practice* 39(3): 329–336.

Part I

INFLUENCES THAT SHAPE LOVE, INTIMACY, AND RELATIONAL PATTERNS AMONG AFRICAN AMERICAN COUPLES

1

INTRODUCTION

Katherine M. Helm and Jon Carlson

The status of the African American couple has changed dramatically from being marginalized and not allowed to marry to having an African American First Couple in the White House. There is a paucity of literature on the unique experiences and struggles of Black couples. Most therapists are trained to "give a nod" to cultural factors, but there is little written about the *specific* issues of couples of color. Instead we frequently assume a colorblind approach to couples' treatment with a superficial acknowledgement of cultural factors in the therapeutic process. Some things have changed for the African American couple while other things have remained the same. Threats to Black marriage remain both internal and external and these residual threats from the time of slavery still impact every African American couple today. To provide therapy to African American couples as though they are the same as couples from other cultural backgrounds will lead to ongoing treatment failure.

This chapter is an overview about love and intimacy issues with African American couples. The current literature will be reviewed in brief and the structure of the book will be defined. Chapter topics will be explained as to their relevancy in treating African American couples. An overview of treatment implications is provided and each will be explored more extensively in other chapters. Finally, threats to couples' intimacy will be introduced. Readers should note that in this book, the terms "African American" and "Black" will be used interchangeably as many African Americans self-refer by both terms. Culturally sensitive clinicians should ask their African American clients about preferred racial terminology instead of assuming that all Black Americans self-identify with the United States Census (2010) term—African American. Additionally, as we highlight in Chapter 5, some Black Americans are not African American at all but may instead refer to themselves as Haitian American, Jamaican American, Nigerian American, etc.

Introduction

Romantic and marital relationships in the United States are in a period of transition. More families are being led by single women, the divorce rate for the general population is between 40 and 50 percent depending on whether it is a first, second or third marriage for the couple (http://divorcerate2011.com/divorce-updates/) and the numbers of cohabiting couples continues to rise. Society has traditionally recognized marital relationships as the only legitimate relationships in which sex and having children occur (King, 2008). This is no longer the case. The structure of couples and families in the United States is rapidly changing. Influences changing the demographics of traditional marriages include individuals marrying multiple times, step-families, geographic distance from one's family of origin, changing gender roles, delaying marriage until one's late 20s or 30s, and wide-reaching economic uncertainty. This is even more the case with African American couples and families. In 1963 over 70 percent of Black families were led by married couples. Today that number is around 40 percent. Forty-three percent of Black men and 41.9 percent of Black women have never been married compared with 27.4 and 20.7 percent respectively for whites. The percentage of African American women who are married declined from 62 percent to 36.1 percent between 1950 and 2000 (Blackman, Clayton, Glenn, Malone-Colon, and Roberts (2005). It is hypothesized that given current trends, many Black women will never marry. Since the late 1970s, African American marriages have been on the decline and are currently in a crisis state due to the multiple forms of oppression Blacks face.

Why a Book on African American Couples?

The literature has long recognized the unique struggles African American couples face because of: historical and current racial oppression, the negative impact of racial stereotypes of Black men and women (and how these can be enacted upon one another in romantic relationships), unequal gender ratios, lower levels of economic and educational attainment than majority couples, higher incarceration rates than the general population, and the role strain African Americans can feel due to having to survive in multiple racial worlds (i.e. double-consciousness issues). When Blacks do marry, their divorce rates are higher than whites (67 percent versus 50 percent for whites) and Blacks are less likely to remarry—especially Black women (Pinderhughes, 2002). Literature about gay and lesbian Black couples and intercultural (e.g. African and African American marriages) scarcely exists (Greene, Boyd-Franklin, & Spivey, Chapter 6). Pinderhughes (2002) states that "It is not possible to understand African American marriages fully without attention to the social, economic, racial, and historical factors that have stressed male-female relationships beyond those stresses experienced by majority couples" (p. 269). The dismal incarceration rates of Black males and the number of Black women and children living below the poverty line plays a role in weakening the stability of Black romantic and marital relationships. In 1985, there were 73 African American males to 100 females in the general population. Among marriageable (i.e. employed) males there were 43 males to 100 females (Pinderhughes, 2002). Today this number is much worse. Almost 1 in 5 Black men 20 years old and older is unemployed and many more are underemployed. The United States Bureau of Statistics reports that 34.5 percent of Black men and 26.3 percent of Black women are unemployed which is three times the national average. Statistically race appears to be a bigger factor in their unemployment compared to age, income or even educational level. Several researchers note (Bryant & Beckett, 1997; Davis, Williams, Emerson, and Hourd-Bryant, 2000; Pinderhughes, 2002; Staples, 2007) that Black men who are unemployed or underemployed are much less likely to marry. Additionally, Black heterosexual women, many of whom prefer Black male partners, are less likely to consider a man "marriageable material" if he is unemployed or underemployed.

Research shows that Blacks highly value marriage and many report a desire to be married; however, Blacks, independent of educational level, tend to marry at later ages than their white counterparts (28.6 for Black men and 28.1 for Black women versus 27.2 for white men and 26.6 for white women) and many Blacks are simply declining marriage overall. Blackman et al. (2005) discuss the pros of marriage specific to African Americans. They state that "On average, married African Americans are wealthier, happier, and choose healthier behaviors than their unmarried peers; their children typically fare better in life – differences that indeed seem to stem largely from marriage itself" (p. 4). In their groundbreaking review, *The Consequences of Marriage for African Americans: A Comprehensive Literature Review*, Blackman et al. (2005) state ten major findings about African American marriage:

1 Marriage clearly appears to promote the economic, social, familial, and psychological well-being of African American men and women.
2 While both Black men and Black women receive a marriage premium, this premium in most cases appears to be larger for men.
3 Economically, marriage appears to benefit Blacks more than whites.
4 Overall, Black women appear to benefit from marriage substantially less than do white women.
5 Black–white differences in marital quality seem to constitute an important reason why Black adults, and particularly Black women, typically benefit less from marriage than do whites.
6 Parental marriage produces important benefits for African American children.
7 Parental marriage appears to be especially important for the well-being of young African American males.
8 In some areas, Black children seem to benefit more from parental marriage than do white children, whereas in others, the reverse is true.
9 The reasons for some apparent racial differences in the consequences of marriage for children are not clear; and further research in this area is needed.
10 For policy makers who care about Black Americans, marriage matters.

The Blackman et al. (2005) review highlights many of the reasons that Black couples come to therapy—they recognize the economic, psychological, intimacy, and social benefits of marriage and long-term romantic relationships, and also see it as important to raising children. Although their review focused specifically on marriage, many of the same benefits can be found within stable, long-term, romantic relationships as well. Clinicians should recognize that couples may choose to cohabitate or have long-term commitments to one another without being married. This is especially true amongst African Americans and these couples also present for counseling. Non-married couples face both similar and unique issues in their relationships to married couples.

One of Blackman et al. (2005) findings that we focused on in this book is why African Americans report a lower level of marital quality than whites (finding #5). They state that "on average, the marriages of Whites appear to be marked by more happiness and less conflict than those of African Americans. The lower average quality of African American marriages, in turn, seems to reduce the benefits to adults that those marriages might otherwise yield" (p. 5). We discuss many of the threats to intimacy that support this finding. These threats will be reviewed later in this chapter and throughout the book.

There is very little independent literary analysis and empirical study of African American couples. Nancy Boyd-Franklin's (1989) foundational foci on African American families and couples provides a critical groundwork for study; however, there remains a paucity of literature that focuses on African American couples independent of the Black family. Bryant's (Bryant & Wickrama, 2005; Bryant, Wickrama, Bolland, Bryant, Cutrona, & Stankik, 2010) study of African American couples has recently begun to change this. To separate Black couples for independent study outside of their families is an artificial distinction. This is both a strength and weakness of this book. We decided to focus on African American couples only, because there is substantial exploration in the literature on the Black family (McAdoo, 2007). Clinicians who primarily work with couples only are less likely to be exposed to family literature—thus a book on African American couples is in order. It is critical, though, that those who see African American couples also study the literature on Black families as this is a rich source of necessary information critical to the treatment of African American couples and families.

Additionally, similar to other couples' therapy texts, we do not focus on children's impact on the couple. Literature exploring child-raising practices and the impact children have on couples' relationships is examined at length in the family therapy literature. We decided to limit our focus to the couple themselves, given the lack of critical analysis of African American couples. We realize that these are artificial distinctions; however, these foci are beyond the scope of this book and these topics are covered more comprehensively elsewhere in the literature (e.g. Boyd-Franklin, 1989; McAdoo, 2007; Dixon, 2007)

Finally, there is a great deal in the popular media about African American women's struggle to find "good black men." For example, comedian Steve Harvey's book *Act Like a Lady, Think Like a Man* (2009) was immensely popular. His book was a frequent topic on talk shows, radio, and television and has recently become a popular film. Some African American women began to see this book as a guideline for having a successful relationship and key to their understanding African American men. Other popular books focusing on problematic African American relationships include: *The Conversation: How Men and Women Can Build Loving, Trusting Relationships* (Harper, 2010); *Is Marriage for White People? How the African American Marriage Decline Affects Everyone* (Banks, 2011), and *The Denzel Principle: Why Black Women Can't Find Good Black Men* (Izrael, 2010). None of these authors are mental health professionals, yet their works are shaping popular discourse on African American male–female relationships. Earlier versions of these current books were popular in the 1990s and also explored similar issues (e.g. Chapman, 1995; Goldsby-Grant, 1995); however, these books were written by mental health professionals. CNN has produced news stories about declining African American marriage rates and the plight of the single, middle-class, Black woman (http://racerelations. about.com/gi/o.htm?zi=1/XJ&zTi=1&sdn=racerelations&cdn=newsissues&tm =36&gps=90_272_1020_612&f=00&tt=2&bt=0&bts=0&zu=http percent3A// articles.cnn.com/2010-08-10/living/black.church.women.single_1_black-women-black-church-black-men percent3F_s percent3DPM percent3ALIVING, August 10, 2010) and the George W. Bush Administration was so concerned about the decline of Black marriage in the African American community that it developed initiatives to improve Black marriage rates by providing funding to churches to encourage and train couples on how to get and stay married.

Thus it appears that everyone seems to be discussing Black couples' issues and publishing anecdotal data about African American romantic relationships except the mental health professionals who see the struggles these couples face first hand in treatment. The view of African Americans and African American couples is distorted within the American psyche, which provides further justification for this book. Popular media certainly influences our views of family, marriage, couples' ways of relating to one another, and gender roles. We frequently ingest a steady diet of negativity when it comes to our views on Black couples, as there are few positive portrayals in the media. Even in the 1980s when the immensely popular *Cosby Show* was on the air, it was criticized for being unrealistic given that it depicted a positive professional African American couple raising children. Such positive portrayals continue to be sparse, although part of the renewed interest in Black relationships may be attributed to President and First Lady Obama, another positive Black professional couple raising their two children.

We want treating therapists to be informed through the psychological literature and through interviews with African American couples and expert therapists who regularly see African American couples in counseling. We do not want clinicians to rely on the popular media as a primary source of information about these couples. African Americans have a long history of being pathologized and problematized in the popular media and in the psychological literature. These views are frequently one-sided, sensationalized, stereotyped, and often discriminatory. We therefore attempt to provide a deeper understanding as to why society depicts Black couples negatively and then unpack the damage these views have on such couples.

Threats to Intimacy

This book focuses on the threats to intimacy in African American couples' relationships. Specifically, common threats to African American couples' intimacy include: a gender imbalance (more women than men) which frequently distorts the distribution of power in couples' relationships and especially in the dating arena; negative stereotypes of African American men and women (which couples unconsciously internalize and then view and treat one another according to these stereotypes); the lack of financial, educational, and health care resources working class couples have which can be stressful on their relationships; lack of significant positive models of healthy long-term relationships within the African American community; the damaging legacy of slavery on the African American psyche; consistent societal racism, sexism (for women), and oppression on Black Americans; damaging media portrayals of African Americans and African American romantic relationships; and many more that will be explored in-depth through the book.

As stated previously, clinicians need a comprehensive understanding of these influences in the lives of their Black couples. The treatment of African American couples should always include an assessment of how these threats influence their presenting issues. This is discussed at length in Chapter 7. Couples themselves may not be aware of these influences; however, they may be significant barriers to intimacy all the same. Clinicians unaware of these threats simply cannot do effective treatment with African American couples. Non-African American clinicians may be especially vulnerable to minimizing the role of oppression, racism, and the internalization of negative stereotypes in the lives of their couples, which is precisely why we spend a great deal of time reviewing these contextual factors and explaining how they can manifest within African American couples' lives.

Couples' Clinicians

Couples' clinicians are taught how to do couples therapy; however, the majority of therapeutic models still do not adequately address culture, and/or cultural issues are considered as an afterthought to the overall approach, as opposed to being a central consideration. This is problematic as it assumes that all couples are the same. Racial issues in the United States have typically focused on African and European Americans. The racial discourse of colorblindness can significantly limit couples' clinicians' ability to effectively do counseling with African American couples and is disrespectful of clients' racial identity and experiences. The assumption that "we are all the same" is both ludicrous and disrespectful to oppressed groups in our society. The experience of being Black in the United States is unique. There are many similarities that oppressed groups face; however, there are also significant differences. These differences are highlighted in this book. Understanding the unique experiences of African Americans and the impact these experiences have on couples' relationships is critical to effective couples' treatment. Without a significant understanding of these issues, couples' clinicians will not be able to understand couples presenting issues at the level of depth necessary to form solid rapport and do quality therapy.

Conversely, assuming that all clients of the same racial/ethnic background have the same traits and issues is equally offensive. Couples' clinicians must balance their perspective and understand that African American couples have both similar and unique issues to non-African American couples. This will enable them to use their global training as a foundation in treating Black couples while still incorporating the culturally sensitive approaches and issues specific to this group explored in this text. This balanced perspective is critical to effective treatment of African American couples in therapy.

Uninformed/culturally insensitive clinicians can actually harm Black couples. Historically and currently, Black couples have had to form romantic relationships against the backdrop of racial and gender oppression. This book will sensitize clinicians to how these factors impact Black couples' issues with intimacy and love.

Socio-Historical Influences

Each chapter in this book begins with a socio-historical perspective. This is a unique focus of this text which contextualizes the influences of African American couples' presenting issues in therapy. Black people in the United States continue to be negatively influenced by the legacy of slavery, the onslaught of stereotypic media influences, the suspicion they face in society as a "problem people," the struggle to find positive images of themselves on television, in the classroom, and in non-African Americans' treatment of them as a collective. These damaging influences are frequently (and often unconsciously) internalized and impact the ways in which Black couples relate to one another. This is why a socio-historical lens is vital in unpacking issues unique to these couples. Clinicians need a critical awareness of these underlying influences and this text can be used to help the conceptualization of Black couples' presenting issues in couples counseling. To date, there are very few texts aimed at mental health practitioners working with Black couples. Historically the psychological literature has pathologized Black romantic and marital relationships because they have always been compared to a white majority model of how these relationships are "supposed to occur." These views have shaped Black relational patterns and clinicians frequently judgmental understanding of them. Black, non-nuclear, female-led families have historically been labeled as dysfunctional although, in today's world, many majority families are also female-led. These damaging views have contributed to a distorted view of Black romantic and marital relationships.

Problem-Focused versus Strengths-Based

Despite the multiple negative influences on Black romantic relationships, many are enduring and consistent over time. Black couples frequently struggle to get together, stay together, and be emotionally and psychologically intimate with one another. Black couples benefit from and utilize kinship networks (extended family and friends), spirituality and religious community support, and community resources to strengthen their relationships and get through stressful times (Boyd-Franklin, 1989). Clinicians who understand and utilize the strengths Black couples bring to counseling can provide their clients with supportive, informed, and culturally sensitive approaches to counseling. Quite simply, Black couples, and probably most couples, respond better to treatment that highlights their strengths and allows them to use these strengths as effective coping tools for problem-solving.

This book highlights many of the obstacles and problems Black couples face in getting together and staying together. In fact at times, many of our co-authors were simply overwhelmed by the number of problems depicted in the literature about Black couples. It *can* be overwhelming; however, this text serves to educate couples' clinicians and counselors-in-training about issues and contextual factors they may be unaware their Black couples face. Thus, it can seem at times that this book focuses overmuch on problems. Our intention is to inform readers of these problems but also educate them about Black couples' strengths. Both are critical components of successful couples' treatment with Black couples. Strengths-based approaches are the key to successful resolution of barriers to intimacy. In our interview with author and popular couples' therapist Audrey Chapman she reflected that, "once Black couples get together, especially if there are children, they tend to work very hard to stay together. We are all about family. Family is very important to who we say we are." This is an incredible strength of the African American couple and family.

Format and Intended Audience

This book will explore the current literature on how clinicians can effectively work with Black couples in counseling. It will review clinically relevant practices for working with different types of Black couples and include specific intervention strategies and assessment practices. This text is directed at practicing clinicians and counselors-in-training. We assume the reader has some basic knowledge of couples' treatment and psychological theory and uses this text to supplement their knowledge of African American couples' treatment specifically. This book is written for practitioners by practicing clinicians. Each chapter reviews an important sub-topic relating to love, intimacy, and the African American couple. Each author has significant expertise in the treatment and analysis of African American couples' issues.

Overview of Chapters

The book is divided into four parts and includes 11 chapters. Each part groups together similar topics to allow the reader an easy-to-navigate structure. Many clinicians read chapters most relevant to the current couples they are working with and this book was written with that in mind. Each chapter stands alone—therefore, readers can explore chapters out of order and still get a comprehensive view of intimacy issues and barriers to treatment, specific to Black couples. This is why each chapter provides an individual socio-historical context. Interviews with experts in the field are distributed throughout the book and provide a rich, well-rounded context for support of the literature and treatment interventions discussed in this book. Additionally, several Black couples were interviewed. These interview data are summarized at the end of the book. The chapter overviews follow.

Part I: Influences That Shape Love, Intimacy, and Relational Patterns among African American Couples

The opening chapter by Katherine Helm and Jon Carlson provides an overview of love and intimacy with Black couples. They provide a literature review and then clearly define the book's structure. The reader will be able to better understand the threats to intimacy that Black couples face and the corresponding treatment implications.

In the second chapter, Sharon Bethea and Tennille Allen describe past and present societal influences on African American couples impacting love and intimacy. These influences include slavery, differences in the ways African Americans define family (e.g. non-nuclear), the imbalanced gender ratio, the pathologization of Black romantic relationships, socioeconomic, educational and employment issues as they relate to couples' relationships, stereotypes of black men and women that erode couples' intimacy, and other major influences on the lives of African American couples that impact all aspects of their relationships. Treatment implications are also examined. Clinicians are provided with a necessary context in which to identify and assess when and how these influences are impacting couples. The authors also provide specific strategies for addressing the negative impact of these influences on couples within their relationship including strengths-based, culturally sensitive approaches.

Part II: Socialization Factors of Black Love and Intimacy

Chapter 3 by Feliesha Shelton-Wheeler begins a new section on the socialization factors of Black love and intimacy. Shelton-Wheeler explores the nature, structure, dynamics, gender attitudes, formation, and maintenance of Black male–female relationships. She utilizes a developmental perspective on African American relationships from childhood to adulthood to educate clinicians about how these influences shape Black male–female romantic relational patterns. This chapter examines current sexual attitudes in the Black community and how these attitudes are communicated to Black men and women. After reading this chapter, clinicians will understand specific treatment implications based on chapter topics enabling them to view Black couples through a culturally appropriate lens and develop culturally sensitive treatment plans. Shelton-Wheeler concludes the chapter by exploring implications for emotional intimacy within African American male–female relationships.

In Chapter 4, Tenille Allen and Katherine M. Helm discuss specific threats to *emotional intimacy* for African American couples. Their chapter provides an in-depth critical socio-historical and political analysis of past and present threats to emotional intimacy within Black couples' relationships. The authors explore how power and gender dynamics influence African American relationships and couples' patterns of relating to one another. Differences between African American and majority couples' operationalization of gender roles, the distribution of household tasks, sexual norms, and communication patterns are explained. Allen and Helm also examine the multiple threats to the couples' friendship and sense of "we-ness" and how clinicians can address these threats in counseling. A thorough review of treatment implications for intimacy threats as it relates to the therapeutic process with Black couples is provided. Specific clinical strategies to address emotional intimacy threats are discussed.

Part III: Subgroups within African American Couples

Chapter 5 is a unique chapter not extensively covered in the couples' and family literature. Black couples are typically viewed as a homogenous group, neglecting the immense diversity within these couples, thereby contributing to a rather limited view of Black couples' relationships. Many Black couples are not simply "African American." Black, a racial distinction, covers all people of African descent from the African diaspora. In the United States, many Black couples are comprised of African American, Haitian, Caribbean, Nigerian, Cameroonian, Black British, Afro-Cuban, and other ethnic unions. The literature has largely ignored the existence of these couples. The issues of Black intercultural couples are unique and worthy of study. Chante' DeLoach, Marissa Petersen-Coleman, and Shena Young explore issues unique to Black couples of different ethnic backgrounds. When intercultural Black couples date or marry they face distinct cultural challenges including values differences, communication and/or language issues, differing worldviews, and sometimes divergent views on the role of extended family, gender roles, and child-raising practices, all of which can threaten intimacy. DeLoach et al. provide clinicians with specific guidelines for working with intercultural Black couples including: specific strategies for increasing clinicians' sensitivity and awareness of how cultural differences between couples of the same race but different cultural backgrounds influence Black couples' relationships, as well the unique treatment issues that may result from these pairings. DeLoach et al. also review treatment implications with intercultural Black couples and demonstrate how to use treatment strategies through a case study.

Chapter 6 is an especially important chapter in that love and intimacy issues in gay and lesbian African American couples are significantly under-explored. Authors Beverly Greene, Nancy Boyd-Franklin, and Philip Spivey take an in-depth look at socio-historical, political, and contextual factors impacting gender, sexual orientation, and race amongst Black gay and lesbian couples. They sensitize clinicians to the multiple issues of oppression and identify what these couples frequently have to face in their relationships as well as the impact these stressors can have on those couples. Greene et al. explores couples' "double-minority" status and how gays and lesbians often have to negotiate their place in society and their legitimacy and status as a couple in ways that heterosexual couples never do. These authors utilize a case study to explore how these dynamics are sometimes operationalized in the relationships of gay men and lesbian women. Greene et al. review treatment implications and threats to emotional intimacy, allowing clinicians to assess for these threats in their couples' counseling practices with gay and lesbian couples.

Part IV: Assessment and Treatment of Black Couples in Counseling

A critical part of the counseling and therapeutic process begins with a thorough assessment of the couple. Katherine Helm and Torrey Wilson outline important areas of assessment for and specific to African American couples. These authors guide clinicians in culturally specific assessment practices and provide a detailed background as to why assessment with African American couples differs in many ways from assessment with majority couples. Chapter 7 provides a "how to, hands-on assessment approach" that is easy to use with couples and gives specific strategies for how to perform culturally sensitive assessments with African American couples. The authors highlight rapport-building techniques and provide suggestions for how to anticipate and cope with the cultural mistrust that some Black couples may demonstrate in counseling. Because many Black couples are aware that historically and currently the field of mental health has pathologized their relationships, they may be reluctant to share certain details about themselves with mental health practitioners, for fear of being judged. Helm and Wilson also provide a list of assessment instruments that have been normed on Black populations that can be helpful in performing thorough assessments with African American couples.

Chapter 8 provides specific treatment strategies and techniques with African American couples. Chante' DeLoach examines current theoretical models' application to counseling with Black couples and explores culturally sensitive ways of providing Afrocentric, solution-focused, Adlerian, family systems, emotion-focused, and insight therapies in the provision of counseling African American couples. DeLoach also discusses ways to make traditional theoretical approaches appropriate for Black couples.

Khyana Pumphrey's Chapter 9 provides culturally sensitive guidelines for non-Black therapists working with Black couples. She reviews the literature on culturally competent counseling strategies and sensitizes clinicians to the challenges non-Black therapists may face in working with Black couples in treatment (e.g. working with cultural mistrust). Pumphrey explores how racial similarity/dissimilarity can influence the counseling relationship. She details culturally sensitive approaches with couples and provides specific strategies for clinicians to increase their cultural sensitivity in working with the African American couple.

In Chapter 10, Byron Waller provides an overview of pastoral counseling with African American couples. Given that a significant majority of African American couples report high levels of spirituality and religiosity (approximately 79 percent), clinicians working with African American couples need to understand how the couples' spiritual life impacts their issues and presentation for counseling. Black couples are far more likely to seek counseling from their pastor and church community than from a professional counselor. Waller provides a historical overview of the Black church's role in the African American community and discusses its changing role today. He explains that both historically and currently the Black church has been one of the few places Black men and women have been able to escape the oppression of negative societal views about Blacks and Black culture and hold leadership positions. The church is one place African American couples can find positive role models of other committed couples. Waller emphasizes that couples' clinicians working with Black couples need to be aware of the role that religion, spirituality, the church community, and values socialized through the church (or other religious communities) influence the couple. Waller implores counselors to utilize couples' spiritual identity as a strength in the counseling process and also discusses the importance of counselors working collaboratively with pastors in the counseling process. Waller explores specific ways to integrate a spiritual focus into counseling for Black couples desirous of such an approach. Spiritually focused counseling is a culturally sensitive approach for many Black couples and understanding most Black couples necessitates an understanding of their spirituality.

In the final chapter, Katherine Helm, Anton Lewis, and Jon Carlson summarize the book's findings, implications for effective counseling practice, and provide resources for couples' clinicians doing counseling with African American couples.

Two other exciting features of the book include our "Interviews with the Experts" and "Interviews with African American Couples." These interviews make the material discussed in the book come alive in genuine and relatable ways. Our experts, Thomas Parham, Ph.D., Chalandra Bryant, Ph.D., Audrey Chapman, M.A., Daryl Rowe, Ph.D., and Sandra Lyons-Rowe, Ph.D., have significant clinical experience working with African American couples. They have seen them in treatment, and written and studied them extensively. We asked our experts about culturally specific strategies in working with African American couples, specific issues they perceive as threats to intimacy with these couples, strengths and weaknesses of Black couples, and other questions specific to their areas of expertise. Our experts provide a critical analysis of the issues these couples present with for counseling and their etiology. Each has a unique perspective.

14

Conclusion

It is our hope that clinicians and counselors-in-training use this book as a tool to augment their existing knowledge on couples' treatment and to sensitize them to the unique issues faced by African American couples. We include a review of already-existing treatment approaches and discuss specific ways to make them more culturally sensitive to African American couples. We also include several African-centered approaches to couples' treatment. Most of these approaches require some specific training; however, the ideology and African-centered focus behind these approaches can be practiced and should further sensitize clinicians to effective treatment strategies. African American couples are less likely than majority couples to seek couples' treatment from a professional counselor. As discussed in Chapter 10, many prefer to seek counseling through their church/religious communities. The fact remains, however, that some Black couples can and do seek treatment—most often when they are in crisis. A culturally sensitive clinician who can quickly assess the couples' issues and understands the unique contextual factors African American couples face is more likely to form solid relationships with their couples and to provide quality treatment. This book serves to provide clinicians and counselors-in-training with a critical set of tools and to expand worldviews to incorporate the unique issues Black couples face in their relationships and in couples' treatment.

References

Banks, R.R. (2011). *Is Marriage for White People? How the African American Marriage Decline Affects Everyone*. New York: Penguin.

Blackman, L., Clayton, O., Glenn, N., Malone-Colon, L., & Roberts, A. (2005). *The Consequences of Marriage for African Americans: A Comprehensive Literature Review*. New York: Institute for American Values.

Boyd-Franklin, N. (1989). *Black Families in Therapy: A Multisystems Approach*. New York: Guilford.

Bryant, C.M. & Wickrama, K.A.S. (2005). Marital relationships of African Americans: A contextual approach (pp. 111–134). In V. McLoyd, N. Hill, and K.A. Dodge (Eds.). *African American Family Life: Ecological and Cultural Diversity*. New York: Guilford Press.

Bryant, C.M., Wickrama, K.A.S., Bolland, J.M., Bryant, B.M., Cutrona, C.E., & Stankik, C.E. (2010). Race matters, even in marriage: Identifying factors linked to marital outcomes for African Americans. *Journal of Family Theory and Review*, 2(3), 157–174.

Bryant, S.A. & Beckett, J.O. (1997). Marital quality in Black and White marriages. *Journal of Family Issues*, 26, 431–441. Effects of status resources and gender on role expectations of African American couples.

Chapman, A.B. (1995). *Entitled to Good Loving: Black Men and Women and the Battle for Love and Power*. New York: Henry Holt & Company.

Davis, L.E., Williams, J.H., Emerson, S., and Hourd-Bryant, M. (2000). In M.L. Hecht, R.L. Jackson, II, S.A. Ribeau (Eds.). *African American Communication: Exploring Identity and Culture, 2nd Edition*. Mahwah, NJ: Lawrence Erlbaum Associates, Inc.

Dixon, P. (2007). *African American Relationships, Marriages, and Families: An Introduction*. New York: Routledge.

Goldsby-Grant, G. (1995). *The Best Kind of Loving: A Black Woman's Guide to Finding Intimacy.* New York: Harper Collins.

Greene, B., Boyd-Franklin, N., & Spivey, P.B. (in press). African American lesbians and gay men in couples relationships: Threats to intimacy and considerations in couples psychotherapy. In K. Helm & J. Carlson (Eds.) *Love, Intimacy and the African American Couple.* New York: Routledge.

Harper, H. (2010). *The Conversation: How Men and Women Can Build Loving, Trusting Relationships.* New York: Gotham Books.

Harvey, S. (2009). *Act Like a Lady, Think Like a Man: What Men Really Think About Love, Relationships, Intimacy, and Commitment.* New York: Amistad Harper Collins Publishers.

Izrael, J. (2010). *The Denzel Principle: Why Black Women Can't Find Good Black Men.* New York: St. Martin's Press.

King, B.M. (2008). *Human Sexuality Today*, 6th edition. Englewood Cliffs, NJ: Prentice Hall.

McAdoo, H.P. (Ed.). (2007). *Black Families* (pp. 157–171). Thousand Oaks, CA: Sage.

Pinderhughes, E.B. (2002). African American marriage in the 20th century. *Family Process* 41(2), 269–282.

Staples, R. (2007). An overview of race and marital status. In H. P. McAdoo (Ed.), *Black Families* (pp. 281–296). Thousand Oaks, CA: Sage.

The United States Bureau of Statistics. (2010). http://2010.census.gov/2010census/.

EXPERT INTERVIEW

Dr. Chalandra M. Bryant is a Professor of Child and Family Development at the University of Georgia. Her research focuses on close relationships and the ability to sustain close intimate ties, particularly the manner in which social, familial, economic, occupational, and psychosocial factors are linked to marital and health outcomes.

Describe your empirical research with Black couples

My current research focuses on African American married couples. I take a contextual approach as a means of understanding the behavioral and cultural processes underlying African American marital relationships. We are currently studying 700 African American couples. Relationships function within a complex context involving social factors, individual characteristics, and resources which may contribute to the manner in which spouses interact with their partners. If we want to improve our understanding of marital behaviors and attitudes, then context needs to not only be considered but carefully examined as well. This reminds us that relationships do not function in a vacuum; they are shaped by the world around us. My colleagues and I show various stressors (which characterize the context in which many Blacks live) can contribute to couple interactions and marital outcomes. Our data show that husbands' perceptions of disorder in their community are associated with the manner in which they behave toward their wives. We also found that the manner in which spouses behave toward their partners is associated with their own, in addition to, their partner's health. Health is a key aspect of the project, not simply because health and marriage are linked, but also because Blacks experience a disproportionate number of physical illnesses. They are also more likely to experience ill health throughout life. Our analyses show that among Black wives, the association between body mass index (BMI) and depressive symptoms is mediated by couples' behavioral closeness, which we assessed in terms of spending time together on a hobby, going out with one another, talking, and intimacy. This means that, interestingly, the direct path from wives' BMI to wives' depression was significant, but when behavioral closeness is added to the model, the direct path is no longer significant. This suggests that increasing

17

the activities that spouses engage in together would be a way of reducing that link between depressive symptoms and body weight.

Describe the strengths and weaknesses of Black couples

Strengths

Some studies have suggested that Black couples are typically willing to share household tasks. This is a great strength given that, for economic reasons, in many cases, both partners need to work outside the home. Another strength is that despite numerous adversities and stressors, many Blacks do, indeed, marry.

Challenges

I prefer the term "challenges" rather than "weaknesses." A few of the challenges include trust and obligations to extended family.

Trust is a concern among Black couples, yet little research examines how Black couples generate a sense of trust and maintain it over the course of marriage.

Obligations to extended family. Throughout the literature, we read about the importance of extended family among Blacks. Extended family members serve as an important, supportive base. People typically think about the recipients of that support rather than those providing the support. Many Black couples who are better off than their family members share their resources with extended family—even when those resources are not particularly plentiful. Moreover, Blacks are willing to take in relatives (whether they are related by blood or not) in need of help. This, too, is sometimes done when resources are not particularly plentiful. These are issues that (although they can be considered strengths) can contribute to stress, which, in turn, can affect the marriage.

Blacks tend to be more likely to enter marriage with children than are other groups. Studies indicate that marital satisfaction decreases with the birth of children. Those two findings would suggest that some Black couples entering marriage with children may start out with relatively lower levels of marital satisfaction simply because the presence of children may add stress to the newly formed union. Just think about the new responsibilities that accompany instant parenthood. Think about spouses learning how to co-parent with their partner's former spouse or with their own former spouse, for that matter. This could contribute to stress in a newly formed marriage.

Why do so many Black marriages fail?

First, I think it is important to note that for two decades—between 1940 and 1960—most African American families were marriage-based. People tend to overlook that—thereby making it sound as though marriage has never worked for Blacks, and that simply is not true. The number of married African Americans peaked during that period. That said, there are obstacles contributing to marital discord. For example, due to socioeconomic conditions, many Blacks live in economically disadvantaged neighborhoods which are characterized by high levels of stress, unemployment, and sometimes violence. Such conditions or pressures can negatively impact interpersonal relationships. Daily experiences of racial discrimination operate as a powerful chronic stressor that can contribute to emotional distress, which, in turn, can also impact relationships. Thus, researchers and therapists need to understand that racial disadvantages are not entirely confounded by socioeconomic factors.

Issues faced by middle class versus working class Black couples

First, I'd like to commend you! You didn't ask about poverty-stricken Blacks. Much research focuses on economically disadvantaged Blacks; few acknowledge other social classes in this population. Ignoring these other socioeconomic groups hinders our ability to understand the heterogeneity among Black families. Furthermore, a myopic focus makes it difficult to determine whether research findings are generalizable across various socioeconomic groups within the Black population.

When addressing the issue of middle class Blacks, we must acknowledge time. Time is an issue—that is, time spent in middle class status. Blacks who are relatively new to this status are especially likely to provide economic support to their relatives who are struggling financially.

Let's get back to sharing of tasks. Although Black men do help with household tasks, women still perform a substantial amount of the child care and domestic duties. Decades ago, we know that Black women experienced more domestic related stress than Black men. This has been linked to class. Some researchers note tensions between the sexes in middle class Black families, even though Black, middle class women have clear advantages compared to Black women in lower socioeconomic groups.

Suggestions for therapists working with Black couples in counseling

Therapists may want to become familiar with the cultural nuances and communication patterns characterizing, as well as the unique stressors experienced by, any particular group they are serving. Context is an integral component of working with couples, and this might be particularly true for minority couples. Our framework underscores the complexity of intrapersonal, interpersonal, familial, community, and environmental factors that impact marriages among Blacks. This framework is especially significant because it incorporates race-specific factors— and by so doing, acknowledges context. Interpersonal interactions and the way one perceives such interactions are intricately tied to race and culture.

2

PAST AND PRESENT SOCIETAL INFLUENCES ON AFRICAN AMERICAN COUPLES THAT IMPACT LOVE AND INTIMACY

Sharon Bethea and Tennille Allen

Introduction

This chapter will describe in detail the past and present societal influences on African American couples that impact love, intimacy, and presenting issues in therapy. These influences include slavery, differences in the ways African Americans define family (e.g. non-nuclear), the imbalanced gender ratio, the pathologization of Black romantic relationships, socioeconomic, educational, and employment issues as they relate to couples' relationships, stereotypes of African American men and women that erode couples' intimacy, and other major influences on the lives of Black couples that impact all aspects of their relationships. Clinicians will be provided with a necessary context in which to identify and assess when and how these influences are impacting the couples as well as provide some specific strategies for addressing the impact of these influences on the couple and within their relationship.

Synthesizing the dearth of literature concerning African American female and male intimate/romantic relationships is challenging at best. Any attempt to conceptualize African American romantic relationships must consider possible variations in structure as well as the influence of historical, cultural, social, and psychological factors. This chapter briefly outlines socio-historical factors such as African traditions, the MAAFA (also known as the Transatlantic Slave Trade System), daily lives of enslaved African communities, and racist/ oppressive institutional structures and ideologies specific to the African American experience. In addition, more contemporary issues will be explored including: African American family structure and function, mate selection and availability, and gender socialization.

As this chapter will illustrate, many African American couples persist in a celebrated cultural context characterized by cultural strengths and resiliency against a backdrop of racism and oppression. Resiliency is associated with "a set of inner resources, social competencies, [and] cultural strategies that permits individuals not only to survive, recover and thrive after stressful events, but also to draw from the experience to enhance subsequent functioning" (Stanton-Salazar & Spina, 2000, p. 229). Utilizing a strengths-based model, an examination of treatment implications that incorporate past and present societal influences on African American couples impacting love and intimacy will be explored. Clinicians will be provided with specific culturally relevant, contextual treatment strategies.

Historical Constraints on African Americans

In America there have always existed constraints on the intimate relationships of African Americans. The first African Americans, brought to the United States against their choice, had incredible strictures placed on their humanity, bodies, and their sexuality. Survival and adaptation under a system of racial, sexual, and economic domination and hostility has led to relationships that have deviated from traditional African principles that stressed "interdependence, cooperation, unity, mutual responsibility, and reconciliation" (Bell et al., 1990, p. 170). The relationships they did form were under social and cultural conditions far different than those they had experienced in their pre-colonial African homelands. The intimate relationships of African Americans have historically fused West African cultural practices with the oppressive conditions faced during enslavement and subsequent disadvantaged economic, social, and political positioning of African Americans. Slaves were not afforded the right to marry, not allowed partners of their own choosing, treated as breeders, coerced into sexual relationships, and forcibly raped (Collins, 2000; A. Y. Davis, 1983; Marable, 1983; McGruder, 2010). As is explored throughout this chapter, the legacy of slavery continues to impact African American romantic relationships today.

African Traditions that Influence the Intimate
Relationships of African American Couples

Research on African American intimate relationships is incomplete without attention to African/African American culture. African Americans are part of a cultural group whose ancestors are originally from many cultural groups of the African continent. Whereas no collection of people that relocate can transport their culture and way of life completely intact (Mintz & Price, 1992) many scholars believe that African influences continue to impact every aspect of the lives of African Americans (e.g. Akbar, 1979; Ani, 1994; Hilliard, 1992; Nobles, 1991; Warfield-Coppock, 1992). Through intergenerational transmission processes, African Americans retained specific and communal Africanisms of West and Central African cultures (Kambon, 1992; Nobles, 1991). Africanisms refer to a particular African reality, worldview, and cultural value system that African-descended enslaved people throughout the Diaspora acknowledge and/or actively participate in (Hilliard, 1997; Holloway, 2005; Kambon, 1992).

The African worldview is a holistic conception of the human condition made up of a series of interlocking systems (White, 1984). While families in the United States, following a Eurocentric framework, have long been modeled upon a nuclear family created through conjugal ties as the ideal form, West African families had been typically organized around a kinship group created through consanguineal or blood ties (Johnson & Staples, 2005; Strmic-Pawl et al., 2011; Sudarkasa, 2007). One of the key responsibilities of African culture is the establishment of institutions that maintain order, promote a system of values, and provide equal distribution of social, material, security, and economic benefits to all their members (Foster, 1983; Holloway, 2005). These features are known to have existed for centuries on the African continent and are therefore legitimately termed a part of African heritage (Strmic-Pawl et al., 2011; Sudarkasa, 2007).

For example, traditionally marriage extended ideas and cultural customs. The practices of polygyny and polyandry formed multifaceted families known as extended family consisting of two or more generations (Foster, 1983; Johnson & Staples, 2005). The structure of extended families in African societies was long-lasting, self-perpetuating over numerous generations, and transcended death. These collectives operated under a set of rules and values that supported collective survival (White, 1984). Female and male unions in traditional African societies were not only partnerships between two individuals but two kin or clan groups (Foster, 1983; Strmic-Pawl et al., 2011; Sudarkasa, 2007). Today these traditions are continued in African American families through contemporary kinship networks, which will be reviewed later in this chapter. Kinship formed the core of Africa's pre-colonial social structure and provided both the expression and the symbol for social relations (Holloway, 2005). The kinship group consists of all people in a society that acknowledges they belong to their kinship group regardless of geographic proximity or blood relationship. Individuals who are part of a kinship group share moral responsibility for helping each other and monitoring each other's behavior (Blassingame, 1972; Strmic-Pawl et al., 2011). Kinship family groups still exist today within the African American community (Blassingame, 1972; Piper-Mandy & Rowe, 2010).

Sudarkasa (2007) described two traits found in African American marriage and family patterns that are thought to be cultural retentions from West Africa: the significance of bloodlines and the essential role of extended family. Like West African families, many African American families' stability today is dependent upon the extended family. Divorce in traditional African communities did not threaten family structures because it did not lead to the disbanding of family. Sudarkasa (2007) surmises that the same trend may apply to African American marriages and families. Because of the support of extended family networks, divorce may seem less detrimental, making it more of an option when marriages are faced with challenges.

Relationships, then, were rooted in the community and, as such, ties to the entire group, rather than to one's partner, had primacy. Ironically, slaves' inability to legally wed, their lack of legal and physical control over their bodies, sexuality, and children, and those adaptations they made, such as continuing the West

African practices of "jumping the broom" as a signal of marriage, and communal forms of childcare, were seen as further proof of their inferiority and justification for their utter oppression. This was further compounded by African Americans' inability to establish conventional gender roles because of their place in the economic structure of slavery that required both men and women to work together as unpaid labor, rather than in separate spheres. Never allowed to fully participate in American culture and life, African Americans were simultaneously castigated for this supposed failure. Such patterns and practices remain ascendant currently. The majority of Africans arrived in the United States via the Transatlantic Slave Trade System (Nobles, 2008). The Transatlantic Slave Trade System can be broadly characterized by "the socio-economic power matrix presided over by a dominant group and a superstructure of racist oppression with detrimental consequences for enslaved African people and their descendents" (Payne-Jackson, 2008, p. 1a.1).

Not only did an enslaved human-based economy and subsequent economic and political arrangements block African Americans' access to full equality and educational, economic, and other structural opportunities but they also have had a deleterious impact on a more individual level, including their romantic interactions. West African gender structures were disrupted by slave's sexual exploitation. Male slaves could not provide for their families and female slaves could not take care of the children. Enslavement prevented Black men and women from fulfilling the socially acceptable gender roles of the time and forever shapes Black male and female relations in the United States.

Legislated Reproduction: The Sexual Economy of Slavery

Just as African Americans' productive labor was controlled, so was their reproductive labor. A. D. Davis (2009) expounds upon this in what she calls the sexual economy of slavery. Male enslaved Africans were often used for breeding purposes, forced to have sex with women owned by his and other Whites who enslaved Africans (Bridgewater, 2005; Hutchinson, 1997). Likewise, from the onset of puberty, female enslaved Africans/African Americans were encouraged to bear children, often through non-consensual sexual relationships, creating a natural yield to increase their enslavers' profits. Though certainly enslaved Africans/African Americans exercised some agency regarding their sexuality and partnering, it was also the case that both men and women were forced into sex with partners not of their choosing. Relationships that were established could be severed at an enslaver's whim, for financial reasons, or a punishment for perceived impudence. White men often coerced and raped Black women and as children inherited the status of their mothers, any progeny were defined as Black and were born enslaved. In these ways, African Americans were neither allowed dignity, humanity, or personhood nor were they allowed the opportunities to fully exercise agency in bonding with loved ones and ensuring their stability and security. Slaves were portrayed as hypersexual—a stereotype that persists today.

The impacts of this on African American women, men, their families, and their relationships has never been fully measured and will never be fully known, though they continue to be felt (Bell, 1999). However, it was within this environment that African American male and female relationships endured. Despite the deliberate and persistent attack on Africans/African Americans during the United States enslavement system, African influences persisted in the lives of enslaved African/ African American people in the United States (Blassingame, 1979; Foster, 1983; Holloway, 1995). African traditions and values gave African descendent people a sense of worth, dignity, belonging, meaning, and direction in this hostile environment (White & Parham, 1990). By holding on to African culture, Africans and their descendents created a "collective existence and a collective psychological space independent of White domination" (White & Parham, 1990, p. 38.). This shared African ethos served as a protective factor against "shattered black identity, legal status as property, a scientific classification as inferior beings, social invisibility, cultural suppression and lifestyles and community structures deemed pathological" (Nobles, 2008, p. 6.40).

John Blassingame (1979) documented monogamous marriages and nuclear and extended families amongst enslaved African/African American people in the United States. Blassingame asserts that these historical records indicate a strong sense of family. When the enslavement of Africans/African Americans disrupted traditional family structures, the strengths of African/African American families became the foundation and structure for survival. Despite sexual exploitation, monogamous relationships and marital fidelity were highly valued and supported (Blassingame, 1979). To preserve stability of the family, fictive aunts, uncles, and cousins were created to maintain kinships groups. Family ties were maintained by Africans/African Americans that freed themselves from their enslavers by living in the surrounding area; often risking re-enslavement (Blassingame, 1979). Blassingame concluded that these communal lives were a blend of Africans and African Americans who "shared a cultural past, a brutal reality, and an uplifting ethos of resistance and that the very existence of families, friendships, kinships and communities was one of the most tangible forms of resistance and liberation struggle" (p. 29). Thus, even today, the Black family exists outside the boundaries of a Eurocentric nuclear family model.

The intimate relationships of African Americans have historically fused West African cultural practices with the structures and strictures faced during slavery and subsequent disadvantaged economic, social, and political positioning of African Americans. At the same time, assuredly, African Americans have been exposed to, influenced by, and have internalized mainstream conventions toward partnering. The confluence of historical and contemporary racially discriminatory policies and practices has meant that Black couples have numerous barriers in completely replicating mainstream partnering patterns, however. Consequently, African Americans and their relationships have long been seen as deviant and pathological in this uniqueness as they diverge from the mainstream (Blassingame, 1979; Collins, 2000; Gutman, 1976; Hill, 2005; D. White, 1999).

In Love and Trouble: A History of Fissures within African American Male and Female Relations

In a sociological analysis that draws from African American slave narratives, oratorical, literary and musical forms, Collins summarizes the state of Black female–male relations as rooted in a tradition of "love and trouble" (2000, p. 152). She contends that this long-standing pattern of adoration and antagonism, of respect and retreat, of cooperation and conflict derives from the implementation of White patriarchal capitalist systems that have touched all aspects of African American life. These have their genesis in the United States' foundation through the enslavement of people of African origin.

For example, care work was differently arranged for African Americans and Whites during slavery. While the prevailing gender ideology meant that White women were relegated to the home and often used slave labor to raise their children, prepare their meals, and clean their homes, African American women did not have the same luxuries they provided their owners. Instead, their enslavement precluded their ability to offer these to their own families as they desired. As an adaptation to their conditions under slavery and in line with the West African cultures they came from, childcare for those too young to work was a communal effort, and was provided by other women in the community while most African American females over the age of 16 were sent into the fields. For African American men, slavery significantly limited their ability to exercise their patriarchal authority, seen as the province of men at the time.

As Black men were unable to provide economic security for their families, Black women had to seek employment in the paid labor force. This in turn necessitated that Black men contribute to care work at home. Taken together, these could be seen as further signs of Black men's inferior masculinity and a devaluation of Black femininity. Not only were men not able to access the traditional route to masculinity—economic provision for their family—but they were also feminized in their doing of tasks traditionally performed by women. At the same time, women were masculinized as they had more access to economic stability and provision compared to African American men. These stereotypes still exist today.

Powerless to challenge this system but buffeted by it nonetheless, the table was set for interpersonal strains between African American men and women. According to Collins, these "tensions characterizing Black women's necessary self-reliance joined with our bona fide need for protection, as well as those characterizing Black men's desire to protect Black women juxtaposed to their admirations and resentment of Black women's assertiveness and independence, result in a complicated love and trouble tradition" (2000, p. 157). One source of this can be found when African Americans' sexuality and sexual relationships are explored in the next section. Another major hindrance to intimacy referenced by Collins comes in negotiating gender egalitarianism and power within relationships, which is the focus of the next section.

25

The Impact of Internalized and Projected Stereotypes on Sexuality and Intimacy

The sexual exploitation mentioned above was normalized and justified through a lack of legal recognition of persons, let alone the crimes committed against them, the development of a collective blind eye, and the creation of myths around African Americans' sexual promiscuity and deviance (Higginbotham, 1992; McGruder, 2010). These historical circumstances continue to bear fruit, leading to a hesitancy to establish sex-positive discourses within institutional spaces within the Black community, such as churches, schools, and families, that began in the period after the Civil War and remains today (Douglas, 1999; C. West, 1993). Cast as hypersexual and bestial in their sexual desire and practices, many African Americans responded by donning a cloak of respectability, downplaying and dismissing the objectified and fetishized sexual images of themselves in public, with others, and to themselves so as not to reinforce the racist notions that formed these ideologies and images. As a result, fear remains that public discussions of sexuality will reaffirm the stereotypes of promiscuity, wantonness, and lustfulness, and other forms of sexual deviance long-held by Whites and internalized by African Americans. Indeed, though such sexual stereotypes may have a genesis in the antebellum United States, they continue today as they have been transmitted through messages passed from generation to generation and through various forms of popular culture, including film, television, and, most visibly, hip-hop music and videos. Therefore, it remains important that clinicians are aware of their roots as they continue to manifest in the lives and relationships of contemporary African Americans.

Though both genders are plagued by these destructive representations, their content is not identical. Throughout their residence in the United States, African American men's sexuality has been framed as violent, dangerous, and predatory (Anderson, 1999; Collins, 2000; hooks, 2004; Patterson, 1998). African American women have been considered wild and exotic sexual temptresses (Collins, 2000; Stephens & Phillips, 2003). These views are both historical and current. Exposure to these images has come in numerous forms, as they were developed to support the sexual exploitation discussed above.

Current Implications of Sexual Stereotypes on African American Relationships

The historical endurance and current inundation of these portrayals has implications for viewing one's partner as inferior, unworthy, and undesirable (Bell, Bouie, and Baldwin, 1990). Negative images that some African American men may hold of African American women include seeing them as emasculating, aggressive, controlling, unfeminine, and unattractive (Bell et al., 1990; C. Franklin, 1984; Lawrence-Webb et al., 2004). Some African American women likewise may perceive African American men as passive, unreliable, irresponsible, unfaithful, less likely to contribute, and less committed to long-term romantic relationships

26

(Bell et al., 1990; Browning & Miller, 1999; Cazenave & Smith, 1990; C. Franklin, 1984; Lawrence-Webb et al., 2004). Both African American women and men view men more negatively than they do women (Cazenave & Smith, 1990) which has significant implications for Black couples' relationships.

Indeed, insidious stereotypes shape the way that African Americans see themselves and each other, fomenting relationship and communication problems (Cazenave & Smith, 1990). These stereotypes also impair couples' ability to develop honesty and trust (Willis, 1990). Gillum (2007) suggests that men who most subscribe to negative stereotypical images are those least likely to have the ability to maintain a successful committed relationship. Successful and healthy relationships are further diminished by the socialization, personal experiences, and observations though which men and women receive messages about sex and potential romantic partners.

The Influence of Racialized Sexual Scripts

Women often receive dating and relationship scripts that are predicated upon romance in contrast to men whose scripts emphasize sex (Anderson, 1999; O'Sullivan & Meyer-Bahlburg, 2003). Negotiating within these disparate and coincidental systems often leads to ambiguity and confusion that then culminates in conflict for couples (Seal & Ehrhardt, 2003; Seal et al., 2008). Indeed, changing and divergent expectations of sex and the role it plays within relationships are a large potential source of disharmony. Gender differences around sexual attitudes, desires, frequency, activity, and attitudes around fidelity are an important source of relational tension to explore, especially as they intersect with racialized and gendered sexual stereotypes. African American women may see Black men with high sex drives or desires for certain forms of sexual activity as confirming their anxieties that he is oversexed or may seek another partner to fulfill his needs. African American men may see African American women who are sexually assertive as promiscuous, assuming that her freedom with him means that she is sexually free with other men, as well (Carey et al., 2010). These anxieties are also based in the lived experiences and observations that African Americans have around infidelity as well as the historical stereotypes about the high sex drives of African American men and women discussed earlier in this chapter. African Americans have higher infidelity rates than other racial and ethnic groups and African American men are more likely to cheat than are women (Adimora & Schoenbach, 2005; Adimora et al., 2007; Carey et al., 2010; Patterson, 1998; Pinderhughes, 2002).

A lack of emotional commitment is negatively associated with sexual fidelity (Bowleg et al., 2004). Negative images associated with African Americans and their sexuality are also implicated here: African American men who support the stereotype of promiscuous, sexually aggressive African American women, for example, also show increased concern with a partner's potential for infidelity, according to one study (Gillum, 2007). When taken with stereotypes that posit one's own infidelity as an outgrowth of one's fear that their partner is being unfaithful, such as in the Fosse (2010) study, a correlation between negative stereotypes and infidelity can be seen. Furthermore, in a situation where negative stereotypes are endorsed or internalized and negative romantic relationships are experienced, stereotypes are reinforced and self-fulfilling prophecies ensue (Marbley, 2003).

Infidelity by African American men may also be explained by the sex-ratio imbalance that first finds African American men in relative short supply compared to the number of available African American women seeking to partner with them. This provides men with a wider range of relationship options which may make monogamy less attractive.

An Imbalanced Sex Ratio

Many arguments have been made that part of the lack of monogamy stems from the sex imbalance between African American men and women. At every stage, African American men exist in lower numbers than African American women. This can be seen in their higher infant mortality rates and higher rates of death from disease and violence through each step of the life course. The African American population in the United States has the lowest ratio of men to women of any group in recent history (Adimora & Schoenbach, 2005). Social scientists began to take note of a supposed lack of suitable Black male marriage partners in the 1980s. Chief among these are William Julius Wilson who notes, along with various colleagues (Wilson, 1987; Wilson & Neckerman, 1986) that structural transformations in the economy, educational, and criminal justice systems mean that African American men have fewer opportunities to mark financial stability and are thus unable to fulfill their, potential mates, and societal expectations for a good partner.

As such, African American women who seek romantic relationships with a man of the same race are limited in their search. Furthermore, the quality of the relationships that do transpire may also be hampered, Harknett and McLanahan (2004) state, as there is an inverse association between perceived partner availability and relationship quality. The low number of African American men available for partnering can mean that those who do enter relationships are not fully committed to them (Carey et al., 2010; Lane et al., 2004). The sex imbalance can lead African American women to "settle for less, and 'like' what they settle for even less" (C. Franklin, 1984, p. 145), and thus setting the stage for lowered levels of self-esteem, happiness, and satisfaction (C. Franklin, 1984).

The sex imbalance also contributes to women's socialization towards independence and self-reliance (Dickson, 1993). The realization that there are simply not enough African American men, to say nothing of those available and interested in partnering with African American women, means that those African

American women who want a male partner of her same race will have to expect to spend at least some time alone and therefore be self-sufficient.

With such high rates of infidelity, sexually transmitted infections, and reservations about a partner's faithfulness, intimacy is stifled. This certainly reinforces stereotypes, ignites distrust, and dampens intimacy. Intimacy is also compromised through the intersection of African Americans' socialization, experiences of racism, and enactment of masculinity and femininity. These complex issues reinforce the notion of a "gender war" existing between Black men and women (Chapman, 1986) which further complicates intimacy in romantic relationships.

Damaging Gender Trends

As is found among most American men, African American masculinity is tied up in ideas about hypersexuality, including copious previous sexual experiences and having multiple, concurrent sexual partners (Majors & Billson, 1992; Whitehead, 1997). African American males' blocked access to traditional routes of success (e.g. employment, education, etc.) due to racism and oppression mean that achievements must be channeled into other, available domains. This has largely been enacted through hypermasculine practices around physical aggressiveness and overt sexuality (Anderson, 1999; A. Franklin, 2004; C. Franklin, 1984; hooks, 2004; Majors & Billson, 1992). This is certainly a contributing factor to problems in romantic relationships. According to hooks (2004, p. 74), "sex becomes the ultimate playing field where the quest for freedom can be pursued in a world that denies black males access to other forms of liberating power." Dunn frames it thusly, "the elevation of sexuality as a site for black males to demonstrate their masculine manhood further hints at its role in counteracting the historic devaluation of black men and their sexuality" (2008, p. 41). Concomitant with this hypersexual image is a man who presents a lack of caring, thoughtfulness, and emotionality, traits requisite for love, commitment, and intimacy (hooks, 2004; Majors & Billson, 1992; Sternberg, 1986). The aloofness, detachment, and projection of fearlessness that many African American males have had to adopt is self-protective on the one hand, but engenders a general sense of distrust, anger, and isolation on the other hand that is manifested within relationships and leads to disconnection with a partner, assuming that a connection is made in the first place (Dickson, 1993; A. Franklin, 2004; Majors & Billson, 1992). For those who wear the mantle of Black machismo as a safeguard from the threats, hurt, and hostility they face so regularly, sexual intimacy, rather than intimate relationships, may be their focus and lost emotional connectedness with women may be an unintended byproduct.

African American women are not immune to displays of learned barriers to intimacy (Browning & Miller, 1999; Thomas & King, 2007). Women who have experienced pain and disappointment in previous relationships may display hostility, distrust, and other negative attitudes that launch self-fulfilling prophecies of new experiences of hurt and disillusionment. Indeed the frustrations that they feel and display lead to self-defensiveness and emotional guardedness which are evidenced when they lash out at their partner, seek and exercise control within their relationships, or employ a "play or get played" attitude (Chapman, 2001).

Women hear stories and warnings from their peers that revolve around men cheating, men only wanting sex, and men lying to women for their personal gain. From their older family members, they hear about and observe men's financial instability and their violence and abuse (Grange et al., 2011; Jarama et al., 2007). Both sets of messages posit African American men as untrustworthy and undependable. As these messages are relayed, so are lessons about the need for women's self-reliance and self-esteem. Although highly valuable, and part of the reason African American women have been able to manage their multiple oppressions, these may also hamper emotional intimacy as women are reluctant to let men in fully.

Their socialization to be strong and independent can make African American women reluctant to demonstrate vulnerability and reliance on a partner. In popular culture this is known as the *Strong Black Woman Syndrome*. At the same time, men's socialization in all quarters of American life place them in the same position. The defenses erected can be an impediment to demonstrating the love that one feels for their partner while also preventing one's partner from feeling and being able to reciprocate love (Fosse, 2010). For both men and women, this fear of vulnerability seriously impinges on the development of intimacy within their romantic lives (Seal & Ehrhardt, 2003; Seal et al., 2008) and may be a presenting issue for Black couples in counseling. Indeed, Seal and Ehrhardt (2003) illuminate this point as they describe the tension within relationships that mounts as men try to reconcile the vulnerability that accompanies emotional connectedness with a partner with the allure of sexual freedom and exploration they think they should relish. They also find that similar tension arises as men attempt to square their desires for emotional intimacy with their desires for sexual intimacy. This becomes all the more difficult as they are inundated with messages from peers and various cultural sources that encourage them to focus on sexual intimacy. Whatever the antecedents, both African American men and women learn, develop, and show a reluctance to rely on others and their express needs (Thomas & King, 2007). For clinicians who treat African American couples, understanding and addressing these barriers to intimacy, commitment, and self-disclosure is a vital step in any treatment plan.

If early lived experiences with Black men and women are negative, this can create suspicion and lower expectations for positive romantic relationships for both genders (Clarkwest, 2007) which, in turn, threatens the stability of African American couples and families (Furstenberg, 2001). For African American men, embracing and seeking intimacy may be considered a display of weakness, and invoke a potential for rejection by their peer group (Anderson, 1999; Boyd-Franklin, 2003; Majors & Billson, 1992). The appraisal and socialization of

African American males through their peers is particularly salient given that they may stand in as proxies for fathers with whom they are not actively involved (Anderson, 1999; Dickson, 1993; Majors & Billson, 1992). In addition, male peers may be seen as more reliable than female partners (Anderson, 1999; Fosse, 2010). Phrases like "bros before hos" are forged from such a belief. In these instances, women, through stereotypes, socialization, and experience, are seen as a threat, manipulative, untrustworthy, and deceitful while friends are there, through all manner of problems. Mothers and fathers raising children of the opposite sex often unconsciously bring these damaging views into their parenting practices, thereby passing this damaging legacy of gender mistrust on to their children. This is how these stereotypes are powerfully transmitted through the generations and how the "gender war" continues. This is then enhanced by stereotypical media depictions of negative African American male–female relationships.

The Compounding Negative Impact on Romantic Relationships

If a couple is not reasonably confident that their relationship will make it, the amount of effort and dedication they devote to it will be diminished. The same can be true if they lack a template for what relationship success should look like (Dickson, 1993). This lack of commitment is a risk factor for intimacy's creation, sustenance, and expansion. Additionally, chronic stressors, such as exposure to disadvantaged neighborhoods, individual and institutional racism, and persistent financial insecurity can produce expectations of poor relationships, displays of hostility, less warmth, and decreased relationship quality and satisfaction (Broman, 1993; Clark-Nicolas & Gray-Little, 1991; Guyll et al., 2010; Wickrama et al., 2010).

Though many conceptualize racism as overt acts of discrimination, typified by the hurling of racial insults, *de jure* segregation, and visible and active White supremacist organizations such as the Ku Klux Klan, contemporary forms of racism are far more subtle and covert and embedded in institutional and societal practices and arrangements (Bonilla-Silva, 2006). As such, African Americans are consistently subjected to a new racism, one that is more amorphous and difficult to identify. Regardless of the form, African Americans experience and perceive racism in their daily lives and respond to it. They may unwittingly act out the negative effects of racism on one another since institutionalized racism is impossible to confront (and sometimes even identify) on an individual basis. In times of trouble, these external factors mean that the couple cannot focus on just their relationship, and their bond may suffer. Another impact of racism is deeply felt mistrust that limits their ability to connect with a partner (Willis, 1990). This occurs when stereotypes of African Americans are believed, internalized, and acted upon. This also occurs when African American couples turn on—rather than to—each other after experiencing discrimination. They can exhibit rage and anger that they fear expressing to the perpetrators of their mistreatment, taking it out on a safer target

(Willis, 1990). At the same time, internalized racism brings with it a great deal of pain and has a negative effect on couples' ability to come together, bond, love, and be loved (Boyd-Franklin, 2003; Boyd-Franklin & Franklin, 1998; Carolan & Allen, 1999). African American men, devalued and degraded in the public mind, in their economic and educational settings, and within the criminal justice system, have few opportunities for positive affirmation or reassurance (A. Franklin, 2004). Interactions with a romantic partner may provide one of the only sources where he can go for the rejuvenation, comfort, and support he needs to conquer such indignity. If, however, she evaluates this as a sign of neediness, weakness, an additional burden or is unwilling or unable to fulfill these needs, he can come to see her and their relationship as further proof of his exclusion and isolation in a hostile world. Because both Black men and women often endorse the stereotype of hypermasculinity—i.e. he can show no emotional vulnerability, lest he be perceived as less than a man—this often leaves men emotionally isolated from their romantic partners. This is yet another cost of internalized racism, sexism, and the damaging intersection of both in the form of gender stereotypes.

Neighborhood contexts that facilitate social isolation may also inhibit successful relationships (Wilson, 1987, 1996). The lack of social connectedness, or enforceable trust, that would make a cheating partner susceptible to not only their partner's scorn but their neighbors as well may be lacking, which can have a negative effect on the development of trust within a relationship (Raley & Sweeney, 2009).

The negative messages received about the other are also internalized as messages about the self and lead to self-esteem problems as well as future disillusionment and discord with partners (C. Franklin, 1984). A lifetime of exposure to negative images for African Americans may mean that "they hate the qualities they see in each other and themselves, becoming destructive toward each other" (Willis, 1990, p. 143). This is evidenced as African American romantic relationships are often seen as in crisis, as highly conflictual, and marked by mutual apprehension that stems from the sources discussed above. Recently, African American relationships have been referred to using militaristic language such as "battlegrounds", "war zones", and "gender wars" (Chapman, 2001; Cole & Guy-Sheftall, 2003; A. King, 1999; Kitwana, 2003; Morgan, 2000). Although this is certainly not the case for all African American relationships, it is frequently the case with couples who come in for treatment. This is emblematic of struggles over control within relationships on the parts of both women and men. Relationships where there is a battle for control and power experience a derogation of intimacy as these fights limit closeness, reciprocity, and support (Bell et al., 1990). Similarly, when relationships are rooted in an ethos of conquest rather than partnership, emotional commitment, honesty, and reliability are seriously compromised (A. Franklin, 2004). However, trusting a partner may be seen as ceding too much power and control (Fosse, 2010). Likewise, having to have an egalitarian relationship because of men's marginalized place in the labor market rather than as a signal of an inherent commitment to this ideal, posits harm to relationships.

Being Black, Doing Gender: Egalitarianism and Its Challenges

Through its dehumanization and exploitation, along with its perversion of acceptable gender roles, slavery brought with it a certain, if uneasy, gender equality between women and men of African descent (Martin & Martin, 1978). Since slavery's end, African American women have had a long history in the paid labor force. While poor and working-class women of all races and ethnicities have worked, middle class and professional African American women emerged well before their White counterparts. Their professional status occurred in concert with role sharing in the work of the home, including economic contributions, care work, and housework.

Willie and Reddick (2003) note that egalitarian family relationships were not just the purview of professional and middle-class Black couples but were also adopted by working-class and low-income Black couples. African American couples remain highly egalitarian (Boyd-Franklin, 2003; Hines & Boyd-Franklin, 1996; Hunter & Sellers, 1998) in terms of shared household and parenting responsibilities (Allen & Conner, 1997; Coltrane, 2000). Both African American women and men demonstrate greater levels of flexible and egalitarian gender roles in their relationships, support for a feminist agenda, and a recognition of gender-based discrimination and disparities (Boyd-Franklin, 2003; Hunter and Sellers, 1998; Kane, 2000). However, an exploration of gender roles and egalitarian ideologies must include both one's preferences and lived experiences. This distinction is especially important for clinicians to understand as it can signal dissatisfaction in the couple's relationship. This is more thoroughly discussed in Chapter 4.

Antecedents to the "Gender War"

African Americans often internalize gender rules common in mainstream or traditional partnerships but are impeded from truly adhering to them because of their lowered social and economic positions in society. As such, both women and men had to work, defying common gender roles at the time of slavery. As stated previously, 19th and 20th century Black women worked outside the home because of economic necessity (Jones, 1985; D. White, 1999). Collins (2000) argues that economic necessity was such that African American couples were never able to maintain the separation of the public and private spheres seen as desirable and even natural in mainstream life. This was compounded through the ways that ideas of *proper* man- and womanhood were tied to their involvement within these constrained spheres. These structural factors have ensured that African American women have had access to non-male controlled financial resources in ways that many White women did not until later in the 20th century. The flexible gender roles encouraged by this system have often been read not as a strength or as revolutionary, but as pathological. It results in stereotypes of aggressive Black women and passive Black men (Jewell, 1983).

Subsequently, Cazenave finds that "some black men appear to be resentful that black women today seem to have more opportunities than they do" (1983, p. 30). His subsequent research illuminates this further as the majority of African American men and women agreed with the idea that African American men had fewer opportunities than African American women and the idea that African American women were actually holding men back through their lack of regard for them (Cazenave & Smith, 1990, p. 157).

That African American men contribute more to the invisible and unpaid labor that occur within the private domain reflects their marginalized economic positions. Under such circumstances, the enactment of egalitarianism and power sharing within African American's romantic relationships may reflect that "gender ideologies are probably less potent predictors of behavior than economic factors" (Hill, 2005, p. 107). Life in a social system based upon male privilege and patriarchal authority becomes difficult to navigate when one's access to these statuses are blocked. Frustration ensues and relationships become marked by discord and conflict (Tucker & Mitchell-Kernan, 1995).

Resultant Relational Strain

Trying to fulfill the traditional male role of authoritarian and provider in a relationship where the female partner has equal or greater levels of income, education, prestige, for example, may lead to such strain that the male partner retreats rather than reconcile these juxtapositions (A. Franklin, 2004). Men who feel they cannot live up to the expectations that they are the main or sole economic provider can react to this inability by withdrawing emotionally or physically from their relationship (Lawrence-Webb et al., 2004). Rather than see their contributions in other ways, such as in care- and housework, they can see this engagement in "women's work" as further proof of their worthlessness as men. Rather than seeing egalitarian relationships as a strength of African American communities or as the culmination of various and interlocking structural oppressions, couples often view these as failures and can turn their disillusionment and distress inwards and on each other (Bell, 1999; Lawrence-Webb et al., 2004).

Wilson (2008) presents data that show how this has increased in the last three decades. In 1979, African American women completed college at a rate 1.4 times larger than African American men; today, twice as many African American women complete college as men. These disparities manifest in the maintenance and formation of intimate partnerships. Today, African American women, much like women through U.S. history and across race and ethnicity contemporarily, express a desire to marry "up"—that is to marry someone with higher levels of education and income than themselves. It is therefore unsurprising when Nitsche and Brueckner (2009) conclude that for highly educated Black women, marriage and children are becoming more elusive. These Black women are twice as likely as comparable White women to never have married by age 45 and twice as likely to be divorced, widowed, or separated. For those Black women who do marry, they are less likely than similarly educated Black men, White men, and White women to have a spouse with a college degree. Certainly these educational mismatches wherein African American women have higher levels of education than their partners can impact a couple's bond. In such pairings, lower levels of warmth are observed (Cutrona, et al., 2003) and for men, marital quality is lowered (Bryant et al., 2008). Banks (2011) highlights problems that can occur between what he terms "power wives"—driven, well-educated, and professional African American women—and less ambitious, less-educated, and blue collar African American men. Such women may see their partners as an improvement project or a burden and men may see their partners as condescending or not being satisfied. Both may experience disappointment and resentment that can rip the fabric of the relationship. These relationships become difficult to navigate, since, in their upending of preferred gender norms and expectations, those within them have few successful models of which to emulate.

Indeed, though African Americans enact gender roles that are more flexible and egalitarian than in couples and families of other racial and ethnic backgrounds, their *preferences* can reflect more traditional roles. Hunter and Davis (1992) report that Black men are more likely to support equality in the public sphere while simultaneously holding positions that uphold both egalitarian and traditional gender roles in the private sphere. For example, most African American men believe that their partners should work outside the home; however, they also may believe that men are the head of the household. This reflects both a traditional and non-traditional gender worldview and is consistent with Black couples' gender egalitarianism *and* preference for traditional gender roles (e.g. man as primary breadwinner). Blee and Tickamyer (1995) note that the realities of shared household and economic labor can be belied by a desire for more traditional gender roles within relationships. African Americans couples, both men and women, tend to agree that men should be strong, independent, and possess the resources to provide financial support (Cutrona et al., 2003). An acceptance and implementation of egalitarianism in wage-earning, care work, and household labor is not the same as a desire for such equity (Hill, 2009; Landry, 2000).

Such mismatches between what Black couples have and what they want can lead to tensions and conflicts, which then pose challenges to intimacy. Bryant et al. (2008) postulate that when expectations around gender roles are not met, dissatisfaction ensues. This is contrasted by research that suggests that marriage stability and satisfaction are higher among couples who report they are equals (Marks et al., 2008). Problems also arise when there are differences in gender ideologies within relationships. Black women are less wed to traditional ideas about gender than Black men or Whites of either gender (Carter et al., 2009; Hunter and Sellers, 1998). There can be an inverse relationship between men's endorsement of traditional gender roles and overall relationship quality (Carlson, 2007). Part of African American women's lower relationship quality and dissatisfaction stems from their having to reconcile their relationship's reality with their ideals amid flexible and variable gender roles and expectations (Bryant et al., 2008). Other mismatches come to bear, as well.

For example, couples may have discord over how money is acquired and spent (Staples & Johnson, 1993) which can also lead to feelings that a partner lacks faith and support in one's dreams (Dickson, 1993). A man whose partner discourages his ideas for a new business venture because of the risk it entails may see this as another example of his being held down and his larger devaluation and inability to fully realize society's expectations for masculinity. A woman whose partner presents lofty dreams and ambitions may see this as his lack of practicality and yet another instance where she has to shoulder responsibility on her own, which is at odds with larger societal expectations. This speaks to a source of incompatibility within relationships and the way that larger forces conspire within the most personal settings.

Similarly, African American women may enter relationships with stereotypic assumptions that African American men will not carry their own weight economically or emotionally or will not work to enhance himself, his partner, or their relationship while men may come in believing that African American women will not trust or believe in him or will be reluctant to take emotional or financial risks that could pay off for both parties (Dickson, 1993). These perceptions are mutually constitutive and reinforcing and lead to cycles of pain, distrust, and conflict. African American women and men may also have differing expectations and goals in relationships such as when women look for partners who can provide financial stability and men seek partners who will offer companionship (Pinderhughes, 2002). If these expectations are too incompatible or irreconcilable with the couples' reality, as is often the case given African American's economic and social conditions, tensions can mount, leading to dissatisfaction, emotional withdrawal, and dissolution (Clarkwest, 2007).

There could also be incongruity between what people say they want in a partner and their true desires. As Dickson (1993) points out, the characteristics that African Americans say they want, such as good partners and stability, can be read as signs that their partner is boring and weak. These negative evaluations can lead to infidelity and manipulation by one partner, frustration and anger by the other, and resentment for both. These disconnections between one's ideal relationship and the reality enforced by African Americans' social and historical context and between what one says they want and what they actually want or exhibit are sources of relationship tension, lead to disengagement, and depresses intimacy (Clarkwest, 2007; C. Franklin, 1984; Hill, 2005) which can be a significant presenting issue in couples' treatment.

African American relationships assuredly suffer from these same flexible and egalitarian roles and power-sharing arrangements that have allowed them to survive in the U.S. If they perceive of these patterns as a result of their exclusion from mainstream success, a failure to measure up to their ideals, or further evidence of the deficiencies of themselves and/or their partners, then the stage is set for relationship disharmony and conflict (Lawrence-Webb et al., 2004). When placed in historical context, it is apparent that "two centuries of negotiation around gender roles has been a source of great stress and strain on intergender relationships between African Americans" (Lawrence-Webb et al., 2004, p. 629).

Intersections of Race, Class, and Gender Discrimination

The intersections of racial, class, and gender-based discrimination have long colluded to deprive African Americans of the opportunity to establish and maintain healthy romantic relationships and discussions thereof have been the mainstay in academic and popular treatments of Black female and male relationships since the 1960s. In 1965, sociologist, key official in the Kennedy and Johnson administrations, and later U.S. Senator, Daniel Patrick Moynihan published his influential work. From this work flowed the enduring notions that Black families are trapped in a "tangle of pathology of unmarried mothers and welfare dependency." The outgrowth of this was his framing of Black women as the "strong, castrating matriarch" and Black men as the "weak, ineffective male." Black women as controlling and domineering matriarchs may have fallen out of vogue with scholars but remains part of the discourse within social policy, popular culture, communities, and relationships. For example, the strong and angry Black woman mythos continues to exist and dominates popular culture. Likewise, African American men are very much still seen as weak and ineffective as is evident in the multitudinous descriptions and depictions of them as unable and unwilling to act in accord with mainstream expectations for masculinity. Society currently projects Black men as both weak and lazy yet hypermasculine and over-sexed. Society enhances these stereotypes on a daily basis through media portrayals of the "strong Black woman," single mother, and the absentee, unemployed Black father. There are few positive portrayals of either Black men or women, but positive portrayals of Black men are almost non-existent. This can significantly damage the psyche of Black people and makes emotional intimacy between romantic partners a powerful challenge.

In the wake of the Moynihan Report, the blame for the emasculation of Black men shifted from powerful White men and the economic, cultural, social, and political systems they controlled and onto Black women (hooks 2004; Neal, 2002). Indeed hooks (2004: 14) states, "this blaming ignited the flames of a gender war so intense that it has practically consumed the historical memory of black males and females working together equally for liberation, creating love in family and community." Cazenave and Smith offer that such a "false dichotomy distorts the nature of intimate relationships and social movements and may result in the fragmentation and failure of both" (1990, p. 167) as time is spent fighting each other, shattering bonds, and distracting from the true roots of their oppressions. Hill (2005) maintains that some African American men became more sexist, and enlisted a host of traditional gender expectations as they clung to patriarchy as their only privilege. Instead of viewing the nontraditional gender roles exposed in the Moynihan report as liberatory, i.e. a signal that African American families deviated from White families as an act of resistance to inequality and the near-total impacts of racial and economic exclusion, some viewed them as another sign of marginalization and pathology.

Therapeutic Work with Black Couples

Despite all of these significant issues, most Black men and women still desire relationships with one another. The clinician's challenge is to capitalize on this strong desire for couples to be together all while recognizing the destructive influences that can tear them apart. Indeed, African American couples often display low levels of generalized and interpersonal trust and the highest levels of distrust within relationships (Harknett & McLanahan, 2004). The preponderance of distrust is so great that relationships may be seen as proving grounds where trust is earned through various tests and trials and is never just given (Dunham & Ellis, 2010; Fosse, 2010). This is an extremely high bar to clear, and while some couples succeed, many times couples fall short. While distrust does not inhibit desire for, entry into, or lifetime number of relationships (Carlson et al., 2004; Estacion & Cherlin, 2010), it is implicated in the transition to more serious relationships such as from cohabitation to dating or from cohabitation to marriage (Carlson et al., 2004; Estacion & Cherlin, 2010; Waller & McLanahan, 2005).

Intersecting and long-standing systems of oppression can lead to problems of self-esteem, worthiness, and self-disclosure that have bearing for individuals and within an interpersonal context (Carey et al., 2010; Lane et al., 2004). This historical context, along with a host of structural, institutional, cultural, and interpersonal factors, leads to difficulties in establishing and maintaining intimacy within the romantic relationships of heterosexual African American couples. Exploring the social, historical, and economic contexts of African Americans will enable clinicians to more fully understand the social locations and thus the practices and understandings their clients describe.

African Americans reside in a variety of environments and it is important to remember that individuals cannot be made to acclimate to any preconceived notion of how they are supposed to be or act. According to Akbar (2009) what becomes important in our analysis and work as psychologists, social workers, counselors, and researchers is not to base our thinking and counseling practices on scholarship that perpetuates the vilification of African male and female relationships. He states that we have increasingly focused on the "crisis" of African American couples; we have excluded from our analysis stable healthy relationships between African American men and women. When we solely engage in academic discourse concerning problems in African American female and male intimate relationships without also examining these couples' strengths, we are engaging in simulated idiosyncrasies, further disenfranchising African American male and female partnerships. This is harmful as it negatively biases the process of counseling African American couples (Akbar, 2009).

There is a growing trend toward the delivery of culturally competent counseling services for African Americans (Belgrave & Allison, 2006). The following section will utilize the tenets of African-centered psychology as a relationally based approach to culturally consistent therapeutic practices with African American couples that are inclusive and respectful of African/African American heritage/traditions, and socio-historical context and experiences. While the scope of this chapter prohibits detailed specifications of culturally consistent therapies and interventions (additional training and knowledge is needed to fully practice these therapeutic paradigms), it is important to provide examples of culturally relevant therapies, interventions, and general guidelines for doing counseling with African American couples that can be used to address the contextual factors discussed in this chapter.

There are a growing number of scholars that have moved away from a deficit view of African American people and their families to strengths-based ideologies and paradigms (e.g. Belgrave & Allison, 2006; Boyd-Franklin & Franklin, 1998; Chapman, 2007; Grills & Rowe, 1998; Sudarkasa, 2007; Sussman, 2004; Washington, 2010; White & Parham, 1990). Utilizing a strengths-based perspective, we will reframe the usual practices of traditional literature's propensity to discuss African American couples' relationships from a victimization perspective. Although African American couples come to therapy presenting with negative relationship issues, utilizing cultural strengths-based approaches and models are essential to effective and culturally relevant counseling with African American couples.

African American cultural strengths are culturally based beliefs and values unique to African Americans. Whereas every worldview has its own set of predicaments, some of the strengths and protective factors of African descended people include: religiosity, spirituality, belief in ancestors, respect for elders, and the focus on family and community including blood-related family and fictive kin (Blassingame, 1972; Boyd-Franklin & Franklin, 1998; LaTaillade, 2006; Sudarkasa, 2007). Other strong values include cooperation, interdependence, collective responsibility, the concept of oneness, and harmony with all life on earth (Nobles, 1998). African-descent people are linked by oral tradition and time is defined by events shared with others in the past and present (Hilliard, 1992; Kambon, 1992). These attributes are functional for the survival, stability, and advancement of African Americans (LaTaillade, 2006; McAdoo, 1998).

These attributes also inform cultural healing systems developed by African Americans. These cultural healing systems include collectively held knowledge and convictions regarding origin and alleviation of mental health concerns among African Americans (Sussman, 2004). Given the socio-historical circumstances unique to African Americans and African Americans' tendency not to utilize traditional therapies, these alternative healing systems are critical to health and well-being (Myers & Speight, 2010). Consistent with cultural strengths specific to African Americans, Boyd-Franklin & Franklin (1998) suggests that counseling strategies with African American couples utilize cultural healing systems such as churches, community programs, and family doctors.

African-Centered Psychology: A Brief Overview

African centeredness is

> a concept which categorizes a "quality of thought and practice," is rooted in the cultural image and interest of people of African ancestry and represents and reflects the life experiences, history and traditions of people of African ancestry as the center of analysis. It represents the core fundamental quality of the "Belonging," "Being" and "Becoming" of people of African ancestry. Furthermore, it represents the fact, that as human beings, people of African ancestry have the right and responsibility to "center" themselves in their own subjective possibilities and potentialities, and through the re-centering process reproduce and refine the best of human essence.
>
> (Nobles, 1998, p.190)

African-centered ideologies suggest that defining African American relationships by the strengths of African/African American culture and precepts contributes to the well-being of African American male and female unions (LaTaillade, 2006). For example, embracing flexible egalitarian gender roles necessary for the survival of the community is consistent with an African ethos. Counselors applying a Eurocentric patriarchal analysis of gender roles concerning African American couples may misinterpret the couples' dynamic (i.e. hypermasculinized African American men, overbearing African American females) (Lawrence-Webb et al., 2004; Strmic-Pawl et al., 2011). According to Lawrence-Webb et al. (2004) the system of patriarchy is one of the most negative influences for African American couples and couples counselors should assess the presence of this influence within the couples with which they work.

African-centered therapeutic paradigms for African descended people are based on research by African-centered scholars and rest on four basic assumptions. They: 1) advance the re-ascension of African cultural patterns and styles for understanding human behavior; 2) reflect the various ways in which African people understand, articulate, and project themselves to themselves, others, and the world; 3) utilize scientific and moral criteria that emerge out of the study of African cultural patterns (i.e. criteria that emphasizes values that are more situational, collective, dynamic, and circular assumptions that are more integrative or "diunital," and methods that are more affective, symbolic and metaphorical or reliant upon an inclusive metaphysical epistemology); 4) verify the reality of African human processes through an examination of historical moments and movements, relying upon African sources, including oral literature (proverbs, songs, tales/stories), spiritual system "scripts," prayers, praise songs, and moral teaching, the dynamic interdependences of community, nature, and spirit and Sankofa (Piper-Mandy & Rowe, 2010, p. 8). African-centered scholars and practitioners advocate that the success of therapy with African American couples is dependent upon integrating culturally sensitive therapeutic paradigms into counseling practices.

40

African American couples are part of an interdependent system that relies upon cultural strengths for support, well-being and to facilitate change (Boyd-Franklin & Franklin, 1998; LaTaillade, 2006; Piper-Mandy & Rowe, 2010).

Given that the development of African American culture is a fusion of traditional African customs and American socio-historical experiences, African centered psychologists have created a meta-theoretical paradigm that utilizes the analysis of ancient African ethos and the unique experiences of African people in the United States as its philosophical base. African-centered meta-theory addresses the historical, cultural, psychosocial, community contextual issues, and environmental stressors as well as cultural strengths and preferences relevant to African descended people (Rowe & Rowe, 2009). To illustrate, *Obi-Dan-Bi*, Rowe and Rowe's model of mental health, utilizes African-centered meta-theory in psychotherapy. *Obi-Dan-Bi* is a communal healing model for African American families and couples that is "rooted in the cultural image and interest of people of African Ancestry and represents and reflects the life experience, history and traditions of African Ancestry as the center of analysis." This model of mental health effectively addresses many of the socio-historical-contextual factors about African American couples discussed in this chapter. Specific interventions utilized in couples counseling for African Americans may include having couples participate in groups to create a sense of community and common [communal] purpose and utilizing African proverbs (brief axioms that assert wisdom, morals, and values) to express truths, provide guidelines for conduct and behavior, and discuss values in the relationship (Rowe & Rowe, 2009). Couples' groups are in alignment with the collectivistic nature of African American cultural values and norms. In addition, the utilization of community spiritual leaders in conjunction with traditionally Western trained therapists can enhance counseling outcomes when addressing problems specific to African American couples (Ojelade et al., 2011).

Towards a More Culturally Consistent Paradigm for African American Couples

African-centered psychology views personality as an amalgam of the spiritual, mental, and physical and is concerned with "understanding systems of meaning of human beingness, features of human functioning, and the restoration of natural order to human development, to resolve personal and social problems and to promote optimal functioning" (Association of Black Psychologists, 2012). Mental disorder does not refer solely to individual intra-psychic malfunction but includes a larger context of social and political reality (Kwate, 2005). Kwate further posits that African-centered theories of "psychopathology" are unique to individuals of African descent and do not use the Diagnostic and Statistical Manual (DSM) but instead view mental illness as a collective (community) issue. Clinicians emphasizing this approach with couples from the first meeting may decrease some cultural mistrust/suspicion of psychotherapy. Mkize (2003) states, "African centered psychotherapy does not consider mental illness as something to be cured or controlled but as something to be understood and acknowledged" (p. 3).

When working with African American couples, an important aspect of counseling is having couples discuss their perceptions of different aspects of their human beingness. For example, counselors can facilitate African American couples in discussing their cultural values, roles, attitudes, cultural stressors, and connectedness to the African American community. In doing so, counselors can ascertain important information concerning ethnic identity, gender identity, and cultural values. The literature clearly suggests that a strong racial identity among African Americans serves as a protective function against environmental (e.g. racism, discrimination, oppression, negative stereotypes) and psychological stress (Cross, 1991; LaTaillade, 2006; Sellers et al., 2003), therefore ascertaining information about a couple's racial identity is an important assessment tool. Obviously, a couple's ability to deal with such stressors significantly influences marital satisfaction and the level of support African American couples have within their own communities (Bell et al., 1990; Boyd-Franklin & Franklin, 1998).

Another important aspect for counselors to address is the impact of racism and oppression on the lives of African American couples (both experienced and internalized). Given that one of the tenets of African psychology is the belief that mental distress amongst African Americans is steeped in a shared social and political reality, having African American couples sort through their responses to external oppressive and racist conditions may expose and explain dysfunctional interactional behaviors that have manifested in their relationship. This is an important step in that interconnectedness can be fostered as couples exercise "empathetic joining" to discuss their day to day problems instead of being at odds with each other or taking it out on each other while they maneuver through oppressive circumstances that they may deal with externally on a day to day basis.

A Contemporary Framework for Indigenous African/African American Healers

Indigenous traditional healers are established health care workers in the African/ African American community (Washington, 2010). Healers utilize alternative healing practices that are sanctioned by the community. Many healers in the African American community have their own field of expertise and may be referred to as diviners (called to duty by Ancestors and are intermediaries between humans and the Supernatural) and/or herbalists (diagnose everyday illnesses and prescribe healing herbs) and faith healers (use prayer, candlelight or water and frequently participants become members of the churches of the faith healer) (Washington, 2010). The concept of "healing" as opposed to "treatment" is critical when working with African American couples, as healing implies a collaborative process by which the healer is emotionally invested with his/her clients (Ojelade et al., 2011). Treatment invokes a perception of the medical model where people and their issues are problems to be solved/treated. Culturally sensitive treatment with African American couples should involve a reconceptualization of treatment as a healing process in which couples are co-creators in their own healing. "Healing" is a more culturally consistent construct than is "treatment" (Monteiro & Wall 2011; Ojelade et al., 2011) and is seen as an act of love and service for the community. Healing skills and power were passed on within families through the use of special rituals. African/African American healers refer to this power as a gift from God and receiving power through a *ritual* as a blessing (Monteiro & Wall, 2011; Nobles, 2008). According to Monteiro and Wall, *ritual* focuses on the individual being as an integral part of a community. Also a *ritual* empathetic exchange occurs between the healer and the client. Koss-Chioino, (2006 as cited in Monteiro & Wall, 2011) states that interactions in rituals also foster social insight and interpersonal sensitivity and judgment. According to Ojelade et al., in indigenous African healing practices mental health concerns emanate from three sources 1) supernatural forces (more severe psychotic behaviors); 2) natural causes (mind-altering substances and food taboos); and 3) personal choice (identified as *Ori* and *Iwa Pele*, maintaining good character). When counselors consider doing counseling with African American couples in conjunction with Western interventions, counselors would benefit from understanding the conceptual framework underlying African indigenous/spiritual healing practices (Mbiti, 1969; Ojelade et al., 2011).

Discerning the difference between religion and spirituality with African American couples will give counselors insight into the validity of utilizing this intervention modality. Strategies that can be utilized with African American couples are: assessing cultural beliefs and values and the couples' adherence to them; the couples' understanding of Karma; the couples' relationship with familiar ancestors and the resolution of those transitions; assessing family dynamics for the purpose of participating in intervention processes; and monitoring use of substances and of dietary restrictions. Once these assessments have been made, a collaborative culturally consistent intervention plan can be put in place.

In this aspect communal healing is paramount (Monteiro & Wall, 2011). Healers believe that suffering is caused by the event that happened, the strategies utilized to heal the suffering, the recall of the injurious events and that which reminds the person of the injurious event. Prayer is an important part of treatment and some healers want their patients to continue with their medication from their Western doctors, others insist that no other medication be taken (Monteiro & Wall 2011; Ojelade et al., 2011).

Again, "healing" implies a collaborative, strengths-based approach which is inferred, as opposed to an individualistic, expert-driven, problem approach which tends not to be culturally sensitive to African/African American clients. Healers are a part of the community, thus counselors working with African American couples should be a part of, or at least knowledgeable of, the inner workings of the African American community (including strengths of the community and challenges faced by the community) and community resources (Ojelade et al., 2011).

Counseling Paradigms Specific to African Americans

Therapeutic work with African American people should be rooted in their interest, life experiences, history, and traditions as the center of analysis (Nobles, 1998). The following section will provide a brief introduction to alternative African-centered therapeutic paradigms, strategies, and models that are more consistent with the ethos of African descent people. These conceptualizations are specifically designed to address the socio-historical and contextual factors discussed in this chapter. This section will briefly review a theoretical conceptualization of an African-centered theory of optimal psychology. The construct of *Ubuntu* will be introduced as it relates to African-centered therapeutic paradigms and NTU, pronounced "in-to" and means life force, psychotherapy will be outlined. A case study will be provided to illustrate the tenets of NTU psychotherapy

Theory of Optimal Psychology

The theory of optimal psychology was developed as an attempt to assist African/African American people in understanding the impact of oppression, discrimination, and racism on their lives (Myers, 1993). According to Myers, optimal psychology (OP) is a Black/African/Africana theory of human "beingness" grounded in a holistic, integrative cultural worldview and wisdom tradition traceable from ancient Africa to present day. Optimal theory emphasizes the interdependence and interrelatedness of spiritual, mental, physical, social, and environmental well-being and consists of mental cleansing, liberation, and cultivating the ability to distinguish between the real and unreal, right and wrong, discerning ego self and true self, and illumination of the soul and radical transformation of consciousness (Myers & Speight, 2010).

The optimal conceptual system consists of integration of the spiritual, the material, harmony, communalism, intrinsic self-worth, self-knowledge, diunital logic (union of opposites), extended self-identity and a holistic worldview (Myers, 1993). Myers describes the suboptimal conceptual system as materialism, competition, extrinsic self-worth, dichotomous thinking, individualism, and a segmented worldview. The therapeutic processes and practices for achieving mental health in optimal psychology consist of a belief system analysis, whereby individuals are assessed on their adherence to an African-centered worldview (Myers et al., 1996). Myers et al. found that individuals who were spiritual, holistic, and communal (tenets of an African-centered worldview) were least likely to report psychological distress. The next step is for the counselor/healer to engage the individual in the optimization process.

The optimization process consists of developing increased knowledge of the multi-dimensional self, and to master the Ten Cardinal Principles described by the ancients:

the ability to distinguish between the real and the unreal, and right and wrong, learning to be free from resentment under persecution and wrong doing, believing and coming to know the truth can be found and lived, being devoted to realizing union with Supreme Being, having faith in the ability for truth to be revealed, and learning to control your thoughts and your actions.
(Myers & Speight, 2010, p. 76)

According to Myers and Speight, commitment to this process will maintain well-being. As stated previously, positive racial identity is also a salient factor for positive outcomes in African American couples' relationships (LaTaillade, 2006). Once this construct is evaluated counselors can utilize information to assess cultural strengths, relational styles, cultural identities, cultural traumas, and resources to address presenting problems of the couples.

Ubuntu in African Psychology

Ubuntu refers to the interrelatedness of all things in the universe. *Ubuntu* places a high value on relationships (Washington, 2010) and involves sensitivity to the needs and wants of others (Mkize, 2003). Utilizing an African collectivistic philosophy, *Ubuntu* in African psychology addresses trauma in the African/African American community by considering the impact and/or the collective memory of the MAAFA (African enslavement) on the current lives of African/African Americans (Washington, 2011). Washington states that the lingering traumatic effects of the MAAFA include psychological, spiritual, emotional, economic, and political devastation, and cultural trauma. Cultural trauma refers to a loss of identity and cultural meaning for an entire cohesive group of people (Alexander, 2004). Elements of cultural trauma may include poor thinking abilities, numbing of affect, feeling broken/alone, insomnia, intrusive memories, self-injury, feelings of guilt, social shrinking, and boundary challenges (Washington, 2010). *Ubuntu* in African psychology seeks to alleviate the effects of the specific traumatic experiences of African descended people.

Ubuntu is grounded in traditional healing practices that acknowledge the impact of internal and external variables on optimal growth and development of human beings and recognizes *ukufa kwabantu*, which are metaphysical disorders that exist among African/Black people (Washington, 2010). Interventions in *Ubuntu* include: tracking trauma, identifying areas of vulnerability (psycho-spiritual, physical etc.), identifying emotional triggers, and cultural healing. Identifying *ukufu kwabantu* challenges (African metaphysical challenges) are often addressed in the communal context through rituals, such as: directing the power of the UniverSoul optimally through ritual, movement, rhythm, and spoken word as the therapy (ritual) of African spirit healing, African drumming (counting, rhythm expression), African dance (rhythm, movement, expression), African *Nommo* (spoken word) (Washington, 2011).

A therapeutic intervention consistent with this paradigm is the notion of the healing cycle from MAAFA (disaster or terrible occurrence) to MAAT (truth justice, order, adjustment honesty, and a harmonious relationship among people and the world) (Mickel, 2005). In this therapeutic intervention, *Sankofa* (return to the past to seek knowledge where wellness exists) is the answer to MAAFA. Counselors can utilize role plays, stories, and therapeutic teachings to assist couples in selecting pictures of wellness from their past (ancestral or personal) and bringing them into their current worldview. According to Mickel (2005), the counselor can engage the family to utilize these pictures of wellness to confront trauma and pain and move to MAAT.

NTU Psychotherapy

NTU psychotherapy (Phillips, 1996) is a pluralistic, evidenced-based therapy that utilizes ancient Eastern principles of healing, New Age conceptualizations of the mind–body relationship, a humanistic perspective, and an African-centered worldview and methodologies (Gregory & Harper, 2001). NTU is based on the assumptions that people are innately good by nature, have good intentions, and want to be happy. NTU further posits that behavior is purposed to be representative of one's actualized potential. Healing is considered a natural process and the therapist is the facilitator/conduit for the healing process; skill development and the creation of vision are all part of the therapeutic process (Gregory & Harper, 2001).

NTU psychotherapy is a spiritually oriented, family focused, culturally competent, competency-based, holistic, and systemic approach. The principles of NTU are harmony, balance, interconnectedness, cultural awareness, affective epistemology, and authenticity (Phillips, 1996). There are five phases to NTU psychotherapy. Phase one is harmony. The objective in the harmony phase is the establishment of a shared trusting relationship. The second phase is awareness. There are two aspects of awareness: cognitive awareness (recognition of destructive behaviors) and affective awareness (awareness of needs, wants, strengths, weaknesses, and emotions). The third phase is alignment. Alignment is considered the heart of the counseling process. Phillips (1996) calls this the "working through" phase where clients begin to confront their fears. The fourth stage is actualization. In this phase practice and planning occurs in the context of the clients' environment. The final stage is synthesis. Integration is on a physical, mental, and spiritual level. The synthesis phase is a reflection phase in which the therapist assists the client in looking back on the experience and evaluating it (Phillips, 1996).

NTU Case Study

Darryl and Shaunice are each 30 years old and have been together for eight years and married for three. During that time, Shaunice received her Master's degree and secured a well-paying executive position at a pharmaceutical company while Darryl worked as an auto mechanic at a local car dealership. They met in college, although Daryl dropped out to help his mother who became ill. They began having problems in their marriage while Shaunice was in graduate school. Darryl complained about her absence, which led to arguments about her role as his wife and her commitment to the marriage. In the heat of the moment, Shaunice often had a tendency to lash out at Darryl reminding him of his inability to support her in her academic endeavors. Their arguments became more frequent once she graduated. In anger on several occasions Shaunice reminded Darryl that she was making more money than he and that she could handle things on her own if they split up. Darryl would frequently storm out of the house and come home late at night reeking of alcohol and agitated to a point that he would continue the argument and blame her for his unsatisfying career choice. During the last argument Darryl stated that he wanted a divorce. Shaunice initiated counseling and Daryl reluctantly agreed to attend.

Socio-Historical and Contemporary Variables Operating in the Relationship

Darryl seems to have some anxiety around the educational and career attainment of his partner. Given the socio-historical marginalization of the economic positions of African American males, the fact that his wife makes more money than he may conflict with his ideas concerning gender roles and socioeconomic status. Shaunice's flaunting her success in anger at her husband may activate feelings of insecurity that Darryl may have around these issues. This dynamic may cause frustration, conflict, and discord in their relationship (Tucker & Mitchell-Kernan, 1995). As a result, both may be overly sensitive to the power dynamics within their relationships (Chapman, 2007). Assessing their gender roles/expectations and how they were informed of those roles in their socialization process would be appropriate for this couple.

The Process of NTU Psychotherapy

Phase One: Harmony

In the harmony phase of therapy an NTU therapist realizes the importance of a committed interconnectedness with his/her clients (Phillips, 1996).

Libation rituals involving pouring liquid to honor God and Ancestors can be utilized to make connections to spirit, ancestors, and cultural rituals. Meeting the couple "where they are" is an important aspect of the first phase of NTU (Phillips, 1996). The therapist must have a clear understanding of the couples' strengths and weaknesses, as well as gaining insight into the outside forces (discussed at length in this chapter), operating in their relationship. To foster connectedness with the couple, the NTU therapist might utilize self-disclosure regarding some dynamic of his/her own intimate relationship (if the therapist is in a relationship) to develop a shared experience between the therapist, Darryl, and Shaunice.

Darryl's reluctance to come to therapy should be sensitively addressed. The counselor (if male) can work to bond with Darryl around similar gender issues as it relates to male–female relationships. If the counselor is female, she should work to bond with Darryl to make him more comfortable with the counseling process. Couples counselors should use any similarities they might have between themselves and the couple as a relationship-building tool early in couples' work, all while being respectful and knowledgeable about any differences that exist between couples and counselors. Being well-read in the specifics of African American socio-historical cultural precepts as well as how these socio-cultural factors continue to influence African American couples is important in the rapport-building process, as it helps the counselor demonstrate a more thorough understanding of the couple and the context in which their issues occur.

Phase Two: Awareness

Once the counseling relationship is established, the counselor can facilitate a process by which Darryl and Shaunice begin to talk about their self-barriers to closeness. Utilizing the technique of *realness* (Phillips, 1996), the therapist creates structure in the process so that they do not play the blame game. As they began to talk about their self-barriers the therapist can also have them discuss their cultural and personal strengths, needs, and boundaries as they relate to creating an interconnected family unit. Important techniques in this phase include reframing, relabeling, and feedback of clients' thoughts and feelings (Phillips, 1996). To ascertain the impact of family and community support systems a family and community genogram can be constructed. To aid in the assessment of cultural/racial identity, genograms can include connections to extended family, fictive kin, and community supports. In doing these exercises cultural strengths can be reinforced. Phillips calls this stage the development of NTU energy.

Phase Three: Alignment

In the alignment phase "the client confronts his or her fears in order to achieve the outcome of assimilation and reconciliation of these psychological anxieties into a maturing confident, and harmonious self" (Phillips, 1996, p. 92). During this phase, strengths, fears, and anxieties around gender roles in their marriage can be discussed, role-played, worked through, and resolved. Darryl and Shaunice can discuss their fears around their place in the world and their roles as husband and wife. In the heat of arguments, Darryl and Shaunice revealed issues concerning power dynamics: Darryl told Shaunice that he was tired of her belittling him and Shaunice made it quite clear that she could be independent and didn't need him. The phase of *alignment* is integrative since the objective of the phase is not to necessarily get rid of client fears and anxiety, but rather to come to terms with them (Phillips, 1996). According to Phillips in this phase anger and confrontation may occur. Utilizing techniques that distinguish between self-awareness and cultural awareness can be used in this phase. Cultural awareness exercises can promote the realization of the clients' own cultural background issues, and relationships. Also as the task of therapy becomes more difficult the utilization of cultural, spiritual, familial, and community supports are necessary. Helping the couples get in touch with these supports as they continue to face challenges in their relationship is important, especially given that many African Americans are collectivistic and family/community-centered.

Phase Four: Actualization

For the actualization phase, clients have been prepared in phase three to practice new behaviors with the support of therapeutic safety. In this phase clients are encouraged to practice and record new behaviors in their regular environments (Phillips, 1996). As you recall Darryl was increasingly utilizing alcohol to handle the problems between himself and Shaunice. He would then utilize his altered state of consciousness to communicate his fears and anxieties by blaming Shaunice for his perceived inadequacies. Shaunice would validate those fears and avoid her own anxieties and fears around her relationship with Darryl by throwing it in his face that she made more money than he did. Through NTU therapy, Darryl and Shaunice have learned alternative ways to problem solve and have identified and practiced utilizing their cultural strengths and community and familial support. Therapy sessions can now be utilized to talk about outcomes, responses, and attitudes within their own environment and to validate successes (and disappointments) of goals and tasks (Phillips, 1996).

Phase Five: Synthesis

The synthesis stage is the culmination of the knowledge and processes that were learned in stages one through four. NTU is a circular integrative process by which all phases of therapy support and validate each other. NTU therapy is based in *Nguzo Saba*, which are seven principles concerning cultural precepts of African American culture. For instance, given that one of the tenets of *Nguzo Saba* is *Ujamaa* (cooperative economics) strategies to address mutual financial interdependence are embedded in the therapeutic process. An important construct of NTU is the *extended self* (Phillips, 1996). These techniques might include family budgeting and the process of creating cooperative ventures (Chapman, 2007). For Darryl and Shaunice, a positive intervention would include helping them see themselves as a collective instead of independent of one another. For example, every time Shaunice emphasizes that she does not need Darryl and is more financially successful than he is, she encourages her individual identity over her marital one. Healthy marriages have both (as seen in the above concept of *extended* self); however, interdependence in couples and a "couple identity" is also important to a healthy functioning partnership. A discussion of finances would encourage the couple to think in terms of the common financial goals they have together. In this phase of NTU, the couples' energy occurs on a physical, mental, and spiritual level (Phillips, 1996). Consistent with African American cultural traditions, NTU empowers not only the couple but strengthens the couple's relationship to their system as well (i.e. family, school, culture, community). According to Phillips (1996) this happens because the couple's perceptions of themselves within their environment is different, so their responses to and how they interface with their environment is different.

Conclusion

D. Franklin's words are instructive when she advises that "to understand the tensions and turmoils in the relationships of black men and women today, we must come to grips with the distinctive relational patterns whose roots extend deep into the history of blacks in America" (2001, p. 22). As African Americans enter into romantic relationships, they bring with them a host of long-standing and overlapping racial, gender, and class stereotypes that have been internalized and projected onto their partners (D. Franklin, 2001). Indeed, African American couples live within "entrapment in the societal projection process and having to live with constant conflict, confusion, and contradiction while trapped within a system that undermines functional roles" (Pinderhughes, 2002, p. 272).

Survival and adaptation under a system of racial, sexual, and economic domination and hostility has led to relationships that have deviated from African principles that stressed "interdependence, cooperation, unity, mutual responsibility, and reconciliation" (Bell et al., 1990, p. 170). Absent these, couples' interactions and relationships suffer as intimacy flounders. As Americans, African Americans are also impacted by larger cultural shifts in ideas on romantic partnering. Dickson (1993) illuminates the problems that an overall shift to personal fulfillment and individualism throughout all of American culture pose for couples in general, adding that African Americans are at particular risk, given their marginalized structural and cultural positions. This change means that there is less expectation and support for enduring the ebbs in the course of a relationship as exiting becomes a vehicle to achieve personal fulfillment.

Looking at these societal, structural, and cultural processes allows a perspective that does not hinge on blaming or pathologizing individuals. Viewing constraints through understandings of the self and the relationship will help to mediate negative perceptions that African Americans may have of themselves and of their partners. Realizing the structural impediments to employment for Black men, for example, can remedy perceptions of them as lazy or economically unreliable. Similarly, realizing that Black women have been socialized to be independent and self-sufficient can remedy perceptions of them as domineering and controlling. Understanding these complex contextual factors and how they manifest in couples' relationships is critical to sensitive and effective treatment.

Utilizing the philosophies in African-centered treatment approaches, which are based on African/African American cultural precepts and strengths and are designed to assess these contextual factors while embracing the couple and family, will go a long way in helping couples resolve their presenting issues in therapy. African American couples are members of a community whose cultural accomplishments, strengths, and precepts have been documented throughout perpetuity. In addition, African/African Americans indigenous healing strategies have documented effectiveness and are culturally consistent. The "Africanisms" of African American culture is why African Americans have survived such insidious maltreatment and exploitation and somewhat "countered the lingering effects of human alienation and spirit illness caused by the 'memetic infection' [contagious information patterns] of the Transatlantic Slave Trade experience" (Nobles, 2008, p. 6.46). These counseling modalities may be more appealing (and more effective) for African Americans. Thus, it is our contention that these celebrated indigenous constructs be utilized as a model for well-being for African American couples. Just as all cultures present with mental health concerns, all cultures have ways of achieving mental health and well-being that is consistent with their cultural beliefs morals, values, and behaviors. This notion is no different for African descent people (Grills & Rowe, 1998; Hanks, 2008; Mbiti, 1969; Nobles, 2006; Sudarkasa, 2007; Washington, 2010).

References

Adimora, A. A., & Schoenbach, V. J. (2005). Social context, sexual networks, and racial disparities in rates of sexually transmitted infections. *The Journal of Infectious Diseases*, 191(Supplement 1), S115–S122.

Adimora, A. A., Schoenbach, V. J., & Doherty, I. A. (2007). Concurrent sexual partnerships among men in the United States. *American Journal of Public Health*, 97(12), 2230–2237.

Akbar, N. (1979) African roots of Black personality. In W. Smith, K. Burlew, M. Mosley, & W. Whitney (Eds.), *Reflections on Black Psychology*. Washington, DC: University Press of America.

Akbar, N. (2009). Black male and female relationships (Video file). Retrieved July 15, 2009 from http://www.youtube.com/watch?v=xeLMKuW9pvA.

Alexander, J. C. (2004). Toward a theory of cultural trauma. In J. C. Alexander, R. Eyerman, B. Giesen , N. J. Smelser, and P. Sztompka (Eds). *Cultural Trauma and Collective Identity*. Berkeley, CA: University of California Press.

Allen, W., & Conner, M. (1997). An African American perspective on generative fathering. In A. J. Hawkins & D. C. Dollahlite (Eds.). *Generating Fathering: Beyond Deficit Perspectives* (pp.52–70). Newbury Park, CA: Sage.

Anderson, E. (1999). *Code of the Street: Decency, Violence and the Moral Life of the Inner City*. New York: Norton & Company.

Ani, M. (1994). *Yurugu: An African-Centered Critique of European Cultural Thought and Behavior*. Trenton, NJ: Africa World Press.

Association of Black Psychologists (2012). Retrieved January, 2012 from http://www.abpsi.org/

Banks, R.R. (2011). *Is Marriage For White People? How the African American Marriage Decline Affects Everyone*. New York: Penguin.

Belgrave, F. Z., & Allison, K. W. (2006). *African American Psychology*. Thousand Oaks, CA: Sage.

Bell, D. (1999). The sexual diversion: The Black man/Black woman debate in context. In D. W. Carbado (Ed.). *Black Men on Race, Gender, and Sexuality: A Critical Reader* (pp. 237–248). New York: NYU Press.

Bell, Y. R., Bouie, C. L., & Baldwin, J. A. (1990). Afrocentric cultural consciousness and African American male female relationships. *Journal of Black Studies*, (21)2, 162–189.

Blassingame, J. W. (1972). *The Slave Community: Plantation Life in the Antebellum South*. New York: Oxford University Press.

Blassingame, J. W. (1979). *The Slave Community: Plantation Life in the Antebellum South*. New York: Oxford University Press.

Blee, K., & Tickamyer, A. (1995). Racial differences in men's attitudes about women's gender roles. *Journal of Marriage and the Family*, 57 (1), 21–30.

Bonilla-Silva, E. (2006). *Racism without Racists: Color-Blind Racism and the Persistence of Racial Inequality in the United States*. Lanham, MD: Rowman & Littlefield.

Bowleg, L., Lucas, K. J., & Tschann, J. M. (2004). "The ball was always in his court": An exploratory analysis of relationship scripts, sexual scripts, and condom use among African American women. *Psychology of Women Quarterly*, 28(1), 70–82.

Boyd-Franklin, N. (2003). *Black Families in Therapy: Understanding the African American Experience*. New York: Guilford Press.

Boyd-Franklin, N., & Franklin, A. J. (1998). African American couples in therapy. In M. McGoldrick (Ed.). *Re-Visioning Family Therapy: Race, Culture, and Gender in Clinical Practice* (pp. 268–281). New York: Guilford Press.

Bridgewater, P. D. (2005). Ain't I a slave: Slavery, reproductive abuses and reparations. *UCLA Women's Law Journal*, 14(1), 89–162.

Broman, C. (1993). Race differences in marital well-being. *Journal of Marriage and the Family*, 55(3), 724–732.

Browning, S., & Miller, R. (1999). Marital messages: The case of Black women and their children. *Journal of Family Issues*, 20(5), 633–647.

Bryant, C. M., Taylor, R. J., Lincoln, K. D., Chatters, L. M., & Jackson, J. S. (2008). Marital satisfaction among African Americans and Black Caribbeans: Findings from the national survey of American life. *Family Relations*, 57(2): 239–253.

Carey, M. P., Senn, T. E., Seward, D. X., & Vanable, P. A. (2010). Urban African-American men speak out on sexual partner concurrency: Findings from a qualitative study. *AIDS and Behavior*, 14(1), 38–47.

Carlson, M. J. (2007). Trajectories of couple relationship quality after childbirth: Does marriage matter? (Working paper 897). Princeton, NJ: Princeton University, Woodrow Wilson School of Public and International Affairs, Center for Research on Child Wellbeing.

Carlson, M. J., McLanahan, S., & England, P. (2004). Union formation and stability in fragile families. *Demography*, 41(2), 237–262.

Carolan, M. T., & Allen, K. R. (1999). Commitments and constraints to intimacy for African American couples at midlife. *Journal of Family Issues*, 20(1): 3–24.

Carter, J. S., Corra, M., & Carter, S. K. (2009). The interaction of race and gender: Changing gender-role attitudes, 1974–2006. *Social Science Quarterly*, 90(1), 196–211.

Cazenave, N. A. (1983). "A woman's place": The attitudes of middle-class Black men. *Phylon*, 44(1), 12–32.

Cazenave, N. A., & Smith, R. (1990). Gender differences in the perception of Black male-female relationships and stereotypes. In H. E. Cheatham, & J. B. Stewart (Eds.). *Black Families: Interdisciplinary Perspectives* (pp. 149–170). New Brunswick, NJ: Transaction Books.

Chapman, A. B. (1986). *Man Sharing: Dilemma or Choice, a Radical New Way of Relating to the Men in Your Life*. New York: William Morrow.

Chapman, A. B. (2001). *Seven Attitude Adjustments for Finding a Loving Man*. New York: Pocket Books.

Chapman, A. B. (2007). In search of love and commitment. In H. P. McAdoo (Ed.). *Black Families* (4th ed.) (pp. 285–296). Thousand Oaks, CA: Sage.

Clark-Nicolas, P., & Gray-Little, B. (1991). Effect of economic resources on marital quality in Black married couples. *Journal of Marriage and the Family*, 53(4), 645–655.

Clarkwest, A. (2007). Spousal dissimilarity, race, and marital dissolution. *Journal of Marriage & Family*, 69(3), 639–653.

Cole J. B., & Guy-Sheftall, B. (2003). *Gender Talk: The Struggle for Women's Equality in African American Communities*. New York: Ballantine Books.

Collins, P.H. (2000). *Black Feminist Thought*. New York: Routledge.

Coltrane, S. (2000). Research on household labor: Modeling and measuring the social embeddedness of routine family work. *Journal of Marriage & Family*, 62(4), 1208–1233.

Cross, W. E., Jr. (1991). *Shades of Black: Diversity in African American identity*. Philadelphia, PA: University Press.

Cutrona, C. E., Russell, D. W., Abraham, W. T., Gardner, K. A., Melby, J. N., Bryant, C., & Conger, R. D. (2003). Neighborhood context and financial strain as predictors of marital interaction and marital quality in African American couples. *Personal Relationships*, 10(3), 389–409.

Davis, A. D. (2009). "Don't let nobody bother yo' principle": The sexual economy of American slavery. In S. M. James, F. S. Foster, & B. Guy-Sheftall (Eds). *Still Brave: The Evolution of Black Women's Studies* (pp. 215–239). New York: The Feminist Press, CUNY.

Davis, A. Y. (1983). *Women, Race, and Class*. New York: Vintage Books.

Dickson, L. (1993). The future of marriage and family in Black America. *Journal of Black Studies*, 23(4), 472–491.

Douglas, K. B. (1999). *Sexuality and the Black Church: A Womanist Perspective*. New York: Orbis Books.

Dunham, S., & Ellis, C. M. (2010). Restoring intimacy with African American couples. In J. Carlson, & L. Sperry, *Recovering Intimacy in Love Relationships: A Clinician's Guide* (pp. 295–316). New York: Routledge.

Dunn, S. (2008). *Baad "Bitches" & Sassy Supermamas: Black Action Films*. Urbana, IL: University of Illinois Press.

Estacion, A., & Cherlin, A. (2010). Gender distrust and intimate unions among low-income Hispanic and African American women. *Journal of Family Issues*, 31(4), 475–498.

Fosse, N. E. (2010). The repertoire of infidelity among low-income men: Doubt, duty, and destiny. *The Annals of the American Academy of Political and Social Science*, 629(1), 125–143.

Foster, H. J. (1983). African patterns in the Afro-American family. *Journal of Black Studies*, (14)2, 201–232.

Franklin, A. J. (2004). *From Brotherhood to Manhood: How Black Men Rescue Their Relationships and Dreams from the Invisibility Syndrome*. Hoboken, NJ: John Wiley & Son.

Franklin, C. W. (1984). Black male-Black female conflict: Individually caused and culturally nurtured. *Journal of Black Studies*, 15(2), 139–154.

Franklin, D. (2001). *What's Love Got To Do With It?: Understanding and Healing the Rift Between Black Men and Women*. New York: Simon & Schuster.

Furstenberg, F. F. (2001). The fading dream: Prospects for marriage in the inner city. In E. Anderson, & D. S. Massey (Eds.). *Problem of the Century: Racial Stratification in the United States* (pp. 224–246). New York: Russell Sage Foundation.

Gillum, T. L. (2007). "How do I view my sister?": Stereotypic views of African American women and their potential to impact intimate partnerships. *Journal of Human Behavior in the Social Environment*, 15(2/3), 347–366.

Grange, C. M., Brubaker, S. J., & Corneille, M. A. (2011). Direct and indirect messages African American women receive from their familial networks about intimate relationships and sex: The intersecting influence of race, gender, and class. *Journal of Family Issues*, 32(5), 605–628.

Gregory, W. H., & Harper, K. W. (2001). The NTU approach to health and healing. *Journal of Black Psychology*, 27(3), 304–320.

Grills, C. N., & Rowe, D. M. (1998). African traditional medicine: Implications for African centered approaches to healing. In R. Jones (Ed.). *African American Mental Health: Theory, Research and Intervention*. Hampton, VA: Cobb & Henry Publishers.

Gutman, H. G. (1976). *The Black Family in Slavery and Freedom, 1750–1925*. New York: Random House.

Guyll, M., Cutrona, C., Burzette, R., & Russell, D. (2010). Hostility, relationship quality, and health among African American couples. *Journal of Consulting and Clinical Psychology*, 78(5), 646–654.

Hanks, T. L. (2008). The *Ubuntu* paradigm: Psychology's next force? *Journal of Humanistic Psychology*, 48(1), 116–135.

Harknett, K., & McLanahan, S. (2004). Racial and ethnic differences in marriage after the birth of a child. *American Sociological Review*, 69(6), 790–811.

Higginbotham, E. B. (1992). African-American women's history and the metalanguage of race. *Signs Journal of Women in Culture & Society*, 17(2), 251–274.

Hill, S.A. (2005). *Black Intimacies: A Gender Perspective on Families and Relationships*. Lanham, MD: Rowman & Littlefield.

Hill, S.A. (2009). Why won't African Americans get (and stay) married? Why should they? In H. E. Peters and C. M. Kamp Dush (Eds.). *Marriage and Family: Complexities and Perspectives* (pp. 345–364). New York: Columbia University Press.

Hilliard, A. G., III. (1992). Behavioral style, culture, and teaching and learning. *Journal of Negro Education*, 61(3), 370–377.

Hilliard, A. G., III. (1997). *SBA: The Reawakening of the African Mind*. Gainesville, FL: Makare Publishing Company.

Hines, P., & Boyd-Franklin, N. (1996). *African American Families: Ethnicity and Family Therapy*. New York: Guilford Press.

Holloway, J. E. (Ed.). (2005). *Africanisms in American Culture (2nd ed)*. Bloomington, IN: Indiana University Press.

Holloway, K. F. C. (1995). *Codes of Conduct: Race, Ethics, and the Color of Our Character*. New Brunswick, NJ: Rutgers University Press.

hooks, b. (2004). *We Real Cool: Black Men and Masculinity*. New York: Routledge.

Hunter, A. G., & Davis J. E. (1992). Constructing gender: An exploration of Afro-American men's conceptualization of manhood. *Gender & Society*, 6(3), 464–479.

Hunter, A. G., & Sellers, S. L. (1998). Feminist attitudes among African Americanwomen and men. *Gender & Society*, 12(1), 81–99.

Hutchinson, E. O. (1997). *The Assassination of the Black Male Image*. New York: Simon & Schuster.

Jarama, S. L., Belgrave F. Z., Bradford, J., Young, M., & Honnold, J.A. (2007). Family, cultural and gender role aspects in the context of HIV risk among African American women of unidentified HIV status: An exploratory qualitative study. *AIDS Care*, 19(3), 307–317.

Jewell, K. S. (1983). Black male/female conflict: Internalization of negative definition transmitted through imagery. *The Western Journal of Black Studies*, 7(1), 43–48.

Johnson, L. B., & Staples, R. (2005*). Black Families at the Crossroads: Challenges and Prospects*. San Francisco, CA: Jossey-Bass.

Jones, J. (1985). *Labor of Love, Labor of Sorrow: Black Women, Work, and the Family from Slavery to the Present*. New York: Basic Books.

Kambon, K. K. (1992). *The African Personality in America: An African Centered Framework*. Tallahassee, FL: Nubian Nation Publication.

Kane, E. (2000). Race and ethnic variations in gender-related attitudes. *Annual Review of Sociology*, 26(1), 419–439.

King, A. (1999). African American females' attitudes toward marriage: An exploratory study. *Journal of Black Studies*, 29(3), 416–437.

Kitwana, B. (2003). *The Hip Hop Generation: Young Blacks and the Crisis in African American Culture*. New York: Basic Civitas Books.

Kwate, N. O. A. (2005). The heresy of African-centered psychology. *Journal of Medical Humanities*, 26(4), 215–235.

Landry, B. (2000). *Black Working Wives: Pioneers of the American Family Revolution*. Berkeley, CA: University of California Press.

Lane, S. D., Keefe, R. H., Rubinstein, R. A., Levandowski, B. A., Freedman, M., Rosenthal, A., Cibula, D. A., & Czerwinski, M. (2004). Marriage promotion and missing men: African American women in a demographic double bind. *Medical Anthopology Quarterly*, 18(4), 405–428.

LaTaillade, J.J. (2006). Considerations for treatment of African American couple relationships. *Journal of Cognitive Psychotherapy: An International Quarterly Volume*, 20(4), 341–358.

Lawrence-Webb, C., Littlefield, M., & Okundaye, J. (2004). African American intergender relationships: A theoretical exploration of roles, patriarchy, and love. *Journal of Black Studies*, 34(5), 623–639.

Majors, R., & Billson, J.M. (1992). *Cool Pose: The Dilemmas Of Black Manhood In America*. New York: Simon & Schuster.

Marable, M. (1983). *How Capitalism Underdeveloped Black America: Problems in Race, Political Economy, and Society*. Boston, MA: South End Press.

Marbley, A. F. (2003). "Hey there Ms. Jones!": A qualitative study of professional African American males' perceptions of the selection of African American females as partners. *Journal of African American Studies*, 7(3), 15–30.

Marks, L. D., Hopkins, K., Chaney, C., Monroe, P. A., Nesteruk, O., Diane D., & Sasser, D. D. (2008). "Together, we are strong": A qualitative study of happy, enduring African American marriages. *Family Relations*, 57(2), 172–185.

Martin, E., & Martin, J .M. (1978). *The Black Extended Family*. Chicago, IL: University of Chicago Press.

Mbiti, J. S. (1969). *African Religions and Philosophy*. New York: Praeger Publishers.

McAdoo, H. P. (1998). African American families: Strength and realities. In H. I. McCubbin, E.A. Thompson, A. I. Thompson, & J. A. Futrell (Eds.). *Resiliency in Ethnic Minority Families. Vol.2: African American Families* (pp. 17–30). Thousand Oaks, CA: Sage.

McGruder, K. (2010). Pathologizing Black sexuality: The U.S. experience. In J. Battle & S. Barnes (Eds.). *Black Sexualities: Probing Powers, Passions, Practices, and Policies* (pp. 101–118). New Brunswick, NJ: Rutgers University Press.

Mickel, E. (2005). African centered family therapy in transition: Healing cycle as an answer to terrorism. *International Journal of Reality Therapy*, (24)2, 33–37.

Mintz, S. W., & Price, R. (1992). *The Birth of African-American Culture: An Anthropological Perspective*. Boston, MA: Beacon Press.

Mkize, D. L. (2003). Towards an Afrocentric approach to psychiatry. *South African Journal of Psychiatry* 9, 3–6.

Monteiro, N. M., & Wall, D. J. (2011). African dance as healing modality throughout the Diaspora: The use of ritual and movement to work through trauma. *The Journal of Pan African Studies*, 4(6), 234–253.

Morgan, J. (2000). *When Chickenheads Come Home to Roost: My Life as a Hip-Hop Feminist*. New York: Simon & Schuster.

Moynihan, D.P. (1965). *The Negro family: The Case for National Action*. Washington, DC: Office of Policy Planning and Research.

Myers, L. J. (1993). *Understanding an Afrocentric World View: Introduction to an Optimal Psychology*. Dubuque, IA: Kendal Hunt.

Myers, L. J., & Speight, S. L. (2010). Reframing mental health and psychological well-being among persons of African descent: Africana/Black psychology meeting the challenge of fractured social and cultural realities. *Journal of Pan African Studies*, (3)8, 66–82.

Myers, L. J., Montgomery, D. E., Fine, M. A., & Reese, R. (1996). Belief system analysis scale and belief and behavior awareness scale development: Measuring an optimal, Afrocentric world-view. In R. Jones (Ed.). *Handbook of Tests and Measurements for Black Populations.* (2 vols). Hampton, VA: Cobb & Henry Publishers.

Neal, M. A. (2002). *Soul Babies: Black Popular Culture and the Post-Soul Aesthetic.* New York: Routledge.

Nitsche, N., & Brueckner, H. (2009). Opting out of the family? Social change in racial inequality in family formation patterns among highly educated women. Paper presented at American Sociological Association, San Francisco, CA.

Nobles, W. (1991). African philosophy: Foundations for black psychology. In R. L. Jones (Ed.). *Black Psychology*, (3rd ed.) (pp. 47–63). New York: Harper & Row.

Nobles, W. W. (1998). To be African or not to be: The question of identity or authenticity some preliminary thoughts. In R. L. Jones (Ed.). *African American Identity Development.* Hampton, VA: Cobb & Henry Publishers.

Nobles, W. W. (2006). *Seeking the Sakhu: Foundational Writings for an African Psychology.* Chicago, IL: Third World Press.

Nobles, W. W. (2008). Shattered consciousness & fractured identity: The lingering psychological effects of the Transatlantic Slave trade experience. *Illinois Transatlantic Slave Trade Commission 2008 Report II: v2*, Chicago, IL: Illinois Transatlantic Slave Trade commission.

Ojelade, I. I., McCray, K., Ashby, J. S., & Meyers, J. (2011). Use of Ifá as a means of addressing mental health concerns among African American clients. *Journal of Counseling & Development*, 89, 406–412.

O'Sullivan, L., & Meyer-Bahlburg, H. (2003). African-American and Latina inner-city girls' reports of romantic and sexual development. *Journal of Social and Personal Relationships*, 20(2), 221–238.

Patterson, O. (1998). *Rituals of Blood: Consequences of Slavery in Two American Centuries.* Washington, DC. Basic Civitas Books.

Payne-Jackson, C. (2008). The impact of racism on enslaved Black mothers and the implications for birth outcomes. *Illinois Transatlantic Slave Trade Commission 2008 Report II: v2*, Chicago, IL: Illinois Transatlantic Slave Trade commission.

Phillips, F. B., (1996). NTU psychotherapy: Principles and processes. In D. Azibo (Ed.). *African Psychology in Historical Perspective and Related Commentary* (pp. 83–97). Trenton, NJ: Africa World Press, Inc.

Pinderhughes, E. B. (2002). African American marriage in the 20th century. *Family Process* 41(2), 269–282.

Piper-Mandy, E., & Rowe, T. D. (2010). Educating African-centered psychologists: Towards a comprehensive paradigm. *The Journal of Pan African Studies*, 3(8), 5–23.

Raley, R. K., & Sweeney, M. M. (2009). Explaining race and ethnic variation in marriage: Directions for future research. *Race and Social Problems*, 1(3), 132–142.

Rowe, D. M., & Rowe, S. L. (2009). Conversations in marriage©: An African-centered marital intervention. In M. E. Gallardo & B. McNeill (Eds.) *Intersections of Multiple Identities: A Casebook of Evidence-Based Practices with Diverse Populations* (pp. 59–84). New York: Routledge.

Seal, D. W., & Ehrhardt, A. A. (2003). Masculinity and urban men: Perceived scripts for courtship, romantic, and sexual interactions with women. *Culture, Health and Sexuality*, 5(4), 295–319.

Seal, D. W., Smith, M., Coley, B., Perry, J., & Gamez, M. (2008). Urban heterosexual couples' sexual scripts for three shared sexual experiences. *Sex Roles*, 58 (9/10), 626–638.

Sellers, R. M., Caldwell, C. H., Schmeelk-Cone, K. H., & Zimmerman, M. A. (2003). Racial identity, racial discrimination, perceived stress, and psychological distress among African American young adults. *Journal of Health and Social Behavior*, 43, 302–317.

Stanton-Salazar, R. D., & Spina, S. U. (2000). The network orientations of highly resilient urban minority youth: A network-analytic account of minority socialization and its educational implications. *Urban Review*, 32, 227–61.

Staples, R. & Johnson, L.B. (1993). *Black Families at the Crossroads: Challenges and Prospects*. San Francisco, CA: Jossey-Bass Publishers.

Stephens D. P. & Phillips, L. D. (2003). Freaks, gold diggers, divas, and dykes: The sociohistorical development of adolescent African American women's sexual scripts. *Sexuality and Culture*, 7(1), 3–49.

Sternberg, R. J. (1986). A triangular theory of love. *Psychological Review*, 93(2), 119–135.

Strmic-Pawl, H. V., Phyllis, K., & Leffler, P. H. (2011). Black families and fostering of leadership. *Ethnicities*, 11(2), 139–162.

Sudarkasa, N. (2007). Interpreting the African heritage in African American family organization. In H. P. McAdoo (Ed.). *Black Families (4th ed.)* (pp. 29–48). Thousand Oaks, CA: Sage Publications, Inc.

Sussman, L. (2004). The role of culture in definitions, interpretations, and management of illness. In J. Gielen, M. Fish, & J. Draguns (Eds.). *Handbook of Culture, Therapy, and Healing* (pp. 37–65). Philadelphia, PA: Erlbaum.

Thomas, A. J., & King, C. T. (2007). Gendered racial socialization of African American mothers and daughters. *The Family Journal*, 15(2), 137–142.

Tucker, M. B., & Mitchell-Kernan, C. (1995). Trends in African American family formation: A theoretical and statistical overview. In M. B. Tucker & C. Mitchell-Kernan (Eds.). *The Decline in Marriage Among African Americans: Causes, Consequences, and Policy Implications*. New York: Russell Sage Foundation.

Waller, M., & McLanahan, S. (2005). "His and "her" marriage expectations: Determinants and consequences. *Journal of Marriage and Family*, 67(1), 53–67.

Warfield-Coppock, N. (1992). The rites of passage movement: A resurgence of African-centered practices for socializing African American youth. *Journal of Education*, 61, 471–482.

Washington, K. (2010). Zulu traditional healing, Afrikan worldview and the practice of *Ubuntu*: Deep thought for Afrikan/Black psychology. *The Journal of Pan African Studies*, 3(8), 24–39.

Washington, K. (2011). The practice of *Ubuntu*: Deep thought for Afrikan/Black psychology, Symposium Presented at Annual Meeting of the Association of Black Psychologists Conference, Washington, DC, July

West, C. (1993). *Race Matters*. New York: Vintage Books.

White, D. (1999). *Too Heavy a Load: Black Women in Defense of Themselves 1894–1994*. New York: W. W. Norton.

White, J. L. (1984). *The psychology of Blacks*. Englewood Cliffs, NJ: Princeton Hall.

White, J. L., & Parham, T. A. (1990). *The Psychology of Blacks (2nd ed.)*. Englewood Cliffs, NJ: Princeton-Hall.

Whitehead, T. L. (1997). Urban low-income African American men, HIV/AIDS, and gender identity. *Medical Anthropology Quarterly* 11(4), 411–447.

Wickrama, K. A. S., Bryant, C. M., & Wickrama, T. K. A. (2010). Perceived community disorder, hostile marital interactions, and self-reported health of African American couples: An interdyadic process. *Personal Relationships*, 17(4), 515–531.

Willie, C. V., & Reddick, R. (2003). *A New Look at Black Families*. Walnut Creek, CA: AltaMira Press.

Willis, J. T. (1990). Some destructive elements in African-American male-female relationships. *Family Therapy*, 17(2), 139–147.

Wilson, W. J. (1987). *The Truly Disadvantaged: The Inner City, the Underclass, and Public Policy*. Chicago, IL: University of Chicago Press.

Wilson, W. J. (1996). *When Work Disappears*. New York: Alfred A. Knopf.

Wilson, W. J. (2008). The economic plight of inner-city Black males. In E. Anderson (Ed.). *Against the Wall: Poor, Young, Black, and Male* (pp. 55–70). Philadelphia, PA: University of Pennsylvania Press.

Wilson, W. J., & Neckerman, K. M. (1986). Poverty and family structure: The widening gap between evidence and public policy issues. In S. H. Danziger & D. H. Weinberg (Eds.) *Fighting Poverty* (pp. 232–259). Cambridge, MA: Harvard University Press.

Part II

SOCIALIZATION FACTORS OF BLACK LOVE AND INTIMACY

3

AFRICAN AMERICAN MALE–FEMALE ROMANTIC RELATIONSHIPS

Feliesha Shelton-Wheeler

This chapter will explore the development of Black male–female relationships from childhood to adulthood. Gender socialization and romantic relationship patterns will be examined. Treatment implications based on chapter topics will be reviewed as it is critical that clinicians understand these specific influences on Black couples' relationships to do culturally sensitive and effective treatment. Emotional intimacy within Black male–female relationships will be discussed and strategies for treatment of Black couples will be provided.

Relationship Development

Our ideas about romantic relationships come from a variety of sources: our families, cultural background, the media, peer group, and our worldview. We develop romantic relationship and sexual scripts (King, 2009) based on these multiple influences. In an attempt to understand the process of relationship development further, there are some questions that may be useful to explore. Specifically, where do we learn about intimacy? How do we learn how to be intimate with another person? A primary place to begin exploring the answers to these questions is to examine the development of relationships from childhood to adulthood. It is helpful to examine the formation of attitudes, behaviors, and gender roles that impact the ways in which Black children and adolescents develop intimate relationships. There are many ways in which intimacy is defined. One definition of intimacy entails the sharing of oneself in a way that promotes a sense of connectedness with someone else (Dixon, 2007). As with many things, culture and family have a significant role in shaping the way we assign meaning to and define emotional intimacy. From a Western perspective, intimacy tends to be perceived as a process that involves sharing feelings, thoughts, experiences, empathy, and support of another person (Marshall, 2008). The interpersonal process model explains that intimacy is a feeling of closeness that arises from an exchange of self-disclosure between partners (Marshall, 2008). Thus, intimacy not only entails that both partners provide empathic and supportive responses to one another's self-disclosures, but that they also perceive each other's responses as supportive. In this model, when a person feels validated and understood by his or her partner the process of intimacy is achieved (Marshall, 2008).

Intimacy occurs in various contexts, such as friendships, dating, and marriage. Different types of intimacy exist within each of these contexts. For example, the physical aspect of intimacy involves sharing one's body with another person and being attracted to the physical features of another person (Dixon, 2007). The mental aspect of intimacy involves exchanging thoughts and values with a person; while the emotional part of intimacy involves sharing one's feelings (Dixon, 2007). Research suggests that emotional intimacy is an important aspect of human development and can promote the health and well-being of a person (Gaia, 2002). In a Westernized model of romantic scripts, this type of intimacy is highly allured. A final type of intimacy is the spiritual component of intimacy. This aspect of intimacy entails exchanging spiritual beliefs and connecting on a religious level with another person (Dixon, 2007). Many African Americans most especially prize spiritual intimacy.

Today, romantic scripts tend to include a desire for emotional intimacy. Most couples have the expectation that their partners will be loving, supportive, sexually faithful, and contribute to the growth of both people in the relationship. Intimacy failures are frequently what bring couples to treatment. In American culture, adolescence is the time in which we begin to explore our romantic ideals about love, lust, intimacy, and romantic relationships. Adolescents typically do this through crushes and dating relationships. Thus, we will review romantic script development amongst African American couples through a developmental lens.

Adolescence

Adolescence is the phase of human development that represents the transition from being a child to becoming a young adult. It is a significant time in which an individual attempts to gain and establish his/her identity, and becomes strongly impacted by peer influence. Wolfe, Jaffe, and Crooks (2006) explain that adolescents rely heavily on their peers for intimacy and nurturance. In addition, they either replicate or challenge the relationships that were modeled for them by the media and their families. These modeled relationships (whether negative or positive) help to shape an adolescent's expectations and ideas about their sexuality, intimacy, and gender roles within relationships. African American adolescents typically begin dating and sexual relationships earlier than their white peers (Mandara, Murray, & Bangi, 2003). Because so many of the media images about African American romantic relationships are negative, and adolescents are significantly influenced by media culture, this can negatively shape Black teens attitudes towards dating relationships and gender roles.

Media and African American Adolescent Sexuality

From childhood, we develop romantic and sexual scripts. A sexual script is a schema we develop in childhood that influences our beliefs and values regarding how sexual relationships are supposed to occur and is influenced by our environments, family, culture, and society (King, 2009). The media is also a powerful socializing influence on these scripts. Television, magazines, video games, music, and the Internet constantly relay written and visual messages to adolescents about sex. Many of these messages focus on physical appearance, identity, and how they should be interacting with their peers. For example, some music videos show very provocative images of female sexuality. Rouse-Arnett and Long Dilworth (2006) explain that females are twice as likely as males to be portrayed as seductive and aggressively encountered by a person in the video. This is especially true in hip hop culture where females in videos are typically objectified sexually and males are viewed as dominate connoisseurs of female sexual favors. Further, these authors suggest that youth who view a high rate of television content that is sexual tend to initiate sexual behavior. If, however, the television content conveys the risks of sexual behavior then adolescents may be inclined not to engage in sexual behavior. A study on African American youth found that adolescents who watched television shows that discussed sexual risks and safety were less likely to initiate sexual intercourse the following year (Rouse-Arnett & Long Dilworth, 2006); however, the opposite is also true, television shows with high levels of sexual content appear to encourage adolescent sexual behavior.

Romantic relationships begin to transpire during adolescence. In response to peer influence, many adolescents begin experimenting with their sexuality and sexual intercourse (Wolfe et al., 2006). This may be especially true for African American adolescents as research demonstrates that African American teens tend to have intercourse earlier than their white peers. Mandara et al. (2003) identify three areas within African American adolescents' lives that may impact their decision to engage in sex early. Specifically, the authors explain that personal, familial, and extrafamilial factors impact African American adolescents' decision to engage in early sexual activity. With regard to personal factors, the use of alcohol has been linked to an increased probability (96 percent) of African American male adolescents as being sexually active while alcohol use in relation to African American female adolescents has been linked at 85 percent (Mandara et al., 2003). Mandara et al. (2003) explain that because alcohol use can lower one's inhibitions, and disrupt one's abilities to make appropriate decisions and judgments, the chances are high for adolescents who abuse alcohol to make unsafe and poor choices regarding sex.

With regard to familial influences, Mandara et al. (2003) explain that the onset of early sexual intercourse for adolescents may be impacted by the degree of parental monitoring that is/ is not present. Adolescents who have a significant degree of parental monitoring (e.g., parents are at home when their child comes home from school or a parent is aware of their child's peer interactions and activities), are likely to have limited abilities to engage in sexual activity. In contrast, adolescents who have minimal parental monitoring are likely to have more opportunities to seek and engage in activities that might promote early sexual exploration. While there are exceptions, the presence of two parents who are actively monitoring their child's activities may likely exhibit a higher level of monitoring their child than a single parent. Single parents' resources may be more limited than dual parent households. African American adolescents tend to represent the highest number of children who are raised in single parent households (66 percent versus 24 percent of Caucasian kids) (Kids Count Data Center, 2009), thus increasing the possibility of early sexual activity. With regard to extrafamilial influences Mandara et al. (2003) explain that the socioeconomic status (SES) of an adolescent's family can influence his/her choices to engage in sex early. Adolescents in lower SES households may be likely to engage in sex early. While there are exceptions, lower SES families may have limited education and limited access to resources and information regarding sex related prevention. Mandara et al. (2003) explain that families with higher education levels may have more financial resources to provide adolescents with alternative activities that promote self-confidence, positive coping, and positive engagement with peers. In 2010, the median income of African American families was identified as having the lowest level of household income within the U.S. ($32,068) in comparison to Asian households who held the highest level of income at $64,308 (U.S. Census Bureau, 2011). African American families were also identified as having the highest percentage of poverty within the U.S. (27.4 percent) compared to 9.9 percent for non-Hispanic Caucasian families.

Crockett and Randall (2006) state that by age 15 or earlier, most adolescents will have a boyfriend/girlfriend. A reason why romantic relationships begin at this age is because of the elements that exist within their peer relationships. For example, the elements of similarity (e.g., age), power, and social status contribute to the development of these romantic relationships. These elements are also important in helping adolescents establish a sense of respect and mutual selflessness toward one another (Crocket & Randall, 2006). Adolescents in general frequently shape their young lives around their current romantic interests and the status of their romantic relationships and African American adolescents are no exception to the cultural drive to express romantic interests around this age. Authors Simons, Simons, Lei, & Landor (2011), explain that teen dating can serve as the catalyst for shaping the ideas and expectations adolescents have about marriage. Further, teen romantic relationships often serve as the developmental precursor for the romantic relationships adolescents may experience later as adults. If a teenager experiences negative dating relationships (e.g., chronic conflict and disappointment or abuse), they may develop a negative outlook on the benefits of adult relationships and marriage (Simons et al., 2011). For African American adolescents, this is where issues of gender stereotypes begin to surface romantically. For example, if a male adolescent has heard older male relatives or experienced media influences that convey Black women in a negative manner (e.g., Black women are controlling and bossy—don't let yourself be controlled by a Black woman or you won't be a man), this is the attitude he may bring to his dating relationships. Conversely, if Black female adolescents have heard that Black boys/men are "no good" and will cheat on you, this is the attitude she may bring to her dating relationships. As per Bandura's social learning theory (Anderson & Kras, 2005), we often model behaviors we have seen. Adolescence is the time these romantic relational models and influences become operationalized and negative racial and gender stereotypes can be internalized where Black female teens do not trust one another if they have been socialized to believe that other girls/women are after their boyfriends. The same is true for African American males. This early internalization of negative racial and gender stereotypes can have devastating consequences for both adolescent and adult romantic relationships. By the time adolescents grow up, these stereotypes may be deeply ingrained and may have already negatively impacted intimacy in romantic relationships.

Parents and Adolescent Sexuality

While adolescence is the stage where romantic interests begin to flourish, the literature suggests that attitudes about sexuality develop much earlier. By age three or four, a child's ideas about nudity and displaying affection have been shaped by his/her parents (Rouse-Arnett & Long Dilworth, 2006). The manner in which parents communicate and model their ideas about sexuality and intimacy can impact the way in which adolescents display both. Rouse-Arnett and Long Dilworth (2006) explain that individuals whose parents model for them that sexuality and intimacy are inappropriate/should be avoided, will likely perceive sexuality and intimacy with feelings of shame and guilt. As a result, adolescents are then likely to turn to their peers to learn about sexuality and intimacy (Rouse-Arnett & Long Dilworth, 2006). Seeking information from their peers only heightens their risk for becoming sexually active as research suggests that adolescents whose friends are engaging in sexual intercourse are more likely to do the same (Rouse-Arnett & Long Dilworth, 2006).

Because more African American children grow up in single parent homes than their white counterparts many may not have the benefit of growing up in a household where they regularly see how adults relate to one another in a romantic context which also shapes children's romantic and sexual scripts.

Research suggests that mothers tend to be the primary parent to initiate or talk with their children about sex (Rouse-Arnett & Long Dilworth, 2006). In fact, a mother's influence can have strong implications for their daughter's sexual behavior. The literature suggests that African American youth, in particular, who intend to abstain from sexual intercourse are strongly influenced by their mothers, more than their father and peers (Rouse-Arnett & Long Dilworth, 2006). Research also suggests that parents tend to have more conversations about sex with their daughters than sons (Rouse-Arnett & Long Dilworth, 2006). Perhaps this is because parents fear their daughter may get pregnant. Still, many parents fear that talking about sex may initiate their child's sexual behavior or interest; however, these parents fail to realize is that there are several benefits to talking with their teenager about sex. Research indicates that talking to teenagers about sex can decrease premarital intercourse, decrease promiscuity, and increase the proper use of contraception (Rouse-Arnett & Long Dilworth, 2006). Additionally, as discussed in Chapter 2, because African Americans are stereotyped as being hypersexual, both historically and currently, it is important that parents instill a positive sense of one's sexual self and help their teens understand the physical, spiritual, and emotional consequences of having sex. Parents should also discuss abstinence, sexual values and morals, and contraception use as appropriate so that teens are empowered in their sexual decisions instead of inadvertently encouraging them to be secretive by not having discussions about sex.

African American Female Sexuality

When it comes to discussions about sexuality for African American females, Rouse-Arnett and Long Dilworth (2006) explain that most literature tends to focus on teenage pregnancy, out-of-wedlock births, contraceptive use, and the prevention of sexually transmitted diseases. The authors explain that other aspects of sexuality, such as a female's values, attitudes, and emotional states in relation to sexuality are rarely discussed. In an effort to address this deficiency, the authors conducted a study that examined how African American women's sexuality is influenced by parental, peer, and media influences. The study included a sample of African American single mothers who discussed the influences on their sexuality and how these influences shaped the way in which they saw themselves. One of their findings revealed that the women's family of origin had a strong influence in how they saw themselves. Their mothers/female caregivers had a significant impact on relaying negative/positive messages about their sexuality. Most participants stated that conversations regarding sexuality in adolescence centered primarily on contraception use and sexually transmitted diseases.

Many participants described ambivalence, fear, and ignorance when it came to their first menstruation because they received unclear (and often negative) messages about their body from their parents which may reflect the parents' own discomfort with talking about sexuality and their own bodies. Unfortunately, this discomfort is easily communicated to children and teens and influences them well into adulthood as evidenced by many of the women in the study who expressed feelings of shame, guilt, and inadequacy regarding their bodies. These early experiences deprived many of these women the opportunity to connect with their sexual experiences and bodies (Rouse-Arnett & Long Dilworth, 2006). This may explain why African Americans tend to be more conservative in sexual behavior than their white peers (King, 2009).

Thomas, Crook, and Cobia (2009) explain that there are a range of messages African American women can receive about sexuality in childhood, including nudity and masturbation being viewed as unacceptable and premarital sex as sinful. In addition to the negative media influences Black girls receive about the standard of beauty (thin, blonde, and white), and the media's portrayal of Black girls/women as sexually promiscuous, these rigid messages can create a disconnect between African American women and their bodies and create a negative view of sex and female sexuality. Thomas et al. (2009) state that these stereotypes negatively impact the sexual identity development of African American females. Stereotypes include: Black women as Jezebels (promiscuous), mammies (asexual, dark skinned, overweight, showing deference to others' needs instead of their own), the welfare mother (irresponsible in bearing an excessive amount of children, creating financial strain on society due to the excessive births), the matriarch (controlling and condescending), divas, and gold diggers. These images can have a significant impact on the way in which African American men may perceive their female partners.

African American Male Sexuality

Just as African American women learn different messages about sexuality during childhood, African American men receive them as well. African American males are taught, early on, that to be masculine means they must be sexually assertive. Bowleg (2004) asserts that boys/men are often encouraged to engage in sexual activity for pleasure and recreation, have multiple partners, and take a dominant stance within the sexual relationship. African American males that portray this ideology of masculinity have been found to engage in sexual intercourse early (Bowleg, 2004). With regard to specific messages about masculinity, Bowleg (2004) explains that, within the U.S., the idealized masculine role includes an element of economic wealth, including success and power. African American males have been at a disadvantage in being able to attain this ideal role because of the historical barrier of slavery and current racist practices that disproportionately discriminate against African American men. While many Caucasian males are intermittently at an economic advantage due to their ancestral connection to slave owners and white skin, most African American males have never received the same economic advantage due to their ancestral connection with slaves and black skin. As a result of this disadvantage and inability to consistently succeed at society's hallmarks of masculinity (e.g., high income and prestigious employment), Bowleg (2004) explains that African American males have had to establish alternative expressions of masculinity. Specifically, some African American males have learned to utilize sexual promiscuity, acts of aggression and violence, risk taking, emotional suppression (e.g., vulnerability, sadness, fear), emotional expression of anger, and rejecting feminine qualities and homosexuality as surrogate forms of ideal masculinity. These behaviors are often learned in and encouraged during adolescence. It should be noted that while emotional suppression is a common, learned male behavior, in general, it is has a unique impact for African American males who already live within a society that invalidates their existence in many ways. Bowleg (2004) explains that some African American males have learned, early on, to adapt a *Black machismo identity* (e.g., a *cool pose*). Black machismo identity is defined as that identity which embraces a sexual conquest over females and displayed aggression toward other African American males or authority figures. The underlying purpose of this identity is to create a sense of power that African American males would otherwise not have within a society that often reiterates racist/diminishing messages that can negatively impact the self-worth of African American men. Black boys/men may internalize the same racist stereotypes that society projects onto them. This alternative masculine identity appears to be more strongly demonstrated among some African American males who are among the lower SES (Bowleg, 2004), although it is not exclusive to lower SES African American males. It is also likely to interfere significantly with the way in which African American men are able to establish relationships with African American women and vice versa.

Understanding Relationship Development from the Perspectives of Role Theory, Social Learning Theory, and Family Systems

There are three theories that help to explain how individuals learn about relationships and develop ideas about gender roles—role theory, social learning theory, and family systems—and they offer interesting perspectives on this subject. A brief description of these theories will be provided.

Role Theory

According to Turner (2000) role theory asserts that people exhibit social behaviors based on roles they are assigned and learn from others. Each of these learned and assigned roles are based on gender. From this perspective, a person evaluates his/her self-worth based on whether he or she can perform his/her gender role adequately. With regard to gender roles, Wolfe et al. (2006) stated that "...gender becomes a simple way of assigning expectations and roles. If a child sees that most childcare workers, housekeepers, and grocery shoppers are women...he or she easily comprehends that these are the tasks that women do..." (p. 35).

The way in which a child interprets his or her role, based on gender, will likely transfer into his or her relationships as adults. Thus, if a male child has seen his mother solely perform household duties (e.g., washing clothes), it is very likely that that child will expect that same task to be performed by his girlfriend or wife. Similarly, if a female child grows up watching her father be the sole financial provider, she is likely to expect that her husband will be the breadwinner, as well.

70

Social Learning Theory

Albert Bandura's social learning theory views human behavior as learned through experience and observation (Anderson & Kras, 2005). From this perspective, observing (*modeling*) and then imitating the actions of others is thought to be one of the most influential ways that human beings learn behavior. Modeling comes from various sources, such as peers, the media, and families and is a primary way in which a person learns how to be in relationships with others. We learn the roles men and women have within relationships by watching how men and women relate to one another. We also learn how to communicate, behave, think, and feel in our own relationships by watching other men and women engage with one another.

Bandura's concept is applicable to individuals and families of any culture, including African Americans. If learning how to be in a relationship occurs through observing men and women in relationships, then there may be factors that may hinder this process for African Americans, such as the media. For example, Entman and Rojecki (2000) explain that the images of African Americans in advertisements (e.g., commercials) depict fewer images of African Americans speaking to other African Americans or displaying forms of intimacy (e.g., caressing one another's skin, kissing, or hugging) compared to the way in which Caucasians are depicted in commercials and movies. They find that advertisements tend to depict African Americans as being sexualized rather than engaging in intimacy (e.g., hugging and kissing). Interestingly, the authors also explain that the networks designed primarily for an African American audience (e.g., BET) have shown ads where there were few or peripheral roles depicting African Americans. Even more disturbing, the authors explain, is that intimate images that were displayed on networks like BET were those depicted by Caucasian actors. The absence of these integral intimacy images can negatively influence the way in which African American couples learn how to relate to one another. Thus, many African Americans lack positive romantic relationship role models within the home, media, and community. Obviously this can significantly impact one's relational and sexual scripts.

Within the African American community, not only are relationships and gender roles modeled, but cultural aspects are interwoven within these modeled behaviors, as well. Throughout history, African Americans have had to endure and overcome various racial and economic challenges in the U.S. For this reason, the training and modeling of African American households tends to include different elements that may not be present within white households. For example, research suggests that there is a tendency for many African American mothers to model behaviors for their daughters that show they must succeed and survive in society (Dickson, 1993). The messages of independence and self-sufficiency, for females, can likely be traced back several generations within the African American community and may be interpreted as signs that a woman does not need a man in her life to obtain the things she wants. While being self-sufficient has many benefits, it can also have negative implications in a relationship and create friction as some African American males may perceive her independence as a sign that their female partners do not need them.

With regard to African American males, Dickson (1993) explains that in an effort to overcome various societal oppressions, many men have been taught to exhibit a *cool pose*. A cool pose is a pose that exudes fearlessness, aloofness, and emotionlessness to society (Dickson, 1993). The cool pose serves as a protective factor which allows an African American male to maintain a sense of pride, dignity, and self-respect (Dickson, 1993). There is a risk, however, that these characteristics may transfer into relationships which could create a barrier to communication and affection. Specifically, if an African American male exhibits emotional detachment in a relationship, his partner will likely interpret him as non-caring and emotionally unavailable. Literature suggests that more than half of African American households are headed by African American women who are raising children under 18 (Bush, 2000). Among those children are male children who are being raised by their mothers. While there are various factors that influence the way in which African American males are socialized, as reviewed above (e.g., media and peers), similar to females, parents play a significant role in the way in which they perceive masculinity and their gender role. Sharp and Ispa (2009) state that African American males raised by single mothers have a tendency to be more firm with their daughters than their sons. African American mothers tend to view their sons as vulnerable (perhaps due to their high risk for incidents, such as homicide and imprisonment) and thus have a tendency to be very protective of them. This form of extensive protection that African American mothers extend to their sons has been labeled as "loving their sons and raising their daughters" (Sharp & Ispa, 2009). Bush (2000) found in his study on how African Americans raise their sons, that African American women's definition of masculinity tended to include aspects of both feminine and masculine qualities. Their integrated definition of masculinity, however, appeared to fall within a traditional European concept of masculinity and femininity. Examples of this traditional concept include being financially independent, reliable, Christian, and honorable. Bush (2000) found that many of the mothers were aware of the societal challenges their sons had to endure, such as stereotypes and racism. Many of the mothers in the study shared the belief that their sons needed the presence of a man in their lives to teach them how to be a man. It is possible without having a positive male role model to demonstrate certain prosocial male behaviors; however, a male partner within a relationship may feel a sense of inadequacy with how to engage with, communicate, and convey expectations to their partner if this has not been modeled to him by other males. These feelings of inadequacy could create barriers between partners where their needs are not being met, which could lead to unsatisfying relationships. It should be noted by clinicians, however, that not all African American men are negatively impacted by the above factors. Culturally sensitive clinicians should assess for the existence of these factors but not assume that all African American men are negatively influenced by them.

Unfortunately, some African American couples may have expectations of one another that are based on stereotypes. This has been discussed at length in the previous chapter. African Americans have had to develop coping skills to deal with society's dysfunctional racist and discriminatory barriers that many have to face on a daily basis. Thus, the development of survival skills, such as appearing tough, masculine (for both men and women), and invulnerable has enabled African Americans to survive in a society that projects negative images about them on a consistent basis. Unfortunately, this way of surviving ultimately costs many the ability to develop trusting, emotionally intimate, romantic relationships. Couples' clinicians can work with them to ascertain how to maintain necessary survival skills in society, but also develop new ways of being in intimate relationships so that they can reap the benefits of supportive unions.

Family Systems Theory

Family systems theory is another theory that offers a perspective of how people learn about relationships and develop ideas about gender roles. Specifically, family systems theory offers insight on the ways in which families of origin impact adult couples. This theory suggests that various dynamics within a person's family unit, such as family roles and rules, can shape the way in which one thinks, feels, and behaves. Family roles and rules tend to be carried over into relationships outside of the family. The impact is so significant that literature suggests families of origin can have an effect on the quality of romantic and marital ties (Cui, Fincham, & Pasley, 2008). For example, the quality of a child's parents' marriage can have a profound impact on a child's marriage as an adult. Research suggests that children who come from families whose parents divorced are at risk for experiencing marital conflict as well as divorce themselves (Cui et al., 2008). Thus, the way in which a child's parents experience and model their marriage can shape the way in which that child feels about his or her marriage as an adult.

One way in which the family of origin impacts African American families is through the modeling of gendered aspects of power. Parents model the way in which their own gender (as a male or female) expresses power. Cowdery, Scarborough, Knudson-Martin, Seshadri, Lewis, and Mahoney (2009) explain that gendered power is shaped by various factors, such as historical, cultural, and structural factors. The disempowering impact of racism on African Americans shapes the ways in which couples express, exchange, or inhibit power with each other (Cowdery, et al., 2009). In the U.S., African American couples live within a society that operates from a predominately Caucasian, male dominant leadership creating a top/dominant–bottom/subordinate relationship, where African Americans or people of color tend to be in the subordinate role in society (Angelique, 2008). Subordinates have their power controlled, contained, and/or eliminated. For African American couples the effects of slavery and racism can be projected into their relationships and resultant tension/conflict can develop. The impact may be invisible to the couple, because of the systemic psychological depths to which racism operates. As a result, African American women not only find themselves subject to living within a society that is dominated by Caucasian males, they are also subject to the unequal power that exists between them and males in general (including African American males). Thus, they end up enduring the power differential from outside of their family unit, as well as the inside (e.g., from their own husbands). African American males, however, must endure similar but different effects of the power differential within a Caucasian, male dominant society (because their power is limited and they do not have the same access to the resources that validate their masculinity as those of a Caucasian male), so they may attempt to exert their male dominant position within their own home. Thus, you have both members of the couple attempting to exert some form of power within their family unit, possibly to compensate for their lack of societal power. As a result, this may create tension that may result in arguments, fights, mental health problems, or even divorce. Sometimes in an effort to protect their husband's compromised societal power African American women may negotiate their own power by decreasing it within the relationship and promote their husband's power (e.g., identifying their husband as the head or leader of the household) (Cowdery et al., 2009).

Positive Coping Skills of African American Couples

Many African American couples do adapt positive and healthy collectivistic behaviors, despite the power differentials that exist for them in the world. African American couples tend to put the needs of their family before their individual needs, and decisions and actions they make tend to be for the good of the unit (or family) (Cowdery et al., 2009). In a sense, some African American couples develop a motto of "it is us against the world" and pull together as a united front in order to overcome challenges. African American children are privy to observing these types of unique interactions between their parents. Thus, clinicians should use the collectivistic nature of many African American couples to help them pull together and support one another since this is already an established value system amongst most African Americans.

As reviewed in Chapter 2, the West African tradition of kinship networks (extended family and friends) is an enduring pattern in African American families today and can serve as a significant source of support or stress for the couple. The challenge for some couples is trying to establish a balance within their own relationships without allowing outside relationships (e.g., family members and friends) to intrude upon the space and facets of the couple's relationship (Whitfield, Markman, Stanley, & Blumberg, 2001). These forms of intrusion can have devastating effects on the couple's ability to establish a bond and trust between one another. Two other important strength areas within most African American couples include a strong sense of spirituality (see Chapter 10) and gender egalitarianism within their relationships (see Chapters 2 and 4). Clinicians should attend to these strengths in their work with African American couples.

African Americans Marriages and Expectations of Marriage

Most of the research that exists about African American couples reveals a dismal outlook. Literature suggests that African Americans are the least likely to marry, the most likely to divorce, and tend to maintain fewer enduring and committed relationships than any other group (Banks, 2011). As many experts would agree, the primary reasons for the disparaging outlook for African American couples have to do with economic hardship and the effects of racism. Again, African American's feelings/expectations about marriage and relationships are shaped in childhood and adolescence by what they see and experience. Despite all of the unique negative influences African American couples face these couples continue to get together and stay together. Clinicians can help facilitate couples' staying together through crisis times and teach them coping skills for enhancing the emotional intimacy and problem-solving within their relationships. African Americans continue to highly value long-term romantic partnerships.

White and Parham (1990) identified four areas within African American couples' relationships that can significantly impact the degree to which couples experience their relationship as rewarding or challenging. The four areas include: trust, control, sex, and social roles. The ability to trust (to have confidence in someone's ability or intention), and to feel that someone is being real and genuine is an important concept within the African American community (White & Parham, 1990). It appears that in the beginning of relationships, couples tend to go through a transitional process and exchange of trust. As White and Parham (1990) explain, the trust process begins by each partner initially ensuring that the needs of their partner are met and making their needs secondary. Every effort is made by each partner to ensure that the other feels validated and that his/her needs are satisfied. As this process unfolds, each partner gains a sense of trust that his/her needs will be met by the other. Once this initial level of trust is established, and each partner feels secure that the other will meet their needs, a shift eventually occurs where each partner moves from being *other centered* (putting the partner's needs before his or her own) to becoming more *self-centered* (putting one's needs before his or her partner's). The shift may or may not be intentional. Regardless of the intention, the consequences of this shift can make either partner feel neglected, taken advantage of, and resentful toward their partner. The challenge then, for African American couples, becomes finding a way to rekindle the initial trust they had that their needs would be met by the other (White & Parham, 1990). Without this level of trust being reestablished, the dynamics of the relationship can feel separate, stagnated, fruitless, and unsatisfactory.

In addition, issues of control can manifest themselves within relationships. As White and Parham (1990) explain, control (the need or desire each partner has to influence the course of the relationship and/or behavior of their partner) is ultimately under the guise of trust. Control issues are related to trust in that the degree to which one is able to trust his or her partner can impact the degree to which one is willing to surrender control in the relationship. For example, common issues of control with relationships tend to be conflict related to money management (e.g., shared or separate bank accounts), significance of careers and potential demographic relocation (e.g., type and length of position held), and pre-existing relationships (e.g., maintaining or ending male–female friendships that may support or diminish the couple's marriage).

Research suggests that African American couples experience conflict and distrust in their marriage at a higher degree than white couples (Hill, 2009). Yet, despite this distrust, studies suggest that African Americans continue to have a supportive attitude about marriage (Hill, 2009). In fact, in comparison to white families, Hill (2009) explains that African Americans appear to embrace the traditional ideas about marriage, sexuality, and family. She states, "African Americans are as likely as white Americans to idealize marriage and are less accepting of sex before marriage, cohabitation, and divorce than whites" (p. 352). Yet, research suggests that despite the supportive attitudes African Americans have about marriage, more couples who are white tend to marry (Chaney & Marsh, 2009).

White and Parham (1990) explain the importance of African American couples actively working together to define the parameters of their relationship and expectations that they have for one another. One of the areas that can have different meanings for couples includes sex. It is not uncommon in relationships for sex to be used as a primary means of intimacy. However, the authors suggest that African American couples need to identify additional meaningful ways to communicate their feelings and intentions toward each other. As the authors suggest, while sex can be a very healthy way of expressing one's affection for his or her partner, it can also be a distraction from the verbal communication that is necessary in relationships. Thus, it is important for couples not to rely solely on one aspect of the relationship but also to make every attempt to integrate all forms of communication within the relationships.

A final area that White and Parham (1990) identify as significant to African American couples includes social role expectations. The authors suggest that couples tend to conform to the gender-appropriate roles modeled within Western society. The socialized roles specific to males tend to include men being the primary financial supporter and decision makers in the relationship. In contrast, women tend to be socialized to defer to male authority and be the emotional caregivers in the relationship. While some couples may be able to adapt to the traditional gendered roles, African American couples may find it difficult to integrate into roles that do not reflect their authentic life experiences. For example, research suggests that financial strain is one of the most common problems African American couples experience, due to a lack of economic resources (Lincoln & Chae, 2010). Financial strain can evoke negative emotions among African American couples, resulting in resentment and marital dissatisfaction and possibly divorce (Lincoln & Chae, 2010). Thus, as stated previously, African American couples may find it difficult to operate within the traditional gender roles of the male being the primary breadwinner but instead may have to operate within a household where either or both partners take on that role. Whitfield, Markman, Stanley, and Blumberg (2001) describe gender-based racism (unjust treatment toward people of color as well as their gender) as being a common occurrence within the relationships of African American couples. Specifically, in today's world, African American females are more likely to be offered more financial opportunities than African American men, which may be due to women's advancement in the educational realm. Of all degrees awarded to African Americans, Black women account for 58 percent of college degrees and 62 percent of masters degrees (*The Journal of Blacks in Higher Education*, 2009). Educational discrepancies between African American men and women can sometimes cause problems in African American partnerships (Banks, 2011). Although this follows the national trend of women achieving college degrees at higher rates than men, it has special bearing on African American dating and marriage rates. The inability of many African American men to meet the traditional standards may, in turn, create feelings of incompetence, low self-worth, and a desire for him to separate himself from his spouse due to feelings of shame and inadequacy.

Understanding the types of challenges African American couples face, one might wonder why African American couples decide to establish a relationship and get married. One reason, perhaps, is that there are benefits to being married. Research suggests there are emotional, psychological, and physical benefits that arise from marriages. For example, some studies indicate that people who are married experience more happiness, better health, and less stress than those who are single (King, 1999). In addition, married couples have been found to have lower rates of alcoholism, suicide, and mortality rates than those who are single (King, 1999). As discussed in Chapter 1, Blackman et al. (2005) discuss ten specific benefits to marriage for African Americans (see p. 5).

Another reason African American couples may marry is because of their expectations about marriage and being able to build a future together (Dickson, 1993). This process of *building* may include having children, becoming financially prosperous, and owning a home, although partners should not assume that their definition of *building* is the same as, when these differing expectations do not merge, it can create dissention toward each other which can create unfair expectations and stereotypes of each other. The following case study illustrates many of the concepts discussed in this chapter.

Case Study

Shawn (25) and Carmen (27) have been married for six years. Shawn grew up in a lower middle class single parent household where he was raised primarily by his mother. His household included his mother, maternal grandmother, and a younger brother and sister. His parents were never married but he has spent time with his father, occasionally seeing him during his childhood. Since that time, however, his relationship with his father has improved and they now often spend time together. In the absence of his father, Shawn assumed the head of household role. Although his mother was the primary financial caretaker, she often allowed him to guide his younger siblings with making decisions and taking care of them when she was unavailable. At 16, he worked and attended school using the money he earned to help his mother with the household bills, as well as purchase items his mother was unable to afford for himself and his siblings. Household responsibilities were shared between Shawn and his siblings. Due to his extra family responsibility, he frequently missed school to take on extra shifts at work. As a result, he dropped out of high school but earned his GED and later his associate's degree in business. He currently works as a manager for a cell phone store.

Shawn and Carmen met at a fundraising event. She is a project manager for a consulting firm and grew up as an only child in an upper class dual-parent household. Although her parents were able to afford service staff to help with cleaning, cooking, and household responsibilities, Carmen was used to seeing both of her parents engage in household duties. She, however, was rarely asked to complete household chores.

Both Shawn and Carmen had romantic relationship experience dating prior to getting married. Shawn's prior relationship was the one he considered to be his most serious relationship with a woman. He ended the relationship two months before dating Carmen. Prior to meeting Shawn, Carmen was in a serious relationship for two years. Shawn and Carmen dated for three years before getting married. They do not have children but both have expressed a desire to have children when they feel they are in a comfortable financial position.

The couple present to a private practice for marriage counseling following months of unresolved arguing. Most of the arguments center on money and career choices. Shawn believes Carmen takes money for granted and that her frivolousness with money has to do with her privileged upbringing. Carmen, however, believes that she is financially responsible. She shares that her father taught her about investments and that she has a general understanding about how to save money. She also does not understand why Shawn feels she is irresponsible with money as she rarely purchases items for herself, other than food and household items. Carmen expresses resentment toward Shawn for how he feels about money and believes that if he would return to school to pursue a higher degree, he could put himself (and her) in a better financial position. Shawn expresses resentment toward Carmen when she urges him to go back to school stating that he feels as though she is belittling him for only having an associate's degree.

Shawn and Carmen's arguments have escalated to the point that they are no longer sleeping in the same bed. Shawn tends to respond to the arguments by leaving the house while Carmen attempts to resolve the arguments by urging Shawn to continue talking about his concerns even when he has verbalized a desire to stop talking about it. She becomes angry, cries, and stops speaking to him for days after the argument has taken place. Carmen initiated counseling. Shawn feels they should be able to handle their own problems. Carmen has spoken with her minister on occasion about their marital difficulties but has not revealed this to Shawn citing that "he doesn't attend church anyway." Carmen eats excessively to deal with her stress. Shawn consistently criticizes her weight gain and her ability to "keep house." He becomes angry when Carmen expects him to share in the household responsibilities, such as cooking and washing clothes; although he admits he is capable of completing household chores and had to do them growing up, he states that because she is the woman of the house, she should take the initiative in making sure that the house is always clean and that she cooks the meals. Carmen is resentful of this attitude and feels that since they both work they should both share in the household responsibilities. Carmen and Shawn present to counseling seeking ways on how to decrease their arguments and how to find a common ground with regard to money.

Strategies for Working with Shawn and Carmen

As previously mentioned, research suggests that one of the key areas to explore with couples, in general, is the degree of mutual exchange of self-disclosure and responsiveness between them. Specifically, this element within a relationship revolves around how much (for example) Shawn and Carmen are able to disclose difficult feelings and needs to each other in a manner where their expression is received openly, without judgment and criticism from the other (Laurenceau, Feldman Barrett, & Rovine, 2005). The more Shawn and Carmen are able to share their feelings openly with one another, the more likely they will be able to move toward establishing intimacy. Therefore, in this case, the clinician should spend time addressing both Shawn and Carmen's feelings about their conflicts and their expectations for their relationship, gender roles, and power dynamics. Additionally, the counselor should work with Shawn and Carmen on their perceptions of themselves as a unit, given the collectivistic nature of African American culture. Finally, their definition of family should be assessed: who do they include in their family? Extended family? Church family? Fictive kin? It is important to assess this couple's support system, particularly as they are at a crisis point and need the support of their family and community.

With Shawn, specifically, the therapist will need to be sensitive to his needs as an African American male client. It is important to understand the challenges he may have with emotional intimacy. Garfield (2010) explains that is important to understand these challenges by examining the historical and cultural context in which the male partner exists. Specifically, Garfield (2010) explains that, historically (within the Western culture), men in general have been groomed to be the financial providers of their household and have learned to abdicate the emotional and domestic responsibilities of the family to their female partners. He also explains that men have been socialized to avoid strong emotions because it can be seen as weak and feminine. Men learn that asking for help is considered a weakness. Thus, going to therapy may be seen as asking for help, weak, and interpreted as relinquishing control and power. It would be helpful, Garfield (2010) explains, for the therapist to guide Shawn in how to be confident within his own authority and to give himself permission to share power with his spouse. However, it will be critical for the therapist to address the issue of power within Shawn's context as an African American male and within his relationship to his female partner. Power can be experienced quite differently among African American couples than Caucasian couples. Therapists working with Shawn and Carmen will need to understand how racial oppression plays a role in the way in which Shawn and Carmen experience power in public and privately within their relationship. Another useful area to focus on with Shawn is friendship skill development. A good counseling strategy would help this couple become emotionally in tune with one another and teach them how not to disconnect when they are having problems. For example, Shawn leaves the house and Carmen cries and then emotionally withdraws. It will be important to teach this couple new ways of connecting even in crisis so that they can learn how to communicate without engaging in rejection behaviors of the other.

Garfield (2010) identifies four areas of difficulty men may have in friendships, which likely present themselves in marriage as well. They include: (1) connection (the ability to find a common emotional place with others); (2) communication (the ability to share and express feelings); (3) commitment (the ability to form meaningful bonds of loyalty); and (4) cooperation (the ability to share power and be flexible with a position of authority). When strengthened, these areas can help men make deeper emotional connections with their partners. Women can also recognize that society does not socialize most men to expect or develop emotional intimacy with others; therefore, the counselor can sensitize Carmen to the difficulties Shawn may face in this realm and allow her to be supportive of his efforts. The counselor, though, should not automatically assume that because Carmen is female, she has more sophisticated intimacy skills then Shawn. Intimacy expectations, skills, and previous experiences with emotional intimacy (e.g., familial, romantic relationships, and friendships) should be assessed in the early phases of counseling which will give the clinician a better idea of what the couple needs, wants, and expects of one another and their relationship.

Additionally, part of therapy for couples should entail an examination of their ideas of what it means to be a man and a woman. Part of this process includes helping the couple understand what is a healthy and effective definition of the gender roles under which both partners operate. Therapists can assist the couple in understanding how they have interpreted and integrated various cultural stereotypes into their relationship (Garfield, 2010). The couple's relationships (or absent relationship) with same gendered-parents should also be explored. For men, although applicable to women as well, Garfield (2010) suggests it would be important to examine what they believe to be their strengths and weaknesses as a husband and a father (if the couple has children) and his relationship to sex and money. Therapists should teach communication skills, such as "I" statements, as they help couples learn how to be responsible for their words. For men, this would aid them in learning how to provide feeling responses when talking with their spouse, rather than responding analytically, intellectually, or as a problem-solver. This process, as Garfield (2010) explains, will also teach the couple empathy. This would be helpful to Shawn and Carmen because both could come to understand their respective worldview and how each goes about problem-solving. Couples can be critical of the ways in which the other solves problems when they are unaware of their combined strengths in this realm. Shawn and Carmen can be sensitized to how their respective backgrounds influence these issues and how this can be a strength in their relationship.

Laurenceau et al. (2005) discuss using a multi-stage model geared toward providing therapy for African American men as, traditionally, men may be less supportive of counseling than women. However, this model would appear to be useful for working with both Shawn and Carmen. The multi-stage model with Shawn and Carmen would include (1) developing rapport, (2) pacing the counseling process, (3) disclosing information about oneself as the therapist (where appropriate), (4) engaging Shawn and Carmen in an introspection process, (5) exploring spirituality, (6) addressing racism, and (7) providing psychoeducational counseling.

Conclusion

In this chapter we have explored the various factors that contribute to the formation and maintenance of Black male–female romantic relationships. Adolescence appears to be a significant life stage where African American males and females initiate the process of emotional and physical intimacy earliest among their peers of other ethnic groups. Media, family, and personal decisions, such as substance use, are factors that can contribute to this early exchange among African American male and female adolescents. There are also a range of messages African Americans receive regarding their sexuality and gender roles. These messages come from society and family. The interpretation of these messages, in some cases, contributes to stereotypes that can impact what African American males and females believe about each other, as well as how they interact with each other. The type of expectations that African American couples have about marriage can also impact the degree of fulfillment they get within the relationship. In spite of the dismal outlook research reveals regarding African American marriages, there are a number of benefits that entice African American couples to marry/engage in long-term relationships. Because African Americans continue to marry, despite the numerous challenges they face, it is important that African American couples have helpful resources to aid them in their marital transition. Counseling can be a resource that can offer African American couples encouragement and support with their marriages. In order for treatment to be effective, however, it should be designed to address the unique issues related to African American couples. Specifically, it will be important for clinicians to make things visible for African American couples such as ways in which racism and historical events have shaped their lives and impact their daily interaction with one another. Additionally, clinicians can demonstrate an openness to discussing difficult issues, such as racism, that will allow African American couples to develop a sense of trust so that that they can talk openly with their therapist about other difficult issues. It will also be important for clinicians' conceptualization of African American couples to include an understanding of the unique internal and external factors that have contributed to their stages of development, such as the rate of sexual activity which can occur during adolescence. Clinicians need to help the couple understand how decisions and behaviors made during their youth may have impacted their marriage. Clinicians should understand the significant role African American couples' families play within their relationship, and how their families have shaped their concept of gender roles. Finally, a main area of importance for clinicians when working with African American couples is to identify the couples' strengths and the benefits of their relationship. It is not surprising that when couples are experiencing difficulties and challenges, they may tend to minimize the areas where they are thriving or the areas in which they are performing well. For example, with regard to our case example, although they may be having arguments about finances, the therapist may want to highlight the fact that they both seem to agree on the importance of finances but seem to have different ideas about how to manage them. Another strength is that although they may need alternative skills in communicating their feelings, they both appear to have concerns for each other's well-being (e.g., Carmen's weight gain and Shawn's career advancement). The therapist would need to teach Shawn and Carmen how to communicate their feelings in a way that allows them to feel less threatened and criticized.

References

Anderson, J. F., & Kras, K. (2005). Revisiting Albert Bandura's social learning theory to better understand and assist victims of intimate personal violence. *Women & Criminal Justice*, 17, 99–124.

Angelique, H. L. (2008). On power, psychopolitical validity, and play. *Journal of Community Psychology*, 36, 246–253.

Banks, R. (2011). *Is Marriage for White People? How the African American Marriage Decline Effects Everyone*. New York: Penguin Group.

Blackman, L., Clayton, O., Glenn, N., Malone-Colon, L., & Roberts, A. (2005). *The Consequences of Marriage for African Americans: A Comprehensive Literature Review*. New York: Institute for American Values.

Bowleg, L. (2004). Love, sex, and masculinity in sociocultural context: HIV concerns and condom use among African American men in heterosexual relationships. *Men and Masculinities*, 7, 166–186. doi: 10.1177/1097184X03257523.

Bush, L. (2000). Solve for x: Black mothers + Black boys = x. *Journal of African American Men*, 5, 31–53.

Chaney, C., & Marsh, K. (2009). Factors that facilitate relationship entry among married and cohabiting African Americans. *Marriage & Family Review*, 45, 26–51. doi: 10.1080/01494920802537423.

Cowdery, R. S., Scarborough, N., Knudson-Martin, C., Seshadri, G., Lewis, M., & Mahoney, A. (2009). Gendered power in cultural contexts: Part ii. Middle class African American heterosexual couples with young children. *Family Process*, 48, 25–39.

Crockett, L. J., & Randall, B. A. (2006). Linking adolescent family and peer relationships to the quality of young. *Journal of Social and Personal Relationships*, 23, 761–780. doi: 10.1177/0265407506068262.

Cui, M., Fincham, F. D., & Pasley, B. K. (2008). Young adult romantic relationships:The role of parents' marital problems and relationship efficacy. *Personality and Social Psychology Bulletin*, 34, 1226–1235. doi: 10.1177/0146167208319693.

Dickson, L. (1993). The future of marriage and family in Black America. *Journal of Black Studies*, 23, 472–491. doi: 10.1177/002193479302300403.

Dixon, P. (2007). *African American Relationships, Marriages, and Families: An Introduction*. New York: Routledge.

Entman, R. M., & Rojecki, A. (2000). *The Black Image in the White Mind: Media and Race in America*. Chicago, IL: The University of Chicago Press.

Gaia, A. C. (2002). Understanding emotional intimacy: A review of conceptualization, assessment and the role of gender. *International Social Science Review*, 77, 151–170.

Garfield, R. (2010). Male emotional intimacy: How therapeutic men's groups can enhance couples therapy. *Family Process*, 49, 109–122.

Hill, S. A. (2009). Why won't African Americans get (and stay) married? Why should they? In H. E. Peters, C. M. Kamp Dush (Eds.), *Marriage and Family: Perspectives and Complexities* (pp. 345–363). New York: Columbia University Press.

The Journal of Blacks in Higher Education (2009). www.jbhe.com/news_views/47_four-year_collegedegree.html.

Kids Count Data Center (2009). In *The Annie E. Casey Foundation*. Retrieved from http://datacenter.kidscount.org/.

King, A. E. O. (1999). African American females' attitudes toward marriage: An exploratory study. *Journal of Black Studies*, 29, 416–437. doi: 10.1177/002193479902900306.

King, B. M. (2009). *Human Sexuality Today, 6th Edition*. Englewood Cliffs, NJ: Prentice Hall.

Laurenceau, J. P., Feldman Barrett, L., & Rovine, M. J. (2005). The interpersonal process model of intimacy in marriage: A daily-diary and multilevel modeling approach. *Journal of Family Psychology*, 19, 314–323. doi: 10.1037/0893-3200.19.2.314.

Lincoln, K. D., & Chae, D. H. (2010). Stress, marital satisfaction, and psychological distress among African Americans. *Journal of Family Issues*, 31, 1081–1105.

Mandara, J., Murray, C. B., & Bangi, A.K. (2003). Predictors of African American adolescent sexual activity: An ecological framework journal of black psychology. *Journal of Black Psychology*, 29, 337–356. doi: 10.1177/0095798403254214.

Marshall, T. C. (2008). Cultural differences in intimacy: The influence of gender-role ideology and individualism–collectivism. *Journal of Social and Personal Relationships*, 25, 143–169. doi: 10.1177/0265407507086810.

Rouse-Arnett, M., & Long Dilworth, J. E. (2006). Early influences on African American women's sexuality. *Journal of Feminist Family Therapy*, 18, 39–61. doi: 10.1300/J086v18n03_02.

Sharp, E. A., & Ispa, J. M. (2009). Inner-city single black mothers' gender-related childrearing expectations and goals. *Sex Roles*, 60, 656–668. doi:10.1007/s11199-008-9567-3.

Simons, R. L., Simons, L. G., Lei, M. K., & Landor, A. M. (2011). Relational schemas, hostile romantic relationships, and beliefs about marriage among young African American adults. *Journal of Social and Personal Relationships*, doi: 0265407511406897.

Thomas, C. M., Crook, T. M., & Cobia, D. C. (2009). Counseling African American women: Let's talk about sex! *The Family Journal*, 17, 69–76.

Turner, R. H. (2000). Role theory. In A. E. Kazdin (Ed), *Encyclopedia of Psychology*, 7, (pp. 112–113). Washington, DC: American Psychological Association.

U.S. Census Bureau (2011). Income, poverty and health insurance coverage in the United States: 2010. Retrieved from http://www.census.gov/newsroom/releases/archives/income_wealth/cb11-157.html.

White, J. L., & Parham, T. A. (1990). *The Psychology of Blacks: An African-American Perspective*. 2nd ed. Engelwood Cliffs, NJ: Prentice-Hall, Inc.

Whitfield, K. E., Markman, H.J ., Stanley, S. M., & Blumberg, S. L. (2001). *Fighting for Your African American Marriage*. San Francisco, CA: Jossey-Bass.

Wolfe, D. A., Jaffe, P. G., & Crooks, C. V. (2006). *Adolescent Risk Behaviors: Why Teens Experiment and Strategies to Keep Them Safe*. Grand Rapids, MI: Yale University Press.

4

THREATS TO INTIMACY FOR AFRICAN AMERICAN COUPLES

Tennille Allen and Katherine M. Helm

Introduction

This chapter will review specific threats to intimacy for African American couples including power dynamics, patterns of relating to one another, gender roles, the distribution of duties between the couple, sexual norms, and communication patterns between couples. A review of treatment implications of the threats to intimacy for African American couples will be explored as it relates to therapy with African American couples.

In order to fully understand and adequately treat the issues raised when working with African American couples in therapy, clinicians must appreciate the contexts within which these couples are located. Knowledge of historical, cultural, and structural influences is vital in gaining insight into a relationship, the individuals within it, and the issues they are negotiating. African American couples share a number of relationship similarities and challenges with couples from all racial and ethnic backgrounds. Pressures from the outside world, interpersonal conflicts, and personal shortcomings know no color and mount barriers to intimacy for any couple. However, African American couples and their relationships are particularly vulnerable to such threats. Financial insecurity, negotiating their status as members of multiply oppressed groups, and historical and contemporary racial prejudice and discrimination collude to threaten African American romantic relationships in ways not experienced by Whites and in ways not typically explored or understood by researchers or clinicians (Bryant et al., 2010). Treating African American couples necessitates a familiarity and sensitivity to the role and interplay of social structure and culture. This includes understanding the legacies of slavery and discrimination, socioeconomic conditions, and racist and sexist stereotypes and imagery. Clinicians must critically evaluate if and how these significant factors impact the couple's lives and how they shape interpersonal dynamics between romantic partners (Collins, 2000, 2004; Pinderhughes, 2002). This is an important part of effective treatment for African American couples. Additionally, gender roles, trust, and intimacy are especially impacted by the confluence of these factors.

There has long been concern over the supposed fragility and instability of African American families (Frazier, 1939; Moynihan, 1965). Only recently, however, has scholarly attention turned specifically to the role of intimacy in the romantic lives of African Americans.

As a remedy to this, researchers and clinicians must employ a broader platform that appreciates the ways that "imbedded inequalities wreck havoc on African American families, [instead of] blaming them for the resulting disruption" (Lane et al., 2004, p. 406) as is often the case in discussions of demographic shifts such as increases in nonmarital childbirths and decreases in marriage rates among African Americans. Clinicians must be especially mindful of maintaining a non-judgmental stance when working with African American couples. Understanding how these negative influences impact African American marriages and other couple relationships will inform practitioners and couples seeking to strengthen these relationships through counseling. We offer a review of recent literature, bringing a contextual perspective to barriers to intimacy for African American couples, as well as suggestions for clinical practice with such couples. Additionally, treatment implications will be reviewed and specific suggestions will be provided to help clinicians recognize and address threats to intimacy.

The Current State of African American Intimate Relations: Identifying and Understanding the Range of Relationship Types

Recent census data (U.S. Census Bureau, 2011) reveal that for African Americans, marriage rates actually declined over the last decade to 36 percent of men and 29 percent of women. During George W. Bush's administration, there was a concerted effort to advance marriage and forestall divorce through the African American Healthy Marriage Initiative (2003). Efforts like these tend to presume that African Americans' declining marriage rates reflect a declining valuation of marriage, which a line of emerging works counters (Cherlin et al., 2008; Edin & Kefalas, 2005). This is actually a false premise. Cherlin (2010), Edin and Kefalas (2005), and Burton and Tucker (2009) all quite clearly demonstrate that African Americans value marriage highly—so highly that survey data finds that many African Americans state that they do not want to marry until they have secure employment, financial security, and social stability. These are factors which frequently elude many African Americans which is why many report that they are delaying marriage. Many, in fact, may simply never marry because they may not feel that they have attained the necessary stability to do so. This is even more the case for men than women (Chaney & Marsh, 2009; Smock & Manning, 2004). Furthermore, these efforts tend to presume that the decline in marriage rates will be remedied solely by those initiatives that focus on individuals in a decontextualized manner, ignoring the larger structural, economic, and cultural conditions that mediate intimate relationship patterns. Additionally, the focus on marriage by scholars and policymakers, at the expense of other relationship types (e.g. cohabiting couples), eludes this reality that marriage is not the norm for the majority of African American couples regardless of race. Indeed, for all couples, there exists an array of partnering possibilities (Amato et al., 2007; Cherlin, 2010). As alternatives to marriage are increasingly employed by African Americans, these must be understood and supported as such, i.e. as an alternative, rather than a stepping-stone to marriage. Clinicians should be respectful of the diversity of coupled relationships in the African American community. Couples presenting for therapy include dating, cohabitating, separated, married, and divorced couples. It is therefore instructive to consider a range of commitments under the rubric of African American intimate relationships. It is also necessary to realize that this diversity of relationship types means that relationships will have varying levels of stability and intimacy within them. As such, African American couples may draw from a number of multiple and sometimes competing relationship scripts in their interactions and understandings (Harding, 2010).

These include the familiar notions of marriage, cohabitation, and dating. It is important to note that though familiar, these are far from static, as a view of shifts within these relationship types over the last four decades reveal. Recent trends demonstrate that, across racial lines, the lines between relationship types and stages have become increasingly blurred (Casper & Bianchi, 2001), that committed or exclusive dating is less common (Bogle, 2007), and that cohabitation, and co-parenting without a couple being romantically involved is both more common, more socially accepted, and less a precursor to marriage than a substitute that closely parallels marriage, for all groups and especially for African Americans (Cherlin, 2004; Manning & Smock, 2002; Smock, Manning, & Porter, 2005). These shifts illustrate changes in the meanings of romantic relationships as marriage is no longer universally seen as the capstone of one's adult life or as the highest form of intimacy one can share with a partner (Cherlin, 2004). Other relationship types, though less common and often demonstrative of lower levels of commitment, stability, and intimacy, exist for contemporary African American couples, including "suspended" and man-sharing relationships. Suspended relationships are unstable and cyclical couplings where partners engage in patterns of dissolution and reconciliation. As Roy, Buckmiller, and McDowell (2008) observe, these relationships are especially likely when there are children present and lead participants to proclaim that they are "together, but not together". In such relationships, parenting and partnering have been decoupled and the participants share children and relationships but not intimacy. In these relationships, partners may also put plans for more a serious relationship on hold until certain conditions—ending patterns of infidelity, completing school, finding and keeping stable and well-paying jobs—are met (Edin, Nelson, and Reed, 2011; Roy et al, 2008). Man-sharing is a phenomenon in which at least two women—acceptingly or reluctantly—are simultaneously involved in a relationship with the same man (Allenye & Gaston, 2010; Chapman, 1986; Cook, 2007). Fueled by the imbalance of Black men to Black women, some women enter and maintain relationships that are not exclusive because they perceive the alternative of not having a relationship at all to be even less desirable.

Such diversity and dynamism within relationships must be recognized, as must the way that these are largely influenced by the racial disparities that African Americans face in the economic, educational, and criminal justice arenas. These are factors implicated in research that shows that African Americans report lower levels of entry into serious relationships, such as cohabitation and marriage (S. Hill, 2005; Marsh et al., 2007) and when they do establish relationships, they are marked by lower levels of quality, stability, and intimacy (Carolan & Allen, 1999; Phillips & Sweeney, 2005; Raley & Sweeney, 2009). Emotional intimacy is especially compromised within suspended and man-sharing relationships as these would otherwise not exist if it were not for the intervening or precipitating factors of the presence of children or the absence of available men (Allenye & Gaston, 2010; Edin et al., 2011; Roy et al., 2008). One commonality revealed by looking at this diversity and the forces that give rise to it is that they reflect and shape the difficulty in creating and maintaining intimacy and enduring relationships for African Americans.

Structural Influences and Threats to Intimacy: Placing African American Couples into Context

Rather than conceive of relationships as steeped solely in individual choices or cultural models, research shows that social institutions and structures, including social stratification systems, racial segregation, and economic restructuring, affect relationship formation and success (Massey & Denton, 1993; South & Crowder, 1999; Wilson, 1987, 1996). Understanding the economic situations of African Americans is crucial in understanding their relationships. Someone who is financially secure is seen as a better partner (King & Allen, 2009). This is reflected as African Americans, and especially those on the lower rungs of the social class ladder, tend to regard economic security as a more important factor in decisions to enter commitments than others (Bulcroft & Bulcroft, 1993; Edin & Kefalas, 2005; Gibson-Davis, Edin, & McLanaghan, 2005). This is also observed as Black men with stable work histories are twice as likely to marry than those without such histories (Tucker, 2000). Given that the earnings of African Americans, at every level of education, are lower than for Whites (Hardaway & McLoyd, 2009; Shapiro, 2004; Wilson, 2008), financial (in)security is a higher hurdle in the establishment and nurturance of their relationships. That African Americans enter into parenthood without or before entering into marriage can be seen as deviant by members of the mainstream culture, the media, and policymakers while at the same time promulgating stereotypes of poor, single African American mothers. Unmarried African American couples presenting for treatment are aware of this negative view which can impact the therapeutic relationship as they may be on guard. Additionally, as stated by Orbuch, Veroff, & Hunter (1999, p. 33), "financial insecurity remains a dominant anxiety for African American males in particular, even when and perhaps especially when their incomes rise". African American couples, fully aware of the compromised economic positioning of African Americans in general and African American males in particular, contend with a host of apprehension and anxiety about men's ability to fulfill the traditional role of economic provider. When they cannot, this may be seen as consonant with stereotypes of irresponsible, lazy, ineffectual African American men. Such a stereotype walks hand in hand with stereotypes that cast African American women as emasculating and eager to take on male roles when their incomes are necessary to meet household needs or when they out earn their male partners. The promotion of these stereotypes and the internalized and projected negative feelings that they inure make it difficult to feel, express, and receive commitment and closeness.

Gendered experiences need consideration here, as well. There are gendered implications to decisions about entering relationships, for example. African American women desire financial security and independence before making serious commitments so that they maximize their partner selection and protect themselves from economic dependency on male partners (Chaney & Marsh, 2009; Osborne & McLanahan, 2007). For some African American women, distrust, fear of intimate partner violence, and concern about losing personal autonomy or one's hard-fought home means that they are hesitant to share financial resources with male romantic partners (Edin, 2000). Women may also maintain separate financial streams in a reflection of their independence and their long employment histories (Moore, 2008). This can foster relational strain and often serves as a threat to emotional intimacy because it signifies a lack of trust, a need for control, and a questionable commitment to the relationship. This emphasis on money often serves to make African American men wary of relationships, fearing that women will mock them for not earning enough, are too calculating in their relationships or will leave if men experience economic loss (Furstenberg, 2001, 2007; hooks, 2001; Stephens & Phillips, 2003). This is an issue that couples may struggle with and clinicians may see in therapy. Indeed, when economic instability does occur, so does a stress point in the relationship, forging a path for instability and dissolution (Furstenberg, 2001). This abuts gendered differences within socialization for African Americans as well. Men of all races are still socialized into the male provider role through their families, peers, popular culture, and public policy (Crook, Thomas, & Cobia, 2009; Pyke, 1996; Roy, 2008). This is also true of African American men, although they may be least able to fulfill the primary breadwinning role due to the social, economic, and educational constraints society places upon Black men as explained earlier in this chapter. When coupled African American women insist on having their own money, this can signal that they doubt their partner's ability to fulfill that role, intensifying his belief that she lacks confidence in him. At the same time, women are socialized into economic independence not only because of African American men's weakened economic and educational positions but also because of beliefs about their financial, emotional, and physical unreliability. In this way, African American women are often taught by their mothers in particular against trust and intimacy with their African American male partners (Furstenberg, 2001). This is obviously a significant threat to emotional intimacy because it fosters independence within the relationship and not interdependence. Trust is eroded from the very beginning of the relationship. Relationships that begin this way struggle to recover and may never do so.

Egalitarianism in African American Relationships

As discussed in Chapter 2, African American couples are more egalitarian in their relationships in regards to traditional gender roles.

While egalitarianism is associated with positive outcomes for African Americans and their relationships, this is premised upon a desire for such a relationship by both members of the couple (Clark-Nicolas & Gray-Little, 1991; Marks et al., 2008).

For clinicians, this is an important dynamic to identify and assess if it is impacting the couples' relationship. The couple, themselves, may be unaware of their dissatisfaction in the relationship because they have not achieved the ideal. This ideal is based on the assumed norm for White couples as White men frequently earn more than their wives. Some African American men seek to establish more control within relationships as a compensatory mechanism (Kane, 2000). Indeed, Black men with less access to socially sanctioned and approved statuses are more likely to show power and control within their relationships (Boyd-Franklin, 2003; S. Hill, 2005) as they have little access to power and control in other avenues. This dynamic may show itself in the form of cheating behavior, emotional withdrawal, consistent threats to leave the relationship, and engaging other women (e.g. flirting, taking phone numbers, texting, etc.) so as to make the female partner feel less secure in the relationship. This significantly threatens to destroy any consistent emotional intimacy as trust is, then, always an issue. African American women could also be resentful and scornful of such men as hooks (2001) recollects hearing women in her community react with scorn to their partners who could not provide them with more economic security. Anderson (1999) locates a large source of tension and conflict within the relationships of young African American couples when men grow resentful of women who expect them to afford them the middle-class lifestyles that their lack of education, income, and opportunities can ill provide. All of these forces erode intimacy between African American couples in damaging and sometimes irreparable ways.

Clinicians should understand that for African American couples, power does not necessarily align along traditional axes of gender. Instead, it is more situational and contextual, relying on particular partners and the resources they possess as determinants of who has greater power (Harvey & Bird, 2004; Senn et al., 2009).

90

It can be difficult for African American couples to reconcile the need for individual autonomy which has been instilled through socialization and cultural messages, with the types of interdependency and compromise that successful relationships need. For example, both African American women and men have often been socialized to be tough (i.e. do not show emotional vulnerability), be self-reliant (depend on no one), and do not trust others lest you get hurt (lack of trust in relationships). Obviously, many parents have instilled these messages in their children to protect them and help them survive in a hostile, racialized world. The intent is to prevent them from getting hurt; however, these messages damage intimacy. Couples themselves are often unaware of them and their negative impact on their relationship. These ingrained messages can set African American relationships up to fail long before they can even begin. These messages are even more clearly conveyed to children when their parents have themselves been in dysfunctional romantic relationships. Many African Americans did not grow up with healthy models of long-term romantic relationships. Additionally, societal stereotypes about Black men and women (e.g. "you can't trust a Black man" and "Black women try to dominate and control their men") can become heightened and subsequently play out amongst couples, especially when there are common misunderstandings or conflicts. These stereotypes can easily be triggered and what began as a small conflict can end up significantly threatening the health and safety of the relationship. Clinicians' awareness of this socialization process and societal stereotypes of African American men and women will help them identify these dynamics as they operate within the relationship and form effective treatment approaches to address them.

Burton and Tucker (2009) note that for some Black women, the task of accepting the reality of their relationships (i.e. men as collaborative financial partners—not primary breadwinners) must be managed while also accommodating Black men's egos and desires for control. They contend that this means "a delicate dance is required of women to balance what is viewed in many African American communities as the need to elevate and honor [Black] manhood (especially those who have committed to families) while carrying out necessary obligations and tasks. A woman's task is to be strong, but not to overshadow her man" (Burton & Tucker, 2009, p. 142). Women also grow frustrated when they feel they must always take responsibility within their relationships, even when this conflicts with their desires to share power or in some cases be taken care of and men grow weary of being judged as "less than" or not pulling their weight in the relationship. This, of course, causes breaches in intimacy.

Gender Stereotypes and Their Impact on Emotional Intimacy

As mentioned in Chapter 2, African American women also run the risk of adopting the "Strong Black Woman (SBW) syndrome", wherein they internalize an image of utter capability and unflappability in the face of tremendous struggle that serves to deny both their pain and the possibility for its healing (Beauboeuf-Lafontant, 2009; Springer, 2002). Men who buy into the SBW mythos do so in ways that valorize her on the surface but that ultimately ignore her needs and vulnerabilities. Many Black men also resent the SBW syndrome because it can be seen to threaten their masculinity, putting forth the notion that Black women do not need them and can do anything on their own. The SBW syndrome is frequently passed down from mothers to daughters. Sons may admire this trait in their mothers but may not desire the SBW syndrome in their romantic partners. The SBW image may also serve as a disincentive for her partner to assume more responsibility within the relationship, leading to more frustration and disappointment (Beauboeuf-Lafontant, 2009). As part of the SBW ideal is invulnerability, African American women may adopt a posture that conveys that she does not need anyone and African American men may respond with hurt, frustration, and withdrawal. This becomes a downward spiral of reinforcing ideas and experiences within a relationship that pave the way for further disconnection from each other. The SBW mythos is damaging to both partners, not allowing either to be vulnerable in their relationship, preventing interdependence, and eroding trust. If partners do not rely on one another, they can become emotionally disconnected from one another and hurt and resentment can result.

As mentioned in Chapters 2 and 3, some African American men adopt the "cool pose" (also known as swagger)—a protective posture that presents a macho image of invulnerability and unflappability. African American men and women frequently hold Black men to an impossible gender standard in which men can never show any sort of vulnerability in society and in their intimate relationships. When African American men are tempted to break out of this rigid gender role, they frequently receive ridicule from their female romantic partners ("act like a man") and male peers to maintain the "cool pose" posture at all costs. Similar to the SBW stereotype, this prevents true intimacy and encourages a view that African American men are to be in control and dominant at all costs. Both the SBW and "cool pose" defensive postures are taught from a very young age and serve to protect from racism and societal hurt but also prevent deep intimate relationships as one can never let one's guard down.

These images reinforce the stereotypes of Black women as unfeminine and aggressive and Black men as hypermasculine and lazy. When these stereotypes play out in relationships, not only do couples not trust one another, they often do not even like one another. This makes it difficult to stay together, especially when times get difficult for the couple. Common marital struggles are heightened by these stereotypical images. Thus, couples can end up relating to the stereotypes and not one another, which is very harmful for the relationship.

An Unbalanced Ratio

Another structural underpinning of relationship threat is the imbalance in the number of African American women to men. As discussed in Chapter 2, there are simply more Black women than there are Black men. Recent assessments of the sex ratio for Blacks reveal that for every 100 Black women, there are 90.5 Black men (Marks et al., 2008). This is coupled with the notion that there is also a shortage of marriageable Black men—those single, heterosexual Black men who are seen as good marriage material because of their desire to marry, personality, educational attainment, financial stability, potential to achieve one's desired traits or some combination of these elements. As a result of the academic, popular, and anecdotal accounts of a dearth of eligible heterosexual Black men, there is a belief among some Black women and men that men are valuable and limited commodities. This gives African American men freedom and choice and, in accord with the principle of least interest (Waller, 1937), they have control and power in their relationships (Banks, 2011; Seal & Ehrhardt, 2003; Senn et al., 2009). For some African Americans "the overabundance of desirable women makes it easier for men to avoid a committed relationship" (Pinderhughes, 2002, p. 276), an assertion supported by Banks (2011). When partnered, some of these more advantaged men express lower levels of relationship quality (Bryant et al., 2008). As such, men may consider leaving their long-term relationships when their partners became too demanding, suspicious, or taxing, knowing they could easily exercise better options (May, 2001). Entering and sustaining marriage and other serious commitments can be less attractive when men know the odds are in their favor (Wilson, 2009) which clearly disrupts a healthy power balance in an African American relationship as women may realistically fear that their male partners can leave the relationship for someone better whenever they wish. This skews the power in the relationship in favor of Black men. For some men, this could mean that they no longer have to maintain relational integrity, faithfulness, and commitment to one woman because they can have several simultaneously without much accountability. This dynamic causes some women to feel insecure in the relationship and to become angry with their partners and their own perceived lack of power.

Some African American women then tolerate behaviors from their partners they otherwise would not (Allenye & Gaston, 2010; Bowleg, Lucas, & Tschann, 2004; Lane et al., 2004). In addition to the man-sharing mentioned earlier, the sex-ratio imbalance may also contribute to the higher infidelity rates reported for Black men (Pinderhughes, 2002) who feel they are a valued asset and have more room to stray than Black women. This pattern is occasioned by growing mortality, incarceration, underemployment, and unemployment rates amongst Black men (Dixon, 2009).

Another threat to intimacy and feelings of solidarity can be found in exploring the supposed "down low" phenomenon in which heterosexual-identified men engage in covert sexual activity with men; although greatly exaggerated, this has caused suspicion among some Black women and resentment among some Black men as they feel this questions their masculinity.

Another intimacy threat is the growing educational disparities between Black men and women, so pronounced that the possibility for a well-remunerated and relatively secure career is largely impossible for someone who does not have post-secondary education (Wilson, 2009). Indeed, when African American parents could only afford to send one child to college, it was often their daughters, whose only other employment opportunities were largely limited to domestic work (S. Hill, 2002). The confidence that sons could find good-paying blue-collar jobs has disappeared. At a time when the credentialization and professionalization of careers and occupations increases the need and desire to attend college (Arum & Roksa, 2010), currently, in a trend impacting all races, African American women are attending college in far larger numbers than African American men. Marital quality declines when African American women have higher educations, incomes, or occupational prestige than their male partners (Banks, 2011; Creighton-Zollar & Williams, 1994). These educational disparities between women and men are a development that "poses a formidable threat for intimate relationships" (Burton & Tucker, 2009, p. 141). Interestingly, this is a greater peril in relationships than income differentials favoring women (Furdyna, Tucker, & James, 2008).

Internalized Racism and Gender Stereotypes as Threats to Intimacy

This litany of potential threats and real barriers to closeness and intimacy within African American relationships reflects the ways that centuries of persistent racial, economic, and gender exclusion have combined to place significant hurdles along the path to close, stable, and satisfying unions. Certainly anger and frustration from experiencing racism can be taken out on one's partner and often, unconsciously, lead to conflict (Boyd-Franklin & Franklin, 1998). As S. Hill (2009, p. 355) points out "this sense of being disrespected and disvalued in the larger society can adversely affect the quality of intimate relationships and the likelihood of marriage" as well as that of marriage success.

Pitting one set of struggles over another is counterproductive, especially as, when these battle lines are drawn, a couple's sense of connectedness is eroded and intimacy is lost. As African Americans feel the enormity of their racialized oppression, they can attack the most convenient target—the person they are presumably closest to rather than the true source of their mistreatment. This misdirected anger increases hostility and perceptions of disrespect and depresses trust and feelings of intimacy (Boyd-Franklin & Franklin, 1998; Bryant et al., 2008; A. Franklin, 2004; Willis, 1990). Clinicians may see these themes in couples who present for treatment. African American men, for example, ravaged by covert and overt forms of contemporary racism, may react with rage and then an emotional withdrawal that decreases their likelihood to find satisfaction (Taylor, 1990) and initiate/accept connection (A. Franklin, 2004) with their female partners. African American women similarly can shift their anger and frustration with racism to anger and frustration with their male partners and by reacting in ways that are harmful to herself (e.g. overeating, staying in an emotionally or physically abusive relationship, male bashing to friends, etc.) and her relationship (Murry et al., 2001; Wimberley, 1997). Similarly, raising one's defenses at home can be seen as an extension of the defenses that African Americans utilize in their dealings outside the home (Chapman, 2001). This is devastating to relationships because one never truly trusts anyone—not even one's partners. Also, if African Americans are always hyper-vigilant against threats, one cannot ever relax and get away from it, not even at home. Defensiveness and withdrawing from one's partner or reacting with anger offers power and control against a larger context that offers very little of either. These responses mitigate the pain of racism while also mitigating the comfort and closeness one can share with their partner. Rather than seeking each other for comfort and commiseration over shared experiences of racism, African American couples can turn against each other, engaging in a sort of "Oppression Olympics" (Martinez, 1998, p. 5), or a symbolic contest over who is more exploited that inevitably ends in the participants seeing each other as competitors without realizing their shared oppression and discounting the possibility for cooperatively fighting against this and finding sanctuary together. Indeed, experiences of racism and the protective mechanisms used to manage these decrease African Americans' ability to foster and maintain intimacy within their relationships (A. Franklin, 2004). Still, shelter from these storms must be found—historically, one safe haven from the vicissitudes of racism has and continues to be within the extended family. Clinicians should be able to anticipate and identify the negative impact this "gender war" has on couples.

The Weakness of Strong Ties: The Extended Family as a Threat to Intimacy

One key to understanding African American couples is realizing their place within the extended family, "a multigenerational, interdependent kinship system which is welded together by a sense of obligation to relatives;...extends across geographical boundaries to connect family units to an extended family network; and has a built in mutual aid system for the welfare of its members and the maintenance of the family as a whole" (Martin & Martin 1978, p. 1). As a cultural group, African Americans are collectivistic. Because of this, the benefits of the Black extended family are many and crucial for the survival for African Americans as individuals and as a community (Boyd-Franklin, 2003; R. Hill, 1999; Martin & Martin, 1978; Stack, 1974; Stack & Burton, 1993). Influenced in part by their West African cultural heritage, the fragility of families under slavery, and the economic disruptions experienced in particular in the urban North during and after deindustrialization, the extended family remains an integral part of many African Americans' lives as they continue to grapple with disproportionate economic and social challenges (Billingsley, 1992; Collins, 2000; D. Franklin, 1997; Frazier, 1939; Gerstel, 2011; Stack, 1974; Sudarkasa, 1997, 2007). Though often pathologized and seen as a reflection and source of dysfunction (Burton et al., 2010; Furstenberg, 2007;

Moynihan, 1965), extended families within African American communities have been a longstanding cultural and literal survival mechanism. This is, in fact, a strength of Black families and couples and also allows for care work (e.g. child or elder care), emotional support, and economic cooperation across generational and household lines, a practice vital for people whose families have been continuously threatened, disrupted, and marginalized throughout their tenure in this country. Clinicians must understand the influential roles of grandmothers and grandfathers, aunties and uncles, "play sisters, brothers and cousins" (i.e. a beloved peer, not a blood relative), in the structure and maintenance of the Black family. Without this understanding, clinicians could underestimate the familial influences that have the most impact on the couple.

Given this West African legacy and continued need, some African Americans emphasize the ties in one's family of origin over the ties to one's romantic partner (Anderson, 1999; Stack, 1974; Sudarkasa, 1997). Indeed, some scholars find "the strong ties generally heralded in African American families are not between spouses or lovers but between blood and adopted kin" (Boyd-Franklin & Franklin, 1998, p. 274). As this conflicts with the idealized norm of the primacy of the couple and their resultant nuclear family found in mainstream and popular American culture, a potential for stress and a risk to intimacy arises as couples negotiate this incongruity. Because African Americans have been influenced by West African and European cultures, Black families differ in regards to their loyalty to extended and married families. It is easily possible to have a husband with little ties to his extended family and a wife with significant extended family ties (or vice versa). He may expect loyalty to him over her family of origin and she may view this as impossible. This would then pose a threat to intimacy. Additionally, if both members of the couple are more committed to their extended families and less to one another, this can threaten the marital bond. This dynamic is distinct from what is typically seen in most White couple relationships. Alternatively, the varied forms of support from other members of the extended family can also lessen relational strain caused by financial or emotional troubles, thus lessening a potential threat to intimacy.

Furthermore, while extended family relationships provide vital material, instrumental, and emotional supports to couples in need, they can also be draining in that both members of the couple are also expected to provide these same resources to other members of the kin group. Indeed fulfilling this expectation is one of the contributing factors in the Black–White wealth gap (Chiteji & Hamilton, 2002; Heflin & Pattillo, 2006).

Conflicts with and interference from a partner's family can be especially off-putting and serve to fragment the dyadic bond as one partner feels they must choose between their family of origin and their new family while the other partner feels rejected and disrespected (Bryant & Conger, 1999; Bryant et al., 2001, 2010; Hatchett, Veroff, & Douvan, 1995; Stack, 1974; Tucker & Mitchell-Kernan, 1995). There is also concern that commitments to the extended family can curb couple's bonding with each other. As they invest within the collective, there is less left to invest within the couple's relationship and involvement with the extended family can decrease a couple's sense of themselves as a couple, independent of their relationship to their larger familial unit (Bryant et al., 2010).

Relationships can also fray when pulled in different directions by members of one's immediate and procreative family. Multi-partnered fertility—having children with more than one partner—is also a stress point as resources, such as money, time, and commitment, are attenuated and possibilities for conflict between the couple and the other parent(s) are increased. The possibility for conflict within the couple around issues of jealousy, resentment, distrust, and infidelity is also exacerbated (Carlson & Furstenberg, 2006; Edin & Kefalas, 2005; Harknett & Knab, 2007; H. Hill, 2007). Many African American families are blended and issues of step-parenting, multi-partnered fertility, and relationships with former romantic partners and children outside the current relationship potentially cause major conflicts and drain the emotional resources of the couple and their commitment to one another. Feelings and experiences of closeness can be compromised if one feels insecure as their partner interacts with the mother or father of a child from a previous relationship. Likewise, sharing a child can also mean that some feelings for the other parent never die and that some hold out hope that a fire can be rekindled (Roy & Dyson, 2005; Roy et al., 2008; Singer et al., 2006). Many current partners find this very threatening and may always see former romantic partners as "the enemy" and suspect cheating behavior as a result. Additionally, relationships with children outside the current relationship can be damaged as the current partner is sometimes threatened by the time spent with these children. Under such scenarios, commitment to one's current partner and therefore intimacy are strained. This is of particular concern for the health and functioning of relationships as multi-partnered fertility is on the rise and is expected to only increase, amongst several populations in the United States, especially among urban and African American populations (Carlson & Furstenberg, 2006; Guzzo & Furstenberg, 2007; Harknett & Knab, 2007). Issues around sexual jealousy and multi-partnered fertility also pose another threat to intimacy if they are seen as connected or contributing to destructive ideas and images of African American sexuality. These are common areas of conflict for some African American couples in therapy.

Conversely, there are times in which step-parents form wonderfully nurturing and loving relationships with children outside their romantic relationship and serve an active role in their upbringing, also a common dynamic in African American families. Clinicians, then, would be wise to assess which dynamic is occurring in the relationship instead of making negative assumptions about blended families' level of functioning. These issues can subsequently tear the relationship apart due to the significant stressors involved with negotiating these multiple relationships among blended families. Clinicians should be well-versed in understanding these stressors on the couple and in finding helpful ways to assist couples in managing the inevitable conflicts that can arise amongst blended families.

Constructions of Black Sexuality: Threats to Sexual Intimacy

An additional handicap in establishing intimacy can be found in the historical and contemporary constructions of Black sexualities. In the case of African Americans, besieged with racial exclusion and disparities and barraged with negative images of themselves, many of these expectations and scripts contain destructive elements. This is apparent as hooks (2004, p. 115) says "everything we commonly hear about romantic partnerships between black women and black men is negative. We hear that black men are dogs and black women bitches and ho's [sic].... We hear about the lying and cheating and the lowdown violence. We hear about the mistrust and the hatred." This damaged view of one's own sexuality makes it nearly impossible to positively regard another's, as stereotypes about one's self and members of the opposite sex are internalized and then acted upon within relationships. This significantly interferes with emotional and sexual intimacy between Black couples because, as stated previously in this chapter, they may end up relating to one another through negative stereotypes. These shape and impact the relationship in very damaging ways.

Indeed, possessing negative and stereotypical beliefs about members of the opposite sex is seen as harmful to the formation of trust success in relationships for African Americans (Gillum, 2007; Willis, 1990).

Patricia Hill Collins (2000) advances the concept of "controlling images", depictions developed and utilized within various policies, media, and reified through popular thought. These images (e.g. jezebel, gold digger, welfare mother, etc.) reflect and construct a deviant and often irresponsible and profligate sexuality for African American women that obscures their enduring sexual exploitation and also damage their images of themselves and their sexuality. As African American women were often taught by their parents to exercise sexual restraint, lest they be labeled sexually available and promiscuous—and thereby being targeted for sexual ridicule and rape—they have often denied their reality as sexual beings in need of sexual pleasure (Collins, 2000; Townsend, 2008; Wyatt, 1997). When, however, African American women are sexually assertive and seek control of their pleasure, they can be met with scorn and negative judgment. This poses harm to relationships when men interpret their female partner's sexual interests, desires, and skills as signs of her promiscuity or infidelity or when it reinforces common stereotypes about the hypersexual African American woman (Crook et al., 2009; Gillum, 2007; Staples, 1982; Stephens & Phillips, 2003). This can significantly inhibit Black women's sexual expression and frequently erodes their ability to be comfortable in their sexual relationships with romantic partners.

These controlling images bear on not just African American women but on men as well. As hooks frames it, African American men have been:

> seen as animals, brutes, natural born rapists, and murderers... [and] are victimized by stereotypes that were first articulated in the nineteenth century but hold sway over the minds and imaginations of citizens of this nation in

the present day… black male identity [is] defined in relation to the stereotype whether by embodying it or seeking to be other than it.

(hooks, 2001, p. xii)

Against this, African American men have had to forge alternative concept-ualizations of masculinity. Because there are almost no positive messages about Black masculinity it is not only damaging to Black men as a whole and potentially damaging for one's individual self-image, but it is most especially damaging in romantic relationships. While some of these adaptations are positive and allow African American men to successfully reconcile their realities with their discounted positions within the social hierarchy (Hunter & Davis, 1992), other attempts at such reconciliations have been maladaptive. In a system where masculinity is conflated with high levels of power and economic success, alternative manifestations of masculinity will be displayed when the traditional routes to said success are limited or altogether blocked. Negative economic shifts and concurrent skyrocketing incarceration rates have rocked the economic fortunes of many African American men, heightening the need for these alternative masculinities (e.g. hypersexual, predatory) for some African American men. Hooks (2004) and others assert that Black males learn from an early age that they live in a society that has no room for men seen as sensitive and instead forces Black men to be "cool and dangerous, bad boys" (Majors & Billson, 1992; West, 2001; Anderson, 1999).

Although the same characteristics are initially alluring, they militate against long-term relationships as they are "counterproductive when a man becomes obsessed with being cool just to win a woman's heart, only to find that the relationship sours when true intimacy does not materialize" (Majors & Billson, 1992, p. 44). Furthermore, when a man sees sex as the prize won through courtship, his gain comes at the cost of "genuine closeness and companionship because he has not allowed his deeper feelings to surface" (Majors and Billson, 1992, p. 44), a conclusion also reached by Chapman (1995). Feeling and showing emotions, as is called for in healthy and strong romantic relationships, is antithetical to membership within this cult of masculinity and causes a rupture in the construction of masculinity. Consequently, there are few avenues for African American men to express their feelings in ways that can foster better understandings and nurturance of themselves, their partners, and their relationships (Kelley, 1997; Roy, 2005; Young, 2011). This is an unfortunate positioning for African American men and women because as reiterated throughout this chapter, there is significant damage to emotional intimacy when Black couples relate to one another through a stereotypical racialized façade of Black masculinity and femininity. This means that couples who related to one another in this way may never really get to know one another and never truly emotionally connect.

Another contemporary influence on African American sexuality and sexual scripts is hip hop culture. Since its ascendancy in the 1980s, hip hop has been an important backdrop in the development and negotiation of both gender and sexual identity as well as for relationships for several African American cohorts (Kitwana, 2003; Muñoz-Laboy, Weinstein, & Parker, 2007; Stephens & Phillips, 2003). While it is certainly the case that the misogyny that is often critiqued within hip hop is part and parcel of the larger patriarchal, sexist, and misogynistic culture that we all inhabit, as noted by numerous scholars and critics (e.g. hooks, 1994: Powell, 2003; Rose, 2008), this serves as a particularly salient barrier to intimacy in the relationships of African Americans given the genre's popularity amongst Black youth.

In many ways hip hop is a male dominated genre. In hip hop, Black men are powerful and dominant, a status denied them by White culture and mainstream society. Black women are positioned to be sexually submissive and serve Black men. Repeated exposure can impact gender relations between Black men (boys) and women (girls). Relationships where men are dominant, and women are scantily clad and men and women relate to one another through automatic assumptions of mistrust and suspicion is depicted as the norm. One can see, then, how these powerful negative images of African American male–female relationships come to exert a significant influence on Black romantic relationships and can seriously undermine emotional intimacy.

Clinicians should assess the impact of sexual and gender scripts on couples' relationships. Current scripts have become more liberal and egalitarian allowing for sex to occur without a committed relationship; women are more free to initiate sexual relationships. Certainly changing gender roles and sexual scripts are implicated as a source of tension. Uncertainty about changing economic, social, and cultural climates gives rise to instability in romantic relationships, especially in decisions about whether, how, and whom to trust (Burton & Tucker, 2009). It is an unfair burden on Black men and women that they have to attempt to generate healthy racial, gender, and sexual identities against an environment that reflects little to no positive images about them as a group. These negative images are frequently internalized and can be passed down multigenerationally from within Black families—extending the damage over generations. What makes it worse is that this is often done without conscious awareness.

Distrust in Relationships: The Biggest Threat to Intimacy

Sternberg (1986, p. 120) views intimacy as a constitutive element of love "which encompasses the feelings of closeness, connectedness, and bondedness". It is also facilitated by feelings of trust (hooks, 2000; Sternberg, 1986) and leads to a sense of security, reliability, and predictability vis-à-vis one's partner (Holmes & Rempel, 1989). In the absence of these assessments, relationships are often conflictual, stressful, and likely to fail (Holmes & Rempel, 1989). It is instructive for clinicians treating African American couples to consider and understand how these are experienced. Distrust, when learned through personal experiences, observed through others' relationships, and taught by family members and peers through messages such as "Black men can't be trusted" or through the media, as is the case, for example, in some rap lyrics that cast women as manipulative and gold diggers, functions as a moderating influence on intimacy and other aspects of healthy relationships.

The development and maintenance of trust is particularly hampered within African American intimate relations because of the multiple external strains they face (Kelly & Floyd, 2001). Without trust, there can be no true emotional intimacy which is why mistrust is the most significant intimacy threat.

Technology as an Intimacy Threat

Today's Black couples are just as impacted by technology as the rest of society. Black couples may use websites such as www.blackpeoplemeet.com, blacksingles, match.com, and eharmony to meet one another. Many couples have entire discussions/arguments via text messaging and bring these in as "evidence" against their partners in couples' counseling. Advances in social networking sites and access to the multiple ways of connecting with romantic partners have shifted the ways in which relational boundaries are understood, as well as affording new ways of violating trust (Nelson, Piercy, & Sprenkle, 2005). According to Helm (2010), other problematic issues associated with Internet use include: Internet affairs, compulsive sexual behavior utilizing Internet adult sex sites, and those who compulsively use the Internet as a way of not coping with real life problems. The Internet affords couples opportunities to get their emotional needs met outside of their relationships without ever leaving their homes or even meeting the person they are communicating with online.

Social networking sites allows individuals to post and respond to comments others write, personalize their pages with pictures, and indicate individuals relationship status (e.g. single, married, dating, etc.). This allows couples to make certain aspects of their relationship highly public. Once the information is in cyberspace, it is difficult, if not impossible, to completely remove it. In our work with couples, some present to therapy because they find that their partner has violated their trust by contacting old boyfriends/girlfriends, venting about them online, changing the posted status of the relationship without informing them, etc. Evaluating and understanding the role technology plays in the life of the African American couple (and all couples) is extremely important. Additionally, exploring with couples how technology can potentially violate trust and stretch interpersonal boundaries should be evaluated as a potential threat to intimacy.

Socioeconomic Status and Threats to Intimacy

In all realms of life, the experiences of African Americans are shaped, certainly by race, while simultaneously acted upon by their social class background (Collins, 2000; Pattillo, 2005, 2007; Pattillo-McCoy, 1999). All Black couples face racism, discrimination, and internalized stereotypes as threats to intimacy in their relationships but the degree to which these are experienced and what this experience looks like for the couple is often mediated by their socioeconomic status.

For middle class African American couples, in particular, role conflict may lead to discord and a lack of fulfillment in their relationships as the time that they would spend on developing, giving, and receiving love and support is spent on meeting the demands of children and other family members and on maintaining and advancing their careers. Rooted in this struggle, Coner-Edwards (1988) asserts that "the demands of the multiple roles do not permit adequate development and maintenance and intimacy and affective qualities of the relationship" (pp. 39–40).

In addition, African American middle class/professional couples may be particularly vulnerable to relationship problems heralded by the sex-ratio imbalance present for all African Americans in particular and the perceived scarcity of professional, educated, well-compensated, heterosexual African American men who are interested in partnering with African American women. As stated earlier, both men and women are aware of the perception of such men's rarity and this can make men feel that they have greater power and options in dictating the course of the relationship. At the same time, women might feel that they must do whatever they can in order to keep their partner's interest. Under these circumstances, intimacy may be compromised as positions and interests are maximized or sacrificed, depending on one's gender.

When women desire men who out earn them but their reality dictates that their partners will more likely have comparable, if not lower, incomes dissatisfaction ensues. Indeed Davis, Emerson, & Williams (1997) report that African American males report having partners who are closer to their ideal than do African American women. This is both reflective of the skewed availability of African American men and indicative of a key site for African American women's resentment and dissatisfaction that can target their partner, sparking a cycle of mutual distrust, conflict, tensions, and reduced intimacy.

Social class and race also intersect in the lives of those who are not well-educated professionals. Low-income African American couples are much less likely to get married than both their more affluent African American and their similarly situated White and Latino counterparts (Burton & Tucker, 2009; Edin & Kefalas, 2005). For poor women, there is a reluctance to marry similarly poor men, seen as unable to be a good lifelong partner because of their lack of education, steady incomes, and earning potential, along with possible histories that involve violence, infidelity, incarceration and substance abuse (Burton & Tucker, 2009; Edin & Kefalas, 2005). Indeed, marriage is seen as largely out of reach for poorer African American men and when cohabitation is chosen, African American men are less likely than men of other racial and ethnic groups to marry (Smock & Manning, 2004). When cohabiting, low-income African American women may be reluctant to add their partner's name to their leases which might jeopardize their housing, independence, and autonomy should relationships problems arise (Chaney & Marsh, 2009; Clark, Burton, & Flippen, 2011; Edin & Kefalas, 2005). While certainly protective against uncertainty, these actions signal distrust and lack of commitment to male partners who might feel hurt, resentment, and disrespected as a result. Finally, working class African Americans often live in neighborhoods that do not support marital/committed relationships as there are few relational role models within these communities (Banks, 2011).

South (2001, p. 756) further notes that residents of "disadvantaged neighborhoods lack successful marital role models and durable social institutions that continuously signal the benefits of marriage and provide the normative expectations to remain married". Raley and Sweeney conclude as much when they say that residents of communities "where there is little social integration and few overlapping relationships, may have more difficulty developing trust because others do not monitor the relationship and the social costs for infidelity are low" (2009, p. 138). Additionally, experiencing and bearing witness to relationship failure creates conditions detrimental to relationship formation and stability (Burton & Tucker, 2009; Edin, 2000; Furstenberg, 2001). Thus, middle and working class Black couples face similar concerns but unique ones as well.

Clinicians should be aware of how social class plays a role in African American couples' presenting issues.

Identifying Specific Intimacy Threats

Intimacy threats as well as couples' strengths should be identified at the outset of treatment.

Many threats to intimacy can be identified by exploring the couple's (both as individuals and also as a couple) internal dialogue regarding issues of gender roles, power, stereotypes, trust, intimacy, racial identity, sexual and romantic relational scripts. Identifying vast differences between the couple on their scripts will quickly clarify many of the intimacy threats discussed in this chapter. For example, if a male partner believes that his cohabiting girlfriend should be responsible for an equal part of the finances in the relationship and she believes that men should be the primary breadwinners, this is an obvious threat to intimacy which needs to be addressed. We recommend seeing the couple for an initial intake session in which the clinician assesses the couple's presenting issues and then seeing the couple for one individual session each to ascertain each individual's familial relationships (e.g. evaluating the role each individual's family has played in their lives—both currently and in the past), their individual view of the problem, their past romantic relationship history, etc. and societal (SES, internalized stereotypes, etc.) context. Other areas of assessment are further delineated in Chapter 7).

Teyber and McClure (2011) discuss the importance of understanding clients' initial attachment relationships to primary caregivers. They state that the strength of our early attachment relationships not only shapes our view of future relationships, ability to trust, expectations for and behavior in future relationships, and relationship-seeking behavior, but also how happy and secure we are in our marital/romantic relationships. Teyber and McClure find that individuals tend to recreate attachment relationship patterns in their romantic relationships. Society's typically negative view of African Americans can impact the development of their romantic attachments.

A clinician's understanding of each couple's past relationship history (romantic, parental, familial, etc.) can give important clues into couples' internal dialogue regarding their ability to trust, securely attach to, and be emotionally intimate with a partner. This awareness of the couple's past relationship (and attachment) history will be important in helping to identify specific threats to intimacy. For example, if one member of the couple had an ambivalent attachment relationship with her mother, she may show distancing or game-playing behaviors with her spouse, in attempts to protect herself from getting hurt. She may have difficulty maintaining emotional closeness and may withdraw from emotional intimacy, leaving her partner frustrated, hurt, and rejected. She may also feel rejected, as her partner then distances from her after repeated attempts to emotionally connect, fulfilling her (often unconscious) expectations for a problematic attachment relationship. This understanding of our early attachment relationships, according to Teyber and McClure, provides an essential framework for understanding intimacy, trust, emotional connectedness, and ability to form intimacy bonds within our romantic partnerships. For African Americans, given the numerous negative messages/stereotypes they face on a daily basis regarding their gender, sexuality, and very value as a people, this can significantly impact their ability to trust a partner. Because African Americans are typically socialized to take care of themselves, not to show vulnerability, and not to trust others, this can clearly impact the level of intimacy possible for many black couples, as true intimacy involves a level of emotional vulnerability and significant trust within the relationship. Simply asking couples about their individual and joint backgrounds, their family structure, family and gender roles, and strengths of their familial relationships will help identify many of the threats to intimacy discussed in this chapter. Additionally, evaluating how much the couple has internalized racial and gender stereotypes, especially stereotypes about Black masculinity and Black femininity, is critical. As stated throughout this chapter, Black couples often have the added pressure within their relationships of projecting these negative images onto one another and then relating to one another through these negative projected images, which causes significant damage within their relationship, preventing true emotional intimacy.

Identifying each couple's intimacy threats involves a culturally sensitive understanding of the context in which many African American couples exist and an awareness of what these threats are as well as how they present in treatment. Attending to couples' emotional presentation, facial expression, body, language, tone of voice, and attending behavior (e.g. can they look at their partner or relate to them in session when they are speaking) will provide critical clues to intimacy threats. This is further illustrated in the case study included at the end of this chapter. Finally, with all couples, regardless of racial and cultural backgrounds, an understanding of a couple's "hot button" issues and individual emotional triggers (e.g. within a lesbian couple, a hot button issue might be if one member of a couple is "out" to her family and the other is not) provides more significant clues to specific intimacy threats. These can be initially assessed by asking the couple what they think their "hot button" issues are and how they have coped with them in the past.

Treatment Implications

When couples are made aware of how these intimacy dynamics influence their relationship, and they are motivated to heal their relationships, they can frequently work together to combat these negative intimacy threats. Couples may either be unaware that these threats are operating within their relationship or minimize the impact these threats have on them as a couple. Increasing couples' awareness of these dynamics can enhance the couple's sense of "we-ness" and friendship, since many, although certainly not all, of these intimacy threats are socially constructed for Black couples. Cueing couples into their common values and collectivistic identity as a couple is another tool to help the couple come together and work collaboratively on their issues. If African American couples can support one another in viewing their common and individual struggles as a collective (an African-centered value: "we" over "I"), this can go a long way in improving the couple's bond with one another. Sometimes this is not possible. When it is not possible, clinicians should once again evaluate the couple's expectations about how their relationship should proceed and what specific roles they perceive themselves as having within their relationship. Highlighting these differences for the couple may help them understand their areas of difficulty and basis for them (i.e. their differences in expectations and if they stem from different values and the way each were raised).

Role flexibility within the couple should also be explored. Historically, Black couples have needed to quickly adapt to the changing environment around them, which is how African American couples became more gender egalitarian than White couples. This is a historic and current strength of many Black couples. Identifying ways in which the couple is willing to change and adapt to strengthen their bond can help the couple overcome their intimacy threats as long as they are motivated to work on them. Depending on the damage the couple has had to endure within their relationship (e.g. trust issues, infidelity, multiple incidences of emotional abuse or hurt), poor relational attachment patterns, and the amount of negative impact they have had to sustain from the intimacy threats discussed in this chapter, this can be a complicated process and thus the focus of therapy.

Finally, most couples do not have an equal level of motivation for therapy or to stay together. This is another obvious threat to intimacy that should be clarified early in treatment and, if necessary, explored as an issue. A review of the couple's romantic relationship history together, as well as exploring if there are any ongoing affairs, will provide the clinician with some information about why the couple may be disproportionately motivated in couples' therapy.

Chapter 7 provides a more detailed exploration of specific assessment areas for Black couples.

Conclusion

If the issues of Black couples are viewed in the context of systemic racial and gender domination, Black couples are better able to survive, thrive, reconcile with one another, and understand the impact that these negative forces have on their relationships. This can help inoculate them against further damage as well as understand the forces that can influence their relationship in which they have little control (e.g. racism). Blame, then, is not personal, but societal. Successful clinicians working with Black couples can never understand their presenting issues without fully assessing and understanding the context in which these relationships exist. Some of the influences that threaten emotional intimacy are common among all couples; however, African American couples face additional challenges not faced by majority couples.

Failure to openly address these problems culminates in a "conspiracy of silence" (Collins, 2000, p. 158) that normalizes and reinforces dysfunction and will continue to pose formidable threats to African Americans' romantic endeavors. The assortment of problems that strain African Americans' relationships intersect and act in concert with each other. If partners see this confluence of problems as inextricable and overwhelming, the risk of dissolution rises (Waller, 2008). Addressing the current depictions of men, women, and their relationships as well as the continued forms of institutional discrimination that African Americans face can serve as a corrective and help support their relationships.

Case Study

Jamilla (25) and Carter (23) grew up in a small town in Georgia, where they continue to reside together. Carter is a construction worker and Jamilla works as a Licensed Professional Nurse (LPN) in a nursing home. Both have finished high school but neither went to college. They have been together since their senior year in high school and have two sons together, aged five and four. The couple first sought counseling through their church and the Pastor referred them for additional counseling services after he finished initial pre-marital counseling with them. The couple hopes to be married within the year and pre-marital counseling is required at their church.

In an initial session with the couple, I ask them why their Pastor referred them for further counseling. Jamilla states that she is very angry at Carter because he has cheated on her several times over the course of their relationship together. He has a daughter (three years old) from a previous relationship when Jamilla and Carter were broken up for about a year right after the birth of their second child. Jamilla openly discusses how hurt and angry she is that Carter has another child outside of their relationship.

106

She explains that she struggles with accepting the child into their shared home and often states that "Black men ain't nothin" when talking about her relationship with Carter. Carter, who appears withdrawn and disconnected, states that he is tired of Jamilla's bad attitude and quick temper. He admits that she has aggressed violently against him on several occasions and states that he has never hit her back but he is getting tired of being hit and if she does it again, he's "not going to be so nice". Carter admits that he really wants to raise his sons together with Jamilla but has a significant problem with Jamilla not accepting his daughter into their home. He explains that this could break them up permanently if she does not accept his daughter. He vehemently denies being currently involved with his daughter's mother and gets very tired of "Jamilla throwing that up in my face every time we have an argument. I did not cheat with her. We were broken up!" He further states that neither of them grew up in a two-parent home, as both were raised by single mothers and he really wants his sons to grow up in a two-parent household and he wants his daughter exposed to that as well. However, both were raised in the church and describe themselves as highly religious. Both of them want to follow the will of God, stop living in sin, and get married.

When the couple discusses emotionally difficult issues, their body language is notable. For example, when Carter is speaking, Jamilla sometimes rolls her eyes at him and tries to interrupt him to debate a point he has said. When she is angry, she taps her foot and shakes her head. When Jamilla is speaking, Carter seems to withdraw, look down or away, and emotionally retreat. When he disagrees with what Jamilla is saying, he shakes his head and shrugs his shoulders as if to say, "I just can't win with you" or "I am just about ready to give up."

Threats to Intimacy

Jamilla and Carter clearly love one another—but they have significant issues with trust. Jamilla's father was inconsistently involved in her life, and had several children with other women. She claims "I was just one of many. We never spent time together alone. I swear I only know who *some* of my siblings are. There are several I suspect I'm related to but I have no idea." Carter also did not grow up having a relationship with his father until he was 12. Two years after several positive interactions with his father, his father was killed in a car accident. He reveals that he "finally got to have a dad for two years, and then he got taken away". When asked about how the couple manages daily tasks like household duties and finances, Carter states that he handles the money and Jamilla does many of the household chores—although he helps out when he can. Jamilla works fewer hours than Carter and they have worked out that she will take on more household responsibilities as long as he continues to work overtime. Both state that they are active parents to their boys.

Jamilla's and Carter's mothers help them with the boys consistently, as all of them continue to live in the same town and attend the same church. The couple's financial resources are limited. They describe their financial situation as "just trying to keep our heads above water". Jamilla remarks that if Carter didn't have to pay child support, their financial situation would be better. Carter quietly states: "she is my child just as our boys are and I will do right by her". Carter currently sees his daughter every two weeks and would like to have her over more often to interact with the boys, but "Jamilla makes it very difficult for me to do this and I am getting tired of it." This is clearly a "hot button" issue for the couple and will be incorporated in treatment.

Jamilla states that she and Carter have discussed her taking classes at the local community college. She wants to become a Registered Nurse (RN) instead of an LPN and explains that, as a Black woman, she feels that she would get better treatment on the job if she had more education. She feels that she gets treated like "a slave's cousin" because all of the people in charge on her job are White and all of the "lowly" care workers of the elderly she works with are Black. Most of the elderly residents are White. She frequently refers to her job as "the plantation" and reveals that she is growing very tired of being "treated like dirt" and that every day she has to fight from letting her temper show. Jamilla does feel like she brings this negativity home with her and sometimes unfairly takes it out on Carter. When asked about racism and discrimination on his job, Carter says, "with the guys I work with, someone is always saying something stupid about race, but I just ignore it. I don't think it affects me much. I am just there to make a paycheck. I don't bother anyone."

When asked about their support system, the couple states that besides their mothers (with whom they are both very close and they each also get along well with their respective mother-in-laws to be) they are well-connected in the community. Both grew up in the same small community and have many friends.

From the initial intake interview, this couple's threats to intimacy appear to be: trust, problematic early attachment relationships with their fathers, internalized negative gender stereotypes about Black masculinity and femininity, multi-fertility familial issues, financial strain, racism on the job, anger towards one another from past and present grievances, relational violence, communication issues, and difficulty listening to one another. The couple's strengths include: a strong commitment to their family, gender egalitarian decision-making, a strong history together, a child-focused family, the support of extended family and community support, a unified religious orientation and commitment to a religious value system, a commitment to their community, and a high level of motivation to stay together.

Focus of Treatment

This couple has multiple strengths but also several intimacy threats. The focus of treatment would include: educating the couple on their internalized gender stereotypes of one another, examining their trust issues, evaluating how their poor relationships with their fathers may influence their own relationship expectations and ability to trust one another, an exploration of how anger at one another influences their relationship, a review of how flexible Jamilla can be about including Carter's daughter in their lives, teaching Jamilla other, healthier ways to express her anger, besides striking Carter, incorporating their spirituality in session (possibly including their trusted Pastor), building on their sense of "we-ness" as a couple and shared values, and an exploration on how racism/discrimination on the job contributes to their relational stress. Therapy would build upon the couple's many strengths and identify and work on their multiple threats to intimacy within their relationship.

References

African American Healthy Marriage Initiative. (2003). Why marriage matters: Roundtable Summary report. Washington, DC: Administration for Children and Families, U.S. Department of Health and Human Services.

Allenye, B., & Gaston, G. (2010). Gender disparity and HIV risk among young Black women in college: A Literature review. *Affilia*, 25(2), 135–145.

Amato, P. R., Booth, A., Johnson, D., & Rogers, S. (2007). *Alone together: How marriage in America is changing*. Cambridge, MA: Harvard University Press.

Anderson, E. (1999). *Code of the street: Decency, violence and the moral life of the inner city*. New York: Norton & Company.

Arum, R., & Roksa, J. (2010). *Academically adrift: Limited learning on college campuses*. Chicago, IL: University of Chicago Press.

Banks, R. R. (2011). *Is marriage for White people? How the African American marriage decline affects everyone*. New York: Penguin.

Beauboeuf-Lafontant, T. (2009). *Behind the mask of the strong Black woman: Voice and the embodiment of a costly performance*. Philadelphia, PA: Temple University Press.

Billingsley, A. (1992). *Climbing Jacob's ladder: The enduring legacy of African-American families*. New York: Simon & Schuster.

Bogle, K. A. (2007). *Hooking up: Sex, dating, and relationships on campus*. New York: NYU Press.

Bowleg, L., Lucas, K. J., & Tschann, J. M. (2004). "The ball was always in his court": An exploratory analysis of relationship scripts, sexual scripts, and condom use among African American women. *Psychology of Women Quarterly*, 28(1), 70–82.

Boyd-Franklin, N. (2003). *Black families in therapy: Understanding the African American experience.* New York: Guilford Press.

Boyd-Franklin, N., & Franklin, A. J. (1998). African American couples in therapy. In M. McGoldrick (Ed.), *Re-visioning family therapy: Race, culture, and gender in clinical practice* (pp. 268–281). New York: Guilford Press.

Bryant, C. M., & Conger, R. D. (1999). Marital success and domains of social support in long-term relationships: Does the influence of network members ever end? *Journal of Marriage and the Family,* 61(2), 437–450.

Bryant, C. M., Conger, R. D., & Meehan, J. (2001). The influence of in-laws on change in marital success. *Journal of Marriage and the Family,* 63(3), 614–626.

Bryant, C. M., Taylor, R. J., Lincoln, K. D., Chatters, L. M., & Jackson, J. S. (2008). Marital satisfaction among African Americans and Black Caribbeans: Findings from the national survey of American life. *Family Relations,* 57(2), 239–253.

Bryant, C. M., Wickrama, K. A. S., Bolland, J. M., Bryant, B. M., Cutrona, C. E., & Stanik, C. E. (2010). Race matters, even in marriage: Identifying factors linked to marital outcomes for African Americans. *Journal of Family Theory and Review,* 2(3), 157–174.

Bulcroft, R. A., & Bulcroft K. A. (1993). Race differences in attitudinal and motivational factors in the decision to marry. *Journal of Marriage and the Family,* 55(3), 724–732.

Burton, L. M., & Tucker, M. B. (2009). Romantic unions in an era of uncertainty: A post-Moynihan perspective on African American women and marriage. *The Annals of the American Academy of Political and Social Science,* 62(1), 132–148.

Burton, L. M., Bonilla-Silva, E., Ray, V., Buckelew, R., & Hordge Freeman, E. (2010). Critical race theories, colorism, and the decade's research on families of color. *Journal of Marriage and Family,* 72(3), 440–445.

Carlson, M. J., & Furstenberg, F. F. (2006). The prevalence and correlates of multipartnered fertility among urban U.S. parents. *Journal of Marriage and Family,* 68(3), 718–732.

Carolan, M. T., & Allen, K. R. (1999). Commitments and constraints to intimacy for African American couples at midlife. *Journal of Family Issues,* 20(1), 3–24.

Casper, L. M., & Bianchi, S. (2001). *Continuity and change in the American family.* Thousand Oaks, CA: Sage.

Chaney, C., & Marsh, K. (2009). Factors that facilitate relationship entry among married and cohabiting African Americans. *Marriage & Family Review,* 45(1), 26–51.

Chapman, A. B. (1986). *Man sharing: Dilemma or choice, a radical new way of relating to the men in your life.* New York: William Morrow.

Chapman, A. B. (1995). *Getting good loving: How Black men and women can make love work.* New York: Ballentine Books.

Chapman, A. B. (2001). *Seven attitude adjustments for finding a loving man.* New York: Pocket Books.

Cherlin, A. J. (2004). The deinstitutionalization of American Marriage. *Journal of Marriage and Family,* 66(4), 848–861.

Cherlin, A. J. (2010). *The marriage-go-round.* New York: Random House.

Cherlin, A. J., Cross-Barnet, C., Burton, L. M., & Garrett-Peters, R. (2008). Promises they can keep: Low-income women's attitudes toward motherhood, marriage, and divorce. *Journal of Marriage and Family,* 70(4), 919–933.

Chiteji, N., & Hamilton, D. (2002). Family connections and the Black-White wealth gap among the middle class. *Review of Black Political Economy,* 30(1), 9–27.

Clark, S. L., Burton, L. M., & Flippen, C. (2011). Housing dependence and intimate relationships in the lives of low-income Puerto Rican mothers. *Journal of Family Issues*, 32(3), 369–393.

Clark-Nicolas, P., & Gray-Little, B. (1991). Effect of economic resources on marital quality in Black married couples. *Journal of Marriage and the Family*, 53(4), 645–655.

Collins, P. H. (2000). *Black feminist thought*. New York: Routledge.

Collins, P. H. (2004). *Black sexual politics: African Americans, gender, and the new racism*. New York: Routledge.

Coner-Edwards, A. F. (1988). Mate selection and psychological need. In A. F. Coner-Edwards, & J. Spurlock (Eds.), *Black families in crisis: The middle class* (pp. 37–49). New York: Brunner/Maze.

Cook, C. T. (2007). Polygyny: Did the Africans get it right? *Journal of Black Studies*, 38(2), 232–250.

Creighton-Zollar, A. A., & Williams, J. S. (1994). The relative educational attainment and occupational prestige of black spouses and life satisfaction. *Western Journal of Black Studies*, 16, 57–63.

Crook, T., Thomas, C. M., & Cobia, D. C. (2009). Masculinity and sexuality: Impact on intimate relationships of African American men. *The Family Journal*, 17(4), 360–366.

Davis, L. E., Emerson, S., & Williams, J. H. (1997). Black dating professionals' perceptions of equity, satisfaction, power, and romantic alternatives and ideals. *Journal of Black Psychology*, 23(2), 148–164.

Dixon, P. (2009). Marriage among African Americans: What does the research reveal? *Journal of African American Studies*, 13(1), 29–46.

Edin, K. (2000). What do low-income single mothers say about marriage? *Social Problems*, 47(1), 112–133.

Edin, K., & Kefalas, M. (2005). *Promises I can keep: Why low-income women put motherhood before marriage*. Berkeley, CA: University of California Press.

Edin, K., Nelson, T., & Reed, J. (2011). Daddy, baby; momma maybe: Low income urban fathers and the "package deal" of family life. In P. England and M. Carlson (Eds.), *Families in an unequal society*. Palo Alto, CA: Stanford University Press.

Franklin, A. J. (2004). *From brotherhood to manhood: How Black men rescue their relationships and dreams from the invisibility syndrome*. Hoboken, NJ: John Wiley & Son.

Franklin, D. (1997). *Ensuring inequality: The structural transformation of the African American family*. New York: Oxford University Press.

Frazier, E. F. (1939). *The Negro family in the United States*. Chicago, IL: University of Chicago Press.

Furdyna, H. E., Tucker, M. B., & James, A. D. (2008). Relative spousal earnings and marital happiness among African American and White women. *Journal of Marriage and Family*, 70(2), 332–344.

Furstenberg, F. F. (2001). The fading dream: Prospects for marriage in the inner city. In E. Anderson & D. S. Massey (Eds.), *Problem of the century: Racial stratification in the United States* (pp. 224–246). New York: Russell Sage Foundation.

Furstenberg, F. F. (2007). The making of the black family: Race and class in qualitative studies in the 20th century. *Annual Review of Sociology* 33(1), 429–448.

Gerstel, N. (2011). Rethinking families and community: The color, class, and centrality of extended kin ties. *Sociological Forum*, 26(1), 1–20.

Gibson-Davis, C. M., Edin, K., & McLanahan, S. (2005). High hopes but even higher expectations: The retreat from marriage among low-income couples. *Journal of Marriage and the Family*, 67(5), 1301–1312.

Gillum, T. L. (2007). "How do I view my sister?": Stereotypic views of African American women and their potential to impact intimate partnerships. *Journal of Human Behavior in the Social Environment*, 15(2/3), 347–366.

Guzzo, K. B., & Furstenberg, F. F. (2007). Multipartnered fertility among American men. *Demography*, 44(3), 583–601.

Hardaway, C. R., & McLoyd, V. C. (2009). Escaping poverty and securing middle class status: How race and socioeconomic status shape mobility prospects for African Americans during the transition to adulthood. *Journal of Youth and Adolescence*, 38(2), 242–256.

Harding, D. J. (2010). *Living the drama: Community, conflict, and culture among inner-city boys*. Chicago, IL: University of Chicago Press.

Harknett, K., & Knab, J. (2007). More kin, less support: Multipartnered fertility and perceived support among mothers. *Journal of Marriage and Family* 69(1), 237–253.

Harvey, S. M., & Bird, S. T. (2004). What makes women feel powerful? An exploratory study of relationship power and sexual decision-making with African Americans at risk for HIV/STDs. *Women and Health*, 39(3), 1–18.

Hatchett, S., Veroff, J., & Douvan, E. (1995). Marital instability among Black and White couples in early marriage. In M. B. Tucker & C. Mitchell-Kernan (Eds.), *The decline in marriage among African-Americans: Causes, consequences, and policy implications* (pp. 1–50). New York: Russell Sage.

Heflin, C. M., & Pattillo, M. (2006). Poverty in the family: Race, siblings, and socioeconomic heterogeneity. *Social Science Research*, 35(4), 804–822.

Helm, K. (2010). Internet infidelity: Guidelines to recovering intimacy. In J. Carlson & L. Sperry (Eds.), *Recovering intimacy in love relationships: A clinicians' guide*. New York: Routledge.

Hill, H. D. (2007). Steppin' out: Infidelity and sexual jealousy among unmarried parents. In P. England & K. Edin (Eds.), *Unmarried couples with children* (pp. 104–132). New York: Russell Sage Foundation.

Hill, R. B. (1999). *The strengths of African American families: Twenty-five years later*. Lanham, MD: University Press of America.

Hill, S. A. (2002). Teaching and doing gender in African American families. *Sex Roles*, 47(11–12), 493–506.

Hill, S. A. (2005). *Black intimacies: A gender perspective on families and relationships*. Lanham, MD: Rowman & Littlefield.

Hill, S. A. (2009). Why won't African Americans get (and stay) married? Why should they? In H. E. Peters and C. M. Kamp Dush (Eds.), *Marriage and family: Complexities and perspectives* (pp. 345–364). New York: Columbia University Press.

Holmes, J. G., & Rempel, J. K. (1989). Trust in close relationships. In C. Hendrick (Ed.), *Close relationships* (pp. 187–220). Newbury Park, CA: Sage.

hooks, b. (1994). *Outlaw culture: Resisting representations*. New York: Routledge.

hooks, b. (2000). *All about love: New visions*. New York: Harper Perennial.

hooks, b. (2001). *Salvation: Black people and love*. New York: William Morrow.

hooks, b. (2004). *We real cool: Black men and masculinity*. New York: Routledge.

Hunter, A. G., & Davis J. E. (1992). Constructing gender: An exploration of Afro-American men's conceptualization of manhood. *Gender & Society*, 6(3), 464–479.

Kane, E. (2000). Race and ethnic variations in gender-related attitudes. *Annual Review of Sociology*, 26(1), 419–439.

Kelley, R. D. G. (1997). *Yo' mama's disfunktional!: Fighting the culture wars in urban America*. Boston, MA: Beacon Press.

Kelly, S., & Floyd, F. J. (2001). The effects of negative racial stereotypes and Afrocentricity on Black couple relationships. *Journal of Family Psychology*, 15(1), 110–123.

King, E. O., & Allen, T. T. (2009). Personal characteristics of the ideal African American marriage partner: A survey of adult black men and women. *Journal of Black Studies*, 39(4), 570–588.

Kitwana, B. (2003). *The hip hop generation: Young Blacks and the crisis in African American culture*. New York: Basic Civitas Books.

Lane, S. D., Keefe, R. H., Rubinstein, R. A., Levandowski, B. A., Freedman, M., Rosenthal, A., Cibula, D. A., & Czerwinski, M. (2004). Marriage promotion and missing men: African American women in a demographic double bind. *Medical Anthropology Quarterly*, 18(4), 405–428.

Majors, R., & Billson, J. M. (1992). *Cool pose: The dilemmas Of Black manhood in America*. New York: Simon & Schuster.

Manning, W. D., & Smock, P. S. (2002). First Comes Cohabitation, Then Comes Marriage?: A Research Note. *Journal of Family Issues*, 23(8), 1065–1087.

Marks, L. D., Hopkins, K., Chaney, C., Monroe, P. A., Nesteruk, O., & Sasser, D. D. (2008). "Together we are strong:" A qualitative study of happy, enduring African American marriages. *Family Relations*, 57(2), 172–185.

Marsh, K., Darity Jr., W. A., Cohen, P. A., & Salters, D. (2007). The emerging Black middle class: Single and living alone. *Social Forces*, 86(2), 735–762.

Martin, E., & Martin, J. M. (1978). *The Black extended family*. Chicago, IL: University of Chicago Press.

Martinez, E. S. (1998). *De colores means all of us: Latina views for a multi-colored century*. Boston, MA: South End Press.

Massey, D. S., & Denton, N. A. (1993). *American apartheid*. Cambridge, MA: Harvard University Press.

May, R. A. B. (2001). *Talking at Trena's: Everyday conversation at an African-American tavern*. New York: NYU Press.

Moore, M. R. (2008). Gendered power relations among women: A study of household decision making in Black, lesbian stepfamilies. *American Sociological Review*, 73(2), 335–356.

Moynihan, D. P. (1965). *The Negro family: The case for national action*. Washington, DC: Office of Policy Planning and Research.

Muñoz-Laboy, M., Weinstein, H., & Parker, R. (2007). The hip-hop club scene: Gender, grinding, and sex. *Culture, Health & Sexuality*, 9(6), 615–628.

Murry, V. M., Bynum, M. S., Brody, G. H., Willert, A., & Stephens, D. (2001). African American single mothers and children in context: A review of studies on risk and resilience. *Clinical Child and Family Psychology Review*, 4(2), 133–155.

Nelson, T., Piercy, F. P., & Sprenkle, D. H. (2005). Internet infidelity. *Journal of Couple and Relationship Therapy*, 4(2), 173–194.

Orbuch, T. L., Veroff, J., & Hunter, A. G. (1999). Black couples, White couples: The early years of marriage. In E. M. Hetherington (Ed.), *Coping with divorce, single parenting, and remarriage: A risk and resiliency perspective* (pp. 23–43). Mahwah, NJ: Erlbaum.

Osborne, C., & McLanahan, S. (2007). Partnership instability and child wellbeing. *Journal of Marriage and Family*, 64(4), 1065–1083.

Pattillo, M. (2005). Black middle class neighborhoods. *Annual Review of Sociology*, 31(1), 305–329.

Pattillo, M. (2007). *Black on the block: The politics of race and class in the city*. Chicago, IL: University of Chicago Press.

Pattillo-McCoy, M. (1999). *Black picket fences: Privilege and peril in the Black middle class neighborhood*. Chicago, IL: University of Chicago Press.

Phillips, J. A., & Sweeney, M. M. (2005). Premarital cohabitation and marital disruption among White, Black, and Mexican American women. *Journal of Marriage and the Family*, 67(2), 296–314.

Pinderhughes, E. B. (2002). African American marriage in the 20th century. *Family Process* 41(2), 269–282.

Powell, K. (2003). *Who's gonna take the weight? Manhood, power, and race in America*. New York: Three Rivers Press.

Pyke, K. D. (1996). Class-based masculinities: The interdependence of gender, class, and interpersonal power. *Gender & Society*, 10(5), 527–549.

Raley, R. K., & Sweeney, M. M. (2009). Explaining race and ethnic variation in marriage: Directions for future research. *Race and Social Problems*, 1(3), 132–142.

Rose, T. (2008). *The hip hop wars: What we talk about when we talk about hip hop and why it matters*. New York: Basic Civitas.

Roy, K. M. (2005). Transitions on the margins of work and family for low-income African American fathers. *Journal of Family and Economic Issues* 26(1), 77–100.

Roy, K. M. (2008). A life course perspective on fatherhood and family policies in the United States and South Africa. *Fathering: A Journal of Theory, Research, and Practice about Men as Fathers*, 6(2), 92–112.

Roy, K. M., & Dyson, O. L. (2005). Gatekeeping in context: Babymama drama and the involvement of incarcerated fathers. *Fathering*, 3(3), 289–310.

Roy, K. M., Buckmiller, N., & McDowell, A. (2008). Together but not "together:" Trajectories of relationship suspension for low-income unmarried parents. *Family Relations*, 57(2), 197–209.

Seal, D. W., & Ehrhardt, A. A. (2003). Masculinity and urban men: Perceived scripts for courtship, romantic, and sexual interactions with women. *Culture, Health and Sexuality*, 5(4), 295–319.

Senn, T. E., Carey, M. P., Vanable, P. A., & Seward, D. X. (2009). African American men's perceptions of power in intimate relationships. *American Journal of Men's Health*, 3(4) 310–318.

Shapiro, T. M. (2004). *The hidden cost of being African American: How wealth perpetuates inequality*. New York: Oxford University Press.

Singer, M. C., Erickson, P. I., Badiane, L., Diaz, R., Ortiz, D., Abraham, T., & Nicolaysen, A. M. (2006). Syndemics, sex and the city: Understanding sexually transmitted diseases in social and cultural context. *Social Science and Medicine*, 63(8), 2010–2021.

Smock, P. J., & Manning, W. D. (2004). Living together unmarried in the United States: Demographic perspectives and implications for family policy. *Law & Policy*, 26(1), 87–117.

Smock, P. J., Manning, W. D., & Porter, M. (2005). Everything's there except money: How economic factors shape the decision to marry among cohabiting couples. *Journal of Marriage and Family* 67(3), 680–696.

South, S. J. (2001). The geographic context of divorce: Do neighborhoods matter? *Journal of Marriage and Family*, 63(3), 755–766.

South, S. J., & Crowder, K. D. (1999). Neighborhood effects on family formation: Concentrated poverty and beyond. *American Sociological Review*, 64(1), 113–132.

Springer, K. (2002). Third Wave Black Feminism? *Signs*, 27(4), 1059–1082.

Stack, C. B. (1974). *All our kin: Strategies for survival in a Black community*. New York: Harper & Row.

Stack, C. M., & Burton, L. M. (1993). Kinscripts. *Journal of Comparative Family Studies*, 24(2), 157–170.

Staples, R. (1982). Black masculinity: The Black male's role in American society. San Francisco, CA: Black Scholar Press.

Stephens, D. P., & Phillips, L. D. (2003). Freaks, gold diggers, divas, and dykes: The sociohistorical development of adolescent African American women's sexual scripts. *Sexuality and Culture*, 7(1), 3–49.

Sternberg, R. J. (1986). A triangular theory of love. *Psychological Review*, 93(2), 119–135.

Sudarkasa, N. (1997). African American families and family values. In H. P. McAdoo (Ed.), *Black Families* (pp. 9–40). Thousand Oaks, CA: Sage Publications.

Sudarkasa, N. (2007). Interpreting the African heritage in African American family organization. In H. P. McAdoo (Ed.) *Black Families* (pp. 29–47). Thousand Oaks, CA: Sage Publications.

Taylor, J. (1990). Relationship between internalized racism and marital satisfaction. *Journal of Black Psychology*, 16(1), 45–53.

Teyber, E., & McClure, F. H. (2011). *Interpersonal process in therapy: An Integrative model*, 6th ed. (pp. 13–16). Belmont, CA: Brooks/Cole, Cengage Learning.

Townsend, T. G. (2008). Protecting our daughters: Intersection of race, class and gender in African American mothers' socialization of their daughters' heterosexuality. *Sex Roles*, 59(5-6), 429–442.

Tucker, M. B. (2000). Marital values and expectations in context: Results from a 21 city survey. In L. J. Waite, C. Bachrach, M. Hindin, & A. Thornton, (Eds.), *The ties that bind: Perspectives on marriage and cohabitation* (pp. 166–187). New York: Aldine de Gruyter.

Tucker, M. B., & Mitchell-Kernan, C. (1995). Trends in African American family formation: A theoretical and statistical overview. In M. B. Tucker & C. Mitchell-Kernan (Eds.), *The decline in marriage among African Americans: Causes, consequences, and policy implications*. New York: Russell Sage Foundation.

U.S. Census Bureau (2011). *America's Families and Living Arrangements: 2011*. Retrieved from http://www.census.gov/population/www/socdemo/hh-fam.html.

Waller, M. R. (2008). How do disadvantaged parents view tensions in their relationships? Insights for relationship longevity among at-risk couples. *Family Relations* 57(2), 128–143.

Waller, W. (1937). The rating and dating complex. *The American Sociological Review*, 2(5), 727–734.

West, C. (2001). *Race matters*. Boston, MA: Beacon Press.

Willis, J. T. (1990). Some destructive elements in African-American male-female relationships. *Family Therapy*, 17(2), 139–147.

Wilson W. J. (1987). *The truly disadvantaged: The inner city, the underclass, and public policy*. Chicago, IL: University of Chicago Press.

Wilson, W. J. (1996). *When work disappears*. New York: Alfred A. Knopf.

Wilson, W. J. (2008). The economic plight of inner-city Black males. In E. Anderson (Ed.), *Against the wall: Poor, young, Black, and male* (pp. 55–70). Philadelphia, PA: University of Pennsylvania Press.

Wilson, W. J. (2009). *More than just race: Being Black and poor in the inner-city*. New York: W.W. Norton.

Wimberley, E. P. (1997). *Counseling African American marriages and families*. Louisville, KY: Westminster John Knox Press.

Wyatt, G. (1997). *Stolen women: Reclaiming our sexuality, taking back our lives*. New York: Wiley Books.

Young, A. (2011). Comment: Reactions from the perspective of culture and low-income fatherhood. *The Annals of the American Academy of Political and Social Science* 635(1), 117–122.

EXPERT INTERVIEW

Audrey B. Chapman is a family therapist, author, trainer, and nationally known relationship expert. She has appeared on dozens of national and television programs, including *Oprah*, has her own weekly radio show, and has authored several books.

Today's Black couples face some challenging issues. How do you think that the issues Black couples face have changed over the last 60 years? How have they stayed the same?

What's changed for single Black men and women is the lack of interest in getting married at all. The marriage rate has dropped. When I talk to men and women, what I find is that they are the generation that experienced the instability and dissolution of marriage more than previous generations. I believe these kids witnessed the instability—thus, while you can get married, it does not mean that you necessarily stay married. So, what many of this generation is doing is resisting marriage—not simply marriage, but they are resisting love and the tradition that you build relationships, and sometimes relationships cause hurt. They assume that if they don't get married or build relationships, they won't have to go through relational pain.

The other issue is the shortage of African American men, which is a reality. This is not something anybody created. There is a shortage over all, but in the Caucasian, Asian, and Latino communities they are more willing to marry across racial lines.

There is more pressure [to marry] if individuals are "church-going" because the church says if you are going to be with someone and you are going to consummate the relationship, then you must be married; however, this does not enable individuals to actually be able to bring that to an end. Today's Black men and women just have a different attitude about marriage and it is not simply about economics. That is too simplistic an assumption to make. It's also an attitude shift. For example, many young women still hope to meet their mates in college; however, there are fewer young Black men in college than women, as Black men graduate high school at lower rates than Black women. This makes for another complicating issue.

What skills do Black couples need in this world to stay together?

Clearly, I think that many people focus on communication. While I think that communication is clearly important, what they also have to have is the ability to be accountable with each other so that they then have the capacity to have emotional intimacy with one another. The media stresses sexual intimacy over emotional intimacy. Obviously with sexual intimacy, there is a risk to one's health—but not necessarily one's heart. Young people today often rely on texting and emailing and do not know how to talk to each other. When these are the primary modes of communication, they risk losing the skill for holding conversations. Many do not know how to do this and it is very tragic. Sometimes couples feel like there is not the "time for conversations" and they substitute texts and emails for real dialogue which is a significant barrier to emotional intimacy.

So we are creating a generation of young people who cannot effectively problem solve or share or let people into their emotional space. Many do not know how to do this which is the basis of holding a marriage together. At the basis of being intimate with one another is dialogue and understanding.. This is what holds a marriage together

Couples have to know how to self-soothe. This is *key* to having a successful relationship. I teach this frequently in couples' therapy because many couples do not know how to do this. Self-soothing helps people to calm down and to feel comforted. Self-soothing in words means being empathetic to one's partner.

In the beginning of my work with couples, I approach couples' therapy as a teaching agent rather than a therapy process. The therapy begins when I take an extensive history of the couple when they come in (e.g. sexual history, trauma, relationship with church, education, etc.). Clients have to be mature and willing to "go there". Thus, doing a comprehensive assessment early in the therapy process is very important.

There is so much attention paid to the negatives of African American romantic relationships.
What strengths do many AA couples bring to their relationships?
What are some of the common weaknesses of struggling AA couples?

We believe in family which is an important part of our culture. We believe very strongly in trying to provide a base, family, home, space, for our children. There is a lot of communication around what being in a family provides. If you are going out to deal in a hostile world where you may have a great deal of difficulty dealing with co-workers and bosses, especially through issues of racism, you may look to your family to hold you together. I think that once Black men and women decide to be a couple, they work hard to remain so.

Discuss the "gender war" and its impact on Black couples

The gender war is actually secondary. I think the primary issue is that one cannot have a good relationship with a romantic partner if you do not have one with yourself. I talk about this every single morning on my Saturday morning radio show. If we want to stop the "gender war" we need to first explore the war within [ourselves]. What I find in my work with couples and individuals is that most people project anything that is unwanted or unacceptable about themselves onto their romantic partners. Thus, one must know what one's own "stuff" [personal baggage] is and one needs to be willing to address his/her own personal issues. If you are working with yourself in a wholesome way—because the goal is to be wholesome and to have a centered self, rather than being self-centered (as there is a big difference between the two)—then you can have a better ability to have a healthy exchange within a relationship. If you are not working with yourself in a healthy way, then, as a therapist, I have to spend more time on an individual, because his/her ego will not allow me to deal appropriately with his/her personal issues. If an individual does not resolve his/her own personal issues, they have relationship issues within all of their relationships (family, friends, co-workers, etc.), not just their romantic relationships. They simply have problems relating.

I frequently see a deficit having to do with low self-esteem and self-confidence, and this must be dealt with in therapy. Once this gets worked through, the individual can begin to relate to others more comfortably and their relationships with males and females get better.

What are the advantages of marriage/long-term committed relationships for Black couples and the Black community?

I believe that it produces more stable children, more social children, a more stable community, and more stability for an individual. Two are better than the individual because they do better financially and have more wealth. Marriage/long-term relationships are also better for one's health and enable people to live longer and survive better. I think that these are important supports for long-term relationships. However, couples need to have good tools to sustain these relationships. There are no problem-free relationships and no relationships without conflict. It is how you manage these issues within a marriage/long-term relationship. If you do not deal with conflicts, there will be bigger problems, so having resources and tools are critical. Sometimes reading a book will help but often the most helpful thing is to go to a retreat with other couples—no matter how long a couple has been married, this can be helpful. On retreats, other couples can help reinforce the tools you are using. It's also good for couples to go to couples' conferences. I do a seminar several times a year with a couples' organization. The goals are to reinforce romance and put it back into marriage and we give tools for how to do this. I think that after a while, for couples who have been together for a long period of time, they begin to take each other for granted.

Part III

SUBGROUPS WITHIN AFRICAN AMERICAN COUPLES

5

LOVE AND INTIMACY ISSUES WITH INTERCULTURAL BLACK COUPLES

Chante' D. DeLoach,
Marissa N. Petersen-Coleman, and Shena J. Young

There is an erroneous common belief that African Americans/Blacks are culturally homogenous. In fact, this group is comprised of U.S. born persons of African ancestry as well as immigrants and their descendants from continental Africa, the Caribbean, and Europe (Rastogi et al., 2011). Similarly, Blacks inhabit every region of the country, yet little focus is given to cultural differences that may emerge as a result of geographic location. This collective distorted view of African Americans as a group has resulted in a limited and myopic understanding of African Americans as a people, including their relationships. While little research has focused exclusively on African American romantic relationships, even less has focused on cultural differences within those relationships (Alex-Assensoh & Assensoh, 1998). Those few studies that have attempted such an exploration have focused primarily on interracial relationships with little acknowledgment or literary consideration of intragroup cultural diversity. To this end, discussions of intercultural relationships, even within couples' discourse, presume that partners are of different racial groups. Such assumptions negate 1) the cultural diversity within the "Black/African American" racial category, 2) the rich cultural traditions within this diverse racial group, and 3) the needs and challenges that may emerge from Black people of different cultural backgrounds joining together. The purpose of the present chapter is to acknowledge the heterogeneity across persons of African ancestry residing in the U.S., give voice to the range of experiences of Black couples of different cultural backgrounds, and provide an overview of: a) how culture-related stressors impact Black intercultural romantic relationships, and b) how cultural resiliencies can serve as clinical strengths within a therapeutic setting. Moreover, the authors intend to emphasize the challenges and strengths associated with balancing cultural differences within a committed relationship for this particular group; specific recommendations for helping professionals will be provided.

Defining Black and Intercultural Black Couples

In light of the conflicting definitions of *intercultural*, and range of interpretations for the *Black/African American* racial category, these terms will be operationalized as they are being utilized in the present discussion. According to the 2010 U.S. Census, "Black or African American" refers to a person having origins in any of the Black racial groups of Africa (Rastogi et al., 2011). This racial category includes people who self-selected the "Black, African American, or Negro" categorical option as well as respondents in the multiple-race Black population indicative of those who identify as Black and/or multiracial (Rastogi et al., 2011). This category also includes those who reported Sub-Saharan African lineages such as Kenyan and Nigerian, as well as Afro-Caribbean lineages such as Haitian and Jamaican (Rastogi et al., 2011). It is noteworthy that individuals of African ancestry from the Spanish speaking Caribbean, Central and South Americas are excluded from the Black/African American racial category and typically are categorized as "Hispanic/Latino" (Ennis, Rios-Vargas, & Albert, 2011). Such classification further underscores the continued social construction of race, negation of cultural ancestry, and obfuscates the cultural diversity and complexity of each racial category.

The term *intercultural couples* most commonly refers to "domestic partnerships comprised of partners from different ethnic, racial, religious, or national backgrounds" (Bystydzienski, 2011, p. 1). However, this chapter will focus only on couples in which both partners identify as Black and also represent different cultural backgrounds (e.g. Haitian, Jamaican, African American, etc.), as existing racial categories are limited in capturing the range of cultural differences.

Presently, accurate statistics for intercultural couples living in the U.S. are difficult to come by given the above mentioned deficits in racial categorization; however, previous data suggests that intercultural couples may be in the tens of millions (Passel, Wang, & Taylor, 2010) although they remain an understudied aspect of American life (Bystydzienski, 2011), and even more so in Black couples' discourse. Given the increased number of immigrants of African ancestry and their descendants, more attention in this area is warranted. Specifically, the unique history and sociocultural factors of these groups that undoubtedly influence the dynamics of Black intercultural couples are central to understanding their presenting issues.

Black Immigration

It is important to consider immigration and acculturation patterns as persons who select the categories reviewed above reflect those of African descent from around the world. As immigration continues in the U.S., so does ethnic and cultural diversity. Unfortunately, Black immigrants in the U.S. are considerably understudied in comparison to Hispanic/Latino and Asian immigrants, and existing data tends to focus mainly on Caribbean immigrants (Dodoo, 1997).

Reports on immigration patterns, however, indicate that the U.S. is the top migrant destination country in the world and hosts over two thirds of Latin American and Caribbean migrants, accounting for fifty-three percent of the total foreign born population in this country (International Organization for Migration, 2010). In regards to the Black immigrant population, about two thirds of foreign born Blacks are from the Caribbean and Latin America and nearly one third were born in Africa (Kent, 2007). The number of foreign born blacks more than tripled between 1980 and 2005 and forty percent of African born blacks arrived between 2000 and 2005 (Kent, 2007).

Immigration of Blacks to the U.S. from Africa, the Caribbean, and some Latin American countries is often influenced by economic and political forces, as foreign born Blacks are seeking educational opportunities, jobs, and sometimes individual safety (Kent, 2007). Further, they inherit two distinctive social labels in the U.S., immigrant and Black, which inevitably impacts adaptation to their new country (Kent, 2007). Such a dynamic poses a significant challenge for Black immigrants and their adaptation to U.S. life and extends beyond first generation immigrants. Despite often being part of the majority culture in their home countries, Black immigrants often encounter discrimination embedded in the U.S. culture (Kent, 2007). Thus, while Black immigrants may be racially categorized or viewed phenotypically as "Black/African American," many may not have viewed themselves as "Black" pre-immigration and some may maintain different value systems and political views than this group. Others still may consciously view themselves separate and distinct from U.S. born African Americans and choose to identify differently racially as a result (Gaines & Ramkissoon, 2008; Waters, 2000).

Additionally, references to Caribbean immigrants as the "model minority" due to their economic standing, entering more prestigious jobs, and experiencing less crime and unemployment poses a different type of pressure in the acculturation experience and may influence their relationships with African Americans (Kent, 2007). On the contrary, African born Blacks are often not privy to such an immigrant advantage, as Americans, including African Americans, often hold negative misconceptions about them (Kent, 2007). These notions negatively impact immigrants as reflected in earning patterns, socioeconomic status, and social exclusion (Kent, 2007). For example, Caribbean immigrants are reported to earn more money, enter more prestigious jobs, and experience less unemployment when compared to African immigrants, and African immigrants' incomes and jobs do not commensurate with their educational levels (Shaw-Taylor & Tuch, 2007).

Fortunately, many Black immigrants have joined together to form resources, develop enclaves, and maintain essential aspects of their native communities (Kent, 2007; Wilson, 2009). Research has indicated the importance of continued communication with family members in one's home country, community-building with others from their respective region, and self-defining strategies to maintain their ethnic identities (Wilson, 2009). Further, a common experience amongst immigrants can be described in terms of their respective beliefs and upbringing that becoming a U.S. citizen is an act of transgression; however, this is often an emotional journey as the choice itself can signify abandonment of their home culture (Wilson, 2009). It is clear that little is known about these issues for Black immigrants. Future studies should investigate the adaptation, adjustment, and acculturation experience for Black immigrants and their unique migrant ideology.

African Worldview and Cultural Continuity

Clearly, the Black/African American racial category is diverse, inclusive of persons of African ancestry who may identify very differently and embrace myriad perspectives as a result. Yet, the present authors take a decidedly Pan-Africanist perspective in honoring the shared African ancestry and cultural traditions that survived centuries of colonial praxis, continued global European hegemony, and that transcend continental and geographic divides (Diop, 1974; Kambon, 1998). Accordingly, while cultural differences exist, there appears to be a shared core worldview that is cosmologically African despite patterns of acculturation and assimilation that allow continental and Diasporic African people to connect and share experiences. Dixon (1976) suggested that an African worldview emphasizes communalism, harmony and balance, and values a human-to-person relationship. In terms of time, value is placed on past and present; time is seen as cyclical. To this end, being is emphasized over doing. Epistemologically, the focus is on the *how* of knowledge; multiple ways of knowing are valued including through affective/symbolic engagement strategies and intuition versus sole emphasis on cognition. Lastly, as Diop (1974) noted, logic is understood to be diunital, reflecting a "both/and" approach—things are considered to be simultaneously true and false—depending upon the subjective perception of the observer-participant. Thus, an African worldview juxtaposed against a European worldview that separates persons from the phenomenal world in that it values a human-to-object relationship; emphasizes individualism; a future, linear time orientation; and doing over being. Thus, the African worldview is seen as qualitatively different from the European worldview. While there may be core worldview similarities across persons of African ancestry, factors such as country of origin, acculturation/assimilation, and familial variables may impact the degree to which a person endorses an African worldview. Thus, within an intercultural Black relationship, differences may exist in areas such as: degree to which one prioritizes family/community over self, time orientation, or understandings of the cycle of life.

Beyond the shared tumultuous history of enslavement for people of African descent, namely African Americans, African Caribbeans, and Afro-Latinos, a number of core similarities have emerged. Black (1996) lists several areas of experience that Black people in the New World share that set them apart from all other ethnic groups. These areas include:

(a) the African legacy, rich in culture, custom, and achievement; (b) the history of slavery, a deliberate attempt to destroy the core and soul of the people, while keeping their bodies in enforced servitude; (c) racism and discrimination, ongoing efforts to continue the psychological and economic subjugation started during slavery; and (d) the victim system, a process by which individuals and communities are denied access to the instruments of development and advancement, and then blamed for low levels of accomplishment and achievement, while their successes are treated as anomalies.

(p. 59)

Alex-Assensoh and Assensoh (1998) note that this shared racial plight of Otherness for Africans, African Americans, and Blacks from the Caribbean may serve as a "unifying force, attracting, and subsequently bridging Africans and their African American partners together" (p. 103).

African Immigrant/African American Relations

As mentioned previously, many Black immigrants may come from contexts in which they are in the numerical majority, yet one must recall that these spaces were colonized (some may argue remain so). Thus, continental and Diasporic Africans, including those in the Caribbean, continue to suffer from internalized colonialism/racism, which may manifest in specific ways that impact relational decisions such as: notions of inferiority, perceptions of beauty, social class distinctions, and inform mate selection to name but a few (Gaines & Ramkissoon, 2008). For example, in Jamaica, its population is over 90 percent persons of African ancestry, yet continued privileging of lighter skin color is common. It is not uncommon in the Caribbean for children to be socialized that White and lighter skinned playmates are preferable (Fanon, 1967). Similarly, implicit and explicit messages are provided that Whiter features are preferred in mate selection (Gaines & Ramkissoon, 2008). These messages are consistent with the booming market and availability of skin bleaching products in Africa and throughout the Caribbean (Christopher, 2003; also see for example popular media sources such as the Jamaican healthy campaign: "Don't Kill the Skin."). Thus, colorism and light skin privilege continue to exist across many areas of the Diaspora.

Socialization within systems of racism inherently impact how Africans and African Americans view and relate to one another. Interestingly, first-generation Black immigrants tend to be less supportive of ethnic assimilation and support maintaining strong cultural ties, yet also endorse strong positive relationships with Whites and perceive less racial discrimination (Gaines & Ramkissoon, 2008). Such differences are thought to negatively influence Black Caribbeans' relationships with U.S. born African Americans, some of whom grew up in the numerical minority experiencing chronic racial discrimination (Gaines & Ramkissoon, 2008). Yet, second-generation Caribbeans report more negative attitudes toward

Whites and less optimism about their status in the U.S. (Waters, 2000). Thus, second generations' relationships with U.S. born African Americans appear to be less influenced by immigration experiences, yet marked with similar challenges to many African American romantic partnerships (Gaines & Ramkisson, 2008).

Hence, while some authors may emphasize the potential impact of Black immigrants coming from a numerical majority, the far-reaching impact of colonialism and racial hatred transcends geographical divides and is irrespective of experiencing being in the demographic majority. Despite this phenomenon, African Americans and Black immigrants are joining together in romantic relationships. To this end, Alex-Assensoh and Assensoh (1998) predict that as the number of marriageable African American men decline, other Black immigrants may be more highly sought after by African Americans for romantic relationships. Yet, Alex-Assensoh and Assensoh also theorize that African Americans (and those of the majority culture) have little awareness of culture-specific practices or pertinent cultural differences between African Americans and African immigrants (ibid). Moreover, as mentioned previously, there is little training for helping professionals who work with these couples and families.

Cultural Differences in Persons of African Ancestry

The lack of homogeneity within the Black racial group, specifically for American born Blacks, can pose a daunting task for clinicians working with intercultural couples and families. As previously mentioned, racial similarities do not necessarily translate to cultural similarities (Bustamante et al, 2011; Reiter, 2008; Waldman & Rubalcava, 2005). Interestingly, considerations of power and oppression are not solely associated with racial differences but are also factors within Black intercultural relationships (Sullivan & Cottone, 2006). Some theorists note that in the pursuit of a common Pan-African identity, cultural differences as a result of global displacement, continued oppression, and internalized racism may be minimized. Alex-Assensoh and Assensoh (1998) note that "these differences include 1) the clash between a self-oriented culture and a communal culture; 2) the clash between definitions of marriage based on extend family ties and one based on the union of two individuals; and 3) the clash between conflicting images and stereotypes Africans and African Americans may have of each other" (p. 106).

Such differences and cultural nuances are important to identify that cultural differences are at the heart of intercultural unions and present couples with different challenges than couples of similar cultural backgrounds. These differences could influence couples' presenting issues in therapy. Black intercultural couples may initially bond by their cultural similarities; however, cultural differences are likely to arise. The role of culture in human development is such that individuals of all cultures will tend to presume that their cultural values are representative of truth and/or the way things ought to be (Waldman & Rubalcava, 2005). This presumption, understandably, may cause dissention within Black intercultural couples.

Clinical Issues in Black Intercultural Relationships

Gottman's (1999) research has identified several primary sources of conflict across couples including stress, finances, sex, delineation of domestic responsibilities, and having a child. There is a growing amount of literature on cultural influences within relationships; however, as noted elsewhere in this volume (see DeLoach, Chapter 8), empirical research on African American couples is limited. This want of research is even more pronounced for Black intercultural relationships (Bustamante et al., 2011; Molina, Estrada, & Burnett, 2004). Black intercultural relationships are likely to experience many of the same stressors facing many culturally homogenous Black couples including racial discrimination, economic challenges, gender role strain, and communication to name a few. However, these issues may strongly be influenced by cultural differences in ways that the couples themselves may be unaware.

Hsu (2001) states, that "intercultural couples have a greater likelihood of encountering problems because they hold even more diverse values, beliefs, attitudes, and habits than couples who are of similar culture" (p.225). Bustamante and colleagues (2011) reviewed available literature on "intercultural couples" (defined broadly by the researchers) and found that overall, five primary sources of stress for intercultural couples are discussed in the literature: 1) differences in cultural values and worldviews; 2) systemic issues, or negative messages from family or dominant culture; 3) distinct culturally patterned communication and conflict resolution styles; 4) religious, spiritual, and ethnic beliefs; and 5) an unbalanced view of cultural differences. While some of these issues are foundational, some of these challenges constitute what Ting-Toomey & Oetzel (2001) call the "emotional tasks" of relationships or the daily ins and outs of a relationship that may indicate that partners differ personally or culturally in how to manage such tasks. In the interest of organization of the present discussion, we will present these categorically as 1) differences in cultural values; 2) familial and gender roles; 3) cultured patterns of communication and conflict resolution; and 4) systemic influences. Each of these will be reviewed, specifically as it relates to Black intercultural relationships.

Differences in Cultural Values

Differences in ethnic and racial identity, immigration status, and the impact of internalized racism on African/African American relationships have already been discussed. Notably, social disapproval and negotiating cultural differences may intensify these stressors within Black intercultural relationships. According to Bustamante et al. (2011), "cultural differences can place internal strains on a marriage" (p. 155). Intercultural research indicates that through close cross-cultural relationships one can develop genuine interpersonal empathy that transcends rigid cultural stereotypes (Ting-Toomey & Oetzel, 2001). Even the most open-minded partner may unwittingly perpetuate relational ethnocentrism in which they privilege the way in which they were socialized to do things; this may be even more pronounced during relational tension and conflict. Indeed, "individuals presume that his or her perception of the other is objective, true and factual. Each partner makes sense of the other's affect, behavior and expression in terms of his or her own unconscious cultural organizing principles" (Waldman & Rubalcava, 2005, p. 230). For example, issues such as child rearing practices are often culturally based. A new couple may experience conflict if one partner believes his or her disciplining practices are "right" and methods contrary to this, specifically those disciplinary practices rooted in the partner's culture, are "wrong".

Many contemporary, psychodynamic authors view personhood as a cultural construction (Waldman & Rubalcava, 2005; Yi, 1999). This assumption implies that individuals cannot separate the personal from the cultural because they are so intimately intertwined (Bronfenbrenner, 1979). Therefore, cultural differences are at the heart of intercultural unions. Again, Black intercultural couples may initially bond by their racial similarities; however, inevitably cultural differences will arise.

Yet, all intercultural couples may not perceive cultural differences as a source of distress (Falicov, 1995). Specifically, Falicov (1995) states that couples in distress may have an unbalanced view of cultural differences in which partners may minimize or exaggerate differences. Conversely, couples with a balanced view tend to have an integrated, more complementary perspective of cultural similarities and differences (ibid). Attending to the way in which a couple perceives these differences is important as it may be emblematic of how they deal with other areas of difference or disagreement. Moreover, she notes that "…any difference or similarity can be maximized by the spouses at different times and in different areas for psychological reasons or purposes" (p.233). Thus, it would behoove clinicians to attend to the meaning in which couples make of similarities and differences as well as the process by which these issues emerge.

One way such issues may emerge is through problems of cultural code, or the culturally based rules that govern life, including relational rules (Falicov, 1995). Conflicts of cultural code are thought to emerge from differences in governing rules, power, and authority over what and whom are included and excluded from the couple system. Others discuss the process of *cultural camouflage*, or using cultural practices or even stereotypes to explain one's behavior and avoid or minimize conflict (Falicov, 1995; Molina et al., 2004). For instance, a Jamaican partner using his nationality to condone drug use perpetuates a negative cultural stereotype while attempting to avoid spousal conflict.

Familial and Gender Roles

As mentioned previously, family is central within an African worldview. How family is defined specifically including understandings of dependents and financial responsibility to extended family is defined culturally and historically (Alex-Assensoh & Assensoh, 1998). There are many similarities in family constellation across African cultures. Family structure for African Americans and African Caribbeans is often similar having been comparably impacted during enslavement resulting in single parent and female-headed households, which continue today (Barrow, 1996).

One might hypothesize that comparable similarities exist in romantic partnerships as well, yet little research is available in these areas. Gender roles and gendered expectations may vary across Black ethnic and cultural groups and appear to be influenced by numerous factors including economic needs and religion.

Current relational discourse would benefit from increased historical and political contextualization. For example, Gaines & Ramkissoon (2008) describe how economic realities influence Jamaican women's partner selection and relationship decision-making. While these authors discuss Jamaican romantic relationships in an arguably less than culturally nuanced manner, they describe one identified relational pattern for Jamaican women to have children with different fathers, maintain multiple relationships to have her diverse needs met, and to expect financial support from male partners. They note further that Jamaican men may seek sexual relationships with multiple partners yet endorse more traditional gendered domestic roles, particularly when there is an increased degree of commitment or marriage. For some Jamaican men, being able to house, clothe, and feed a mistress may be a sign of status and wealth (Brice-Baker, 1996). Finally, Gaines & Ramkissoon conclude that, "romance appears to be secondary to more practical and utilitarian considerations for forming and maintaining relationships among Black Caribbeans at home and abroad" (2008, p.236).

Clearly within Jamaican culture, like others, there are many gender role paradoxes. Young girls are taught to be obedient and pretty but not sexually alluring while young boys are praised for drawing the attention of the opposite sex (Brice-Baker, 1996). While this research is limited and therefore should be interpreted with caution, it provides information on gender roles and relational expectations and illustrates the importance of viewing relational patterns within nuanced cultural contexts. This data coupled with the previously mentioned socialization messages around skin color and social class may inform mate selection, relationship, and sexual decision-making, and contribute to issues within romantic partnerships with African American partners who may hold counter values.

Thus, beliefs about sex, gender, and power within a family are directly connected to the specific cultural values represented within the relationship. Molina et al. (2004) illustrate an example of common attitudes held by African-American women: "I work at home and on the job. I expect my husband to share the work at home while he holds a job. I expect us to share family responsibilities and I do not have to compete with him about work at home or work on the job" (p. 142). This attitude about gender roles is contrasted with Roopnarine and colleagues' (2009) study on the beliefs about parental roles and the division of childcare and household labor in Indo-Caribbean immigrants. The researchers found that: "Fathers saw their role primarily as financial providers, followed by their role as emotional caregivers, and finally as physical caregivers; mothers saw their role primarily as physical caregivers, then as emotional caregivers, and finally as financial providers" (p. 177). These findings, like that mentioned for the Jamaican families, illustrate a greater adherence to traditional gender ideologies than seen in their African American counterparts, thus further emphasizing that, despite cultural similarities, there may be cultural differences that Black partners of different cultural backgrounds carry into relationships.

The differences of gender roles, traditions, and values may contribute to relationship dissatisfaction within intercultural relationships. Internalized racism and negative media portrayals may contribute to stereotypes and fantasies about narrowly prescribed gender roles that may play a role in Black intercultural relationships (McFadden & Moore, 2001). Stereotyped gender roles may initially appear attractive within intercultural couples; however, this is likely to later lead to dissatisfaction (Sullivan & Cottone, 2006). Such an initial attraction may be novel or even "different" (if it is acknowledged at all). Yet, as previously noted, ethnocentric bias can be present even within intimate partnerships. Further, many intercultural couples do little intensive exploration of cultural differences. Thus, cultural understanding may be superficial or uninformed. Dissatisfaction is likely to occur when couples examine their unfulfilled expectations that undoubtedly are rooted in their differing cultural backgrounds. Alex-Assensoh and Assensoh (1998) note that in their research, despite stereotypes of African female submission and widespread paternalism, African/African American marriages demonstrated low spousal conflict over gender roles. They further note that many African men who immigrate to Europe and the U.S. have had sociocultural, educational, and economic opportunities that may lead them to eschew more traditional gender roles in favor of a more egalitarian approach. Yet conversely, the little data available reportedly indicates that African women married to African American men ascribe to more restrictive gender roles and are often described by their African American husbands as "...more supportive and less domineering" than U.S. born Black women (Normant, 1982, as cited in Alex-Assensoh and Assensoh, 1998, p.109).

Relatedly, in an exploration of Nigerian immigrants who entered a courtship and married in the U.S., researchers found they often experienced tension within their African family of origin because the roles of middlepersons, diviners, and dowries were not utilized (Nwadiora, 1996). Culturally, loyalty to one's individual ethnic group is of the utmost importance regardless of one's location and education level, causing the choice to marry outside of their specific ethnic group to be met with resistance from extended family members. Thus, there are myriad social and cultural factors that influence Black intercultural couples.

There is an insufficient amount of specific research on Black intercultural couples' coping strategies, yet Bustamante and colleagues' (2011) research may be helpful. They indicate six primary ways in which intercultural couples (broadly defined in their study) coped with culture-related stressors including:

> a) gender role flexibility, b) humor about differences, c) cultural deference or tendency to defer to the culture-related preferences of a partner, d) recognition of similarities, e) cultural reframing or an ability to redefine relational identity into a unique way of relating that blends and transforms traditional culture-related values into a new set of values particular to an intercultural couple, and f) a general appreciation for other cultures.
>
> (p.159)

These results exemplify how critical personal and cultural flexibility are in coping and developing a new, shared relational culture for the couple. Moreover, it demonstrates that communication, cultural reframing—even through humor—are essential in how couples make meaning of and resolve culture-based conflict.

Communication and Black Intercultural Relationships

Communication is a critical issue for couples and has been identified as a primary reason couples present for counseling (Whisman, Dixon, & Johnson, 1997). Molina et al. (2004) recognize that gender and cultural differences impact communication patterns within relationships. While a detailed analysis of different cultural typologies is outside of the current exploration and tends to be more aligned with a cultural differences' approach to understanding intercultural (read: interracial) relationships, it is prudent to acknowledge 1) that all individuals of African ancestry may not endorse comparable degrees of collectiveness (i.e. a collective identity as Black people) and 2) socialization largely informs mate selection, relational patterns, and communication styles (Gaines & Ramkissoon, 2008). Thus, a brief overview of culture-based communication will be provided. Anthropological research offers that individualistic cultures tend to be more supportive of open disclosure of feelings while those in more collectivistic cultures tend to conceal feelings and express less verbally (Gudykunst, Ting-Toomey, & Nishida, 1996). Others discuss cross-cultural communication based upon high- and low-context cultures (Gudykunst et al., 1996; Hall, 1976) whereby high-context cultures tend to place higher value on interdependency, harmony, and balance and low-context cultures tend to place greater emphasis on independence, self-efficacy, and direct, open communication (ibid). Partners who are more individualistic may have more discreet boundaries around "privacy" and the couple subsystem. Accordingly, they may be more open to seeking assistance from a mental health professional. More collectivist oriented partners or couples may view this as intrusive or as an invasion. It is important to remember that while individuals of African ancestry tend to be more collectivistic, individual differences exist based upon acculturation, assimilation, and country of origin, among others. Research comparing worldviews and value orientations across individuals of African ancestry is lacking (Hunter, 2008). Yet one recent study found that a sample of Caribbean born Blacks endorsed higher rates of individualism than U.S. born Blacks (Hunter, 2008). Thus, generalizations are difficult to make regarding which Black cultural groups may be collectivistic or individualistic. Clinicians should explore specific value orientations with couples as part of routine assessment.

Such cultural typologies have also informed the way in which researchers specifically consider conflict resolution styles. Psychologically intimate conflict modes developed by Rusbult (1987; Healy & Bell, 1990) may be helpful in understanding the intersection of cultural communication and conflict resolution. They describe *exit, voice, loyalty,* and *neglect* conflict resolution styles. *Exit* strategy is active and often hurtful and destructive, relying primarily on the use of threats, intimidation, verbal aggression, and may abruptly exit the relationship or situation. *Voice* is an active yet constructive strategy where verbal communication is utilized to improve situation and resolve conflict. *Loyalty* is described as a passive yet constructive strategy in which a partner utilizes a "wait and see approach" and seeks to accommodate the other partner. *Neglect* is described as a passive and destructive process through the use of avoidance or passive-aggression to minimize or ignore a partner's needs.

It should be noted that 1) this model is innately Western and 2) meanings that partners make are culturally grounded. Therefore, the same strategies may or may not be experienced as destructive or passive across varying cultural systems. Despite its limitations, the model may provide a loose framework for mental health professionals to begin assessing and considering differing relational conflict strategies and, more importantly, to use as a point of departure to discuss specific meaning making with the couple.

Communication and Interpersonal Conflict

How couples make meaning of conflict informs how they respond to and resolve conflict (Johnson, 2008). The relational equity model maintains that a partner may emphasize norms and rules of fairness/justice to resolve personal conflict and tends to privilege outcomes (e.g. one's own happiness and satisfaction) over process (e.g. feelings and relationships) (Ting-Toomey & Oetzel, 2001). A communal-based model is one in which importance is placed on using norms that focus on one's group and relational harmony. Accordingly, it is more process based and other-focused (e.g. being sensitive to the needs of the couple/group) than self-focused and outcome based (ibid). Thus, understanding if someone is operating from a more relational equity model or communal model may provide greater insight into the *why* (a partner's focus and relational priorities), as well as the *how* (communication and conflict resolution processes).

Similarly, relying upon social psychology research, particularly in the area of attribution studies, one can see that how a person attributes or makes meaning of a partner's behaviors is critical, particularly during protracted times of relational conflict. This research demonstrates that, during these times, one may tend to view a partner's behavior as global, stable over time, and attribute it to their overall personhood while viewing our own behavior as situational and not a negative dispositional character trait (Jones & Harris, 1967). This is of particular importance for intercultural couples because a partner may incorrectly attribute culturally based behaviors as behaviors that are intentionally malicious or destructive to the relationship, thereby influencing negative sentiment and relational satisfaction. Consider the following example: Carlos is a Black Dominican male engaged to Monica, an African American from Brooklyn, New York. They describe their relationship as passionate but rather volatile at times. When Carlos becomes angry or jealous, he yells and swears (sometimes in broken Spanish) and frequently storms off. Monica notes that she has responded similarly: when she is upset she yells and often erupts into tears, sometimes in response to what Carlos has said or done. Monica's view is that Carlos is "always" angry and yelling: "He's an angry person, typical jealous, controlling Dominican man." In this example, Monica makes a global attribution about Carlos' behavior while angry to his entire personhood. Further, she generalizes such behavior based upon his cultural identification into known stereotypes about Dominican men.

Systemic Influences on Black Intercultural Couples

Black couples bring their experiences with various systems—oppressive and liberating alike—to their relationships. Hunter (2008) states that "clients of African descent feel that they must be hyper-vigilant to obstacles to success in the environment or the extent to which clients may feel interdependently connected with members of their social groups" (p. 330). As a result, it is vital to fully assess the couple's experiences and interpretations of external, impacting systems. Bronfenbrenner's (1979) ecological theory of human development specifies four types of environmental systems that influence individuals in multi-directional ways. The four systems include: 1) Microsystem: immediate environments (family, school, peer group, neighborhood, and childcare environments); 2) Mesosystem: the connections between immediate environments (i.e. a child's home and school or workplace and religious center); 3) Exosystem: external environmental settings which only indirectly affect development (i.e. a parent's workplace); 4) Macrosystem: the larger cultural context (national economy, political culture, subculture, Eastern versus Western culture) and; 5) Chronosystem: the patterns of environmental events and transitions over the course of a lifetime (i.e. segregation, apartheid, civil rights laws).

Thus, an ecological and culturally based perspective holds that it is important to consider that in addition to the systems in which they are embedded, intercultural couples also develop their own intricate systems (Rosenblatt, 2009). Rosenblatt (2009) emphasized key areas of system dynamics for the intercultural couple:

a) key aspects of the ecosystem which the couple lives; b) interpersonal power in the couple relationship; and c) changes in couple system dynamics as the relationship evolves over time (p. 3). These areas are considered important as each couple is embedded within a "complex array of shoulds, limits, interactions, competing pressures, expectations, and models of how to be a couple" (Rosenblatt, 2009, p. 4). These cultural understandings are often manifested in many ways, including, but not limited to, cultural standards for an appropriate spouse, degree of obligation to provide care and/or financial support for spouse's parents, ideas regarding having children, what it takes to achieve economic well-being, and cultural standards of sexuality and erotic satisfaction (Rosenblatt, 2009).

Further, understanding the intercultural relationship's historical systemic influences is vital, as the fundamental basis of the relationship may have been established centuries before the couple became acquainted (Rosenblatt, 2009). This could potentially pose a point of discourse as "colonization of one partner's country by the other partner's country may have established power relationships between individuals from the cultures involved" (Rosenblatt, 2009, p. 7). Consequently, families of origin may oppose or disapprove of the joining of two cultures and couples may face racism, ethnocentrism, and other forms of bigotry in their respective communities (Rosenblatt, 2009). Lastly, a developmental perspective suggests that many of the couple's cultural differences evolve over time and in accordance with significant life events, for example, childbirth or death of a parent (Rosenblatt, 2009). Despite the potential for cultural friction within the systemic structures, it is vital to consider that "couples do not necessarily experience their differences the way an observer might see them" (Rosenblatt, 2009, p. 16).

Social messages, family influences, and the degree of community agreement impact the effects of miscommunication within relationships (Molina et al., 2004). Healthy communication within any relationship, especially Black intercultural relationships, is critical for long-term relationship satisfaction (Biever, Bobele, & North, 1998; Hines & Boyd-Franklin, 1996; Molina et al., 2004). Such perspectives underscore the necessity of helping professionals to acknowledge the cultural influences within each unique intimate relationship and learn how to effectively navigate potential relationship conflicts in a culturally syntonic manner.

Therapeutic Strategies

A primary purpose of this chapter is to highlight the culture-related stressors for intercultural Black couples. Despite any differences in cultural identities, these are "Black" couples that are likely to face similar issues as same-culture Black couples in addition to those unique challenges intercultural Black couples face outlined in the previous section. Black couples face challenges and continue to persevere, likely because of shared protective cultural factors. The collectivist nature of African culture serves as a relational strength that, when supported in a therapeutic environment, can draw out the innate resiliencies within Black intercultural couples. Specifically, the deep value of kinship, emphasis on family, dependence on community, and spiritual connectedness are characteristics likely to enhance many therapeutic goals in couples' therapy. The authors acknowledge that while advocating for a culture-centered approach, counseling in the U.S. necessarily privileges a Eurocentric model of healing based primarily on talk therapy. This may represent a parallel process to the ever-present quandary of being of African ancestry (and in the numeric minority in many cases) in the U.S. and the balancing of histories and identities. Several models may be appropriate in working with intercultural Black couples, given their sensitivity to cultural and contextual factors. They include: Boyd-Franklin's multisystemic therapy (1989; Kelly & Boyd-Franklin, 2009); Dunham & Ellis' (2010) contributions on culture-centered couples' work, especially with regards to internalized stereotypes; and Gottman's (1999) work on increasing positive sentiment within the couple and emotion focused therapy. These are discussed at length in Chapter 8, so will not be reviewed here. Obviously, an essential part of doing effective counseling with intercultural couples requires an initial thorough assessment (see Chapter 7) enabling the clinician to understand the couples' individual and combined values and worldview, as influenced by their respective cultures.

Finally, Black and non-Black clinicians alike working with intercultural couples must first be comfortable with their own cultural identities and have awareness of how they are perceived in the room, how *who* they are or who they represent may influence the therapeutic encounter, and be comfortable in discussing cultural issues. This culturally competent approach arguably serves as a foundation of therapeutic relationship with Black clients, particularly in explorations of cultural issues.

Clinical Strategies and Cultural Differences

As mentioned previously, cultural differences may present challenges in intercultural relationships. Yet, it is the *perception* of these differences that seems to be paramount (Falicov, 1995). Clinicians must assess the cultural identities of couples and further assess if culture-based stressors are a source of tension or distress for the couple. This may include questions on an intake form, questions during initial consultations, or the inclusion of assessment measures such as the Multiple Heritage Couples Questionnaire (MHCQ) (Bustamante et al., 2011; Henrikson, Watts, & Bustamante, 2007). Briefly, Henriksen and colleagues (2007) note the MHCQ, grounded in existential theory, is a measure developed to aid clinicians and couples in sharing thoughts and emotions as sources of strength and cooperation. As a clinical tool, it allows clinicians to take a constructivist approach in premarital, couples, and marriage counseling, particularly to increase couples' awareness of internal/external influences of culture and race and communicate these. Moreover, therapists can use the measure to explore their own personal views related to multiple heritage couples and how this might influence the counseling process.

Crohn (1998) also advocates for mental health professionals to take a cultural history, which may not only be beneficial for the counselor, but also helpful for partners to hear and experience. He notes that asking questions such as: Have you ever lived in another country? Speak a second language fluently? Identify strongly with a religious faith as a child? Identify strongly now with a religious faith? Identify strongly with a cultural/racial identity? Ever wished for a stronger sense of cultural identity? Such questions may serve as a point of departure around discussions of identities and particularly any areas of shared experiences or sources of distress.

Another aspect of cultural assessment is the area of gender role ideology. As previously discussed, cultural nuances of gender roles are important and may serve as a source of relational distress. Yet, some couples may not have had open dialogue about family histories and any cultural or religious teachings that may influence these beliefs. While there are a wide number of measures available to assess gender roles, few are specifically developed for and/or normed with Black populations. The Bem Sex Role Inventory is widely referenced particularly with regard to desired/preferred gender characteristics, yet it may also be important to assess gender role stress which refers to the amount of stress that results from the perceived failure to meet the traditional gender role standards. One measure utilized to assess gender role stress is the Masculine and Feminine Gender Role Stress scales (MGRS and FGRS).

Research with another measure, the Gender Role Conflict Scale (GRCS), indicated that the GRCS was an adequate measure of gender role conflict; however, the reliability was lower for African American men (Norwalk et al., 2011). Researchers concluded that gender role conflict (GRC) likely impacts African American men in many ways but particularly because they are often influenced by two sets of cultural values and therefore two sets of unique gender norms. As a result, African American men may struggle to identify with the gender role values of dominant European American culture, while still attempting to maintain the unique gender role values of their own culture (Black, 1996). Similarly, Camp (2002) developed the African American Gender Stereotyping Scale to assess the extent to which individuals endorse same sex and opposite sex stereotypes. Respondents are asked to rate the extent to which they agree or disagree with statements such as:

(a) A White woman will better cater to a man's needs when compared to a Black woman. (b) Many Black women just look for financial stability in a man rather than getting to know him for who he is. (c) Generally speaking, Black women have too much power and control in their families. (d) Many Black men are emotionally unavailable.

(Camp, 2002, p. 70)

The measure has had high internal reliability within a primarily middle class African American sample. Clearly, gender roles are essential in romantic partnerships and can serve as a source of distress, particularly if there is lack of clarity or conflict in these areas.

The distress possibly caused by an unbalanced view of cultural differences, including those around gender, is an important point of intervention. The culturally attuned therapist must be able to listen to and challenge any minimization or denial of cultural differences (Falicov, 1995). Similarly, any exaggeration or scapegoating (cultural camouflage) of cultural issues must also be brought into the room and challenged. The therapist may also need to serve as a "cultural referee," in which part of their role is to help differentiate cultural issues from personal and relational concerns (Hsu, 2001, p. 238). In so doing, the therapist may help facilitate dialogue and engender a mutual understanding of gender and familial roles.

One way that couples may cope with cultural issues is through cultural deference in which one partner defers to the cultural preferences or patterns of the other (Bustamante et al., 2011). While the limited research with couples utilizing this practice has demonstrated that some couples find this practice helpful, therapists are encouraged to facilitate open and honest dialogue about such practices. Specifically, this should be assessed to ensure that one partner does not feel the need or pressure to assimilate or give up parts of one's identity, particularly not within their most sacred and intimate relationship. This may be of even greater importance for Black couples within the U.S. who face racial discrimination and the pressures of cultural hegemony that promotes assimilation. Couples should be encouraged to actively discuss and co-construct the culture of their relationship and family.

As mentioned previously, the role of culture in human development is such that individuals of all cultures tend to presume that their cultural values are representative of truth and/or the way things ought to be (Waldman & Rubalcava, 2005). This presumption, understandably, may cause dissention within Black intercultural couples. Psychodynamic theories such as intersubjectivity and self-psychology illuminate the role that culture places in unconscious psychological organization. Unconscious cultural influences impact the manner in which couples experience each other. Ultimately, one primary role of the therapist in working with intercultural Black couples is to help foster the development of this *relational culture* or *third culture building* (Waldman & Rubalcava, 2005). This refers to the process of the couple bringing unconscious cultural–relational patterns to the couple's awareness to create a relational milieu that encompasses their own couple-defined values and mores (Bustamante et al., 2011; Casmir, 1993; Wood, 2000). A comprehensive understanding of the interaction between culture and self-experience is vital in order to effectively work with intercultural Black couples.

Cross-Cultural Communication Skills Building

Many couples' therapy approaches focus on therapeutic strategies to increase communication. Cognitive behavioral couples' therapy is perhaps best known for its skills-based interventions, which generally involve the therapist instructing the couple in specific skills, such as in increasing communication. The use of Socratic questioning to redress faulty or distorted cognitions is often utilized, as is "guided discovery" which refers to therapist created encounters in which one or both partners are able to challenge and evolve their perspective on the relationship. This may be particularly beneficial in cases in which miscommunication has occurred, perhaps due to cultural reasons.

For purposes of the present exploration, it may also be helpful to consider strategies specific to inter- and cross-cultural communication, particularly it may be helpful to integrate notions of culture-based communication in the way in which we facilitate dialogue between clients. As mentioned previously, culture is a primary determinant of acceptable modes of communication, particularly in the resolution of intimate partner conflict, which is often a primary concern for presenting clients. If cultural identities are assessed as outlined above, this information may be helpful in guiding the therapist's understanding of communication styles and expectations of each partner. Moreover, in the previously presented multisystemic therapy model articulated by Boyd-Franklin, she advocates for the use of enactments in session where clients discuss an issue with one another. This may be an opportunity to observe 1) the structure of the relationship (including gender-based roles); 2) how clients engage one another and communicate, including about cultural issues; and 3) facilitate any conflict resolution around any culture-related sources of distress.

Specific strategies that may be helpful in fostering communication in Black intercultural couples may include:

- Teaching active listening skills. This is often a good point of departure since individuals across cultures want to feel heard and understood by their partner. Specifically, it may be helpful to teach individuals how to sit with a partner's difficult emotion and listen openly, demonstrating that they are listening with their nonverbal mannerisms, minimizing defensiveness, and overly personalizing what the partner may be communicating.
- Teaching and practicing the use of summary and reflective statements. This may foster an environment in which partners both feel heard and that their perspective is valued and understood. (For example, a partner might state: "I heard you say....") Teaching partners how to restate and summarize *before* responding to their partner may foster communication. This sentiment is important in cross-cultural communication in which culture-based values and communications strategies may not always feel honored.
- Teaching partners how to utilize "I statements." This may be helpful for couples who are more open and assertive in the communication to own their own experience and feelings while helping to minimize accusations and defensiveness in one's partner. For instance, "I feel rejected when you

140

express disinterest in sexual intimacy with me" instead of more accusatory language such as "you reject me every night" or "you make me feel rejected."

- Encouraging couples to learn their partner's "love language." Dunham and Ellis (2010) discuss the use of Gary Chapman's discussion of love languages with Black couples and emphasize the value of learning how to communicate in ways in which the partner can best receive it. For example, some individuals need to hear clear verbal expressions of love while others place more emphasis on service or acts.

Conclusion

Sustaining healthy and successful Black relationships is a challenge within an oppressive social context in which one is constantly assaulted by negative portrayals of one's cultural group. Yet, it appears that cultural strengths and community may serve as protective factors for these couples. Alex-Assensoh and Assensoh (1998) note that collective internalized racism including commonly held stereotypical beliefs and endorsement of media portrayals of African and African Americans may negatively impact relations between these groups (and ostensibly other Black immigrants). Even if a couple does not endorse such stereotypes, family members or friends may do so and therefore couples may have to learn how to effectively deal with such issues with one another and respective family members. To this end, issues of race, racism, and acculturation remain ever present for these couples (McFadden & Moore, 2001).

It is clear that clinical work with intercultural couples of African ancestry requires cultural competence, personal and theoretical flexibility, and should be strengths-based and systemic in nature. Theoretical and clinical flexibility may include increased openness to integrating or working with traditional health practitioners, clergy, and spirit- or movement-based therapies. Yet, there is little by way of data regarding the effectiveness of these interventions. In working particularly with Black immigrant clients, additional care should be taken to discuss preferred methods of healing based on cultural traditions. Moreover, systemic considerations around issues of residency, citizenship, visa status, and related issues for the couple or their family members may be areas of concern. Others, particularly second and third generation immigrant families, may not have the same concerns, but there may be issues of loss around cultural identity and language to name but two. Further research should also be inclusive of such experiences.

Case Study

Damien, a 35-year-old African American male from Mississippi and his wife, Asya, a Kenyan-born, 33-year-old woman, presented to counseling reporting communication problems and increased marital conflict. They have been married for four years, have a three-year-old son, and Asya is two months pregnant. They met in college. Asya reports immigrating to the U.S. for college. She comes from a close-knit, middle class family, although her father had a secret family in a nearby town. Her parents remain married. Asya misses her family and continues to struggle with adaption to life in the U.S. due to the cultural differences. Damien was raised in a single-mother household with his two siblings. He reports an "OK" relationship with his father. He admits to "partying" in college until he developed a racial and political consciousness about "being a Black man in America." The couple met at a Black Student Union event and began dating seriously. When Asya had issues concerning her student visa, they decided to marry so that she could legally remain in the U.S.

Asya and Damien both noted that they would joke about cultural differences but didn't see them as a "real issue" for them, particularly early on in their relationship. Asya admitted that she had many stereotypes about Black American men (that they are playas and thugs). Damien admitted that he knew very little about Kenyan cultures in particular and that he glamorized being with a "real African," likely because of his politics and heightened consciousness as a Black man. They talked little about cultural values and differences. He accepted her long trips home and understood because she was studying abroad and homesick. He reportedly thought nothing of her family's strict Christianity and his own emerging agnosticism and figured they would create their own way, although "everything changed" when they got married.

After getting married, much of Asya's family remained with them for two to three months. Damien noted that he had not expected this but Asya argued that she told him they were coming for a visit to which her husband remarked that, "two to three months is NOT a visit!" Asya quit her job to spend more time with her visiting family and began sending money to her family overseas, causing a financial strain between the couple. This was heightened when Asya became pregnant and wanted to stay at home with their son. In the midst of this, Damien was laid off from his sales job and became depressed and angry, often directing his negative feelings towards Asya. She was ashamed to admit to her family that they could no longer afford to send money home, as they were seen as "privileged." Although Damien did find another job six months later, there was already significant damage to their relationship.

Conceptualization and Interventions

An integrative approach, informed by Boyd-Frankin's multisystemic, emotion focused and narrative therapy models, was used with this couple. Because they were rather hesitant in the beginning, we spent considerable time getting to know one another prior to getting into more information about their primary presenting issue. Boyd-Franklin (1989) recommends prioritizing the *joining* process with Black clients and views this as an ongoing process. For this couple, I utilized therapeutic self-disclosure to help facilitate joining. Specifically, I talked about my professional work, my travel throughout Africa and the African Diaspora, and my training and background in family systems and work with Black couples and families. This disclosure seemed to allow them to get to know me better and served as a baseline of understanding. In short, they reportedly felt like I "got them." In addition, I used a conversational method to begin the initial "intake and assessment" and asked simply that they tell me a little about themselves and their "story." My goal in joining was to form an authentic relationship with them as people and for them to begin trusting in the relationship being built.

The couple stated they felt rather discouraged and experienced relational increased tension, yet it was very clear that they were committed to one another. We were able to quickly identify the strengths of their union: they were very loving and supportive of one another (particularly during non-conflict times), both were individually good parents and appeared to parent well together, and had good relationships with extended family. They felt that their primary concern at the time was around being more open in communication, especially about family. There were unspoken expectations and resentment about the extent to which they would help "extended" family members, particularly given their recent financial problems. These issues were generally brought to the forefront only during arguments.

We utilized the two following sessions to work on the identified issue. Through the use of enactments, I helped facilitate conversation about expectations and feelings around Asya's family in particular. I was able to observe the pattern of communication, in which Damien was far more open and direct and Asya was less comfortable articulating her feelings verbally. While both endorsed values consistent with what are labeled high-context cultures, Damien's style of open and direct communication is more consistent with low-context, individualistic cultures. When I identified this pattern, Asya admitted that in general she felt comfortable verbalizing her feelings that she had begun to feel "vulnerable" and "needy" since she was no longer contributing to the household income. She stated that because she was still not a citizen, there was a part of her that feared that Damien would leave her and that she might even lose custody of DJ. This reportedly caused her to avoid conflict and not be as open with her husband. Damien was reportedly shocked (and angered) to hear that she felt this way. He felt that it meant she didn't understand his love for and commitment to her and the family. They were able to have a very emotional conversation about the roots of these feelings, including her own experience with her father. Damien was able to acknowledge that it likely didn't help that he would make hurtful statements about her not working during arguments. This also allowed Damien to be more vulnerable, to *soften*, as articulated by emotion-focused therapy (EFT) and admit that he felt a lot of pressure as husband and provider and felt that he had few exemplars on "how to do this well." He stated that he was committed to not repeating the mistakes of his own father (I also questioned if he was cognizant of the patterns of Asya's father as well), thus trying to break a generational cycle of male absence and/or poor parenting.

I was able to highlight Damien's fear of failing her (likely as her father did). Aysa was able to receive this and first responded that "she didn't know why he would feel that way..." but was soon able to own her own contributions and understand that it was hard for both of them. As she *softened*, she was able to say that she was scared too. She questioned her ability to care for a newborn and a three-year-old son, especially without the help of her mother and aunts.

Part of the dialogue shifted to problem-solving, how they could better utilize the supports and resources they had in place.

Although our work was cut short by a family emergency for Aysa, there are few aspects of this clinical work that are noteworthy. First, I was effective in assessing cultural identity in a way that was at once conversational and informative. Second, my use of disclosure from the beginning, particularly around my own cultural identities and experiences with African people, allowed the couple to feel safe discussing cultural issues from the very beginning, not just as an adjunct to the presenting issues. This set the stage for understanding culture as part of who we all are, including for the therapist. Facilitating open communication with this couple was essential in that there were many unspoken thoughts and feelings that needed to be brought to the forefront. In the process of these discussions, they were both able to be vulnerable and more open, which allowed both of them to *soften*. This appeared to have a dynamic effect: both partners being more open and vulnerable allowed them to soften, which, in turn, fostered greater vulnerability and deeper sharing, particularly about family of origin issues. If I were able to continue working with this couple, I would focus on the power imbalance in the relationship and how these issues would conspicuously manifest during arguments. Specifically, the power imbalance around gender roles (Damien: husband-father-provider; Asya: wife-mother-financial dependent). In addition, there was a clear power differential around legal status or citizenship that would emerge. While Damien would note her lack of citizenship, Asya would threaten to leave the country with their son. Both partners appeared to be exerting power in harmful ways. This was perhaps indicative of an underlying power struggle in the relationship or a reflection of lack of power in society.

References

Alex-Assensoh, Y., & Assensoh (1998). The politics of African and African-American marriages. In R. Berger & R. Hill (Eds). *Cross-Cultural Marriages: Identity and Choice* (pp. 101–112). Oxford: Berg Publishers.

Barrow, C. (1996). *Family in the Caribbean: Themes and Perspectives*. Kingston, Jamaica: Ian Randle Publishers.

Biever, J., Bobele, M., & North, M. (1998). Therapy with intercultural couples: A postmodern approach. In S. Palmer (Ed.). *Multicultural Counseling* (pp. 73–81). London: Sage.

Black, L. (1996). Families of African origin: An overview. In M. McGoldrick, J. Giordano, & J. Pearce (Eds.). *Ethnicity and Family Therapy* (pp. 57–65). New York: Guilford Press.

Boyd-Franklin, N. (1989). *Black Families in Therapy: Understanding the African American Experience*. 2nd edition. New York: Guilford Press.

Brice-Baker, J. (1996). Jamaican families. In M. McGoldrick, J. Giordano, & J. Pearce (Eds.). *Ethnicity and Family Therapy* (pp. 85–96). New York: Guilford Press.

Bronfenbrenner, U. (1979). *The Ecology of Human Development: Experiments by Nature and Design*. Cambridge, MA: Harvard University Press.

Bustamante, R., Nelson, J., Henriksen, R., & Monakes, S. (2011). Intercultural couples: Coping with culture-related stressors. *The Family Journal: Counseling and Therapy for Couples and Families*, 19(2), 154–164.

Bystydzienski, J. M. (2011). *Intercultural Couples: Crossing Boundaries, Negotiating Difference*. New York: New York University Press.

Camp, C. M. (2002). African American male-female alienation: An evaluation of psychosocial and socio-cultural factors that influence attitudes and beliefs about romantic involvement and relationship outcomes among African American singles. Dissertation Abstracts International, 63(02). (UMI No. 3043462).

Casmir, F. (1993). Third-culture building: A paradigm shift for international and intercultural communication. In S. Deetz (Ed.). *Communication Yearbook 16* (pp. 407–428). Newbury Park, CA: Sage.

Christopher A. (2003). Skin bleaching, self-hate, and Black identity in Jamaica. *Journal of Black Studies*, 33(6), 711–718.

Crohn, J. (1998). Intercultural couples. In M. McGoldrick (Ed.). *Revisioning Family Therapy: Race Culture and Gender in Clinical Practice* (pp. 295–308). New York: Guilford Press.

Diop, C. A. (1974). *The African Origin of Civilization: Myth or Reality?* Edited and translated by Mercer Cook. Westport, CT: Lawrence Hill & Company; Paris: Presance Africaine.

Dixon, V. (1976). Worldviews and research methodology. In L. M. King, V. Dixon, & W. W. Nobles (Eds.). *African Philosophy: Paradigms for Research on Black Persons*. Los Angeles, CA: Fanon Center.

Dodoo, F. N. (1997). Assimilation differences among Africans in America. *Social Forces*, 76(2), 527–546.

Dunham, S., & Ellis, C. M. (2010). Restoring intimacies with African American couples. In J. Carlson & L. Sperry (Eds.). *Restoring Intimacy in Love Relationships: A Clinician's Guide*. (pp. 295–316). New York: Routledge.

Ennis, S. R., Rios-Vargas, M., & Albert, N. G. (2011). The Hispanic Population: 2010. U. S. Census Bureau. C2010BR-04.

Falicov, C. (1995). Cross-cultural marriages. In N.S. Jacobson & A.S. Gurman (Eds.). *Clinical Handbook of Couple Therapy* (pp. 231–246). New York: Guilford Press.

Fanon, F (1967). *Black Skin, White Masks*. New York: Grove Press.

Gaines, Jr., S. O., & Ramkissoon, M. W. (2008). US/Caribbean relationships. In T. Karis, & K. D. Killian (Eds.). *Cross-cultural Couples: Transborder Relationships in the 21st Century* (pp. 227–250). Binghamton, NY: Taylor and Francis.

Gottman, J. M. (1999). *The Marriage Clinic*. New York: Norton.

Gudykunst, W., Ting-Toomey, S., & Nishida, T. (1996). *Communication in Personal Relationships across Cultures*. Thousand Oaks, CA: Sage.

Hall, E. (1976). *Beyond Culture*. New York: Anchor Books.

Healy, J. G., & Bell, R. A. (1990). Assessing alternative responses to conflicts in friendship. In D. D. Cahn (Ed.). *Intimates in Conflict: A Communication Perspective* (pp. 25–48). Hillside, NJ: Lawrence Erlbaum.

Henriksen, Jr., R. C., Watts, R. E., & Bustamante, R. (2007). The multiple heritage couple questionnaire. *The Family Journal*, 15, 405–408.

Hines, P., & Boyd-Franklin, N. (1996). African American families. In M. McGoldrick, J. Giordano, & J. Pearce (Eds.). *Ethnicity and Family Therapy* (pp. 66–84). New York: Guilford Publishers.

Hsu, J. (2001). Marital therapy for intercultural couples. In W. Tseng, & J. Streltzer (Eds.). *Culture and Psychotherapy* (pp. 225–242). Washington, DC: American Psychiatric.

Hunter, C. (2008). Individualistic and collective worldviews: Implications for understanding perceptions of racial discrimination in African Americans and British Caribbean Americans. *Journal of Counseling Psychology*, 55(3), 321–332.

International Organization for Migration (2010). World Migration Report 2010, The future of migration: Building capacities for change. Switzerland: International Organization for Migration.

Johnson, S. M. (2008). Emotionally focused couple therapy. In A. S. Gurman (Ed.). *Clinical Handbook of Couple Therapy, 4th Edition* (pp. 107–137). New York: Guilford Publishers.

Jones, E. E., & Harris, V. A. (1967). The attribution of attitudes. *Journal of Experimental Social Psychology*, 3(1), 1–24.

Kambon, K. K. K. (1998). *African/Black Psychology in the American Context: An African-Centered Approach*. Tallahassee, FL: Nubian Nation Publications.

Kelly, S., & Boyd-Franklin, N. (2009). Joining, understanding, and supporting Black couples in treatment. In M. Rastogi, & V. Thomas (Eds.). *Multicultural Couple Therapy* (pp. 235–254). Thousand Oaks, CA: Sage.

Kent, M. M. (2007). Immigration and America's Black population. *Population Bulletin*, 62(4), 1–16.

McFadden, J., & Moore, J. L. (2001). Intercultural marriage and intimacy: Beyond the continental divide. *International Journal for the Advancement of Counseling*, 23, 261–268.

Molina, B., Estrada, D., & Burnett, J. (2004). Cultural communities: Challenges and opportunities in the creation of "happily ever after" stories of intercultural couplehood. *The Family Journal: Counseling and Therapy for Couples and Families*, 12, 139–147.

Norwalk, K. E., Vandiver, B. J., White, A. M., Englar-Carlson, M. (2011). Factor structure of the gender role conflict scale in African American and European American men. *Psychology of Men and Masculinity*, 12, 128–143.

Nwadiora, E. (1996). Nigerian families. In M. McGoldrick, J. Giordano, & J. Pearce (Eds.). *Ethnicity and Family Therapy* (pp. 129–138). New York: Guilford Publishers.

Passel, J. S., Wang, W., & Taylor, P. (2010). Marrying out: One-in-seven new U.S. marriages is interracial or interethnic. Pew Research Center, A social and demographic trends report. ii-37. Retrieved from http://pewsocialtrends.org/files/20 10/10/755-marrying-out.pdf.

Rastogi, S., Johnson, T., Hoeffel, E., & Drewery, M. (2011). Majority of the Black population lived in the south. Random samplings: The Official Blog of the U.S. Census Bureau. Retrieved on December 14, 2011 from http://blogs.census.gov/censusblog/2011/11/majority-of-the-black-population-lived-in-the-south.html.

Reiter, M. (2008). Open communication and partner support in intercultural and interfaith romantic relationships: A relational maintenance approach. *Journal of Social and Personal Relationships*, 25(4), 539–559.

Roopnarine, J., Krishnakumar, A., & Xu, Y. (2009). Beliefs about mothers' and fathers' roles and the division of child care and household labor in Indo-Caribbean immigrants with young children. *Cultural Diversity and Ethnic Minority Psychology*, 15(2), 173–182.

Rosenblatt, P. C. (2009). A systems theory analysis of intercultural couple relationships. In T. A. Karis, & K. D. Killian (Eds.). *Intercultural Couples: Exploring Diversity in Intimate Relationships* (pp. 3–20). New York: Routledge.

Rusbult, C. E. (1987). Responses to dissatisfaction in close relationships: The exit-voice-loyalty-neglect model. In D. Perlman, & S. Duck (Eds.). *Intimate Relationships: Development, Dynamics, and Deterioration* (pp. 209–237). Newbury Park, CA: Sage.

Shaw-Taylor, Y., & Tuch, S. A. (2007). *The Other African Americans: Contemporary African and Caribbean Immigrants in the United States*. Maryland: Rowman & Littlefield Publishers, Inc.

Sullivan, C., & Cottone, R. (2006). Culturally based couple therapy and intercultural relationships: A review of the literature. *The Family Journal: Counseling and Therapy for Couples and Families*, 14(3), 221–225.

Ting-Toomey, S., & Oetzel, J. (2001). *Managing Intercultural Conflict Effectively* (2nd ed.). Thousand Oaks, CA: Sage Publications.

Waldman, K., & Rubalcava, L. (2005). Psychotherapy with intercultural couples: A contemporary psychodynamic approach. *American Journal of Psychotherapy*, 59(3), 227–245.

Waters, M. (2000). *Black Identities: West Indian Immigrant Dreams and American Realities*. Cambridge, MA: Harvard University Press.

Whisman, M., Dixon, A., & Johnson, B. (1997). Therapists' perspectives of couple problems and treatment issues in couple therapy. *Journal of Family Psychology*, 11(3), 361–366.

Wilson, E. S. (2009). What it means to become a United States American: Afro-Caribbean immigrants' constructions of American citizenship and experience of cultural transition. *Journal of Ethnographic & Qualitative Research*, 3, 196–204.

Wood, J. T. (2000). *Relational Communication* (2nd ed.). Belmont, CA: Wadsworth.

Yi, K. (1999). Ethnic identity: From stage theory to a constructivist narrative model. *Psychotherapy*, 36, 16–26.

6

AFRICAN AMERICAN LESBIANS AND GAY MEN IN COUPLES' RELATIONSHIPS

Threats to Intimacy and Considerations in Couples' Psychotherapy

Beverly Greene, Nancy Boyd-Franklin, and Philip B. Spivey

This chapter addresses issues that may arise in couples' therapies with African American lesbians and gay men. We also comment on the historical antecedents of attitudes toward the sexuality of African Americans as a diverse and heterogeneous group, members of sexual minority groups and the contemporary psychosocial contexts of African American lesbians' and gay men's lives and relationships. The aforementioned factors are important determinants of the behaviors that we observe and the issues that arise in therapies with these couples. A familiarity with them is essential for therapists who conduct psychotherapy with this population as they have a strong role in shaping behaviors and expectations. Challenges to better understanding this topic include a dearth of research and published clinical and empirical psychological research, family and couples' therapy literature on African American lesbians and gay men and their relationships. Most of the literature on lesbian and gay couples has focused overwhelmingly on white, middle class, urban respondents just as the focus on African American couples focuses almost exclusively on heterosexual couples (Garnets & Kimmel, 1991; Greene, 1994a, 1994b, 2000; Greene & Boyd Franklin, 1996; Hall & Greene, 2002; Peplau, Cochran, & Mays, 1997). It would be fair to say that the African American couples' literature marginalizes African American lesbian and gay couples in the same ways that African American couples were once marginalized in the couples and family therapy literature. That marginalization contributes to the often stark invisibility of African American lesbian and gay couples or even lesbian or gay children in African American families. The invisibility of this group in their families, communities, society and in the professional literature intensifies the effects of homophobia and racism making treatment more challenging.

Historically we have been unable to "count" the numbers of African American lesbian and gay couples. Changes in the law over the past eight years that permit civil unions and same sex marriage, now in eight states, provide us with an opportunity to obtain more information about these couples, who they are, as well as more accurate information about the duration of their relationships.

We critique the lack of inclusion of these couples in research as well as the limited generalizability of findings on both heterosexual and gay/lesbian couples that is a function of their absence. However, we recognize that there are challenges to conducting research with this population as well as research that includes them and represents the diversity within the group. People who live in rural areas, who have little to no discretionary income, who are not working or attending institutions of higher education, people with disabilities, people of color and those who are very closeted are among the groups who tend to be underrepresented in most of the research on sexual minorities. Bowleg et al. (2008) also documents the methodological challenges of this research and observes that we do not have the adequate analytic and interpretive tools that are necessary to make the intersections between ethnicity, gender, sexual orientation and the social inequities associated with them explicitly available for analysis. Such narrow clinical and research perspectives leave us with a poor appreciation of the realistic social and psychological tasks and stressors that are a component of lesbian and gay identity formation for African American men and women. They also ignore an exploration of how the vicissitudes of racism, sexism and homophobia in interaction with one another effect couple relationships in African American lesbians and gay men. Practitioners, then, are left with a limited understanding of the diversity within African American men and women and within lesbians and gay men as groups threatening practitioners' ability to address the clinical needs of African American lesbians and gay men in culturally sensitive and competent ways (Greene, 1994a, 1994b).

A more detailed exploration of those challenges is beyond the scope of this chapter; however, the reader is urged to consider those we have mentioned when evaluating the generalizability of the research that is currently available. Other challenges to the provision of optimal psychological services to this group include beliefs in persistent stereotypes about African Americans, lesbians and gay men that are not limited to the general public but are also held by mental health professionals and researchers. We offer our observations based on that which we glean from the professional literature and our collective professional experience of over 25 years each doing psychotherapy with African American lesbians and gay men in individual and couples' therapies.

African American Lesbians and Gay Men: Identities at the Intersections and the Margins

African American lesbians and gay men represent a part of the spectrum of diversity among African Americans, men and women and lesbians and gay men. They may also be found in every other social group across the developmental spectrum, which includes persons with disabilities, diverse socioeconomic class and other groups. As African Americans, women (for lesbians) and sexual minorities they face double and triple marginalization in American society. The interaction between race, gender and sexual orientation is complex in ways that single identity paradigms are unable to capture. African American lesbians' and gay males' cultural positioning is in the nexus of those identities and the structural inequities associated with those identities can leave them predisposed to psychological vulnerability as well as psychological resilience depending on other factors in their lives.

The history of African Americans in the United States has played an important role in shaping perceptions of gender roles and perceptions of what are acceptable forms of sexual expression and sexuality. Ferguson (2010), McGruder (2010), Moore (2011) and West (1999) argue that the diverse family structures and expressions of sexuality among African Americans were initially viewed as deviant when compared to Western practices that were deemed normative. This was true even when some of those differences were a function of adapting to limited social opportunities that were a direct function of racism. The treatment of African Americans as slaves and the irrational prohibitions against interracial sexual relations were based on distorted depictions of their sexuality, i.e. that they were morally loose, promiscuous and animal like in their sexuality. Those distortions were required to rationalize the inhumane treatment that they were accorded as slaves that included forced sexual relationships with other slaves and with slave masters. Similarly, prohibitions against same sex desire are based on distorted depictions of lesbians and gay men. Just as the diverse family structures of African Americans challenges the normative position of patriarchal family structures, same sex relationships challenge the rules that frame sex and gender that make them a similar threat to patriarchal domination. Because the very identities of sexual minority group members threatens the validity of patriarchal domination, the identities of group members were discredited, deemed pathological and immoral. Distortions of African Americans were designed to rationalize their sexual exploitation and to shift responsibility for the sexual violence directed toward them onto the victims rather than the perpetrators. West (1996) observes that distortions of Black sexuality and racialized sexual perceptions have always influenced perceptions of race in ways that bring race, sex and class oppressions together. Hence how these social identities interact with one another is something practitioners must always keep in mind.

These historical precursors left African Americans in the position of having to defend themselves against these distortions, usually expressed in degrading sexual stereotypes, by policing their public sexuality and conduct so that it conforms to the dominant cultural moral order. We view this as a function of internalized racism. Moore (2011) observes that this public conduct is also "classed" and suggests that more middle and upper middle class African Americans may be even more eager to fit within the social order and therefore more vulnerable to internalizing the dominant cultural values, values that inherently devalue African Americans. For Moore (2011) an examination of the intersections of race, sexuality and socioeconomic status is necessary to understand the experiences of Black lesbians because these factors shape the social construction and subjective experience of identities behavior and relationships (Moore, 2011, p.4). We believe that this is the case for Black gay men as well. The Black middle class sought to distance itself from negative racial stereotypes, particularly sexual stereotypes, but also from racialized working class stereotypes. They did so by developing a posture of "respectability" in sexual matters and public behavior. In Moore's analysis, Black lesbians who live openly claim a level of sexual and identity autonomy that places them outside of the normative order of "respectability" for women in the world of the Black middle class struggling to gain acceptance in the mainstream of United States society.

Challenges to Intimacy in African American Lesbian and Gay Male Couples

All couples face challenges to healthy intimacy in their relationships. Some threats can be a function of the psychological and family history of each person and the way those dynamics interact with one another. However, for African American lesbians and gay men there are particular challenges based on the legacy of racism, internalized racism, heterosexism and internalized homophobia that forms the historical and contemporary context in which their relationships take place.

In the context of racist ideology, nonconformists among African Americans are often used to reinforce stereotypic beliefs of questionable validity about African Americans in general. Therefore the group's nonconformists are easily scapegoated because of their potential use as an embarrassment and as justification for the ill treatment of African Americans. Cohen and Jones (1999) observe that an environment is created where African Americans "police" one another to assure that the dominant cultural codes are observed. Because heterosexism institutionalizes patriarchal family structures and rewards heterosexual relationships, it punishes and even demonizes same sex relationships as well as alternative family structures, establishing them as being outside of the "respectable" and acceptable moral order of the community. We emphasize that there may be a distinction between the way that public and private behaviors are viewed. We have observed that there has existed an unspoken, silent "tolerance" of lesbian and gay members of African American communities; however, that tolerance is often predicated on silence. Silence usually implies an avoidance of any open discussion about the sexual minority status of a member of the family or community, and on the lesbian or gay member's understanding that it is not to be discussed. When such discussions are broached, when a family member "comes out" overtly and discloses that they are lesbian or gay, has a partner who is introduced to family or community as a romantic or domestic partner, marries or seeks public validation, the previously understood tolerance or acceptance may quickly turn ugly. The culture of silence that exists even within the group that forms the clients' most loved and trusted figures has clear effects on their relationships with partners. When couples are obliged to protect their relationships from hostility, from a community and/or family members, they are challenged in ways that heterosexual couples are not. Cerbone (2011) observes that maintaining a cloak of silence and verdigris of disconnection around their relationships in public spaces does not simply end in private, but lingers in the form of internalized homophobia and problems establishing the trust that is a precursor of intimacy within the relationship, even when those relationships seem to occur in plain sight. Furthermore, those who have internalized negative stereotypes and distortions about themselves may be less likely to trust other African Americans. If this occurs it undoubtedly arises as an issue in the couple relationship.

Spivey suggests that both internalized homophobia and internalized racism may be responsible for a phenomenon that he observes in Black gay male couples that he treats. In this case the couples' history may reveal a familiar pattern. In the early stages of the relationship there is what appears to be a healthy pattern of sexual desire and intimacy. However, as the relationship deepens and emotional intimacy intensifies, the relationship begins to flounder. One partner may begin to express the desire to have other partners or has an affair that threatens and often does undermine or end the relationship. In our struggles to determine what this might mean beyond the obvious issues that members of this group often bring to couples' as well as individual psychotherapy, we thought about the context for these relationships. Prohibitions against same sex relationships as well as interracial relationships targeted legitimized relationships where there is an assumption of a foundation of love and respect. Sexual violence has always taken place across racial lines and within groups of men and women. When perpetrators of this violence are members of the privileged mainstream, it is often treated as their prerogative. Slave masters were never punished for their rape of slave women. We assume that rape of slave men must have also occurred because sexual violence targets both men and women. Gay men are also visible targets of sexual violence from other presumably heterosexual men. While sexual violence is "tolerated", the love that creates healthy bonds of sexual intimacy are not permitted. Spivey offers that in the men he treats, they behave as if they catch themselves doing or having something they are not supposed to have—love. While they wish for such relationships he suggests that many do not really feel deserving of them, nor do they trust one another.

In addition to these factors, same sex relationships as a whole do not receive the same supports from society, family and friends as their heterosexual counterparts. Their relationships may be more likely to be greeted with dismay and conflict than celebration. Hence their survival is seriously challenged and undermined by many societal forces.

Contemporary Psychosocial Contexts: Precursors of Resilience and Vulnerability

The underpinnings of traditional approaches to psychology are replete with androcentric, heterocentric and ethnocentric biases (Garnets & Kimmel, 1991; Glassgold, 1992; Greene, 1994a, 2000), thus reinforcing the double and triple discrimination both lesbians and gay men of color face. Heterocentric thinking often results in misconceptions about lesbians and gay men, as common in ethnic minority groups as the dominant culture, among which are that each wants to be a member of the other sex and expresses their gender identity in that way. Lesbians are presumed to be unattractive or less attractive than heterosexual women (Dew, 1985), are less extroverted (Kite, 1994), are unable to get a man, have had traumatic relationships with men which presumably "turned" them against men, or are defective females (Christian, 1985; Collins, 1990; Greene, 1994a, 1994b; Kite, 1994). Acceptance, in African American communities, of the assumption that sexual attraction to men is intrinsic to being a normal woman, and attraction to women is intrinsic to being a normal man, often leads to a range of equally inaccurate assumptions about their relationships that include the presumption that reproductive sexuality is the only form of sexual expression that is psychologically normal and morally correct (Garnets & Kimmel, 1991; Glassgold, 1992), and that there is a direct relationship between sexual orientation and conformity to traditional gender roles and physical appearance within the culture (Kite & Deaux, 1987; Newman, 1989; Whitley, 1987), i.e. women and men who do not conform to traditional gender role stereotypes must be lesbian or gay, men and women who do conform must be heterosexual. These assumptions are used to threaten men and women with the stigma of being labeled lesbian or gay if they do not adhere to traditional gender role stereotypes in which males are dominant, hypermasculine and females are submissive (Collins, 1990; Gomez & Smith, 1990; Smith, 1982). This often occurs in African American communities despite the history and tradition of gender role flexibility within African American families.

Family of Origin: Another Locus of Vulnerability and Resilience

The African American family has functioned as a refuge to protect group members from the racism of the dominant culture. African American families' responses to gay and lesbian members are diverse and may range from outright rejection to a healthy acceptance of that person and integration into the family system. Family responses may also evolve from more rejecting initially to becoming gradually more accepting. There is also a range of acceptance within families as some may be more or less accepting than others, which can evolve over time as well. Generally there is a wide range of adaptations between those extremes that are as diverse as African American families themselves. For some families, the cultural and familial strength of family ties may mitigate against outright rejection of a gay or lesbian member even when the family disapproves of the person's sexual orientation. Tolerance, however, should not be equated with tacit approval. This can be a function of varying levels of tolerance for nonconformity, denial, or may represent distinct ways of conveying negative attitudes about a family member's behavior that are particular to that family (Greene, 1994a, 1994b, 2000).

As previously mentioned, tolerance within African American families is often contingent on silence. Serious conflicts *may* occur once a family member openly discloses, or labels him/herself lesbian or gay. For example, a lesbian or gay family member's lover may have been treated well and welcome until the relationship is labeled lesbian/gay and the family member seeks family support, or their open acknowledgment of the relationship being more than just "special friends", "sisters", or "brothers". In contemporary environments where some African American lesbians/gay men wish to marry, the public nature of marriage may make a previously acceptable relationship a source of discomfort for that family or for some family members. Even when family members are accepting and supportive, the broader African American or Caribbean community may not be.

Homophobia among African Americans and Afro-Caribbeans is a function of many different determinants. These cultures often have a strong religious and spiritual orientation. For adherents to Western Christian religiosity, selective interpretations of Biblical scripture may be used to reinforce homophobic attitudes (Greene, 1994a, 1994b, in press; Icard, 1986; Moses & Hawkins, 1982) particularly when marriage is being considered. Similarly members of non-Christian sects view homosexuality as a decadent Western practice.

Clarke (1983), Silvera (1991) and Smith (1982) cite heterosexual privilege as another factor in the homophobia of African American and Afro-Caribbean women and men. Because of sexism in both dominant and African American cultures, and racism in the dominant culture, African American men and women may find heterosexuality the only privileged status they may possess (Greene, 1994a, 1994b). As such, they may be reluctant to jeopardize that status and the privileges associated it either by claiming a minority sexual identity or supporting those who do. African American men and women who have internalized the racism and sexism inherent in the patriarchal values of Western culture may scapegoat any strong women or any men who does not adopt the hypermasculine persona, making lesbians and gay men easy targets. Spivey adds that in his experience there has been little support even in the gay male community for stable ongoing relationships among its members. He hypothesizes that this may be a function of envy—many men do not feel deserving of loving relationships and envy those who have them. Those couples are not infrequently on the receiving end of seductive and envious behavior that seeks to undermine their union. It is important to urge such couples to find arenas that are supportive of their relationship, even if it is among heterosexual peers.

African American Gay Men's Relationship Issues: Therapeutic Implications

In Spivey's work with Black gay men he also observes that most of the men he treats *do* want successful relationships; however, they do not really believe they can have them. Both internalized homophobia and internalized racism complicate this endeavor. Furthermore, it is exceedingly difficult in the midst of these complexities to develop a social vocabulary or skill set for interacting in emotionally healthy ways with another man. There are few visible models for doing so. Another complication to finding and maintaining healthy relationships for African American gay men are the unrealistic expectations of partners. In an atmosphere where many men have been victimized emotionally and/or physically, many are seeking safety in relationships but have such high expectations that disappointment is often inevitable. Often partners have fears of abuse and the wish for a relationship that is magical. Many sabotage their own relationships by making choices that are inappropriate. For example, an older man will choose a much younger man as a partner with the expectation of fidelity that is not age appropriate for the younger man. This may be attributable in part to their, like many lesbians and gay men, not having a normal adolescence or developmental period of healthy exploration. Many of their relationships have been constrained or consisted of relationships that were forced on them. Hence there is a form of relationship immaturity that surfaces that therapy must address. This developmental immaturity includes being able to see their masculinity in different ways, and to be comfortable with sexually receptive as well as active roles in the relationship. Another form of immaturity may rest in the belief that power means having the capacity to have multiple partners and perhaps simultaneously appear to not care about being alone. Yet another form of immaturity is reflected in the failure to appreciate the reality that healthy relationships require real work and the ideal is not something that real people can live up to. For those who are stuck in viewing the ideal as the goal, their relationships ultimately collapse under the weight of such unrealistic demands. Spivey also observes that there is frequently a great deal of competition between partners which he sees as a derivative of being a victim of an oppressive society with male gender role socialization, where the emphasis is not on the cooperative skills required for healthy relationships, rather, winning or being right is the only thing that is important.

African American gay men typically have little trust in the therapy process and enter treatment with serious trust issues in their relationships. By the time they come to therapy, problems in the relationship have been present for a considerable time. It is advised that the therapist focus on stabilizing the relationship by exploring those things that are working and that are satisfying and that have enriched their relationship. Informal (not poor) language is suggested to create a relaxed atmosphere in sessions. Spivey observes what he describes as an epidemic of depression in Black gay men that is sometimes masked by sexually compulsive behavior. While he suggests that medications may be important aspects of treatment, the idea of medicines often scare Black men just as the idea of having a mental illness is repugnant. He suggests that when working with these men it is important to use language such as having the big "B" blues, versus the little "b" blues or funk. It is also important to help the depressed partner to acknowledge the effects of his depression on his partner and discuss it with him rather than withdrawing. Partners of depressed patients often become personally offended and angry by the depressed partner's withdrawal when there is no acknowledgement about what is taking place.

African American gay men share historical and cultural origins and circumstances with their lesbian counterparts. Homophobia is, however, gender coded and some of the challenges they face are connected to what is deemed their violation of normative behaviors and desires for men. As previously mentioned, African American gay men may be hypermasculinized in the dominant culture and feminized within African American cultures. Those who do not have more flexible notions of masculinity may be imprisoned between these polarities in ways that are destructive to their relationships. Each is an extreme born of distortions about acceptable male behavior as well as racist stereotypes. The Black brute image of African American men was created to rationalize the brutality and physical violence that was in fact directed at them as a function of racism. The Black brute was one to be feared and presumed dangerous, and if dangerous warranted control by any means needed, even violence.

Spivey observes that African American gay men are often a focus of violence within their families of origin as well as within the broader society and that these encounters with violence affect their relationships. In Black communities, corporal punishment is an accepted form of discipline during childrearing. It is not uncommon for a father to hit a male child who is crying to "toughen him up" or teach him to act "like a man". This may take on stronger overtones if a father senses that his son might be gay or if that son does not fit the "masculine" stereotype society holds for men. In some cases punishment crosses the line and becomes abusive. If the father is gay himself or struggling with his feelings for other men, he may be hypersensitive to his son, especially if that child *is* gay. In this case the son may become the object of the father's projections and concerns about his own "masculinity". Traditional but largely discredited views of the origins of a gay sexual orientation for men suggest that unusually close relationships with mothers and distant relationships with fathers have a causative relationship to gay sexual orientation. While we emphasize that these theories are not supported, we can understand why they may have appeared to be salient. Many gay men report being gender atypical as children and we suspect that this preexisting difference may have elicited distance and in some cases abuse from their fathers for the reasons we have suggested. Mothers of these men often became their place of refuge because they did not feel safe with their fathers. This may well have been a result of their being gender atypical or different in ways that their fathers could not tolerate, rather than the cause. What we suggest is that many of these boys

156

were already different and their fathers were responding to that difference in a variety of ways depending on their own issues. Parental relationships may have ranged from distant and indifferent to brutal and unforgiving. The first loving relationship that a man has with a man is with his father. Difficulty establishing a loving bond between father and son can predispose problems establishing trust in relationships. This is not an explanation for the son's sexual orientation, rather it is what we see as a determinant of a gay man's relationship with his partner, another man.

In this situation a gay man is expected to have a loving relationship with a man when he has no template for what that looks like or how to do so and may have unexpressed rage for men if his paternal relationship was brutal or abusive. When no loving bond has existed between father and son or when that relationship has been punctuated or plagued with violence and rejection, it is likely to affect his relationships with men as well as women, but perhaps more profoundly in intimate relationships with men if he is gay. We understand that people who have been verbally, physically and/or psychologically abused have little opportunity to develop trust in those relationships and that people who have had abusive relationships with parental figures are more vulnerable to seeking out partners who repeat that pattern. Unfortunately this only reinforces the pattern of distrust in relationships.

Spivey observes a pattern in relationships with African American gay men that he describes as "Throwing Shade". It consists of verbal slights, put downs and insults that range from subtle to overt. He suggests that the motivation for throwing shade is distrust within the relationship. There is a belief that you cannot trust another Black man, that he will hurt you. You assert power by hurting him first. What is the legacy of this distrust? Spivey also offers that the more successful relationships that he has observed are mixed race relationships (one African American and one white partner) and puts forth some tentative explanations for this.

African American Gay Men: Mixed Race Relationships

Although a bit beyond the scope of this book, we are including mixed-race relationships as a brief focus because many African American gays and lesbians are more likely to participate in such pairings than their heterosexual counterparts. We know that mixed race relationships are not inherently superior or inferior to monoracial couples and range from healthy to unhealthy types. In the less emotionally healthy types there are more tacit assumptions of inherent worth based on sexual capital (attractiveness) for the Black partner—typically the white partner is not nearly as physically attractive in appearance. However, they seem to strike a bargain, the Black partner finds refuge in the safety and protection of his partner's white privilege (at least the appearance of it) and the white partner finds a handsome "boy toy". In the healthier relationships of this type, there are fewer disparities in age, education, achievement and sexual capital. The ability to share power seems to be the hallmark of health. Spivey offers that in his experience Black men hold one another to a higher standard than the standard to which white men are held. This is perhaps an artifact of internalized racism. We also know that black male and female same sex couples can be publically invisible. There are no visual cues to suggest coupling and many lesbian and gay couples do not wish to be recognized when they are public, thus behaving in ways that reduce the likelihood that they would be identified.

African American Lesbians' Relationship Issues: Therapeutic Considerations

Since their origins in America as objects of the United States slave trade (Greene, 1994a, 1994b), African American women were considered to be property wherein forced sexual relationships with African males and white slave masters were the norm. Afro-Caribbean women, not of Latin descent, often possess cultural values and practices reflective of the country which colonized their island, particularly Great Britain or France.

Ethnosexual stereotypes about African American women have their roots in images created by a white society with an investment in disparaging them. African American and Caribbean women clearly did not fit the traditional stereotypes of women as fragile, weak and dependent, as they were never allowed to be this way. The "Mammy" figure is the historical antecedent to the stereotype of African American women as assertive, domineering and strong. This was to be applauded as long as those qualities were put to the service of her master and mistress.

Stereotypes of lesbians as masculinized females coincide with stereotypes of African American and Afro-Caribbean women. Both are depicted as defective females who want to be or act like men and are sexually promiscuous. It is important to understand the history of institutional racism and its role in the development of myths and distortions regarding the sexuality of lesbians from these groups.

Males in the culture are encouraged to believe that strong women are responsible for their oppression, and not racist institutions. Racism, sexism and heterosexism combine to cast the onus on African American women for the failure of their family structures, which suggests the remedy for liberating people of African descent is male dominance and female subordination. Many African American and Afro-Caribbean women, including lesbians, have internalized these myths, which intensifies the negative psychological effects on African American lesbians and further compromises their ability to obtain support from the larger African American and Caribbean communities (Collins, 1990; Greene, 1994a, 2000).

This legacy of sexual racism plays a role in the response of many African Americans to lesbians in their families or as visible members of their communities. As discussed above, the African American community is perceived by many of its lesbian members as extremely homophobic (Mays & Cochran, 1988). Internalized racism may be seen as another determinant of homophobia among African Americans and Afro-Caribbeans. For those who have internalized the negative stereotypes constructed and held by the dominant culture, behavior outside societal norms is a negative reflection on all African Americans (Greene, in press; Poussaint, 1990). Hence there may be an exaggerated desire to model "normalcy" to the dominant culture (deMonteflores, 1986; Gomez, 1983; Greene, 1994a, 1994b; Wyatt, Strayer & Lobitz, 1976). Since acceptance of lesbian sexual orientation may be inconsistent with the dominant culture's ideal, lesbians may be experienced as an embarrassment to persons who strongly identify with the dominant culture (Poussaint, 1990). Indeed, the only names for lesbians in the African American community, "funny women" or "bulldagger women" are derogatory (Jeffries, 1992, p. 44; Omosupe, 1991).

Clarke (1983) and Jeffries (1992) observe that there was once a greater tolerance for gay men and lesbians in some poor African American communities in the 1940s through 1950s. While Clarke (1983) refers to this as "seizing the opportunity to spite the white man", Jeffries (1992) attributes this behavior to the empathy African Americans felt, as oppressed people, towards members of another oppressed group. However, a strong component to this tolerance was their silence and relative invisibility within the African American community and the dominant culture. The heightened visibility of lesbians and gay men since that era, related in part to greater openness in our society, greater open advocacy for social equality and technology that affords people involved in social movements far less privacy, may place great tension on the denial that may have formed a basis for this tolerance (Greene, 1994a, 1994b). In therapies with African American lesbians, a sense of conflicting loyalties between the African American community and the mainstream lesbian community is often reported. This is especially true in areas outside of large urban centers where there is no Lesbian, Gay, Bisexual, Transgender (LGBT) community per se; however, even in urban centers many may be unwilling to jeopardize their ties to the African American community (Dyne, 1980; Greene, 2000; Icard, 1986). Another factor complicating dual loyalties is the racial discrimination African Americans face in the broader lesbian community regarding social opportunities, i.e. admission to lesbian bars, employment and advertising (Greene, 1994a, 1994b, in press; Gutierrez & Dworkin, 1992; Mays & Cochran, 1988).

There is great diversity within the African American lesbian community. It is crucial for the reader to first understand that the race/ethnicity of the partner of an African American lesbian can greatly affect the dynamics of the relationship as well as its visibility/invisibility and therefore how it is perceived and received by the African American family and community.

Many African American lesbians' relationships are largely unsupported outside of the lesbian community. These women may encounter unique challenges in relationships with partners who have the same gender socialization in a culture which conspicuously devalues their person and devalues their relationships on multiple levels and has few open, healthy models of such relationships. Those in lesbian relationships may find support for their relationship within the African American community. However, this support is often marked by a collusion of silence, ambivalence and denial. Lesbian women of color who have received family support for their struggles with racism, and perhaps sexism, may not presume that this support will extend to their romantic relationships or that their families will empathize with their distress if the relationship is troubled. This is compounded upon seeking professional assistance, only to find few, if any, therapists who have training in addressing issues in nontraditional relationships (Greene, 1994a, 1994b, 1994c).

African American Lesbians and Mixed Race Relationships

We are including a brief section here, on mixed race relationships, as we think it important the clinicians be sensitive to the complications of mixed racial romantic pairings amongst lesbian couples given that they are more likely to be in such pairings than their heterosexual counterparts (Greene, 1995; Mays & Cochran, 1988; Tafoya & Rowell, 1988). This has been attributed in part to the larger numbers of white lesbians than Black (Tafoya & Rowell, 1988). While heterosexual interracial relationships often lack the support of each member's family and community, lesbian interracial relationships face even greater challenges to a situation already fraught with difficulty (Greene, 1994a, 1994b, 1995).

While racial differences and cultural diversities within relationships may pose challenges to them, they should not be regarded as the cause of the presenting problem unless careful exploration reveals that to be the case. It can be tempting for the therapist to collude with clients in their belief that their most visible differences explain their problems. The therapist must explore why each client believes this to be true; however, the therapist must also keep an open mind and be aware that these differences do not *ipso facto* explain anything. It is the therapist's responsibility to assist the couple, when necessary, in exploring when these reasons for their difficulties are preferred or emotionally easier to explore than more complex analyses, and, as such, may be scapegoated. Therapists who avoid this may collude in permitting their clients to avoid an examination of what may be more complex and, as such, often more painful issues and their connections to their respective vulnerabilities within their relationship (Greene, 1994b, 1995). Therapists should be aware that although differences in ethnoracial identity, religious and spiritual orientations etc. *may* serve as relationship stressors, other problems arising out of conflicts over intimacy, other interpersonal and characterological issues, or individual psychopathology may be racialized or experienced as if they are about the couple's racial or ethnic differences, when they have more complex origins both within and outside of the relationship (Greene, 1994b, 1995).

Similarly, choices of partners and feelings about those choices may, but do not automatically, reflect an individual's personal conflicts about their own ethnoracial identity. When such conflicts are present they may be expressed by African American lesbians or gay men who choose or are attracted to white partners, exclusively, or who categorically reject and/or devalue African American or lesbians and gay men of color as unsuitable partners. African American lesbians/gay men who experience themselves as racially or culturally deficient or ambiguous may seek a partner from their own ethnic group to compensate for their perceived deficiency or to demonstrate their cultural loyalty. There may also be a tendency for the African American lesbian or gay man in a relationship with partner of color, who is not African American, to presume a greater level of similarity of experiences or world views between them than is realistically warranted. Their common oppression as persons of color, women and as sexual minorities can mean that they have had the opportunity to have been exposed to certain forms of degrading treatment, threats to their physical safety or social barriers. However, what they make of those experiences cognitively and emotionally are not necessarily the same. Similarly, their views on their preferences for roles, structure of their household, who they consider "family" and who is not, and what that means with respect to desired levels of and frequency of contact with them may be very different (Greene, 1994b, 1995).

A therapist should not presume that participation in an interracial lesbian relationship is an expression of cultural or racial self-hate in the African American lesbian. Similarly, the therapist cannot accurately presume that her presence in a relationship with another African American woman is anchored in either loyalty or respect for that culture. Each relationship has to be explored on its own merit in the specifics of the individuals in it. What is of significance is that the therapist be aware of a wide range of clinical possibilities and explore them accordingly (Greene, 2000).

Culturally Sensitive Therapeutic Considerations for Lesbian and Gay Couples of African Descent

Despite African American lesbians and gay men having greater potential to experience the stress, tension and loneliness that make them psychologically vulnerable, they were and are less likely to seek professional help. The reticence to seek professional help may then leave them with a greater potential for negative therapeutic outcomes when they finally do seek help. An understanding of the meaning and reality of being an African American woman who is lesbian or of an African American man who is gay requires a careful exploration of the impact of factors such as ethnic identity, gender, minority sexual orientation, and their dynamic interactions in the individual; the nature of the culture's traditional gender role stereotypes; the role and importance of family and community; the role of religion/spirituality in the culture; and both the public and private understanding of the role and scope of sexual relations in relationships. Other important factors include the role of racial and ethnic stereotypes, the degree of sexism within their culture, racism from the dominant culture, and how these contribute to ethnosexual myths superimposed on all African American men and women.

In therapy with African American lesbian and gay male clients the family context must be considered: How much do parents or family of origin continue to control or influence children, even when they are adults? How important is the family as a source of economic and emotional support? Other factors to be explored include the degree to which having children and continuation of the family line is valued, closeness of ties to the ethnic community, the degree of acculturation or assimilation of the client and whether it is significantly different from other family members, and the historical oppression the group has faced within the dominant culture. When analyzing the history of discrimination of an ethnic group, group members' own understandings of their oppression and coping strategies must be incorporated. Reviewing or validating only the dominant culture's perspectives on such groups may only reinforce ethnocentric, heterocentric and androcentric biases (Greene, 1994a, 2000).

Another important dimension that must be considered is how sexuality and gender interrelate with culture. Espin (1984) suggests that in most cultures a range of sexual behaviors is tolerated while others are not. It is important for the clinician to determine where the client's behavior fits within the spectrum for her/his particular culture (Espin, 1984). In exploring the range of sexuality tolerated by the person's culture it is helpful to know whether formally forbidden practices are tolerated as long as they are not discussed and not labeled.

It is also important to determine the relationship of ethnosexual mythology to an African American's understanding of a lesbian or gay sexual orientation. These myths perpetrated by the dominant culture often represent a complex combination of racial and sexual stereotypes designed to objectify men and women of color, isolate them from their idealized white counterparts, and promote their sexual exploitation and control (Collins, 1990; Greene, 1994a, 2000; hooks, 1981). The symbolism of these stereotypes and its interaction with stereotypes held about gay men and lesbians are important areas of inquiry. Spivey observes that African American gay men face a circuitous stigma in that they are feminized within Black communities and hypermasculinzed in the dominant cultural gaze. As men who are both Black and gay their only locus of power rests in being male in a patriarchal society. This can give rise to competition within their relationships for power and control as a presumed precursor for safety. "Extramarital" affairs may represent a need to be in control and attain power via promiscuity. Value and power is derived by "getting" as many sexual partners as one can. African American lesbians and gay men come from all socioeconomic levels. Stereotypes of them can lead therapists with limited information or contact with group members to viewing them as only coming from impoverished, drug seeking, street life or poorly educated groups. Therapists are urged to listen non-judgmentally to these clients' stories about how they have been able to put together the social, professional and vocational lives they live. It is most helpful to do this from the perspective that they have often been victimized and while they *have* problems, *they* are not the problem. Being authentic as the therapist is important particularly but not exclusively in therapy with gay Black men because issues of trust are paramount. It is also important to ask questions of the client rather than make assumptions that may be based on attitudes or beliefs of the therapist that may be of questionable validity. Those questions might include how they were treated by parents, what parents' fights or disagreements looked like, what it meant to trust in the family of origin, who was trusted, who was not and why, what did love look like in the family, who was loved and who was not? What all people seek in their intimate relationships is a sense of personal power and agency, safety and the realistic potential to get their needs met. Problems enter relationships when manipulation is required to get those needs met. One of the more important questions we ask when treating these couples is what is wrong or dangerous about being authentic? What happens or has happened to the client when they have said what they felt, believed or wanted? If they were punished for any of those things it becomes no longer safe to ask for them overtly, they must be had by manipulating others, in this case a partner.

Conclusion

It is clear that African American lesbian and gay couples' experiences are significantly underrepresented in the couples' literature. Given the recent attention to gay marriage in various states (e.g. California) and the media, the landscape for gay and lesbian couples is changing, suggesting that more openly gay couples might be more willing to seek psychotherapy to help them cope with relational problems than in the past. Obviously, Black gay and lesbian couples face significant challenges (both different from and similar to one another) given their multiple levels of oppression, discrimination, stereotypes based on gender, sexual orientation and race, and their consistent fight for legitimizing their relationships in society. There is a lack of support for their racial identities within the larger gay community, and heterosexism and homophobia within society as a whole. Clinicians, then, can serve as a strong support for these couples as they enter therapy, providing a safe space for them to strengthen their relationships; however, to do so, clinicians should be aware of and sensitive to the context that informs these couples presenting issues and lives.

African American Lesbian Couples with African American Partners Case Study

The following case discusses a lesbian relationship involving two African American women who are raising a child with extended family involvement. Because of the extended nature of African American families, strong friendship ties between adult women are very common. There is a culturally defined role within the African American community for the nonrelated adult girlfriend who has an often very intense nonsexual, spiritual and emotionally connected relationship with an African American woman friend and her family. This is reflected in the greeting "girlfriend" or "sister" which acknowledges and confers kinship-like status on a close adult female friend who is not blood related but is experienced as intensely as "family". These women are often informally adopted by the family and are referred to by children and younger family members with terms such as "aunt", "play aunt", "play mama" and "sister". Sometimes there is a formal religious aspect to this relationship when this person is a godparent to a child in the family. Given the existence of this role in African American culture, the importance accorded to fictive kin, and because of the proclivity for African American families to deny the existence of lesbian relationships within their midst, it can be easy for African American families to avoid acknowledging the lesbian nature of a relationship between two adult women. African American lesbian couples can sometimes collude in this denial by keeping their sexual orientation a secret. Others may not keep the information a secret but still never fully come out to their family members. Other couples may come out to their families without the families' dealing with the issue of the lesbian relationship and lifestyle but, rather, pretending that the lesbian relationship does not exist and accepting the lover in the culturally accepted role of "girlfriend" or "sister". Some African American families have evolved to the point that a lesbian couple is "accepted" and their relationship acknowledged by the extended family. It is important for clinicians to keep in mind the tremendous diversity of reactions. Different adaptations may exist among the various family members.

This diversity can also extend to the degree of involvement or participation that the lesbian couple has in the Black community and in the community's response as well. African American lesbian women often have children in their relationships. Because of the tradition of "multiple mothering" and grandmother involvement, it is likely that women in the extended family have been more involved in childrearing than their white counterparts (Boyd-Franklin, 1989; Greene, 1990, 1994b). Sometimes the question of who is raising the child or who is the ultimate authority in the child's life can be an issue or a problem in African American families. This is further complicated in the context of a lesbian family in which the generational boundaries are unclear. There are, for example, a number of dilemmas for the lesbian couple who are raising children within an extended family context (many of which are also common to heterosexual relationships). Therapists often view lesbian couples and families through the eyes of the couple. When children are involved, it is easy to assume that one is treating a "nuclear" lesbian family. In many African American couples, this assumption is often incorrect. The following case illustrates one such dilemma.

Background

Kadija, a 29-year-old African American lesbian woman and Aisha, her 35-year-old African American lover of seven years presented for couples' and family therapy. They were raising Kadija's 12-year-old son, Jamal, who was acting out at home and in school. They reported that they were intensely involved in each other's extended families. Within the last two years, they had been experiencing more conflict in their relationship. Both women dated the beginning of that conflict to their move from a separate apartment in Kadija's mother's house to a place of their own. Prior to the move, Kadija's mother had been Jamal's primary caretaker as Kadija had been 17 at the time of his birth.

Aisha, who had been a friend of the family before becoming Kadija's lover, was ambivalently accepted by both her mother and Jamal. While their lesbian relationship was never openly discussed, Kadija reported that she had come out to her mother and that her family "knew" about her involvement with Aisha. It was striking, however, that the couple reported that Jamal did not "know" the true nature of their relationship. As treatment progressed, it became apparent that prior to the move Kadija's mother had served as a buffer between the couple and Jamal. Once the move occurred, they were unprepared for the full responsibility for raising a pre-adolescent child.

The therapist explored their denial of Jamal's knowledge of the true nature of their lesbian relationship. In a session alone with Jamal, the therapist discovered that Jamal was well aware of his mother's relationship with Aisha and he resented it on a number of levels. First, because they were "lying to him"; secondly, because he was being teased by his friends. Finally, it became clear that Jamal had a very close relationship with his grandmother and had discussed his mother's lesbian relationship with her. Ironically, they both participated in the ruse of the denial. In addition, Jamal had been able to camouflage his mother's lesbian relationship from his peers as long as they all lived in his grandmother's house. The move had, in his words, "blown my cover".

The therapist facilitated a number of meetings in which she helped Jamal, Kadija and Aisha to talk more openly about the lesbian relationship. Both members of the couple were surprised at his anger and his embarrassment. As they began to talk about these issues, the tensions in the couple and the acting out on Jamal's part began to ease. At the therapist's suggestion, Kadija's mother was also invited to participate in a few sessions in order to help all parties to negotiate a new way of relating. It became apparent that Jamal and his grandmother often engaged in special alliances and that some of her directives to him were often different from those of Kadija and Aisha.

In the final phase of therapy, additional work was done with Kadija and Aisha to help them to make time in their lives as co-parents in order to nurture their adult relationship.

Discussion

This case illustrates the complexity of extended family relationships within African American families. Therapists working with lesbian couples within this culture should be aware that although it is the couple who presents for treatment, there are often many other family members involved. The collusion and denial evident in this family is not unusual in the African American community.

Therapy often serves the role of helping to open up discussion among family members on the "taboo" subject of the couple's lesbianism. Jamal's response as a pre-adolescent is also a common one. Boyd-Franklin (1989) in her book on black families in therapy discusses the impact of "toxic secrets". For Jamal, his mother's lesbianism is a "toxic secret" which is "known" on some level but denied and never fully discussed. Therapists working with African American lesbian couples with children must be sensitive to these issues and help the couple to begin the process of facilitating discussion with the young person involved. Timing is crucial and therapists may have to work with each family member individually first in order to hear and understand their concerns before bringing the whole family together.

Finally, one of the most important aspects of this treatment is helping the couple to nurture each other and their relationship while these complex family dynamics are being explored in therapy. All of this work takes place in an environment which is antagonistic to African American lesbians and where there is little support for their relationships. Developing supportive networks becomes another important aspect of this challenging work.

References

Bowleg, L., Brooks, K., & Ritz, S.F. (2008). "Bringing home more than a paycheck": An exploratory analysis of Black lesbians' experiences of stress and coping in the workplace, *Journal of Lesbian Studies*, 12(1), 69–84.

Boyd-Franklin, N. (1989). *Black family in therapy: A multisystems approach*. New York: Guilford.

Cerbone, A. (2011, May). What straight and gay couples have in common. In S. Shand (Chair), We do, but we can't (in 45 states): The status of same sex marriage. New York State Psychological Association Annual Convention, New York.

Christian, B. (1985). *Black feminist criticism: Perspectives on Black women writers*. New York: Pergamon.

Clarke, C. (1983). The failure to transform: Homophobia in the Black community. In B. Smith (Ed.), *Home girls: A Black feminist anthology* (pp. 197–208). New York: Kitchen Table-Women of Color Press.

Cohen, C., & Jones, T. (1999). Fighting homophobia versus challenging heterosexism: "The failure to transform" revisited. In E. Brandt (Ed.), *Dangerous liaisons: Blacks, gays and the struggle for equality* (pp. 80–101). New York: The New Press.

Collins, P. H. (1990). Homophobia and Black lesbians. In *Black feminist thought: Knowledge, consciousness, and the politics of empowerment* (pp. 192–196). Boston: Unwin/Hyman.

deMonteflores, C. (1986). Notes on the management of difference. In T. Stein & C. Cohen (Eds.), *Contemporary perspectives on psychotherapy with lesbians and gay men* (pp. 73–101). New York: Plenum.

Dew, M. A. (1985). The effects of attitudes on inferences of homosexuality and perceived physical attractiveness in women. *Sex Roles*, 12, 143–155.

Dyne, L. (1980). Is D.C. becoming the gay capital of America? *The Washington*, September, pp. 96–101, 133–141.

Espin, O. (1984). Cultural and historical influences on sexuality in Hispanic/Latina women: Implications for psychotherapy. In C. Vance (Ed.), *Pleasure and danger: Exploring female sexuality* (pp. 149–163). London: Routledge & Kegan Paul.

Ferguson, R.A. (2010). To be fluent in each other's narratives: Surplus populations and queer of color activism. In J. Battle & S.L. Barnes (Eds.), *Black sexualities: Probing powers, passions, practices, and policies* (pp. 155–168). Piscataway, NJ: Rutgers University Press.

Garnets, L., & Kimmel, D. (1991). Lesbian and gay male dimensions in the psychological study of human diversity. In J. Goodchilds (Ed.), *Psychological perspectives on human diversity in America* (pp. 137–192). Washington, DC: American Psychological Association.

Glassgold, J. (1992). New directions in dynamic theories of lesbianism: From psychoanalysis to social constructionism. In J. Chrisler & D. Howard (Eds.), *New directions in feminist psychology: Practice, theory and research* (pp. 154–163). New York: Springer.

Gomez, J. (1983). A cultural legacy denied and discovered: Black lesbians in fiction by women. In B. Smith (Ed.), *Home girls: A Black feminist anthology* (pp. 120–121). New York: Kitchen Table-Women of Color Press.

Gomez, J., & Smith, B. (1990). Taking the home out of homophobia: Black lesbian health. In E. C. White (Ed.), *The Black women's health book: Speaking for ourselves* (pp. 198–213). Seattle, WA: Seal Press.

Greene, B. (1990). Stereotypes of African American sexuality: A commentary. In S. Rathus, J. Nevid & L. Fichner-Rathus (Eds.), *Human sexuality in a world of diversity* (p. 257). Boston: Allyn & Bacon.

Greene, B. (1994a). Ethnic-minority lesbians and gay men: Mental health and treatment issues. *American Psychological Association*, 62(2), 243–251.

Greene, B. (1994b). Lesbian women of color: Triple Jeopardy. In L. Comas-Diaz & B. Greene (Eds.), *Women of color: Integrating ethnic and gender identities in psychotherapy* (pp. 389–427). New York: Guilford Press.

Greene, B. (1994c). Lesbian and gay sexual orientations: Implications for clinical training, practice and research. In B. Greene & G. Herek (Eds.), *Psychological perspectives on lesbian and gay issues Vol. 1 Lesbian and gay psychology: Theory, research, and clinical applications* (pp. 1–24). Thousand Oaks, CA: Sage.

Greene, B. (1995). Lesbian couples. In K. Jay (Ed.), *Dyke life: From growing up to growing old: A celebration of the lesbian experience*. New York: Basic Books.

Greene, B. (2000). African American lesbian and bisexual women in feminist psychodynamic psychotherapy: Surviving and thriving between a rock and a hard place. In L. C. Jackson & B. Greene (Eds.), *Psychotherapy with African American women: Innovations in psychodynamic perspectives and practice* (pp. 82–125). New York: Guilford Press.

Greene, B. (in press). Intersectionality and diversity in the Minyan: A commentary. In B. Greene & D. Brodbar (Eds.), *A Minyan of Women: Family dynamics, Jewish identity and psychotherapy practice*. London: Routledge.

Greene, B., & Boyd-Franklin, N. (1996). African American lesbians: Issues in couples therapy. In J. Laird & R. J. Green (Eds.), *Lesbians and gays in couples and families: A handbook for therapists* (pp. 251–271). San Francisco, CA: Jossey Bass Publishers.

Gutierrez, F., & Dworkin, S. (1992). Gay, lesbian, and African American: Managing the integration of identities. In S. Dworkin & F. Gutierrez (Eds.), *Counseling gay men and lesbians* (pp. 141–156). Alexandria, VA: American Association of Counseling and Developing.

Hall, R. L., & Greene, B. (2002). Not any one thing: The complex legacy of social class on African American lesbian relationships. *Journal of Lesbian Studies*, 6(1), 65–74.

hooks, b. (1981). *Ain't I a woman: Black women and feminism*. Boston, MA: South End Press.

Icard, L. (1986). Black gay men and conflicting social identities: Sexual orientation versus racial identity. *Journal of Social Work and Human Sexuality*, 4(1/2), 83–93.

Jeffries, I. (1992). Strange fruits at the purple manor: Looking back on "the life" in Harlem. *NYQ*, February 23, 17, 40–45.

Kite, M. (1994). When perceptions meet reality: Individual differences in reactions to lesbians and gay men. In B. Greene & G. Herek (Eds.), *Lesbian and gay psychology: Theory, research and clinical applications*. Thousand Oaks, CA: Sage.

Kite, M., & Deaux, K. (1987). Gender belief systems: Homosexuality and the implicit inversion theory. *Psychology of Women Quarterly*, 11, 83–96.

Mays, V., & Cochran, S. (1988). The Black's women relationship project: A national survey of Black lesbians. In M. Shernoff & W. Scott (Eds.), *The sourcebook on lesbian/gay health care* (2nd ed., pp. 54–62). Washington, DC: National Lesbian and Gay Health Foundation.

McGruder, K. M. (2010). Pathologizing black sexuality: The U.S. experience (pp. 101–118). In J. Battle & S. L. Barnes (Eds) (2010). *Black sexualities: Probing powers, passions, practices, and policies*. New Brunswick, NJ: Rutgers University Press.

Moore, M. (2011). *Invisible families: Gay identities, relationships and motherhood among Black women*. Berkeley, CA: University of California Press.

Moses, A. E., & Hawkins, R. (1982). *Counseling lesbian women and gay men: A life issues approach*. St. Louis, MO: C. V. Mosby.

Newman, B. S. (1989). The relative importance of gender role attitudes toward lesbians. *Sex Roles*, 21, 451–465.

Omosupe, K. (1991). Black/lesbian/bulldagger. Differences. *A Journal of Feminist and Cultural Studies*, 2(2), 101–111.

Peplau, L. A., Cochran, S. D., & Mays, V. M. (1997). A national survey of the intimate relationships of African American lesbians and gay men: A look at commitment, satisfaction, sexual behavior and HIV disease. In B. Greene (Eds.), *Psychological perspectives on lesbian and gay issues: Ethnic and cultural diversity among lesbians and gay men* (pp. 11–38). Newbury Park, CA: Sage.

Poussaint, A. (1990). An honest look at Black gays and lesbians. *Ebony*, September, 124, 126, 130–131.

Silvera, M. (1991). Man royals and sodomites: Some thoughts on the invisibility of Afro-Caribbean lesbians. In M. Silvera (Ed.), *Piece of my heart: A lesbian of color anthology* (pp. 14–26). Toronto, Ontario: Sister Vision Press.

Smith, B. (1982). Toward a Black feminist criticism. In G. Hull, P. Scott, & B. Smith (Eds.), *All the women are white, all the Blacks are men, but some of us are brave* (pp. 157–175). Old Westbury, NY: Feminist Press.

Tafoya, T., & Rowell, R. (1988). Counseling Native American lesbians and gays. In M. Shernoff & W. A. Scott (Eds.), *The sourcebook on lesbian/gay health care* (pp. 63–67). Washington, DC: National Lesbian and Gay Health Foundation.

West, C. (1996). Cornel West on heterosexism and transformation: An interview. *Harvard Educational Review*, 66, 356–367.

Whitley, E. B., Jr. (1987). The relation of sex role orientation to heterosexual attitudes toward homosexuality. *Sex Roles*, 17, 103–113.

Wyatt, G., Strayer, R., & Lobitz, W. C. (1976). Issues in the treatment of sexually dysfunctioning couples of African American descent. *Psychotherapy*, 13, 44–50.

Part IV

ASSESSMENT AND TREATMENT OF BLACK COUPLES IN COUNSELING

CULTURALLY SENSITIVE ASSESSMENT APPROACHES AND CONSIDERATIONS FOR AFRICAN AMERICAN COUPLES

Katherine M. Helm and Torrey Wilson

Couples' treatment poses a set of unique challenges for a clinician. Managing the dynamics of both participants and the reactions (counter-transference) of the clinician, along with the varied expectations of all involved in the process requires a different and more sophisticated set of skills than is required when working with individuals. When the racial/cultural issues and context of working with African American couples are added, this challenge is increased exponentially. Statistically, African Americans are at greater risk for marital discord, including rates of separation and divorce. Two out of every three marriages amongst African American couples (66 percent) will end in divorce (LaTaillade, 2006) as they are generally exposed to a number of chronic stressors such as economic instability, racism, and discrimination that have a disproportionate negative impact on intimate relationships (LaTaillade, 2006). Graduate training across various practice-oriented disciplines lacks any substantive focus on the training of therapists in assessing and working with this population. Additionally, the absence of significant numbers of culturally competent supervisors means that very few novice counselors are receiving the kind of training needed to work effectively with African American couples (Constantine, 1998, 2001, 2002).

This chapter outlines important areas of assessment for African American couples. Effective couples' counseling always begins with an evaluation of the couples' current level of functioning, presenting issues, identified strengths, and the couples' view of their relationship. This chapter will guide clinicians in culturally sensitive assessment practices when African American couples begin couples' treatment. Taking a colorblind approach is not only inappropriate and culturally insensitive, but also harmful as it does not allow the clinician the appropriate context for working with African American couples and assumes all couples are the same. Many Black couples are aware that, historically, the field of mental health has pathologized and misrepresented their relationships, thus they may be reluctant to share certain details about their relationship with practitioners for fear of being judged. LaTaillade (2006) suggests that adapting the timing and depth of assessment should occur to match the couple's comfort level and readiness to share sensitive information. Inclusion of the couple in a collaborative exchange will help to foster an open environment that lends itself to greater disclosure over time. This chapter will address specific relationship-building strategies with African American couples and important areas of assessment, unique to Black relationships.

Assessment as an Ongoing Process

Assessment is important in the therapeutic process, but does not necessarily define treatment in absolute terms. In other words, assessment is a dynamic and continuous process. As more information is gathered throughout the course of treatment, the treatment plan should be adjusted/modified to include new findings (Gurman & Jacobson, 2002); therefore, the direction of treatment should be modified as additional information and understanding of the issues unfold (Gurman & Jacobson, 2002).

Couples come to therapy for various reasons. Presenting issues of African American couples vary widely and can include: pre-marital, co-habitation, marital-separation, divorce, relational discord, infidelity, blended family and step-parenting issues, communications problems, and domestic violence (LaTaillade, 2006). Additional knowledge, training, and expertise are needed when working with gay and lesbian Black couples (see Greene, Boyd-Franklin, & Spivey, Chapter 6). With all couples, the first step in effective assessment is to adequately evaluate the nature of the presenting problems, along with the cultural context of the couple's relationship. Clinicians should investigate the following: How did this couple come to this point? What are the underlying relationship and/or family dynamics and messages about commitment and mating? How do environmental constraints (e.g. financial issues, racial oppression, lack of marital support, differences in child-raising practices, etc.) impact the couple's relationship? Roberto-Forman (2002) suggests the growing number of research papers that have looked at the connection between family of origin problems and later marital issues have the potential for providing a powerful approach to understanding and working with couples in distress. This analysis can provide a means for understanding and decreasing marital discord while simultaneously increasing relational resilience and the ability to prevent future symptoms. Other common areas of assessment for all couples, regardless of racial/ethnic background, include: presenting issue, previous history of counseling, the couples' relational history/narrative with one another, any mental health issues that might be impacting the couple, sexual issues, relational violence, substance abuse issues, domestic violence, presence of suicidal/homicidal ideation, previous history of sexual abuse, if the couple has children or not and how children impact their relationship (e.g. parenting styles, step-parent relationships, etc.), family of origin issues, the role extended family plays in their lives, motivation for counseling, past trauma, familial structure (who lives in the home with the couple), support system, severity, and chronicity of presenting problem, financial issues, relational role strain (e.g. a mother struggling in her roles of wife, mother, and employee), employment and educational status, socioeconomic status (SES), and many other areas. Finally, as Allen and Helm discuss in Chapter 4, the role technology plays in couples' lives should be assessed including: the use of social networking sites to post relational issues and relationship status (e.g. married, single), arguments via text messaging, Internet extra-marital relationships, boundary violations that can happen with technology (e.g. contacting one's ex-romantic partner), etc. as these can have a significant impact on the couple. This chapter will review specific areas of assessment necessary in successful work with African American couples; however, a thorough assessment process takes into account the couple's individual needs and should be tailored to fit the couple with which one is working.

African American Couples Presenting Issues and Strategies for Addressing Them in Counseling

As discussed in previous chapters, understanding and assessing how power and gender dynamics do/do not operate in African American couples' relationships can offer some cultural and contextual variables that may have a disproportionate impact in the couple's relationship. Exploring these dynamics increases awareness of the couple's values, dynamics, and discrepancies between what they value (e.g. man as head of household) and how these roles are actually operationalized within their relationship (e.g. joint decision making). As stated in previous chapters, this is frequently the case with many African American heterosexual couples—they may both wish that the male partner is the primary breadwinner; however, this may not be the case in the relationship.

Feminist therapies frequently employ gender and power role analysis in their approaches to therapy. This could also be very useful for work with African American couples. Gender role analysis involves a collaborative examination by counselor and client regarding the impact of gender on presenting problems (Herlihy & Corey, 2001; Santos De Barona & Dutton, 1997). Foster and May (2003) states that "Gender-role analysis helps clients to identify how societal messages, expectations, and structures related to traditional gender arrangements have influenced their lives. This type of analysis facilitates clients' awareness of how gendered roles are one-dimensional, the male role restricting connectedness to others and the female role limiting the experience of self" (p. 178). Foster and May believe that facilitative questions such as:

1 What is the traditional role of women in your culture?
2 What aspects of the traditional roles have the women in your family followed and which have they not followed?

3 How do you see yourself as similar and different from the women in your family?

Similar questions can be constructed for men. Gender role analysis allows for a deconstructing of gender and an awareness of cultural premises about gender roles. Understanding how gender roles and racial stereotypes impact African American couples is an invaluable part of the assessment process. Finally, as discussed in earlier chapters, gender role expectations also need to be addressed, as some African American couples are gender egalitarian but may wish more male-dominant relationships, especially in terms of the primary breadwinner role.

Also drawing from feminist therapies is the strategy of *power analysis*. A power analysis is a strategy used to explore the power differential between women and men or oppressed and dominant groups (Herlihy & Corey, 2001; Marecek, 2001; Morrow & Hawxhurst, 1998). Foster and May (2003) states that "power analysis helps clients to identify what kinds of power they possess or have access to, and for what reasons. Such an analysis assists clients in understanding both the destructive and effective use of power" (p. 179). Power is socially constructed both within relationships and without. Morrow and Hawxhurst (1998) suggest exploring power along three dimensions: personal power (power within), interpersonal (power with others), and sociopolitical (power in society). This is an excellent assessment tool in working with African American couples, because African Americans continue to experience oppression and powerlessness in society. This culturally sensitive approach easily acknowledges how power (or lack thereof) can impact the couple's relationship and as it relates to their emotional intimacy with one another. It acknowledges both socio-historical-political influences and interpersonal power dynamics within the couple's relationship and is a critical tool in working with African American couples.

Adequate assessment and understanding of the presenting problem(s) ultimately informs the best treatment options for the couple and provides direction to the counseling process. Boyd-Franklin (2003) suggests that because clients come to us to address their pains and difficulties and not their strengths, it is important for the clinician to adopt a strengths-based approach to treatment. In fact, one might argue that assessing a couple's strengths is of equal importance as is assessing their problems. Therapists will rely heavily on these strengths as treatment progresses. Couples, especially African American couples, need to understand the positive characteristics of their relationships, requiring an evaluation of and attention to the cultural and familial strengths that the couple may not be aware of and integrating this into treatment. Strengths-based assessment questions might include:

- What do you see as the strengths of your relationship?
- What has kept you together through previous times of crises?
- How have you collaboratively worked through problematic situations in the past? What has worked for you? What has not worked for you?

- What are your partner's individual strengths? Yours?
- What other relational support do you have as a couple (e.g. extended family, fictive kin, community support, church/religious community support, etc.)?
- How often do you utilize your support system to get you through difficulties in your relationship? What has been helpful to you in the past in using these supports?
- What is your "couple identity"? Who are you as a couple and who do you want to be?

Gottman (1999) suggests that assessment can be a powerful experience for couples as it is experienced as an intervention. For example, when done well, the assessment process helps couples feel understood and hopeful about their relationship and couples' therapy. The assessment process can help couples and clinicians clarify the course and goals of treatment, and provide hope that their specific concerns will be addressed. He also suggests that how the clinician communicates the assessment plan can have a powerful impact on outcome expectations (Gottman, 1999). In this way, assessment is a collaborative process between the clinician and couple. Here, the relationship is established and trust is built.

Culturally Competent Assessment Practices with African American Couples: Specific Strategies

Sue, Fujino, Hu, Takeuchi, & Zane (1991) have suggested that culturally competent care includes: (1) an awareness of one's own culture and its specific impact on the formation of one's values and biases; (2) knowledge of the worldview of the culturally different client; and (3) the use of culturally appropriate treatment strategies and interventions. The therapist's ability to actively attend to these three areas while simultaneously attending to the presenting problems and dynamics is essential to the therapeutic relationship and the establishment of rapport with Black couples because it: (1) provides a more accurate picture of the problems couples experience in their relationships; (2) engenders a sense of trust and rapport between couples and counselors; (3) provides a culturally sensitive analysis of and focus on the couples' issues taking socio-historical-culturally contextual factors into account and how these factors may impact the couple and their presenting issues. Culturally competent couples' counselors address differences between themselves and their clients early in the treatment process. They ask about how racism and discrimination impact the couples' issues, and understand how contextual factors can manifest in African American couples' relationships. Clearly, effective treatment cannot be done with African American couples if the clinician does not understand the context—both past and present—in which these couples exist. This requires a great deal of sensitivity and sophistication from the therapist as they must understand the racialized and oppressed existence of Black couples as well as the overt and nuanced impact this can have on their relationships. An awareness of the aforementioned factors is important in same race (i.e. Black therapist–Black couple) as well as in racially mixed counselor–couple treatment dyads. Culturally sensitive assessment also includes an acknowledgement of the couple's worldview as well as an understanding of the differences that define the intra-racial diversity within the Black community, including SES, geography (e.g. North versus South), level of education, sexual identity, gender roles, and level of religiosity. All interactions, regardless of the counselor's racial/ethnic background, are multicultural at some level reflecting differences in life experiences (clinician–client), cultural identities and values, and understandings around health, illness, and relationships (Sue & Sue, 2003). While it is more common that non-African American clinicians may have a greater set of differences to work through within the therapeutic relationship, the reality is that most clinicians are trained in western-Eurocentric models of assessment and psychotherapy that typically do not offer a fully integrated understanding of diversity. Boyd-Franklin (2003) addressed the need for sensitivity in the assessment process given that traditional sources of counsel and support in the Black community come from the church, extended and immediate family and friends and not psychotherapy. She specifically cautions clinicians against focusing on the suspicious reactions that may arise from African American couples when extensive family histories are taken in the initial intake assessment. Well intentioned interventions on the part of the clinician may evoke "resistance" to treatment when utilized with Black couples and families. Black couples may experience certain interventions as overly intrusive and may feel that traditional psychotherapy labels them as dysfunctional and crazy. African American couples are aware of the negative societal stereotypes about Black families and couples and thus may be "on guard" in initial treatment sessions. For example, Black couples may be reluctant to share information that is consistent with stereotypes about African Americans. Issues of multi-parent fertility or absentee fathers are two such examples. Not sharing this information, however, jeopardizes therapy and the rapport between counselor and couple and does not portray an accurate depiction of the couple's life.

Culturally competent assessment is not just about asking couples a series of questions to ascertain the problem and/or diagnosis. An essential component in beginning the therapy process with African American couples is building rapport. Establishing rapport frequently begins with understanding the differing experiences of Blacks in the United States versus those of other cultural groups and the impact of those experiences on the coupling behaviors of the Black community. The first session is critical to the development of the relationship between couple and clinician. Relationships are typically built on similarity with sensitivity to differences, cultural or otherwise. Couples want to know: Will we be understood and not judged? Can this counselor actually help us? Clinicians' ability to convey their thorough understanding of the couples' presenting issues, empathy and non-judgmental stance, as well as instilling hope and faith that the counseling process can work, are more likely to be successful in establishing trust with their couple and quickly build rapport.

It is important to note that the emphasis on verbally sharing one's feelings, experiences and family history with outsiders is not a part of African American cultural norms and mores. Indeed the process of sharing one's experiences and the subsequent labeling of those experiences as pathological by clinicians has contributed to the negative views that many Blacks have towards therapy and therapists (Boyd-Franklin, 1987; Hines & Boyd-Franklin, 1996; Imber-Black, 1988). Modifying one's approach to the unique experiences and expectations of African American couples will set the stage for a more open and productive exchange. This can be done in several ways. The traditional assessment process for an intake session does not typically include an exploration of racial oppression, which should be included with African American couples, couples of color, and gay and lesbian couples. The intersection of race, gender and sexual orientation (with gay or lesbian couples) should be explored because, for women and gay/lesbian couples, they may experience an identity split (e.g. being both Black and female, or gay and African American) which can strain the relationship. Additionally, the couple's racial identity should be assessed. How important is being African American to who they are as individuals and as a couple? Sometimes couples differ on race (or gender or sexual orientation) as an identity variable which could present problems within their relationships. Finally, the role of the extended family and fictive kin in the couple's relationship should be assessed as many African Americans are collectivistic and view the extended family and fictive kin as an important support system. Assessing these variables will provide both the couple and counselor with critical insights into the couple's relationship and their overall relational dynamic.

Additional information should be gathered when working with Black couples, including religion and the great variability among Black couples across geographic region, socioeconomic level, education, family structure and issues related to complexion (skin color) (Boyd-Franklin, 2002). These issues represent the diversity within Black couples. For many African Americans, skin color issues still shape their cultural landscape and can influence their treatment in society and relationship dynamics. Having lighter versus darker skin—especially for African American women—may be viewed as a beauty ideal and can impact how a Black woman is perceived and treated in society. American society maintains a beauty ideal based on Eurocentric white skin standards. African American women—especially those with darker skin—can never attain this beauty ideal. Some African Americans have painful experiences surrounding the darkness or lightness of their skin which can and does impact their romantic relationships, and families sometimes perpetuate these painful issues by having nicknames for children based on skin color. The impact of skin color within and on a couple's relationship is an area of assessment that should not be ignored. Clinicians' understanding of African American culture-specific issues that underlie each of these areas are a necessary part of effective treatment with Black couples. In sum, Boyd-Franklin (2002) states that these areas of assessment are critical for doing therapy with Black couples.

A final area of focus in the assessment process should be clinicians' attention to and understanding of the apprehensions and fears associated with therapy for the couple. Exploring the couple's fears about entering treatment will better facilitate the counseling process and set a supportive tone for couple's therapy. It can also serve as a clinical "heads up" to the counselor in terms of predicting areas of resistance which may present in the treatment process. Obviously, this chapter does not attempt to provide a comprehensive examination of all of these issues, but does provide a working framework for starting the therapeutic process and assessing the fundamental issues that might present in the assessment of Black couples.

The Clinical Interview

The most important assessment tool in couples' treatment is frequently the clinical interview which provides clinicians the opportunity to build rapport with the couple and let the relationship, and couples' descriptions of their own issues, guide the assessment process. The clinical interview provides clinicians with useful information regarding their individual expectations of couple's treatment, levels of commitment to the relationship, and how congruent their views of the core issues that define the conflictual and healthy elements of the relationship are seen. Additionally, the clinical interview provides couples and counselors with the opportunity to begin collaborating on the therapy's focus and specific goals.

Ivey, Bradford-Ivey, and Zalaquett (2010) provide a basic framework for a culturally competent clinical interview. They include five stages and suggest that when using this five-stage framework the clinician can often predict how clients may respond. The five stages are: *relationship, story and strengths, goals, restory, and action* and is based on a problem-solving model. They stress that each stage requires the clinician's ability to listen, be empathic and non-judgmental. This is especially important for African American couples, as some may demonstrate cultural mistrust due to many of the reasons previously discussed in this chapter. The five-stage model is further delineated below:

- *Relationship*—Involves initiating the session, building rapport and trust, and structuring the upcoming work (i.e. what will our work together look like?).
- *Story and strengths*—Involves gathering specific data, drawing out stories, concerns, problems and issues (why counseling?; couple's strengths?).
- *Goals*—Involves mutual, collaborative goal-setting. What changes do they want to see in their relationship?
- *Restory*—Working together with each other and the counselor. Involves exploring alternatives, confronting the couple's incongruities and conflict *restory*ing. Ivey et al. (2010) describe this as: "Can we generate new ways of thinking, feeling, and behaving?" How can our story be changed? Ivey et al. (2010) emphasize that clinicians "should generate at least three alternatives that may resolve the client's issues" (p. 211) which gives them hope that the

upcoming sessions will be useful. They stress that "creativity is useful here as you seek to find three alternatives so that the couple has choices. Sometimes a valid choice is to accept things as they are" (p. 211).

- *Action*—Is the termination stage which involves generalizing and acting on new stories and shoring up the strengths of the couple. It involves solidifying treatment gains (progress made in counseling so couples understand how far they have come and what improvements they have made) and providing growth areas moving forward.

Ivey et al. (2010) suggest that different cultural groups develop relationships in varying ways. The literature strongly suggests that cultural and ethnic differences need to be addressed in a straightforward manner and relatively early in counseling (such as the clinical interview) as the clinician's ability to recognize and respect differences is essential for the success of the interview and counseling. This may help alleviate issues involving cultural mistrust.

One way of building the relationship with the couple is during the clinical interview; clinicians should ask the couple for their feedback on the treatment plan. Developing the treatment plan and goals by using direct input from the couple is critical to developing a collaborative approach to counseling.

Evaluating the couple's prior experience with counseling (positive or negative) is also important data. Finally, ascertaining what each person believes the problems are is necessary prior to beginning treatment. This knowledge will give the clinician some understanding of the couple's power dynamics as well as their respective worldviews as it relates to their relationship. Traditional clinical interviews include a psychosocial assessment. Additional areas not previously discussed include: description/history of the presenting issues; medications; family of origin, current living arrangement, peer/social relationships and support; vocational/educational information; mental health and diagnostic history; and other relevant assessment areas specific to the couple (Hood & Johnson, 1997).

Areas of assessment specific to African American couples have been suggested earlier in this chapter. A summary is included below.

- power role and gender role analysis
- the impact of socio-historical-cultural factors on the couple's relationships
- immediate and extended family relationships
- fictive kin relationships
- connection to the African American community and/or religious services if applicable to couple
- financial issues
- how racism, discrimination, oppression, skin color (lightness/darkness of complexion) and negative stereotypes impact the couple's relationship and view of one another
- the role children (step-children) and parentage (multi-fertility) play in the couple's relationship

- racial/cultural identity of the couple as a whole and as individuals
- impact of children on the couple's relationship (e.g. multi-parent fertility, step-parenting, etc.).

Assessment of Personal Baggage

In interviewing several African American couples' experts for this book, two specifically suggested that there can be no effective couples' treatment without an understanding of the individual issues that impact the couple as a whole. Both Dr. Thomas Parham and Ms. Audrey Chapman strongly suggested that couples' clinicians should understand how the issues stated below impact couples' relationships.

- attachment (secure attachment history to primary caregivers or damaged attachments)
- identity (who individuals say they are and how they define themselves)
- self-worth
- values
- previous emotional wounds
- ability to trust
- previous romantic relationship history
- relationship (and sexual) scripts
- how each view gender roles
- financial (one's relationship to and with money)
- ability to self-soothe
- individual ability to problem solve
- individual support systems (e.g. friends, family, etc.)
- ability to support one's partner
- ability to compromise
- relationships to family members (family of origin issues)
- emotional maturity
- communication skills

An exhaustive overview of how these issues may be explored is beyond the scope of this chapter; however, in our practice with couples, we have met the couple together for an intake session and clinical interview and then separated them to meet for one to two individual sessions, assessing the above variables. Understanding these issues will also give the clinician a better idea of how the couple perceives their issues on an individual basis. We suggest that individual meetings should be conducted at the beginning of treatment and then couples' meetings should resume. This maintains the focus on the couple. Through this process, clinicians may find that they need to refer one member for individual therapy to work on their respective issues.

Children

The introduction of children into the couple's relationship changes the dynamics between the couple. For example, extra financial and relational stressors are added when children are present and children are usually the focal point of families. Additionally, differences in parenting styles, and values and goals, become apparent when couples have children, which may not have been obvious prior to the couple having children. These issues become even more complicated when couples come to the current relationship with children from previous unions, as their previous romantic partners may still be involved in the lives of the current partner and child. Step-parenting often requires a careful negotiation of roles on the part of the biological parent, child and step-parent, and there is a high potential for missteps, hurt feelings, miscommunication and frustration along the way. Arguments over the distribution of financial, emotional, and time resources, the previous romantic partner's presence in the child's life, jealousy and insecurity, and the step-parent's relationship to the child/children can become highly problematic for the couple. This can stress both new and old relationships. For example, if a child has grown up and moved out, but now comes back home to live and their parent's partner is present, this can cause feelings of torn loyalty and a major relational shift for the couple. These issues require a thorough assessment from the clinician as well as a strong rapport and a high level of sensitivity, as couples may be reluctant to share their honest feelings about their partner's children and previous romantic relationship. These issues usually significantly impact the couple's relationship as they require a high level of emotional maturity and compromise from both partners. These areas should be included in the initial assessment process with African American couples, as they will impact the clinical picture of the couple's issues.

Other areas of assessment, including how matters of disclosure were established in the couple's respective families of origin, and concerns about family secrets and the pathologizing of cultural characteristics by the broader mental community, should be at the forefront of the clinician's thinking as he/she establishes a safe therapeutic environment. This also includes the fundamental structure and functionality of the relationship and the gathering of additional data about culture-specific stressors and other issues that are impacting the relationship (Boyd-Franklin, 1987, 2003; LaTaillade, 2006). Black couples often present to therapy with conscious and unconscious family secrets that they feel culturally bound not to disclose, especially to non-African American clinicians, for concern about being pathologized or negatively viewed. There are often family and cultural expectations that "family business" and sensitive topics are not to be shared with the outside world. The specific prohibition against this can present a particular problem for Black couples that pursue counseling as a means of trying to salvage their relationship (Boyd-Franklin, 2003). These difficult dialogues can and will be revealed over time, once trust and a strong therapeutic relationship is established (LaTaillade, 2006). For example, Boyd-Franklin (1989) states that some African American families tend to keep secrets around sexual abuse, paternity (not informing children who their fathers are or naming a person as a child's biological father who is not), substance abuse, and skin color issues. Domestic violence is another common family secret. These secrets carry shame and guilt for couples and families and clinicians should not try to "uncover" these secrets in an initial interview. Being sensitive to how and why couples hold onto certain family secrets (most often it is fear of judgment) goes a long way in establishing rapport. These secrets are sometimes revealed later in the counseling process; however, "telling the family business" is frowned upon in the African American community, and thus when family secrets are discovered, they need to be handled with sensitivity and respect.

Assessment Tools/Inventories for Couples

Several measures that clinicians can use to augment information gained in the clinical interview are mentioned below. Obviously, before using any assessment tool or evaluating areas of assessment suggested in this chapter, the clinician should use his/her clinical judgment to determine the appropriateness of our suggested assessment practices and have the training necessary to implement these measures. Assessment should be tailored to individual couples' needs because although there are common assessment areas to all couples, others will need to be modified to the specific couple with whom one is working. Hood and Johnson (1997) suggest several assessment inventories for use with couples. Although somewhat dated, the information gained from these inventories remains highly relevant to the couples' counseling process. Only brief descriptions of each are included. As with most currently available inventories, few, if any, have been used exclusively with African American couples. Most have not been tested on Black couples, and may contain an inherent Eurocentric framework; these assessments are simply tools to aid the assessment process and provide the clinician with helpful information about the couple. To use these inventories in culturally sensitive ways with African American couples, the clinician should examine the inventory carefully prior to giving it to the couple to determine if there are discriminatory items. Obviously, a couple's reading ability and level of education should be taken into account before using a paper/pencil measure. If either or both struggle with reading, clinicians might consider administering the instrument verbally or finding a more appropriate assessment tool. Finally, the inventory should be discussed with the couple after they take it to assess the couple's feelings and thoughts about the inventory, whether they believe it provides an accurate reflection of them as a couple and their issues, and the couple's reaction to the inventory's items.

Here are some suggested inventories by Hood and Johnson (1997).

- *The Marital Satisfaction Inventory* (MSI) (Snyder, 1981) is a self-report inventory designed to assess marital interaction and the extent of marital distress.

Scores are obtained on 11 different scales, such as Affective Communication, Problem-Solving Communication, Disagreement about Finances, Sexual Dissatisfaction, Conflict Over Child-Rearing, and a Global Distress Scale.

- *Taylor-Johnson Temperament Analysis* (TJTA) (Taylor, Morrison, & Nash, 1985) is designed for use in individual, premarital and marital counseling. It consists of 180 items equally divided among nine scales measuring traits such as Nervous–Composed, Depressive–Lighthearted, Responsive–Inhibited, Dominant–Submissive and Self-Disciplined–Impulsive. Norms are based on large samples.

- *Family Environment Scale* (FES) (Moos & Moos, 1986) is a social climate scale of 90 items yielding 10 scores from scales such as Cohesion, Intellectual–Cultural Orientation, Active Recreational Orientation, Moral–Religious Emphasis, Expressiveness, and Control.

- *Triangular Love Scale* (TLS) (Sternberg, 1987) is a 45-item scale that measures the three components of romantic relationships Sternberg identified: intimacy, passion and commitment. According to Sternberg, all three components must be assessed in evaluating the quality of a romantic relationship.

- *Myers-Briggs Type Indicator* (MBTI) (Myers & McCaulley, 1985) is often used in counseling with couples and families. Here its use is to help couples understand their differences in the four dimensions measured by the MBTI and therefore help them use these differences constructively rather than destructively. The Myers-Briggs test describes four basic areas of personality: introversion versus extroversion; sensing versus intuition; thinking versus feeling; and judging versus perceiving. This tool can be used to help couples explore these dimensions which shape perception and decision-making:

  1 Extraversion versus Introversion (E vs. I) describes how a person gets energized.
  2 Sensing versus intuition (S vs. N) describes how a person takes in information.
  3 Thinking versus feeling (T vs. F) describes the means a person uses to make decisions.
  4 Judging versus perceiving (J vs. P) describes the speed with which a person makes decisions.

- *Genograms*, which are used in family systems therapies and serve as:

"a map that provides a graphic representation of a family structure. It involves the collection of information about three generations of a family and organizes the information into a kind of family tree. It contains family members' ages, major events such as births, deaths, marriages, divorces, adoptions, and conflicts. It can also contain dysfunctional patterns such as sexual abuse, infidelity, and substance abuse"

(Hood & Johnson, 1997, p. 246)

Gottman (1999) also provides several relevant assessment measures that have strong potential use with African American couples. Reginald Jones (1996) edited two volumes entitled the *Handbook of Tests and Measurements for Black Populations*. He included several measures for Black couples and families, addressing marital quality, racial identity and consciousness, acculturation, spirituality, and worldview. Below are brief descriptions of the three most relevant for couples' counseling.

- *A Typology of Household Structure in the Black Community* (Dressler and Haworth-Hoeppner) which measures the nature of household and family structure in the Black community.
- *Measures of Marital Quality* (Taylor and McMaster-Olmes) which measures marital quality based on four areas: exchange disposition, communication efficiency, receptive accuracy, and instrumental competence which affirm the importance of communication as process and outcome.
- *The Cultural Mistrust Inventory* (CMI) (F. Terrell, S. Terrell, and Nickerson). The CMI was developed to assess the extent to which Blacks mistrust whites in four areas: 1) educational and training settings; 2) political and legal situations; 3) work and business environments; and 4) interpersonal and social contexts.

As will be discussed in Chapter 10 on pastoral counseling, African Americans are overwhelmingly spiritual and largely religious. Therefore spirituality is an important area of assessment for most African American couples. Two of Jones' spirituality measures include:

- *Life Attitude Inventory: A Measure of Spiritual Orientation* (LAI) (Jackson-Lowman, Rogers, Zhang, Zhao, & Brathwaite-Tull). The LAI defines spirituality as spiritual orientation which can be expressed both integratively and disintegratively, and focuses on the everyday expressions of human spirituality.
- *The Armstrong Measure of Spirituality* (AMOS) (Armstrong). This instrument explores several dimensions of spirituality as relevant to African Americans.

In addition, the *Assessment of Spirituality and Religious Sentiments (Aspires) Scale* (Piedmont, 2004) has been shown to be a useful tool. It was developed explicitly to identify those fundamental, motivational aspects of spirituality that underlie all religious traditions. It provides very specific operationalizations for the constructs of religiosity and spirituality. Cross-cultural and cross-faith research has supported the utility and generalizability of the ASPIRES scales (Piedmont, 2004).

A strong working knowledge and training in the use of any assessment tool is needed in order to be an effective and ethical clinician.

Conclusion

The initial assessment process sets the tone for couples' therapy. When done well, couples feel safe, understood and hopeful about therapy and their relationship. This is especially important with African American couples as they are more likely to be wary of counseling and are more likely to drop out earlier in the process than majority couples. This chapter has highlighted specific areas of assessment with African American couples and provided suggestions for rapport-building and strengths-based assessment strategies. The following case study illustrates some of the strategies we suggest in this chapter.

Case Study

Simon (34) and Chandra (42) have come to counseling because Simon wants premarital counseling before they get married next year. He has recently begun seeing an individual counselor to work on issues related to his childhood. Chandra is very reluctant to participate in counseling and is only doing so at the behest of Simon. Simon is a barber and Chandra is a Licensed Professional Nurse. When asked about what brought them to counseling, Simon states that "we can't communicate at all" and Chandra agrees with him. I explained to the couple that the first session is usually where I explore the reasons they came to counseling, get some background and demographic information from them, and collaboratively develop a course of treatment depending on their needs. Although Chandra is reluctant, she is motivated to make Simon happy, so she agrees. Simon has stated that "there will be no wedding without counseling, because we got too many issues to count." The two have been living together for three months. Chandra has an eight-year-old son from a previous relationship. His father is not involved in his son's life.

The Clinical Couple's Interview

When asked, "Why do you want to get married?", Chandra replied that she has been feeling guilty about sleeping with Simon when she is not married, given her religious background. Simon replies, "it's just time—I'll be 35 soon." In interacting with the couple, it is clear that although they love one another, neither appears sure if they want to be married. I observed that the couple often disconnect from one another during areas of conflict in session. In this initial interview, I briefly assess their views on gender through gender role analysis and how they view the distribution of power within their relationship. Simon describes himself as an "emotional man" and apologizes for this. Chandra has said to him in arguments, "Why don't you act like a man?" Simon accuses Chandra of being "emotionally cold." The couple frequently argue over money issues (Simon saves; Chandra spends). Both are religious Christians, although Simon only recently began attending church again after a long absence.

The Clinical Individual's Interview

In interviewing Simon, I find that he initially came from a two-parent home, until his parents divorced when he was six. He remembers taking this very hard, since he was unaware that they were having any problems. Additionally, Simon stated that he "worshipped" his dad, who died when Simon was 14, saying, "he was my idea of what a man should be. He could fix anything and he took me everywhere. I feel like I lost myself and all he would have taught me when he died." When Simon's parents divorced, his mom turned to drugs and his dad's issues with alcohol significantly increased. When Simon was 14, his dad came to pick him up one day, and had a heart attack in front of him and died. Simon states that he's never gotten over it. After his father's death, his mom's substance abuse issues increased, Simon moved out and states that, "I spent the next ten years high and drunk but somehow managed to get a barber's license." Simon also states that he has been involved with many, many women and struggles to remain faithful in all his relationships. I have conceptualized Simon's core (personal) issues as: attachment issues, trust issues, previous trauma, anger issues and unresolved grief. Simon also struggles with his own individual identity as a man.

In interviewing Chandra, she presents herself as "having it all together." When asked how she deals with difficult times, she states, "I just try to keep it moving and not think about it too much. Simon wants to think about everything, I just want to look forward." Chandra is an only child of two middle class parents. Her parents divorced when she was 20—she states that "they should've been divorced much earlier." Her mother is white, her father, African American; however, Chandra considers herself to be African American. Chandra tells me that she had some significant health issues when growing up which prevented her from being involved in physical activity but believes that these issues have "made her stronger." Chandra is a proud single mother. She describes herself as very religious and expresses her feelings of guilt that she is sexually active with Simon without being married. When asked about her relationship with her parents, Chandra describes her relationship with her father as "disconnected and distant" and with her mother as "conflictual at best, since she married a man I don't care for."

I have conceptualized Chandra's core (personal) issues as: trust issues, a tendency to minimize the emotional impact of her past issues with rejections and painful family of origin issues, and she has a fear of becoming emotionally connected to a romantic partner. This accounts for her "coldness/harshness" towards Simon.

Specific Factors to Assess Based on Interview Data

In Simon's individual interview, it became clear that he struggles with post traumatic stress disorder (from witnessing the death of his father), depression and anger issues. He is addressing these issues in individual therapy, but I would work with the couple to educate them on how their individual issues impact their relationship. Additionally, in the initial intake assessment, we discussed some factors unique to Black couples, which helped them contextualize their current struggles. In our second session, we continued exploring how gender and power issues impact them as well as how racial discrimination and the internalization of stereotypes impact their relationship. For example, Chandra stated her mother and grandmother taught her not to trust black men. Simon revealed that he viewed his parent's divorce as his mother's fault and thinks that he has struggled being faithful to women because he does not trust them. A gender role and power role analysis will be performed throughout treatment to help ascertain how this couple is impacted by traditional views of gender and power. Both couples appear to have trust issues deeply impacting their ability to be emotionally intimate with one another. Financial issues are another area of assessment covered within the first two sessions of treatment. Chandra and Simon's financial values appear to be totally different, causing significant conflict in their relationship. Other important areas of assessment with this couple include:

- *Religious differences*—Both Chandra and Simon describe themselves as religious. Although Chandra is more religious than Simon, Simon states that he feels very good about "getting back to church" and is grateful to Chandra for reintroducing him to faith as a foundation for their life together. This couple appears to be on the same page regarding the importance of religion in their lives. This is a strength they share.
- *Emotional maturity*—Chandra is seven years older than Simon. There are times when she appears to be more emotionally mature than Simon; however, Simon more readily admits his weaknesses and emotional responses. Simon is also more motivated to seek counseling to work on his personal issues, but not always willing to explore how his behavior

impacts their relationship. Chandra is less insightful than Simon and also often unwilling to explore how her behavior impacts their relationship. The couple appear to be matched on emotional maturity but are emotionally mature in different ways. It is a strength, if the couple is able to learn from one another; if not, this could be detrimental to their relationship. Currently, it serves as a source of conflict as both find it difficult to understand or respect one another's point of view.

- *Poor problem-solving skills*—This couple does not appear to solve problems well. Their disagreements frequently end with one person leaving and screaming obscenities at the other or threats to break up. This is a problematic area that is a good area of focus for treatment.
- *Fictive kin*—This is an area of significant conflict for the couple as Chandra has an extensive network of friends (male and female) and Simon does not. He is very jealous of this and acts out his jealousy by consistently accusing Chandra of cheating on him. Chandra complains that she has stopped using her Facebook account because Simon always finds something on there to "cross examine her about." This is an area of significant conflict for the couple. Chandra feels that Simon's jealousy is going to destroy their relationship. Simon agrees that this is an issue in their relationship.
- *Racial identity*—Both Chandra and Simon have strong identities as Black individuals. Although Chandra is biracial, she does not identify as such.
- *Communication*—This is an area the couple both agree needs work. This is their stated presenting issue for coming to counseling.
- *Family secrets*—In my joint and individual assessment of the couple, I have, so far, not encountered any family secrets.

Therapeutic tools employed in the assessment process included humor, honesty, directness, warmth, psychoeducation about the counseling process and unique issues Black couples may face that impact their relationship, and self-disclosure about communication issues in my own marriage and how we resolved them. These were effective in helping to establish a solid rapport with the couple.

We have agreed to contract for 12 sessions to work on the issues the couple has presented with as well as other issues discovered in the assessment process. The couple and I are clear about the direction of treatment. We will modify the treatment plan as needed.

No formal assessment measures were used with this couple as they have a clear understanding of the things they wish to accomplish in therapy. Additionally, they are highly motivated for therapy and wish to resolve some of their most serious issues prior to getting married in a year.

This case study highlights both traditional and culturally specific areas of assessment used with a specific African American couple. Because the assessment process with this couple was so thorough, treatment began as an extension of the assessment process and clear areas of treatment were delineated. A treatment plan was collaboratively developed by the counselor and couple. Assessment was ongoing and the treatment plan was modified as things within the couple came up in treatment.

References

Boyd-Franklin, N. (1987). The contribution of family therapy models to the treatment of Black families. *Psychotherapy*. 24, 621–629.

Boyd-Franklin, N. (1989). *Black families in therapy: A multisystems approach*. New York: Guilford Press.

Boyd-Franklin, N. (2002). *Black families in therapy*. New York: Guilford Press.

Boyd-Franklin, N. (2003). *Black families in therapy: Understanding the African American experience* (2nd ed.). New York: Guilford Press.

Constantine, M.A. (1998). Developing competence in multicultural assessment: Implications for counseling psychology training and practice. *The Counseling Psychologist*, 26, 922–929.

Constantine, M.G. (2002). Predictors of satisfaction with counseling: Racial and ethnic minority clients' attitudes toward counseling and ratings of their counselors' general and multicultural counseling competence. *Journal of Counseling Psychology*. 49, 2, 255–263.

Constantine, M.S. (2001). Perspectives on multicultural supervision. *Journal of Multicultural Counseling and Development*. 29, 2, 98–101.

Foster, V.A., & May, K.M. (2003). Counseling women for feminist perspectives. In N.A. Vacc, S.B. DeVaney, & J.M. Brendel (Eds.), *Counseling multicultural and diverse populations: Strategies for practitioners* (pp. 163–187). New York, NY: Brunner-Routledge.

Gottman, J.M. (1999). *The marriage clinic: A scientifically based marital therapy*. New York: Norton.

Gurman, A.S., & Jacobson, N.S. (2002). *Clinical handbook of couple therapy*. New York: Guilford Press.

Herlihy, B., & Corey, G. (2001). Feminist therapy. In G. Corey (Ed.), *Theory and practice of counseling* (6th ed.) (pp. 340–381). Belmont, CA: Brooks/Cole.

Hines, P., & Boyd-Franklin, N. (1996). African American families. *Ethnicity and family therapy* (2nd ed.) (pp. 66–84). New York: Guilford Press.

Hood, A.B., & Johnson, R.W. (1997). *Assessment in counseling: A guide to the use of psychological assessment procedures* (2nd ed.). Alexandria, VA: American Counseling Association.

Imber-Black, E. (1988). *Families and larger systems: A family therapist's guide through the labyrinth (The Guilford Family Therapy)*. New York: Guilford Press.

Ivey, A.E., Bradford-Ivey, M., & Zalaquett, C.P. (2010). *Multicultural interviewing and counseling: Facilitating client development in a multicultural society*. Belmont, CA: Brooks/Cole, Cengage Learning.

Jones, R.L. (Ed.) (1996). *Handbook of Tests and Measurements for Black Populations Vols. 1 & 2. (1996)*. Hampton, VA: Cobb & Henry Publishers.

LaTaillade, J.J. (2006). Considerations for treatment of African American couple relationships. *Journal of Cognitive Psychotherapy: An International Quarterly*, 20, 4, 341–358.

Marecek, J. (2001). Bringing feminist issues to therapy. In B. Slife, R. Williams, & S. Barlow (Eds.), *Critical issues in psychotherapy* (pp. 305–319). Thousand Oaks, CA: Sage Publications.

Moos, R.H., & Moos, B.S. (1986). *Family environment scale manual*. Palo Alto, CA: Consulting Psychologists as cited in A.B. Hood, & R.W. Johnson (Eds.) (1997). *Assessment in Counseling: A Guide to the Use of Psychological Assessment Procedures, 2nd ed*. Alexandria, VA: American Counseling Association.

Morrow, S.L., & Hawxhurst, D.M. (1998). Feminist therapy: Integrating political analysis in counseling and psychotherapy. In M. Hill (Ed.), *Feminist therapy as a political act* (pp. 37–50). New York: Haworth Press.

Myers, I.B., & McCaulley, M.H. (1985). *Manual: A guide to the development and use of the Myers-Briggs Type Indicator*. Palo Alto, CA: Consulting Psychologist as cited in A.B. Hood, & R.W. Johnson (Eds.) (1997) *Assessment in Counseling: A Guide to the Use of Psychological Assessment Procedures, 2nd ed*. Alexandria, VA: American Counseling Association.

Piedmont, R.L. (2004). *Assessment of spirituality and religious sentiments*, technical manual. Baltimore, MD: Piedmont.

Roberto-Forman, L. (2002). Transgenerational marital therapy. In A.S. Gurman, & N.S. Jacobson (Eds.). *Clinical handbook of couple therapy*. New York: Guilford.

Rowe, D.M., & Rowe, S.L. (2009). Conversations in Marriage©: An African-centered marital intervention. In M.E. Gallardo & B. McNeill (Eds.), *Intersections of multiple identities: A casebook of evidence-based practices with diverse populations* (pp. 59–84). New York: Routledge.

Rowe, T.D., & Webb-Msmejai, F. (2004). African-centered psychology in the community. In R. Jones (Ed), *Black psychology*, 4th ed. (pp. 701–721). Hampton, VA: Cobb & Henry.

Santos De Barona, M., & Dutton, M.A. (1997). Feminist perspectives on assessment. In J. Worell, & M.G. Johnson (Eds.), *Shaping the future of feminist psychology: Education, research, and practice* (pp. 37–56). Washington, DC: American Psychological Association.

Snyder, D.K. (1981). *Marriage satisfaction inventory manual*. Los Angeles, CA: Western Psychological Services as cited in A.B. Hood, & R.W. Johnson (Eds.) (1997) *Assessment in Counseling: A Guide to the Use of Psychological Assessment Procedures, 2nd ed*. Alexandria, VA: American Counseling Association.

Somé, S.E. (1999). *The spirit of intimacy: Ancient teachings in the ways of relationships*. Berkeley, CA: Berkeley Hills Books.

Sternberg, R.J. (1987). *The triangle of love: Intimacy, passion, commitment*. New York: Basic Books as cited in A.B. Hood, & R.W. Johnson (Eds.) (1997) *Assessment in Counseling: A Guide to the Use of Psychological Assessment Procedures, 2nd ed*. Alexandria, VA: American Counseling Association.

Sue, D.W., & Sue, D. (2003). *Counseling the culturally different: Theory and practice* (4th ed.). New York: John Wiley & Sons.

Sue, S., Fujino, D.C., Hu, L., Takeuchi, D.T., & Zane, N.W.S. (1991). Community mental health services for ethnic minority groups: A test of the cultural responsiveness hypothesis. *Journal of Consulting and Clinical*. 59, 4, 533–540.

Taylor, R.M., Morrison, W.L., & Nash, L. (1985). *Taylor-Johnson temperament analysis handbook*. Los Angeles, CA: Western Psychological Services as cited in A.B. Hood, & R.W. Johnson (Eds.) (1997) *Assessment in Counseling: A Guide to the Use of Psychological Assessment Procedures, 2nd ed*. Alexandria, VA: American Counseling Association.

EXPERT INTERVIEW

Dr. Sandra Lyons-Rowe is a faculty member and Coordinator of Psychological Services at Santa Monica College, in Santa Monica, California and has been a Clinical Director for EMQ/Hollygrove Children and Family Services where she was responsible for the oversight of several community-based mental health programs. She currently shares a private practice her husband, Dr. Daryl Rowe.

Dr. Daryl M. Rowe is a professor of psychology at the Graduate School of Education and Psychology of Pepperdine University. He is President-Elect of the Association of Black Psychologists and shares a private practice with his wife, Dr. Sandra Lyons Rowe.

Today's Black couples face some challenging issues. How do you think that the issues of Black couples have changed over the last 60 years? How have they stayed the same?

In general, we think therapists need a solid foundation in understanding the nuances of African American culture, history and the broader set of socio-political factors that impact the world in which African American couples must seek common perspectives for negotiating life's dilemmas. What makes working with Black couples unique is that in addition to the everyday struggles of trying to identify suitable mates, maintain commitment, communicate effectively and resolve conflicts about myriad challenges that all couples must negotiate, Black couples must manage these challenges within a socio-political context that discounts, diminishes and dismisses the existence and viability of healthy Black relationships. The assaults on the idea that Black relationships are sustainable—through media (print, movie, literature, music) pose particular obstacles for Black couples. Thus, therapists-in-training must develop an affirmative orientation to the *idea* of viable, sustainable healthy African American relationships and an informed perspective about the socio-political context in which African American couples seek to thrive. Given these structural impediments, from our perspective, therapists must start with a perspective that sustaining African American relationships is *bigger* than the individual couple; our relationships must also serve as beacons to our communities.

What suggestions do you have for training therapists to work specifically with Black couples?
What skills do Black couples need in today's world to stay together?

Skills present an interesting conundrum for African American couples, largely because most of the literature on relational skills discounts and undermines the socio-political issues within which our relationships must take root. Similar to farming in a desert, the sets of cultivation skills must be different [in African American couples' relationships]. To farm in the desert, one has to bring in necessary fluids to nourish the fields, shield the young seedlings from the harsh sun, and be much more attentive to any of a host of environmental threats to the seedlings.

Thus, African American couples need to learn that thriving is dependent on collective collaboration with other couples, so that nourishment happens through more than the individual gifts of the partners. Couples need to rely upon and seek assistance from other couples, both for support and meaning; couples need to learn to separate socio-political issues from uniquely personal issues. African American couples need to develop strong negotiation skills—ways for identifying challenges that emerge from personal or self issues, interpersonal or others' issues and extra-personal or contextual issues that emerge from a broader world that still maintains negative stereotypes and biases towards persons of African ancestry.

Finally, adequate problem-solving skills are essential for managing both the expected and unexpected challenges we must overcome during our relationships. Most of us realize that relationships are fundamentally about compromise—both partners regularly do things or don't do things that create problems within our relationships. Minor problems are routine—we need to expect them to occur, acknowledge them and learn to move forward. However, major problems are also common—life is uncompromising—tough times happen often, irrespective of what we do, and sometimes because of what we do. Thus, couples need to be prepared that problems will emerge—often and regularly—and, as partners, we must learn to bring our best problem-solving skills home to those with whom we seek permanence.

There is so much attention paid to the negatives of African American romantic relationships.
What strengths do AA couples bring to their relationships? Common weakness of struggling
Black couples?

Generally, an important strength for African American couples is their commitment to build relationships that have potential for strengthening and promoting community welfare and well-being. Black couples, especially men, tend to endorse responsibility for supporting community development and empowerment. Similarly, in our experience, African American couples tend to have more flexible gender role expectations—men tend to participate more fully in childcare and household responsibilities and women have long histories of workplace employment.

Another strength for African American couples is a shared tendency towards embracing a spiritual and/or religious family life. Often this shared spirituality provides a foundation to unite couples during difficult times, ties them to other families for support and encouragement, and helps to promote ongoing purpose and meaning outside of themselves.

African American couples who share effective communication skills more easily sort through the various sets of socio-political issues in a way that decreases the chances that these issues serve as a wedge between the partners. Implied is the idea that the communication is honest, responsible, non-accusatory and non-violent. Couples need to learn to develop conversational styles that rise above profanity, name-calling, absolutism and shouting. A practical suggestion that we offer to couples with whom we work is to have their most difficult conversations walking up a steep hill; the effort required to conquer the hill will help minimize the energy available for escalating the conversation.

Finally, consistent with the notion of extended self-identity, where African Americans see their individual senses of self emerging out of collective/communal relationships, Black couples bring a strong reliance on extended families to their relationships and marriages. Extended families, although sometimes sources of considerable stress, more regularly serve as sources of support, encouragement, importance and perseverance. In addition, the reliance on extended communal support often leads African American couples to create extended families when they find themselves separated by distance or circumstance, from their families of origin.

Far too many Black couples underestimate the effects of negative socio-political factors on the sustainability of their relationships; they often personalize contextual challenges and spend a considerable amount of time criticizing each other for these structural problems, often undermining the strength of their relationships.

This lack of critical consciousness can lead to commitment uncertainty, sometimes resulting in infidelity and long-term trust issues. In addition, due to the historical legacy of workplace discrimination and differential compensation for similar work, many African American couples face financial challenges—both hardship and poor financial planning and management.

Lastly, many struggling African American couples are uncertain with how to manage the multiple influences of their extended families and friends. Due to the press of the broader societal value on rugged individualism, many African American couples struggle with finding the balance for incorporating significant others into their relationships. As mentioned previously, from our perspective, relationships are communal—good relationships require the input of others to keep them strong, nourishing and vibrant.

What specific advice would you have for non-Black clinicians working with Black couples? Specific advice for Black clinicians?

Non-Black clinicians need to develop appreciation for the unique cultural history and values of persons of African ancestry and seek to understand the resonance of those values within the sets of problems or concerns that Black couples bring into treatment. Given the longstanding and pervasive impact of racism, African Americans tend to be wary of mental health and psychological treatment, and thus may present in a somewhat more cautious or guarded fashion, being very attentive to a broad array of meta-communication issues, e.g. congruence between what a therapist says and how s/he says it.

When clinicians utilize a more narrative, story-telling conversational style, African American couples tend to be open and responsive to inquiries into the successes and challenges of their relationships. This tendency towards story-telling can be quite productive for effective problem solving.

Non-Black clinicians need to develop comfort with stylistic nuances (vocalisms, volume, speed, gesturing, etc.) and comfort with thematic material (discussions about real and perceived experiences of racism/discrimination, privilege and power).

Similarly, Black clinicians must be capable of responding to emotion—to anticipate and articulate affect that may be unstated or understated. They must be willing to use metaphorical speech and overlaid speech—to communicate using the symbolic and rhythmic flow of conversation, that is, energetic and connective, versus staid and detached. Black clinicians must be more direct and clear about insights instead of tentative and ambiguous; and clinicians must be willing to utilize a higher degree of activity versus a lower degree of activity (Rowe & Webb-Msemaji, 2004).

Therapeutic style is key for producing an environment for change to occur. Since there are few therapeutic approaches and practices grounded in African cultural assumptions, the *person* of the clinician turns out to be the primary technique/tool for forming successful therapeutic/healing relationships. Thus, clinicians must demonstrate a humility that expresses comfort, familiarity and knowledge while relating as collaborator and guide. Implied is clinician appreciation of the various socio-cultural elements of the couples' experiences, which contextualize them more fully.

All clinicians must communicate an open invitation to question—encouraging questions about the therapeutic process, clinician, theoretical leanings, rules of engagement, length of time of treatment, possibility for the involvement of others, expectations about roles, and responsibilities for the couple and clinician. Allowing couples to scrutinize the process enhances clinician credibility. It is important to assume that questions exist, and the therapeutic task is to make the asking of them normal and commonplace.

What cultural competencies are needed for working with Black couples?

The shift that must be emphasized when working with African American couples is to see Black couples as the foundation of vibrant communities, not merely individual relationships. Clinicians must learn to grow and support the re-establishment of strong communities, and communities consist of families— mothers, fathers, sisters and brothers, working hard, living easily, laughing and loving— again.

Other cultural competencies were addressed in answers above.

Are there specific Afrocentric approaches/philosophies you would suggest in working with Black couples?

Sobonfu Somé (1999) in a wonderful small text—*The Spirit of Intimacy*—states that relationships are not private; she argues that relationships belong to the community. Somé's point of view grows out of a West African context, in which the survival of the community directly impacted the survival of its members. As we move into the second decade of the new millennium, it becomes increasingly clear that persons of African ancestry in the United States and throughout the Americas need to recognize more clearly that our survival as individuals is directly impacted by our survival as a community. We believe this is a powerful idea for transforming marriage within the African American community.

Somé defines community as "…the spirit, the guiding light of the tribe, whereby people come together in order to fulfill a specific purpose, to help others fulfill their purpose, and to take care of one another" (p. 36). This notion of community is sufficiently different from that which is common in the United States, where community is defined more by its physical boundaries than its inspiring purpose. Imagine the possibilities, if community was defined more in collaborative terms, where people came together to assist one another in discerning and accomplishing their purposes. Imagine the transformative potential these shared purposes might have on how people—in community—relate to each other. Imagine!

Somé's idea of community places emphasis on the responsibility of community to safeguard the voices of its members, such that each person is heard—valued and affirmed—and each person's gifts are cultivated and freely given to the world. Thus, community, as Somé suggests, serves to anchor persons to something bigger than themselves—a grander scheme, a higher purpose, a reclaimed set of standards—providing both a sense of belonging and purpose. We propose that the basis for those standards is rooted in the social theory of African-centeredness.

Similarly, we share a range of African proverbs that are congruent with the core of our message for and about African American couples (Rowe & Rowe, 2009). Our reasons: to demonstrate that our ancestors provide insight into our current struggles—if we but take time to listen. We believe that marriage allows us to fulfill our life purposes; that we come together in Spirit to fulfill our purpose or destiny; and intimacy—the deeply felt sense of belonging—is also for fulfilling our purpose, for bettering community, and for the expression of Spirit. Marriage is the means for offering the gifts we carry; meaningful marriage happens when we fulfill our life purpose through providing our gifts.

What are the advantages of marriage/long-term committed relationships for Black couples and the Black community?

Traditionally marriage has been the marker of adulthood. It has been seen as the focus of existence—the point where all members of a given community meet—the departed, the living and those yet to be born. Thus, marriage establishes and maintains family, creates and sustains the ties of kinship and is the basis of community. From that historical perspective, marriage is seen as a duty, a requirement for society, and is essential for community—the basis of civilization.

We believe that the rebuilding of African American marriages is the task of serious people—the responsibility of grown men and women. It is our duty, our obligation and our commitment to love again, to build upon our love and marry again, and to re-establish vibrant, healthy, interlocking and supportive communities where our children can laugh, learn and live long productive lives.

Include anything else you believe relevant to this text

We believe that marriage has the capacity to provide us with ongoing insight into who we are, have been and will become. Thus, it is and has to be bigger than mere personal happiness—marriage is as much about building community and preserving community as being in love. Our goal has been to initiate a series of conversations that center persons of African ancestry in the joys and challenges of *holding hands* over time and throughout life. Given the particular challenges with which African/Black folks must grapple in the distinct realities of the United States, we grow more persuaded that we must look back to move forward; that is, we must develop strategies that emerge out of our shared cultural wellsprings to craft solutions to seemingly intractable problems. Strengthening marriages and improving relationships within our community provides a unified approach for addressing multiple complex issues.

8

COUPLES THERAPY WITH AFRICAN AMERICAN COUPLES

Specific Treatment Strategies and Techniques

Chante' D. DeLoach

Little focus has been given to specific strategies and interventions when working with African American romantic partnerships within the larger couples' literature. What little has been done is often generically focused on "diversity" and "multiculturalism" and lacking specificity for the unique needs of African American couples (Sexton, 2008). Thus, the focus of the present chapter is to: 1) provide a brief overview of the strengths and primary issues frequently presented by African American couples seeking counseling; 2) explore the leading behavioral, intrapsychic, relational, systemic, and humanistic therapeutic interventions with a particular emphasis on how these may be utilized with African American romantic partnerships; and 3) discuss culturally centered models for approaching couples work with African Americans.

Couples present to counseling for myriad issues including infidelity, poor communication, child behavioral issues, and overall decreased marital satisfaction to name a few (Whisman, Dixon, & Johnson, 1997). Within the little research that does focus specifically on African American couples, issues such as: the role of racism, sexism, and economic oppression on relational stress, gendered socialization differences and its influence on marital roles, and the role of extended family are highlighted as being prominent (Boyd-Franklin, Kelly, & Durham, 2008). These issues are discussed in detail elsewhere in this text. The current chapter will focus on appropriate therapeutic modalities to use with African American couples.

Empirically Supported Treatments, Evidence-Based Practice, and Practice-Based Evidence

Before exploring leading theoretical approaches to therapeutic engagement with African American couples, a clear understanding of the importance of and cautions in considering empirically supported treatments must be noted.

Within the psychological literature, various terminologies are utilized to describe empirical support demonstrating the effectiveness of particular interventions including *empirically supported treatments* (ESTs), *evidence-based practice* (EBP), and, more recently, *practice-based evidence*. Empirically supported treatments refer to specific clinical interventions that have garnered empirical support for their efficacy in the treatment of a specific diagnosed disorder (Chambless & Ollendick, 2001). EBP refers to a process that involves the use of best evidence in individual clinical decision-making (Sackett et al., 1996; Spring, 2007). It is important to note that efficacy may not translate to patient experienced therapeutic change and therefore does not equal "effectiveness," especially when it comes to African Americans because when this population is included in empirical studies their sample size is usually small (Griner & Smith, 2006). Toward that end, more recent definitions have focused on the integration of the best available research with clinical expertise in the context of patient characteristics, culture, and preferences (American Psychological Association, 2005). Such definitions, however, have been met with much criticism given their detached stance from the evidence of practitioners and clients alike. Yet, it is the paradigm based upon data from clients and practitioners in real clinical settings that has been coined "practice-based evidence" (Barkham & Mellor-Clark, 2003).

Most relevant to the present discussion are the cultural concerns of manualized EST approaches to clinical work with African Americans. As Gallardo and McNeill (2009) indicate, "ESTs have their place in the development of culturally appropriate treatment methodologies. However, we also advocate for the expansion of perspectives in the development of culturally consistent and appropriate treatment methods for individuals representing multiple identities" (p. 313). Bernal and Scharrón-del-Rio (2001) further note that implementing only ESTs in our work across cultures is another form of cultural imperialism. The universal application of empirically supported treatments without consideration of specific cultural norms is hegemonic and may fail to meet the clinical needs of African Americans. Thus, we must move toward a practice in psychology that is grounded in a cultural perspective and supported by multiple forms of evidence. Moreover, empirical findings indicate that culturally specific interventions are four times more effective than those applied universally across client demographics (Griner & Smith, 2006). Therefore this chapter will give particular emphasis not only to interventions receiving the most empirical support, but also to those that are culturally consistent with an African American ethos. With this background, let us consider specific therapeutic models and their applicability with African American couples.

Behavioral Therapies

Behavioral therapies have traditionally received significant empirical support in the reduction of symptoms associated with numerous clinical diagnoses including relational distress (see Baucom et al., 1998; Christensen, McGinn, & Williams, 2009). Modern derivations of behavioral therapies such as cognitive behavioral and integrative behavioral therapies are based upon traditional behavioral couple therapy (TBCT). Briefly, TBCT is focused primarily on the ratio of positive to negative interpersonal exchanges and emphasizes operant conditioning. "A traditional behavioral model posits that behaviors of both members of a couple are shaped, strengthened, weakened, and can be modified in therapy by consequences provided by environmental events, particularly those involving the other partner" (Baucom, Epstein, LaTaillade, & Kirby, 2008, p. 32).

Namely, it is theorized that if a partner receives positive consequences from positive relational behaviors, he or she would be more likely to repeat such behaviors, which is thought to lead to greater relational satisfaction. However, outcome studies have indicated that increased subjectively rated positive behavioral exchanges have not resulted in commensurate increases in relational satisfaction (Baucom et al., 2008; Halford, Sanders, & Behrens, 1993) perhaps because of the discrepancies in partner perceptions of positive behaviors. Results of the empirical research have led to increased focus on the cognitive and affective components of the relational experience, which has been seen in more recent derivations of behavioral therapies. Because more contemporary derivations of behavioral couples' therapy appear to be more prominent in the literature, these will be discussed in further detail and specifically its applicability with African American couples.

Cognitive-Behavioral Couple Therapy

Cognitive-behavioral couple therapy (CBCT) emerged in the early 1980s as a confluence of behavioral couple therapy, cognitive therapy, and research on social cognition and information processing and is an empirically supported intervention for distressed couples. CBCT is most known for its focus on: 1) discrete analyzable (and therefore changeable) aspects of relationships over larger core issues such as emotional intimacy; and 2) couple's cognitive processing and behavioral interactions over enduring personality variables that may shape relational experience (Epstein & Baucom, 2002). While CBCT has not ignored emotion completely, emotions have traditionally been given secondary status and have been viewed largely as a result of the partners' relationship behaviors and cognitions which reflect their roots in behaviorism. Where there has been inclusion of emotion, its focus has been on negative valences of emotions and how to decrease them, which might be considered a weakness of the theory, especially as it relates to couples work. Couples' issues frequently contain a high level of emotional content expressed by both partners (e.g. anger, hurt, disappointment, etc.). Recent theoretical advances, such as within enhanced CBCT, also address characteristics that each partner brings to the couple relationship, explaining why partners behave and interpret events in maladaptive ways.

Some of the critiques of the theory are that for couples to derive optimum fulfillment from their relationships, greater emphasis must be given to the role of positive behavior, cognitions, and emotions (Epstein & Baucom, 2002). Further, couples do not exist in a social vacuum and are influenced by external and environmental stressors, as well as by environmental resources that are available to help them meet their personal and relationship needs (ibid).

The role of the CBCT therapist, then, is one who is active and engaged, and often takes on a directive or didactic approach particularly in assessment and early phases of treatment or with clients who have a difficult time with emotional or behavioral regulation (Epstein & Baucom, 2002). Yet, balancing these roles with the necessary emotional support is deemed critical to the therapeutic alliance. Types of interventions utilized include the use of questionnaires in addition to self-report in the clinical interview to assess such issues as partner satisfaction and individual relational needs as well as screening for domestic violence. "Guided behavior change" or "behavior exchange interventions" refers to behaviorally focused interventions with no skills building focus but may attend to increasing the frequency of positive interactions. Skills-based interventions are also common to CBCT and generally involve the therapist instructing the couple in specific skills, such as communication skills. The use of Socratic questioning to redress faulty or distorted cognitions is often utilized as is "guided discovery" which refers to therapist-created encounters in which one or both partners are able to challenge and evolve their perspective on the relationship.

Efficacy and Applicability with African American Couples

CBCT is the most widely investigated approach to couples' therapy and is based upon TBCT, which has met the most stringent criteria for empirical support (Baucom, et al., 1998). Findings suggest that CBCT is successful in increasing marital satisfaction in previously distressed couples with these results remaining for 6–12 months, but appears to lack long-term sustainability. While CBCT has received laudable empirical support, little research has focused primarily on African American couples. Indeed, Baucom and colleagues (2008) acknowledge that, "although CBCT approaches have made significant strides in focusing on gender issues in couple therapy, they have paid limited attention to the impact of racial, ethnic, and cultural issues, on relationship functioning and treatment" (p. 38). To this end, CBCT has often boasted a color-blind approach that may "obscure cultural and societal influences in individual and couple behavior. Furthermore, treatment tends to emphasize independence and autonomy as optimal outcomes, rather than interdependence and reliance on familial and community support" (LaTaillade, 2006, p. 347). These values go against traditional collectivistic African American values and may be experienced as minimizing or even disrespectful of one's cultural roots and may hinder the development of an authentic therapeutic relationship. Thus, while empirically supported, CBCT should not be employed blindly with African American couples. Most notable in clinical work with African American couples might be the structured approach and tangible skills development particularly in communication, which is often noted as a primary issue in distressed couples (LaTaillade, 2006). Given the research supporting the importance of how couples engage one another as being imperative in relationship sustainability (Gottman, 1999), such tangible skills development is essential for distressed African American couples presenting to counseling. For example, a CBCT therapist might utilize psychoeducation to teach communication skills to a couple. Specifically, the therapist may instruct the couple on how to engage in active listening in which each partner reflects and summarizes what they heard their partner communicate and how to utilize "I" statements. These tangible skills may be experienced as therapeutic within sessions by enhancing communication and optimally foster increased communication outside of therapy.

Emotionally Focused Couple Therapy

Emotionally focused couple therapy (EFT) is rooted in attachment theory and the relational elements central to marital satisfaction and distress yet integrates experiential and systemic perspectives. EFT promotes a non-pathologizing approach in which people are taught to find ways to cope with life challenges but these responses may later be limiting or inadequate in creating fulfilling romantic partnerships. Theoretically, EFT posits that we are formed and transformed by our relationships with others. Systemically, EFT seeks to understand and disrupt destructive cycles of interaction with others while still centering on the core emotional experiences of each partner (Johnson, 2008).

The role of the EFT therapist is that of a "process consultant" whose role is supportive and facilitative, assisting clients in the process of expanding emotional responses within the context of the relationship (Johnson, 2008, p. 107). There is an emphasis on the therapeutic relationship as central in the healing process, particularly given its focus on the acceptance and validation of the client's experience. The therapist must support innate self-healing and growth tendencies in which clients formulate new, healthier responses.

To foster the development of healthier intimate responses, there are two core therapeutic tasks: 1) the exploration and reformulation of the emotional experience, and 2) the restructuring of interactions (p. 120). According to Johnson (2008), the types of interventions utilized to explore and reformulate emotion may include simple reflection and validation of emotion and empathic conjecture. EFT therapists work to increase emotional awareness and open/authentic communication between partners and foster *softening* whereby partners are able to reduce negative sentiment and increase vulnerability with one another. More advanced interventions include evocative responding in which the therapist invites the client to increase awareness of his/her physiological response and behavioral reactions to an emotional stimulus wherein the primary purpose is to identify and integrate elements of a client's experience that may be marginalized or suppressed in some way. This aspect of the theory is particularly relevant to African American couples' therapy given the consistent societal oppression African Americans face based on race and gender. Another intervention may include *heightening*, in which the therapist uses metaphor, enactments, images, or the like to more healthily reorganize the emotional interaction between partners. Restructuring interventions are key to EFT practice and include: 1) tracking, reflecting, and replaying interactions with the purpose of slowing down interactions to clarify steps in the "interactional dance"; 2) reframing in the context of the cycle and attachment processes to help shift and foster more positive and meaningful perceptions of a partner; and 3) restructuring and shaping interventions in which partners are enacting present circumstances and/or choreographing anticipated positive changes in order to clarify negative interaction patterns and create positive cycles of emotional responsiveness (Johnson, 2008).

Efficacy and Applicability with African American Couples

Empirical research indicates that EFT is effective in reducing distress and fostering significant clinical change in couples with myriad presenting circumstances with lasting effects that appear resistant to relapse over time (Johnson, 2008). While there are no empirical investigations focused specifically on its effectiveness with African American couples, there are a few characteristics of EFT that may make it particularly suitable for working with African American couples. Namely, its focus on emotion and attachment may lend it particularly well in working with couples and families who may be emotionally and spiritually expressive. Its emphasis on attachment and adult love may prevent pathologizing the interdependency and close emotional intimacy with one's family of origin and romantic partnerships common in African American family systems. Yet, this same focus may allow an EFT therapist to better understand the enduring impact of attachment issues from experiences such as parental absence or loss, early parentification due to economic strain, or painful previous romantic relationships. Clients who seek a more directive therapist may find an EFT therapist lacking in this area, however.

Structural Couples Therapy

Systems therapies support circular causality (A causes B, which causes A, which causes B...) and posit that individual behavior is interactional, dynamic, both a cause and an effect (Nichols & Schwartz, 2009). They state further that individual behavior is a function of their environment and larger systems of which they are a part. Structural couples therapy (SCT), a systemic therapy, emerged primarily as a result of Salvador Minuchin and his colleagues identifying the ineffectiveness of psychoanalysis with the primarily African American and Latino low-income populations with whom they were working (Minuchin, 1974). While developed as a family therapy, it has recently been applied to couples and individuals, yet it is important to note that couples are viewed within the context of their families. This is especially relevant to work with African American couples given the culture's collectivistic values and the important role the extended family plays in the lives of many African Americans.

Primary SCT concepts include that of *subsystems*, which are thought to develop as a result of differences (Simon, 2008). Through shared experiences a subsystem may emerge. Examples include the couple subsystem and sibling subsystems. Minuchin emphasized the process of socialization and the family's ability to cultivate in its members the skills necessary to function both within and outside of the family. To this end, he emphasized *boundaries* within and around the family and its subsystems as indicators of its health, adaptability, and overall structure. These boundaries were theorized to range from diffuse (referring to a subsystem with little to no differentiation between itself and others) to rigid (the opposite extreme in which subsystems are disconnected). Those with diffuse boundaries are referred to as being "enmeshed' while those with rigid boundaries are characterized as "disengaged."

SCT defines a functional couple as a subsystem that is sufficiently internally resourced and has clearly defined, yet permeable boundaries separating it from its surroundings (Minuchin & Fishman, 2004; Nichols & Schwartz, 2005). Difference is viewed as contributing to a normative, healthy, and adaptable relationship. Dysfunctional/unhealthy relationships are those with overly diffuse or rigid boundaries that may marginalize or alienate the couple, or deprive them of sufficient external connections. Common issues addressed in the SCT literature include diffuse boundaries between the couple subsystem and sibling subsystem (children in the family). In these cases, a core identity and, indeed, emotional intimacy between the couple is rare (Simon, 2008) which leads to a primary focus being on the children. Minuchin (1974) noted that this type of relational dysfunction rarely results in high conflict, which requires greater emotional engagement. Chronic conflict within a couple is also theorized to be a function of diffuse emotional boundaries. Couples may avoid conflict with each other and displace it onto their child.

Accordingly, assessment of the health of the couple is understood within the larger framework of the health, structure, and functioning of the entire family system. Assessment is important in SCT; the assessment of the structure of the family, its boundaries, and ability to adapt is done early and throughout treatment. This is particularly sensitive to African American couples because African Americans are more likely than some other cultural groups to exist within non-traditional (as narrowly defined by dominant American culture) family structures (e.g. grandparents living in the home).

SCT incorporates strengths in that it integrates an *assumption of competence* (Simon, 2008). SCT assumes that couples have internal strengths and resources that need only be re-engaged. This is a change in perspective from those theories that make the assumption of pathology as opposed to competence. Boyd-Franklin (1989) explains that Black couples and families respond best to strengths-based approaches. SCT has this as its thesis.

Insofar as SCT emphasizes the immediacy of partners' experience within the therapeutic encounter, interventions focus on changing partners' experience in the moment. Hence, the primary goal of SCT is the creation of new relational experiences in the moment for the clients (Simon, 2008). The role of the therapist is that of facilitator, primarily vis-à-vis the facilitating of new and different behaviors between partners in the room. There are two interventions in SCT that are especially applicable to work with African American couples: joining and enactment.

Joining is a primary intervention utilized in SCT. This refers to the authentic and intentional process of becoming an insider of the couple system while continuing to maintain the therapeutic posture necessary to activate client resources (Minuchin & Fishman, 2004). Boyd-Franklin (1989) discusses the importance of joining in her work with African American couples. Therapists who successfully *join* the couple's system decrease cultural mistrust (if it exists in the relationship) and increase trust and rapport between the couple and therapist. This is a necessity for effective treatment with African American couples. *Enactment* is the process whereby partners interact directly with one another and therefore have the opportunity to have new relational experiences of one another and the relationship (Simon, 2008). Enactments about partner differences or sources of conflict are noted as particularly helpful in assessing and destabilizing current structural dysfunction. One SCT intervention that has received criticism is that of *unbalancing* in which the therapist instigates conflict between a conflict-avoidant couple (Minuchin & Fishman, 2004). In so doing, the couple is able to *enact* that which they are avoiding but this generally requires acting and provocation from the therapist to elicit such conflict in the room. This intervention, although it has the potential for great success, can be risky if the therapist has not established a secure rapport with the couple. This may be especially the case with non-Black clinicians working with Black couples. Clinicians should assess the strength of their rapport with the couple before attempting the *unbalancing* technique. SCT is concluded when client defined goals are met and when alleviation of presenting symptoms and structural realignment has occurred.

Efficacy and Applicability with African American Couples

There is empirical support for the use of SCT with unmarried, married, and uncoupling partners across demographic groups (Minuchin, Lee, & Simon, 2006). Yet, it should be noted that most of the available research is on structural therapy with families, albeit the same foundational principles and interventions.

This model may feel comfortable for many African American couples given its attention to family structure, relationships, and its directive problem-solving focus

(Boyd-Franklin, 1989). Benefits of using this approach with African American couples include the process of *joining* may feel as if the therapist genuinely cares and is becoming part of the family and is invested in their health. Its openness to multiple family constellations and respect for family hierarchy is aligned with African American cultural values; *enactments* in session can be therapeutic in that couples are actually discussing current relevant issues (and perhaps coming to resolution), within session its structured approach (often important for African Americans wary of counseling), and its ability to instill hope and a sense of empowerment (Boyd-Franklin, 1989). Other ways to increase SCT's applicability with African American couples may include integration of other extended kin, significant others, parents of children from other relationships, and even clergy. While the model is open to multiple family constellations, given the previous discussion of African American blended families, and the importance of extended kin, increased involvement of other relevant parties may make the model better aligned with the range of individuals involved in couples' lives.

Despite these theoretical strengths, SCT has received criticism in a few areas regarding its cultural appropriateness. First, the way in which relational boundaries are described by SCT appear to be based upon Eurocentric normative values and behaviors. SCT potentially pathologizes the emotional closeness typical of African American relational systems as being "enmeshed" while such a boundary may be deemed culturally normative and capable of healthy expression (Kelly & Boyd-Franklin, 2009). Another concern is how *unbalancing* may be perceived by African American couples, particularly if utilized by a non-Black therapist, and it may be ill-received by some couples, contributing to a therapeutic rupture or early termination. SCT should not be used where there is abuse or self/other harm.

Bowenian Therapy

Another popular systems theory is Bowenian therapy (BT) (also referred to as natural systems theory and multigenerational theory). Developed natural systems theory focuses on the "two counterbalancing life forces: *individuality* and *togetherness*" (Nichols & Schwartz, 2005, p. 115). According to Bowen (1978), the core of his theory resides in an individual's ability to distinguish between thoughts and feelings. When feelings completely override thoughts, emotional reactivity occurs, which often leads to fused relationships and unhealthy patterns of behavior. Several of the theory's main concepts will be discussed.

Differentiation of self is what Bowen (1978) referred to as the level at which an individual is able to experience the self as a separate entity yet connected to others: the capacity to differentiate between emotional and intellectual functioning. Thus, a person who is not very differentiated is likely to find that they automatically respond to emotions, regardless of the rationality of the response. A person who is considered differentiated allows his /her thoughts to overrule the tendency to react emotionally and thus is better able to manage stress/anxiety and adapt to change (Bowen, 1978). This same differentiation is important in couples' ability to adapt to change (Roberto-Forman, 2008).

Triangulation is the experience of two people in an intimate relationship who bring in (or triangle) a third person or another issue to decrease anxiety in the two-person relationship. It is theorized that the involvement of the third person may reduce anxiety, yet it can undermine the primary relationship. This is most evident in parents diverting energy to children or the development of extramarital affairs. This can also easily happen with African American couples when issues such as financial concerns, racial and gender stereotypes, step-children and their parents (e.g. baby's mammas, etc.), and extended family issues are allowed to come between the couple. These are common examples of how triangulation can occur and reduce intimacy within African American couples' relationships.

Bowen further noted that often couples find that they are matched in their level of differentiation. Yet, when both members of a couple are poorly differentiated, the relationship may be highly emotional, volatile, and fused (maladaptive closeness) which may contribute to conflict and relational power struggles. For African American families, known for their cultural value of family connectedness, assessment of healthy differentiation remains important. Particularly, it is important to assess healthy connectedness and family boundaries while also exploring the functionality of relationships that are high in conflict or "family drama." For instance, frequent arguments with high emotionality wherein other family members are brought in may be indicative of poor differentiation and the use of triangulation.

Sibling position, Bowen believed, was one of the most important pieces of information a therapist could gather to understand a family's experience, particularly around power, relational experiences, and marital expectations.

Bowen's concept of *societal emotional process* recognizes that the family system exists within a larger society. To this end, Bowen recognized that oppressive forces of racism and sexism impact individuals and relationships and theorized that higher levels of differentiation may serve as a buffer to such deleterious social forces (Nichols & Schwartz, 2009). Bowen's theory is one of the few theoretical frameworks that overtly recognize the impact of racism and sexism on relationships. The level of anxiety present in the outside world has a significant impact on the functioning and level of anxiety of the family unit, which may lead to chronic anxiety. Bowen's family-centered approach is important in the discussion of African American couples for a number of reasons. First, understanding the couple's individual family systems, including any family of origin issues, provides clinically useful information about intergenerational patterns of relating and levels of differentiation that may govern continued relational patterns with one's family of origin as well as inform mate selection and one's boundaries with a romantic partner. In short, it provides information about the "family baggage" one is bringing into a relationship. Second, insofar as African American culture values family-centeredness, such an approach is culturally syntonic. Understanding the individual familial context of African American couples will help shed light on all of the familial variables at play within the relationship.

The role of the Bowenian therapist is to be a coach or consultant, neutral and objective in order to remain de-triangulated from the couple (Guerin, Fogarty, Fay, & Kautto, 1996; Nichols & Schwartz, 2009). As the therapist uses his or her own level of emotional reactivity in the therapy process, he/she may better understand the client's level of differentiation. This role could work very well for African American couples because it is inherently collaborative and does not assume that the therapist is the "expert" on the couple's relationship.

Therapists are urged to focus on the process of the interaction in lieu of content unless such a focus escalates emotion in the room and use nonconfrontational questioning, to stimulate rational thinking and discourse over emotion in the room. De-escalating emotional arguments should be done by talking to one partner at a time (Nichols & Schwartz, 2009). Similarly, Guerin and colleagues (1996) argue for the use of the displacement story or discussion of other couples with similar concerns or even the use of film as a way to create emotional distance, minimize defensiveness, and increase rationality. Perhaps the most well known Bowenian intervention is the creation of a genogram, which is utilized to identify relational patterns across generations of a family or families. Identifying current and multigenerational patterns such as triangulation can lead to deliberate efforts to de-triangulate and eliminate maladaptive patterns. Another common intervention utilized in Bowenian therapy is that of relationship experiments where the goal is to alter identified triangles (Nichols & Schwartz, 2009). In facilitating a relationship experiment, a therapist would help identify each partner's role in a triangle and encourage alternate behavior. For instance, Fogarty (1976) described the "pursuer-distancer" communication pattern whereby one partner pursues the other who, in turn, creates emotional and/or physical distance. A relationship experiment created to disrupt this pattern might encourage the pursuer to: 1) identify what might be contributing to his/her pursuit; 2) refrain from pressuring and pursuing the partner and; 3) distancers are invited to be more open, communicative, and turn toward their partner (as cited in Nichols & Schwartz, 2005). As mentioned previously, African American culture values family. Accordingly, the use of the genogram may be particularly useful with African American couples in identifying current and previous central figures in their lives as well as relational patterns and issues across generations. The visual representation of the family and their issues can allow clients to see their individual and collective issues laid out before them and therefore serve as a powerful clinical tool, particularly in identifying points of intervention.

Finally, Bowen also encouraged the use of psychoeducation, specifically around intergenerational emotional systems and its impact on their current relationship (Nichols & Schwartz, 2009).

Efficacy and Applicability with African American Couples

There is no established empirical basis within clinical outcome studies supporting the effectiveness of Bowenian theory despite its prominence and clinical popularity (Baucom et al., 1998; Johnson & Lebow, 2000; Miller et al., 2000). In a recent review of varying types of research, findings reveal support for the relationship between differentiation and chronic anxiety, marital satisfaction, and psychological distress. Yet, the tenets around sibling position, triangulation, and the theoretical presupposition that partners with the comparable levels of differentiation were not supported (Miller, Anderson, & Keala, 2004).

While there is no research focused specifically on the applicability of Bowenian theory with African American couples, there are a number of aspects of the theory that merit further consideration with African Americans. First, there has been criticism of Bowenian theory in that its values and mores reflect that of a White Christian Protestant population (Ariel, 1999). Yet, Boyd-Franklin (1989) supports the utility of BT, particularly the multigenerational component of the theory and the use of the genogram. She cautions, however, that given the Bowenian focus on historical familial patterns, care should be taken to thoroughly establish trust and safety before using the genogram clinically with this population. Some African Americans may have difficulty tracing their family histories due to social and familial issues such as an absent parent, formal and informal adoptions, and even the deleterious multigenerational effects of slavery. She attests that this is consistent with African American cultural values and family constellations. Additionally, Boyd-Franklin (1989) discusses Black families' tendencies to have secrets they do not want to share outside their own family structure. This could potentially serve as a barrier to rapport in treatment and may be more likely to show up in treatment with non-African American couples' clinicians. Black clients tend to be sensitive to not appearing to fulfill racial stereotypes to White therapists. These dynamics could become apparent when using a genogram as couples may be reluctant to share information that does not show their families in the best light. This cultural mistrust can get in the way of a genuine relationship between the counselor and couple. Boyd-Franklin's method of integrating BT into her own model of multisystems therapy will be discussed later in this chapter.

Other cultural issues to consider are that the therapist use of self in Bowenian therapy may feel more transparent than other theoretical postures and be better received with African Americans who may be wary of counseling. Because of the previously discussed cultural mistrust many African Americans have of the mental health field, many African Americans may be uncomfortable with a traditional posture of the therapist being a "blank slate" who avoids any self-disclosure. Thus, a therapist who is more open and transparent may feel safer and more comfortable for such clients. Therapist self-disclosure and use of self may encourage this. Lastly, the decreased emphasis on emotion in the room may feel inconsistent with African American communication patterns in which expression of emotion may not be experienced as maladaptive or impeding rationality. A benefit of this approach is its openness to flexibility in working with individuals, couples, or families, which may be important given the multiple family constellations for African Americans (Boyd-Franklin, 1989).

Narrative Couples Therapy

Narrative therapy emerges from the social constructionist paradigm that posits that reality is subjective and co-constructed as well as the tradition of post-structuralism articulated by Foucault (1980), which focuses on the storied nature of our life experiences. Instead of problem resolution, the focus is upon externalizing problems, particularly those imposed by dominant culture, to empower individuals and couples to create alternative more positive narratives not defined by the subjugative dominant paradigms (Payne, 2006).

Because of its roots in social constructionism, narrative therapy takes a non-pathologizing stance; narrative therapists do not tend to use categorical or evaluative descriptors of relationships such as diagnoses or terms such as *unhealthy* and *dysfunctional*. Instead, there is a focus on identifying the influence of and subverting problematic discourses on couple relationships. In this way, narrative therapists are viewed as *co-researchers* in a process uncovering truths and new knowledge (Epston, 1999). Because relationships are not viewed as being stable structures over time capable of measurement, narrative "assessment" is about "generating experience rather than gathering information" (Freedman & Combs, 2008, p. 234). Similarly, goal-setting tends to be avoided in that it can restrict the growth process thereby limiting possibilities. Rather, narrative therapists are encouraged to focus on therapeutic and life "directions." The process of narrative couples therapy is generally determined by the couple as they define the problem and its relative influence on their relationship. Thus, treatment planning is dynamic and ongoing. The primary goals of narrative couples counseling include: 1) identifying the influence of dominant cultural discourse; 2) naming and externalizing the problem; 3) taking a stand in opposition to the problem; 4) re-authoring their narrative by creating healthier, more satisfying stories of their relationship; and 5) evaluating the usefulness of the alternative narrative (Freedman & Combs, 2008; Payne, 2006). At its core, narrative therapy considers the impact societally constructed oppression has on clients and their presenting issues—which makes it a culturally sensitive approach.

Therapeutic strategies to achieve these objectives include deconstructive listening and questioning and the process of externalizing in which the problem is intentionally located outside of the individual. Such a strategy is not only deconstructive but may be experienced as personally liberating as one realizes that "rather than *being* the problem, the person or couple has a *relationship* with the problem" (Freedman & Combs, 2008, p. 238). This is especially powerful for African American couples because some of the most damaging influences impacting their relationships are outside of their control (e.g. racism, internalization of negative gender stereotypes, negative depictions of African Americans in the media, lack of consistent role models of healthy couples' relationships for some). Finally, through the therapeutic focus on unique outcomes or events that are contrary to the problem-saturated story, strengths are identified and utilized in the re-authoring process. Multiple resources are utilized to reinforce newly emerging narratives such as letters and other personal documents.

Efficacy and Applicability with African American Couples

The effectiveness of narrative therapy is viewed rather broadly and practically which necessarily makes it challenging to empirically research using the traditional positivist methods most lauded in the scientific community (Etchison & Kleist, 2000). Based upon clinical and self-report data contributing to insider knowledge and the increasing body of qualitative research, narrative therapy appears to be an effective modality, yet little is known specifically about narrative couples therapy. Moreover, little is known specifically about its efficacy with African American couples. However, there are a number of cultural factors relevant to narrative therapy and African American partnerships. Notably, its focus on identifying and subverting the influence of dominant cultural discourse is germane to the experience of couples of African ancestry living in a continuously oppressive environment. Second, as a strengths-based approach that does not inherently find fault within the individual (or couple), this approach may be attractive to African American couples who are consistently challenged to find positive images of themselves or their relationship within an oppressive society. Thus, this appears to be a culturally sensitive treatment that has the potential for success with African American couples.

However, limitations may also exist in the application of narrative therapy with African American couples. Specifically, the less directive role of the therapist may be uncomfortable for many African American couples who come to therapy expecting a more directive therapist. Boyd-Franklin (1989), lauded for her efforts in advancing culturally centered couples' and family therapy with African Americans, notes that often times a more problem-focused and concrete approach is better with African Americans who may find more past-focused approaches as being invasive. Further, while externalizing the problem may be empowering in many circumstances, in others increased accountability may be necessary. Clinicians should evaluate this tendency in couples on an individual basis. Like all treatment approaches, modifications must be made for individual African American couples as different approaches will work better for some couples than others. For instance, in cases of interpersonal violence and abuse, substance dependence, and infidelity, this may be difficult to fully address within the externalizing language of narrative therapy. In such cases approaches such as motivational interviewing, cognitive behavioral approaches, or individual therapy may be warranted to more fully and effectively address these needs.

Solution-Focused Couples Therapy

Like narrative therapy, solution-focused couples therapy is a strength-based and constructivist approach that focuses on the clients' own resources in building solutions to presenting concerns. Toward this end, theory and assessment, particularly that based upon the traditional Diagnostic and Statistical Manual (DSM) nosology is minimized in favor of simpler client self-report of problems and resources. The process of defining tenable goals for therapy is deemed imperative. Specifically, client defined goals should be: 1) small, specific, and behaviorally oriented; and 2) involve the creation of new behavior or processes that signal the beginning of something and not merely the end or cessation of something negative (de Shazer, 1991). Indeed, the basic tenets of solution-focused therapy are to use the client's previously successful solutions, increase more of what has been identified as successful, and if a solution doesn't work, to try something different.

Perhaps, the best known solution-focused technique is the use of the miracle question as articulated by de Shazer: "Suppose that one night there is a miracle and while you are sleeping the problem that brought you into therapy is solved: How would you know? What would be different?" (as cited in Hoyt, 2008). Other therapeutic strategies include "goaling" which can be described as the process of identifying and moving toward new solutions, which often requires negotiation when working with couples.

Efficacy and Applicability with African American Couples

Solution-focused therapy is considered "client-centered and transcultural" and values the "'local knowledge' (individual, familial, social) of those who seek therapy; 'cultural diversity' is honored in that the emphasis is genuinely on learning *from* clients, not just *about* them" (Hoyt, 2008, p.261). It is a collaborative approach. For example, solution-focused therapy views the client as the "customer" and the therapist as the "consultant," thus projecting a collaborative approach. The presenting issue (problem) is known as the "complaint." Solution-focused therapy also assumes that "customers" have the solutions to their own "complaints" making this a strengths-based approach. Yet, these authors also note the apolitical nature of the theory and that cultural and social issues are not generally discussed. African American couples unfamiliar with therapy, especially those who may find the less structured and intrapsychic approaches personally invasive, may find this approach refreshing in its focused nature. Utilizing strengths may also foster confidence in future problem-solving skills of the couple. Yet, couples seeking greater understanding of the social, political, or even familial origins of presenting issues are likely better served using a different therapeutic approach. This approach is also not appropriate for couples who have partners with histories of trauma, substance abuse, or other psychological distress due to its focus on problem solving as opposed to healing. It is probably most appropriately used as a time-limited approach for couples with clearly defined short-term presenting issues (e.g. conflicts over child-raising issues or division of household labor versus infidelity or trauma).

Gottman's Sound Relationship House Theory

Of couples' therapeutic approaches, Gottman's Sound Relationship House Theory is perhaps the one which emanates most from empirical data (Gottman, 1999). Findings from Gottman's proverbial "love lab" (in which he has brought hundreds of couples into his lab, observed them, and followed them longitudinally) have generated an ability to predict long-term relational stability and divorce based upon several factors. Primary findings indicate the following: core personality differences between partners result in "perpetual" unsolvable problems; escalation from mild negative affects to the "Four Horsemen of the Apocalypse" (e.g. criticism, defensiveness, contempt, and stonewalling, which will be discussed at length below) are detrimental to relational stability; the importance of gentle and positive affect during conflict as well as the times when the couple is not in the midst of conflict; and, finally, that nurturing positivity through friendship, humor, romance, good sex, etc. can override conflict and negative sentiment and promote relational stability (Gottman & Gottman, 2008). Couples who divorce early are characterized by patterns of escalating conflict. He also finds that an emotionally disengaged or indifferent affective state within the relationship is equally destructive to couples' ability to stay together.

As mentioned previously, one of the hallmark findings of Gottman's research is the idea that anger and conflict are not solely responsible for relationship satisfaction or sustainability. To this end, he identified the Four Horseman of the Apocalypse: criticism, defensiveness, contempt, and stonewalling. *Criticism* refers to the process of generalizing a complaint to one's entire character instead of focusing on specific problematic behavior. For example, instead of noting that one is upset that a partner failed to clean the kitchen, the partner may state that the partner is an irresponsible, lazy jerk. *Defensiveness* refers to the process of denying a partner's concerns and/or counterattacking. For example, if a partner presented a concern such as: "I really don't like it when you miss the kids' events. I need you to be present." A defensive response or counterattack might be: "You're not perfect, you missed the recital last month." Such a closed and counterattacking position clearly leaves little room for accountability or discussion. *Contempt*, known as the most destructive horseman, refers to being overtly (but sometimes even subtly) disrespectful or insulting to a partner through statements or mannerisms. For example, direct name calling, putting a partner down, or rolling one's eyes are all demonstrative of contempt and are predictors of relational dissolution. Finally, *stonewalling* refers to emotional disengagement, or the times when a partner (more often men) refuses to respond or "checks out." An example of stonewalling is when a wife is talking about her perceptions of relationship issues and her husband does not provide any evidence in mannerisms, verbal or non-verbal behavior that he is listening or has heard what she has said. Like defensiveness, such a posture clearly halts discussion and may therefore be seen as an exertion of power in the relationship.

Overall, Gottman and his colleagues (Gottman & Gottman, 2008) have identified seven primary components to a "sound relationship house" and include: 1) love maps or the map of the inner world of one's partner; 2) a fondness and admiration system referring to an ethos of affirmation of the positive within the relationship in lieu of constant acknowledgment of the negative; 3) turning toward bids for emotional connection, which refers to the daily ways in which partners seek emotional connection and having their needs met. These represent opportunities for partners to choose to turn toward one another and meet these needs instead of ignoring or minimizing them; 4) positive sentiment override refers to an overall state of positive affect due primarily to establishing a core friendship as demonstrated in the first three levels of the house; 5) conflict regulation including either effective problem solving of resolvable issues or healthy coping and dialogue about perpetual problems and physiological soothing during emotional disagreements; 6) making dreams and aspirations come true, which refers to a couple intentionally increasing positive activities and using the relationship in working toward shared dreams; and 7) creating shared meaning, which refers to the formal and informal rituals of connection and overall creation of a shared couple narrative that reflects their life—past, present, and future— together. These are the primary components deemed essential for building a strong foundation or friendship, and promoting overall positive sentiment both during conflict and non-conflict times, through the development and cultivation of a shared narrative guiding the couple forward.

Therapy based upon Gottman's research, then, seeks to engage the meta-emotion mismatches that may disrupt relational satisfaction. The goals of Gottman's model are: 1) to down-regulate negative affect during conflict; 2) up-regulate positive affect during conflict; 3) building positive affect during non-conflict; 4) bridge meta-emotion mismatches; and 5) create and nurture a shared meaning system (Gottman, 1999; Gottman & Gottman, 2008). Therapeutic strategies seek to advance these theoretical goals. Some of the therapeutic strategies utilized to decrease and regulate negative affect are through processing a fight with a couple by having partners take turns discussing their emotions during the incident. Other strategies include having couples validate one another's experience, increase individual accountability, and discuss ways to improve future communication. In this process, the therapist is intentional about heightening awareness of and reducing the Four Horsemen of the Apocalypse by stopping when necessary, segmenting the conversation, and increasing gentle and understanding communication.

In up-regulating (increasing) positive affect, one of the most important strategies identified in this model is to first increase a couple's ability to recognize existing positive affect and to increase a couple's ability to turn toward one another during neutral non-conflict times of the relationship. For example, working with a couple to identify and verbalize to one another the aspects of the relationship with which they are happy and satisfied in addition to "turning toward" one another or increasing physical and emotional intimacy when they are not arguing can increase overall positive sentiment. Such experiences have been demonstrated to increase positive affect during conflict and to help build overall positive sentiment in the relationship. Creating and nurturing shared meaning systems is essential to the joining of two different cultural systems within the couple unit. This can be fostered by building formal and informal rituals of connection, such as regular date nights or ways of making up following a disagreement.

Efficacy and Applicability with African American Couples

Gottman notes that the model is applicable across cultural groups and has diversified the samples in his research to be inclusive of African American couples (Gottman & Gottman, 2008). Yet, his research has not focused specifically on the unique needs of African American couples. Thus, it is unclear if his model is *as* effective in predicting success and stability of these couples over time. It is noteworthy, however, that Gottman's emphasis not only on the challenges of romantic partnership but also increasing and nurturing positive sentiment and shared meaning systems appears to be aligned with African American cultural values. It is also a strengths-based approach and approaches focusing on African American couples' strengths have been found to be an effective treatment strategy (Boyd-Franklin, 1989). Another way of perhaps making these strategies more culturally centered might be a better integration of family and community and the creation of a shared meaning system that intentionally incorporates the ancestors, children, and the yet born. Because many African Americans place value on the continued spiritual presence of deceased family members and, within an African-centered worldview the role of the ancestors, children, and future generations is critical in the understanding of the cycle of life, incorporating these dimensions may help to create a more holistic meaning system. This may be even more critical for couples exploring loss or challenges in life transitions such as the addition of a child or a child leaving the home.

Culturally Centered Models of Couples' Therapy

There is little by way of a clearly developed and articulated therapy specifically for African American couples. Yet, Nancy Boyd-Franklin and her colleagues (Boyd-Franklin, 1989; Boyd-Franklin & Franklin, 1998; Boyd-Franklin et al., 2008; Kelly & Boyd-Franklin, 2009) have spearheaded efforts in integrating African-centered cultural principles in applying primarily systems therapies with African American couples and families. In so doing, they have emphasized African history and praxis prior to enslavement, understanding the historic and continued experience of oppression and White supremacy, and advocate for a strengths-based perspective that highlights African American resilience in light of sustained oppression. They state that work with families of African ancestry necessitates theoretical flexibility and integration. Further, they note that a systemic approach that centers one's understanding of a couple within the larger context of family and community is essential. A strengths-based approach counters a traditional deficit-based perspective that may obfuscate relational egalitarianism and role flexibility often characteristic in African American relationships. To this end, she organized a multisystems model of therapy, which integrates the previously discussed structural and Bowenian theories in what is deemed a more culturally syntonic approach with this population. The model is as follows:

- Axis 1: The Treatment Process
  - Step 1: Joining and engaging new subsystem
  - Step 2: Initial assessment
  - Step 3: Problem solving (establishing credibility)
  - Step 4: Use of family enactment, prescriptions, and tasks
  - Step 5: Information gathering: the genogram
  - Step 6: Restructuring the family and the multisystems
- Axis II: Multisystems Levels
  - Level 1: Individuals
  - Level 2: Subsystems
  - Level 3: Family household
  - Level 4: Extended family
  - Level 5: Non-blood kin and friends
  - Level 6: Church and community resources
  - Level 7: Social service agencies and other outside agencies.

(Boyd-Franklin, 1989, p.135)

Boyd-Franklin (1989) underscores *joining* as being even more critical to the process of gaining trust and building a genuine relationship with African Americans who may be wary of the mental health system. It is the "person-to-person connection [that] is *the* most important in working with Black families; without it, all of the therapists' carefully applied treatment techniques are useless" (Boyd-Franklin, 1989, p. 97, emphasis added).

In this model, initial assessment follows joining as it is the established trust and safety that allows the family to be more open in the assessment. Specifically, a therapist should assess who comprises the family, habitation and living arrangements, and any concerns around co-parenting and/or boundaries in blended families (Kelly & Boyd-Franklin, 2009).

In the next two steps, consistent with the structural therapy approach, she encourages problem solving, use of family enactments, tasks and the like to: 1) utilize a more focused and directive approach to problem solving presenting concerns; and 2) establish further credibility with the couple or family through these efforts. It is this established credibility, mounting trust, and deepened relationship that allows more information gathering and greater utility of the genogram to occur. Boyd-Franklin (1989) notes that this is often when more details about the couple's or family's history emerges; family secrets may be disclosed at this point. The genogram can then be used to identify and trace these patterns while increasing insight into current relational trends. The final stage of the process is restructuring the individual and multisystems based on this increased understanding and movement toward more healthy boundaries and relational patterns. Interventions do not need to occur on every level, but for a contextual understanding of presenting issues is a must given these multisystems. As a couple and family are being restructured, the importance of external community resources in serving as additional supports for the couple should be emphasized (Boyd-Franklin, et al., 2008).

Recently, Kelly and Boyd-Franklin (2009) have further delineated this theory by emphasizing the knowledge, skills, and awareness necessary to best implement this multisystems approach in working with African Americans. These areas are described in detail in Chapter 9.

Dunham and Ellis (2010) provide specific recommendations in recovering intimacy with Black couples which can address specific contextual factors African American couples face including:

a   Orient the couple to therapy process
b   Do not assume familiarity with clients in the first session
c   Address the issue of racism and its effects in their lives
d   Join the couple before gathering sensitive information
e   Maintain a broad definition of family when assessing the couples structure and roles
f   Assess and intervene multisystemically
g   Use a problem-solving focus in treatment
h   Include discussion of spirituality or religion and if appropriate, construct spiritual or religious leaders
i   Use scriptural references or metaphors, and
j   Acknowledge strengths, resources, and successes.

(p. 305)

These traditional approaches are common training models most counselors are exposed to in graduate school. We have attempted to provide specific ways to make them more culturally relevant to work with African American couples. The following section introduces treatment models more specific to African American couples.

Community-Based Educational Programs

There is little discussion within the couples' literature about group and community-based interventions as a way of engaging and responding to the issues of primary concern to African American couples. Ryan and Gottman's (n.d.) program and research are an exception. They find that couples respond well to group interventions (e.g. workshops) which can enhance the gains of individual couples therapy. Similarly, other research on the effects of preventative training programs suggests participating couples experience increased marital satisfaction and decreased rates of divorce (Bodenmann, 1997). This is one reason so many Black churches provide pre- and post-marital counseling and couples' ministries in which couples get together to discuss common relationship issues. The group format may be a low cost, effective therapeutic experience, further supporting the need for group, psychoeducational, community level, and group interventions. Another program which seeks to bridge the gap in group and community intervention and the need for culturally centered intervention is Rowe and Lyons-Rowe (2009) "Conversations in marriage", which is a community intervention program grounded in African-centered metatheory that seeks to empower and promote healthy marriage among African Americans through education about marriage and family and its role in the cultivation of the African American community. Specifically, it seeks to educate through the use of seminars, or a group-based didactic educational and discussion format, the benefits of marriage within the context of African American community development. In their discussion of the importance of community-based therapeutic work with African Americans they note that "community is the outgrowth of family, and marriage is the basis of family" (Rowe & Lyons-Rowe, 2009, p. 67).

Hence, from the authors' perspective, community-based intervention is an imperative given that marriage is the building block of the African American family and community. Their approach to intervention is also contrary to traditional western notions of therapy as it involves an emphasis on the community supporting the couple versus a more westernized individualistic focus. Further, couching marital discussion within the context of family and community building may help to underscore the cultural meaning of marriage beyond the couple as an isolated unit. Indeed, they note that marriage must not be viewed as private: it belongs to the community and is not solely about individual happiness; rather it is a duty, transition to adulthood, and essential for community structure (Rowe & Lyons-Rowe, 2009; Some, 2000).

Broadly, the 12-week curriculum of Conversations in Marriage (CIM) includes an examination and exploration of the meaning and purpose of marriage (contextualized within an historical understanding of African community); realistic struggles of marriage given the historic and continued experience of oppression; myths and gender ideology that influence marital obligations and satisfaction; an understanding of the importance of friendship, choice, and commitment within marriage and the shared construction of marital meaning; the importance of celebrations, ceremony, faith, and forgiveness; and the continued process of rejuvenation and renewed commitment. The authors utilize didactic instruction and discussion to facilitate learning across these broadly defined curricular areas.

Within the program, participatory discussion is emphasized; this is deemed better than didactic instruction alone in that it fostered a more communal environment.

The use of African proverbs stimulated dialogue and new insights about successful marital interaction and intervention. Structuring repetitive group recitations through poetry and proverbs resulted in a shared sense of purpose among group participants. The use of proverbs in this way is deemed essential in the education and empowerment of participants. Specifically, the authors place specific emphasis on the domains in which proverbs can be useful as articulated by Dzobo (1992):

a) to express truths that are difficult to comprehend; b) as guides for conduct – as bases for determining the unacceptability of certain forms of behavior; c) as commentary on human behavior – proverbs help to delineate the styles humans reflect in negotiating life; and d) to express values – to reflect centered values characteristic of Africans, from the psychological, moral, spiritual, humanistic, economic, and intellectual to the material.

(as cited in Rowe & Lyons-Rowe, 2009, p. 69)

While CIM has not been formally evaluated through empirical investigation, participant feedback from couples indicates general satisfaction with the training and increased knowledge pertinent to marital health. Specifically, the authors note that "participants develop a sociohistorical and community perspective toward marriage sustainability within the African American community. Participants reported a deeper appreciation of the broader social and contextual issues that impinge upon African American marriages…" (p. 73). Certainly, further evaluation of this program is warranted, particularly around which particular aspects of the program participants might find most illuminating and specific ways in which marital sustainability, satisfaction, or other outcomes might be influenced. This program is clearly developed based upon the values and needs of African Americans and therefore may feel more culturally familiar for many African American couples, serving as a departure for couples leery of traditional western counseling. This program may not adequately meet the needs of couples in which one or both partners have experienced significant trauma or other psychological distress, or where abuse may be present.

CIM can also serve as a model of how a culturally centered community-based intervention might be effective in promoting marriage and marital sustainment within the African American community, as it challenges couples' therapists to move beyond existing comfort zones and traditional models to engage African Americans in a more familiar milieu. Such a theoretical posture also challenges us to re-examine the notion of the "private" given marriage belongs to the community. Other strategies could include networking and partnering with other therapists or organizations that offer couples' retreats or workshops. Not only does this increase resources for clients, it also allows therapists to be more connected to the communities and individuals providing services to this population. Boyd-Franklin and Franklin (1998) argue that groups with culturally similar members may be an empowering and healing therapeutic tool that may counter the racist and sexist messages of dominant society while also negating conflictual familial messages about relationships. Yet, there are few examples of culturally centered group and community interventions for Black couples in the literature. Given the aforementioned preliminary outcomes, theoretical advocacy in these areas, and data supporting the need for culturally specific interventions, this gap is noteworthy. Clearly, more research and program development is needed in these areas.

Recommendations for Black Therapists

With increased numbers of African American mental health professionals, clients may specifically request a Black therapist and may be heartened to have an opportunity to work with someone whom they perceive as more culturally familiar and understanding of their culture, language, and family issues (Boyd-Franklin, 1989). Yet, clients may view African American therapists as representatives of the White mental health system and may therefore be reluctant to open up. Cultural affinity may assist in the joining process and in understanding complex relational constellations. Boyd-Franklin notes that, "there is a direct relationship between the degree to which Black therapists are comfortable with themselves, their own families, their own racial identity, and their ability to work with Black families" (1989, p. 105).

Hunt (1987, as cited in Boyd-Franklin, 1989) describes a number of potential therapeutic pitfalls and roles that African American therapists should avoid. First, the role of the *saboteur* in which anger and rage with professional peers and hegemonic psychological theories impede one's professionalism and ability to engage therapeutically. Second, the role as *protectors of the race,* in which one's own feelings about the racial collective may impede therapeutic effectiveness in actually addressing the client's specified presenting issues. Therapists may assume the role of the *moralizer* where the focus is on preaching and teaching, which may be experienced as being lectured and may occur at the expense of therapy. Last, *rescuers* assume a role that may reflect guilt of being of a higher social class and educational level and may result in a therapist failing to appropriately challenge clients and overextending oneself or altering boundaries. Overall, this may be disempowering for clients and result in burnout for the therapist. Clearly, there are a number of cultural and relational factors for African American therapists to consider in their work with African American couples.

Recommendations for Non-Black Therapists

Given the low numbers of Black therapists, it is likely that many African American clients will see non-Black therapists. The literature in multicultural counseling is replete with guidelines for engaging in culturally competent counseling, which are also discussed in Chapter 9. Specifically with regard to counseling African American couples, Boyd-Franklin makes specific recommendations. She advises non-Black therapists to be authentic and carefully examine one's own cultural and racial issues. She encourages the use of supervision and consultation and specifically the use of videotaping to review the process and interaction with clients. It should be noted that even seasoned therapists have an ethical obligation to seek consultation and additional training opportunities when practicing outside of areas of expertise, including with cultural groups with whom one may be unfamiliar (American Psychological Association, 2002). Non-Black therapists should never espouse a "color-blind" ideology in which they do not understand nor honor cultural differences; however, they should also not de-skill themselves and assume that they cannot be helpful to racially dissimilar couples. Finally, numerous authors have noted the importance of addressing cultural differences within the therapeutic relationship (see for example American Psychological Association, 2002; Boyd-Franklin, 1989). These recommendations are further delineated in Chapter 9.

Case Study

Jay (age 31) and Carla (age 27), recently engaged, sought counseling to address trust and communication issues prior to their getting married. Jay works in marketing and is completing his MBA. Carla recently finished law school and is currently studying for the bar exam while working full-time in a small law firm. When asked about the history of their relationship, they both chuckled as they looked at one another. When I inquired about the looks, Carla asked if I wanted the "real" story or when they "officially got together." I reassured them that therapy is about the "real story" and that this was their space to be as real as possible; there was no judgment about the circumstances around them getting together. Carla explained that they began as coworkers and developed a friendship while they were both involved in relationships with other people. Their friendship reportedly evolved over time and Carla stated that when their relationship became physical she ended things with her partner at that time. She paused and noted that she was unsure of when Jay ended his other relationship. There was some "miscommunication" and likely some significant overlap of relationships. They both agreed that this created a bumpy start to the relationship but shared the sentiment that they had a good friendship from the beginning.

They began living together one year ago because Carla's lease ended, although this was not the original plan. They both agreed that living together had been a positive experience and Jay noted that he believed it brought them closer together and increased their desire to be married. They described the strengths of their relationship as being their good friendship, having fun together, shared ambition and interests, and being there for one another. Both agreed that they needed to work on improving communication. Jay feels that

Carla doesn't always follow through on her commitments and Carla feels that Jay's quick temper is a problem. When they came in for therapy, they had not yet set a date for a wedding but they were hoping to get married in approximately 9–12 months.

Conceptualization and Interventions

I utilized an integrative perspective, including EFT and narrative therapy, but largely worked in accordance with Boyd-Franklin's multisystems approach. The couple was motivated to seek counseling. In the first two sessions, I worked to join the couple by using their language, particularly the humor that seemed to be central to the way in which they communicated. I utilized professional self-disclosure, answering questions about where I was from and my professional experiences. I sought initial background information on the couple and their families in a joint session. Both partners come from families in which the parents have been married for more than 30 years and remain committed. This was reportedly a source of pride for this couple as they understand that many Black couples may not have this legacy. They noted that their parents' relationships were exemplars for marriage, but had some difficulty in noting anything beyond "they stayed together" as why they were exemplars. In the next sessions, I utilized enactment within the sessions to: 1) assess the couples' structure and communication pattern; and 2) better understand their dominant narrative and influencing factors including familial patterns and present triangles. The couple engaged in discussions about such questions as: Why get married? What does marriage mean to you? What is the importance of children and child rearing, how many children, and when? What does money and financial planning mean to and for you? How do you communicate and how do you argue?

Through these enactments and discussions, I was able to assess a number of potential issues, particularly around the couple's structure, interactional dance, and communication patterns. Their pattern of communication was as follows: Jay gets upset about something that Carla does "wrong" or "she fails to follow through on something." Carla responds by becoming defensive, "makes excuses," to which Jay either becomes more upset and shuts down, becoming silent for some time. Carla responds by stating that she "didn't mean it and won't do it again." She reportedly has a difficult time giving Jay space to "cool off" and usually feels a sense of urgency to resolve matters at the time. This illustrates a clear "pursuer-distancer" pattern (Fogarty, 1976; Gottman, 1999). In addition, a power imbalance and struggle became more evident. Notably, Jay assumed a parental role in which he would identify things that Carla did "wrong." He would respond in a parentified way usually by scolding and yelling. Carla, in turn, would respond in a one-down or more child-like position by apologizing that she "didn't know better," "didn't mean it" and how she would respond differently. Such disagreements were largely around household tasks and while the couple shared responsibilities, Jay would become angered in the process of how things were done and its timeline. He would experience delays in timelines around household responsibilities as Carla's failure to follow on her word. Carla did not understand how such menial disagreements could result in large arguments and decrease relational satisfaction; Jay experienced these disagreements as significantly wounding and responded as such. He experienced Carla's lack of understanding as minimizing his concerns and what he deemed significant issues in their relationship. Communication during heightened emotions was a challenge for this couple. Both partners agreed that Jay had a "bad temper" and that he would "explode, yell, and scream." Jay noted in the first session with apparent pride that Carla "would just take it" and then, when he finally "got it all out" and calmed down, perhaps they could talk. I facilitated discussion between the partners about these issues and during an enactment, witnessed their interactional dance in the room, with Jay shutting down and silencing and Carla beginning to cry softly.

During these times, I used the opportunity to *soften* and to foster dialogue about their feelings in the moment. Jay admittedly had a difficult time with Carla's emotion and noted that he felt it was manipulative because he didn't understand why she needed to cry. Thus, during discussions at home when she cried, this would anger him even more. Carla had difficulty in articulating her feelings but intimated that she felt "attacked" and that she "didn't need him to be her daddy" and questioned his commitment to the relationship. I reflected both partner's feelings and used the *softening* in the moment to discuss the importance of communication and turning toward one another during heightened emotion, given the mutual vulnerability. Jay admitted that this was difficult for him as it felt like "accommodating," which was not positive in his view.

While my work with this couple is ongoing, I want to highlight a few factors. Consistent with much of the couples' literature, I value the experience of the therapist in the room. My own experience of this couple provides me relevant data about this couple. First, I could feel the power imbalance in the room. It is noteworthy that Carla physically appears younger than her stated age and, despite her employment as an attorney, dresses in a manner that is very young. Jay appears to be very image conscious and dresses in a very trendy and perhaps even flashy manner. Moving forward in therapy with this couple, continuing to slow down their interactional dance, realigning this couple with regard to their power struggle (I believe continued enactments and deconstructive questioning will be helpful in this regard), and increasing positive communication are the continued goals. I would also like to encourage the couple to attend a couples' workshop or retreat as this may offer them an opportunity to have a more intensive experience and engage with other young couples who may have comparable struggles and experiences. The psychoeducation of such a community-based workshop/retreat would also be a positive adjunct to our couples' counseling sessions. Ultimately, my goal is to support this couple in fostering healthy communication about their relationship and their struggles in whatever direction they deem most healthy for them at this time.

Conclusion

In reflecting on the discussed theoretical approaches, there are a number of conclusions that can be drawn. First, in exploring dominant theoretical approaches to couples' counseling with African Americans, it is clear that while there is general empirical support for these strategies, there is a dearth of specific research supporting their effectiveness and applicability with this population. Therefore, application of these theories should be done cautiously and with consideration of cultural competence. Yet, there are some collective lessons that may be garnered.

Social constructionist theories clearly demonstrate the healing power of externalizing social ills rather than internalizing oppressive racial and patriarchal ideologies as well as the creation of an empowering shared couple/family narrative (Freedman & Combs, 2008). We must also acknowledge the ways in which dominant cultural, political, and religious discourse has dictated marital and couple pathways in ways that may not be consistent with individual or couple's belief systems or life goals. From the cognitive and behavioral approaches, we learn tangible interventions and skills in supporting the continued importance of communication in relational health and marriage sustainability. Such approaches must be extended beyond the couple to include communication with children and extended family given the potential of extended family as primary supports to the couple as well as frequent reasons African American couples present for counseling. From the emotionally focused theoretical approaches, the importance of attachment and intimacy are underscored. Contemporary African American relationships suffer many internal and external threats to intimacy as previously discussed, such as internalized gender and racial stereotypes and invisibility; effective couples therapists must be willing to confront these issues and assist couples in strengthening in these areas. Given the data around trust and infidelity, alterations in relational boundaries, and increased rates of relationship concurrency, much is to be garnered from EFT and specific interventions focused specifically on attachment, intimacy, and emotional intelligence.

It is evident that African-centered voices are lacking in couples' discourse. The impact of such an absence is pronounced given the lack of empirical research supporting mainstream psychological interventions specifically with African American couples. This is especially problematic because clinicians frequently make the assumption that treatments empirically validated for couples' counseling are empirically validated for *all* couples. As repeatedly stated, strengths-based approaches are critical in working with African American couples. Clearly, an ecological understanding of African American relationships is warranted as is strongly reflected and advocated by Boyd-Franklin and her colleagues (Boyd-Franklin, 1989; Boyd-Franklin et al., 2008). Thus, systemic interventions, such as inclusion of relevant family members, and group and community work, must also be included in any comprehensive approach to the healing and restoration of African American partnerships and families. One area of intervention that is most wanting appears to be in community interventions.

Boyd-Franklin and Franklin (1998) identify the need for therapists of any racial background to seek consultation and supervision to appropriately address their own countertransference issues that may arise in clinical work with African American couples. Moreover, open dialogue among clinicians currently engaging in more culturally consistent strategies may assist in increasing the clinical acumen of couples' therapists as there appear to be deficits in clinical preparation for this work. The theoretical and research limitations as well as gaps in available programming further underscore the need for cultural competence. There is also a clear need to increase the numbers of mental health professionals of African ancestry engaging in culturally consistent clinical practice, relevant research, and program development to ultimately help to provide a better standard of care for the African American couples and families in need.

References

American Psychological Association. (2002). *Guidelines on multicultural education, training, research, practice, and organizational change for psychologists.* Washington, DC: APA.

American Psychological Association (2005). *American Psychological Association statement policy statement on evidence-based practice in psychology.* Accessed online 6/30/2011 at: http://www.apa.org/practice/resources/evidence/evidence-based-statement.pdf.

Ariel, S. (1999). *Culturally competent family therapy.* Westport, CT: Greenwood/Praeger.

Barkham, M., & Mellor-Clark, J. (2003). Bridging evidence-based practice and practice-based evidence: Developing a rigorous and relevant knowledge for the psychological therapies. *Clinical Psychology and Psychotherapy*, 10, 319–327.

Baucom, D.H., Epstein, N.E., LaTaillade, J.J., & Kirby, J.S. (2008). Cognitive-behavioral couple therapy. In A.S. Gurman (Ed.), *Clinical handbook of couple therapy, 4th edition* (pp. 31–72). New York: Guilford.

Baucom, D.H., Shoham, V., Mueser, K.T., Daiuto, A.D., & Stickle, T.R. (1998). Empirically supported couples and family therapies for adult problems. *Journal of Consulting and Clinical Psychology*, 66, 53–88.

Bernal, G., & Scharrón-del Río, M.R. (2001). Are empirically supported treatments (EST) valid for ethnic minorities? *Cultural Diversity and Ethnic Minority Psychology*, 7, 328–342.

Bodenmann, G. (1997). Can divorce be prevented by enhancing coping skills in couples? *Journal of Divorce and Remarriage*, 27 (3/4), 177–194.

Bowen, M. (1978). *Family therapy in clinical practice*. New York: Jason Aronson.

Boyd-Franklin, N. (1989). *Black families in therapy: Understanding the African American experience. 2nd edition*. New York: Guilford Press.

Boyd-Franklin, N., & Franklin, A.J. (1998). African American couples in therapy. In M. McGoldrick (Ed.), *Re-visioning family therapy: Race, culture, and gender in clinical practice* (pp. 268–281). New York: Guilford Press.

Boyd-Franklin, N., Kelly, S., & Durham, J. (2008). African American couples in therapy. In A.S. Gurman (Ed.), *Clinical handbook of couple therapy, 4th edition* (pp. 681–697). New York: Guilford.

Chambless, D.L., & Ollendick, T.H. (2001). Empirically supported psychological interventions: Controversies and evidence. *Annual Review of Psychology*, 52, 685–716.

Christensen, A., McGinn, M., & Williams, K.J. (2009). Behavioral couple therapies. In G.O. Gabbard (Ed.), *Textbook of Psychotherapeutic Treatments* (pp. 603–623). Washington, DC: American Psychiatric Publishing.

de Shazer, S. (1991). *Putting difference to work*. New York: Norton.

Dunham, S., & Ellis, C.M. (2010). Restoring intimacies with African American couples. In J. Carlson & L. Sperry (Eds.), *Recovering intimacy in love relationships: A clinician's guide* (pp. 295–316). New York: Routledge.

Epstein, N., & Baucom, D.H. (2002). Enhanced cognitive-behavioral therapy for couples: A contextual approach. Washington, DC: American Psychological Association.

Epston, D. (1999). Co-research: The making of an alternative knowledge. In *Narrative therapy and community work: A conference collection* (pp. 137–157). Adelaide, Australia: Dulwich Centre Publications.

Etchison, M., & Kleist, D.M. (2000). Review of narrative therapy: Research and review. *Family Journal*, 8(1), 61–67.

Fogarty, T.F. (1976). System concepts and the dimensions of self. In P.J. Guerin (Ed.), *Family therapy*. New York: Gardner.

Foucault, M. (1980). *Power/knowledge: Selected interviews and other writings 1972-1977*, C. Gordon (Ed). London: Harvester.

Freedman, J., & Combs, G. (2008). Narrative couple therapy. In A.S. Gurman (Ed.), *Clinical handbook of couple therapy, 4th edition* (pp. 229–258). New York: Guilford.

Gallardo, M., & McNeill, B. (Eds.). (2009). *Intersections of multiple identities: A casebook of evidence-based practices with diverse populations*. New York: Routledge.

Gottman, J.M. (1999). *The marriage clinic*. New York: Norton.

Gottman, J.M., & Gottman, J.S. (2008). Gottman method couple therapy. In A.S. Gurman (Ed.), *Clinical handbook of couple therapy, 4th edition* (pp. 138–166). New York: Guilford.

Griner, D., & Smith, T. (2006). Culturally adapted mental health intervention: A meta-analytic review. *Psychotherapy: Theory, Research, Practice, Training*, 43(4), 531–548.

Guerin, P., Fogarty, T., Fay, L., & Kautto, J. (1996). *Working with relationship triangles*. New York: Guilford.

Halford, W.K., Sanders, M.R., & Behrens, B.C. (1993). A comparison of the generalization of behavioral marital therapy and enhanced behavioral marital therapy. *Journal of Consulting and Clinical Psychology*, 61, 51–60.

Hoyt, M.F. (2008). Solution-focused couple therapy. In A.S. Gurman (Ed.), *Clinical handbook of couple therapy, 4th edition* (pp. 259–295). New York: Guilford.

Johnson, S.M. (2008). Emotionally focused couple therapy. In A.S. Gurman (Ed.), *Clinical handbook of couple therapy, 4th edition* (pp. 107–137). New York: Guilford.

Johnson, S.M., & Lebow, J. (2000). The coming of age of couple therapy: A decade review. *Journal of Marital and Family Therapy*, 26, 23–38.

Kelly, S., & Boyd-Franklin, N. (2009) Joining, understanding, and supporting Black couples in treatment. In M. Rastogi & V. Thomas (Eds.), *Multicultural couple therapy* (pp 235–254). Thousand Oaks, CA: Sage.

LaTaillade, J.J. (2006). Considerations for treatment of African American couple relationships. *Journal of Cognitive Psychotherapy: An International* Quarterly, 20, 341–358.

Miller, R.B., Anderson, S., & Keala, D.K. (2004). Is Bowen theory valid? A review of basic research. *Journal of Marital and Family Therapy*, 30, 453–466.

Miller, R.M., Johnson, L.J., Sandberg, J.G., Stringer-Seibold, T., & Gfeller-Strouts, L. (2000). An addendum to the 1997 outcome research chart. *The American Journal of Family Therapy*, 28, 347–354.

Minuchin, S. (1974). *Families and family therapy.* Cambridge, MA: Harvard University Press.

Minuchin, S. & Fishman, H. C. (2004). *Family therapy techniques.* Cambridge, MA: Harvard University Press.

Minuchin, S., Lee, W., & Simon, G.M. (2006). *Mastering family therapy: Journeys of growth and transformation.* Hoboken, NJ: Wiley Press.

Nichols, M.P., & Schwartz, R.P. (2005). *Family therapy: Concepts and methods.* 7th edition. New York: Allyn and Bacon.

Nichols, M.P., & Schwartz, R.P. (2009). *Family therapy: Concepts and methods.* 9th edition. New York: Prentice Hall.

Payne, M. (2006). *Narrative therapy: An introduction for counselors.* London: Sage.

Roberto-Forman, L. (2008). Transgenerational couple therapy. In A.S. Gurman (Ed.), *Clinical handbook of couple therapy, 4th edition* (pp. 196–228). New York: Guilford.

Rowe, D., & Lyons-Rowe, S. (2009). Conversations in marriage: An African-centered marital intervention. In M. Gallardo, & B. McNeill (Eds.), *Intersections of multiple identities: A casebook of evidence-based practices with diverse populations* (pp. 60–84). New York: Routledge.

Ryan, K., & Gottman, J. (n.d.). *The effectiveness of the art and science of love: A workshop for couples 1999–2003.* Unpublished manuscript accessed online 6/30/2011 at: http://www.gottman.com/49874/Marriage--Couples-Research.html.

Sackett, D.L., Rosenberg, W.M., Gray, J.A., Haynes, R.B., & Richardson, W.S. (1996). Evidence based medicine: What it is and what it isn't. *BMJ*, 312, 71–72.

Sexton, J. (2008). *Amalgamation schemes: Antiblackness and the critique of multiracialism.* Minneapolis, MN and London: University of Minnesota Press.

Simon, G. (2008). Structural couples therapy. In A.S. Gurman (Ed.), *Clinical handbook of couple therapy, 4th edition* (pp. 323–353). New York: Guilford.

Some, S. (2000). *The spirit of intimacy: Ancient African teachings in the ways of relationships.* New York: William Morrow Paperbacks/Harper Collins Publishing.

Spring, B. (2007). Evidence-based practice in clinical psychology: What it is, why it matters; what you need to know. *Journal of Clinical Psychology*, 63, 611– 631.

Whisman, M.A., Dixon, A.E., & Johnson, B. (1997). Therapists' perspectives of couple problems and treatment issues in couple therapy. *Journal of Family Psychology*, 11, 361–366.

EXPERT INTERVIEW

Dr. Thomas Parham is the Vice Chancellor for Student Affairs and adjunct faculty at the University of California Irvine. He is a Past President of the Association of Black Psychologists, an American Psychological Association and American Counseling Association Fellow, and has authored numerous publications including: *The Psychology of Blacks, Counseling African Descent People.*

What suggestions do you have for training therapists to work specifically with Black couples?

Working with Black couples does not begin by working with couples in therapy but rather begins at the cultural deep structure: therapists have to be able to understand the culture of African people because so many of our relationships are impacted by the way we perceive the world. They have to understand culture and develop a level of cultural competence that is anchored in the cultural realities of Black life in America. Effective counseling needs a cultural basis.

How would you suggest that, especially White, therapists do this?

First, masters/doctoral graduate training programs must [do a better job] of providing culturally competent training [specific to African descent peoples]. We must demand this. Second, they have to couple the didactic elements of their curriculum with experiential elements to give them practical clinical training in doing this kind of work. Although this is easier said than done, [graduate schools] would not let a student go out and give an MMPI [Minnesota Multiphasic Personality Inventory] if they did not provide the student with assessment training, so why would we let them go work on Black couples when they don't have a clue on how to do it? It is no different to me. Third, I think we have to talk to some of the provider agencies that are providing continuing education because most licensed people at a masters or doctoral level have to engage in continuing education and the problem is that a lot of the continuing education provided, is provided in a landscape that is culturally sterile (i.e. does not acknowledge the relevance of culture).

What skills do Black couples need in today's world to stay together?

One, I believe that you have to have basic communication skills because you have to be able to communicate with your partner. You also have to have skills in being able to compromise because relationships are really a partnership where each has to compromise about some element within the relationship so that each can get their own needs met. You also have to have compatible interests. Also, comprise is important but if your whole relationship is built on compromising what your interests are, then you are not being fulfilled and you are not growing. So the 3 Cs are: communication, compromise, and compatible interests.

I also think that the skills that couples have to have is an awareness into their own issues. What is the residual baggage they carry? Secondly, they have to have insight into how that residual baggage manifests itself within the dynamics of the relationship.

For example, let's say you have a client in which his first spouse cheated on him, so now because he was so hurt by that, even though he is now in a happy relationship, he is a little bit more paranoid and sensitive in terms of the flexibility he gives his current mate because he does not really trust her, when trust is not really their issue, it's his issue. However, the way it comes out is him projecting it [into the relationship]. This is what I mean by needing to have insight.

The third element at the deep structure level I think people have to have [is] an analysis of values. What do they value? What do they hold near and dear? How compatible are we on those things?

There is so much attention paid to the negatives of African American romantic relationships, what do you see as the strengths these couples bring to their relationships?

I do not necessarily pay a lot of attention to the negatives even though I know a lot of the negatives are out there. One strength is a cultural value system that is more collective as opposed to individualistic. A second strength is a history of struggle which can be a double edge sword, because if struggle is only related to trauma that you have experienced, then sometimes that gets played out in the context of the relationship you have. But if it is related to some progress that you have had, you are in a good space.

The third important piece is, couples bring a rich legacy, and the legacy is anchored in, not just struggle, but within the essence of what I call "spirituality." I am not talking about religiosity here. What I am talking about is the core of spirituality which is energy and its life force. If you think about the energy and life force within each individual, what is true is that whenever you have spirituality, on the other side of the scale, you always have, particularly for Black folk and Black couples, unjustified suffering, unmerited pain, and undeserved harm. So the question is not, do bad things happen in your life, the question is, how are we are able to sustain some movement and momentum in the face of that adversity? This is why I pair the sense of spirituality with the notion of struggle. I think that this becomes a strength that Black couples bring with them because life is going to present most relationships with hardship,[and spirituality will help them deal with it].

Describe some of the weaknesses of struggling Black couples.

One is I think that there is an adoption of a Eurocentric value system when measuring who is an eligible mate (e.g. he must have a college degree; she must look like a model). I think that both men and women do this, but I think that more sisters do this than men partly because the way the cultural dynamic is set up between males and females: men have to be in the position of initiation; women are in the position of confirmation. So men ask a woman to dance. Women respond yes or no. It is usually male initiated, while women confirm. So because of this, there is a bit more emphasis on women [rejecting men]. I think that anchoring your relationship in the Eurocentric value system puts undue pressure and expectations on people that, in some cases, [is] unrealistic in terms of meeting [a partner].

It used to be that a man was defined by his ability to provide for and protect his family. It used to be a man had to have a tender side that was able to bring out the best in his partner in the same way a woman had to bring out the best in her man. It was a mutual admiration society that fit with this notion. Some of those fundamental values have been traded in these days by this new generation of people, who put criteria on others to determine their eligibility.

The second problem I think we have with relationships in my mind has to do with trust issues. I think that couples have trouble trusting. The [big] problem in relationships if a couple has a tendency to externalize trust and responsibility. Externalizing trust, for example, might be, "I'm going to make you jump through 3, 4, 5, 8, 10 hoops before I decide whether I can trust you or not, based on how much [personal] baggage I have been through." Part what of what I want to suggest to folk, this is one of my "Parhamisms," that I have written about in a couple of my books: real trust is not an external circumstance, but rather an internal virtue.

This means that, the question is not, "Can I trust you?"—the real question is "Can I trust myself enough to take a risk with you?" But it also puts the responsibility back on the individual rather than externalizing responsibility outside him/her.

Another problem is that, in some respects, relationships are built on too much lust and not enough substance. So, we get taught to look at who is fine and who is attractive and we get taught to then cultivate that attractiveness so that each person in the relationship packages themselves to look the most attractive to the other person. Then once we get into the lust phase, where we are very attracted to folk, we end up developing a level of intimacy with them—and find that lust only lasts so long. One needs to look at the substance of the relationship—what is going to help the relationship sustain itself? My position is, and I would argue, that lust is not enough. We just look at people who are fine. And the problem is that beauty fades, and people change, but it is the substance that endures. For example, when you have to face economic hardship, how do you work together on compromise, collaboration, and communication? When you have to go through health issues together (life and death issues) lust wears off quickly, so you have to have something more substantive to be able to sustain relationships in those hard times. So for me, those are among the things that I would be critical about in terms of relationships.

I did a workshop a while back entitled the "Institution of Marriage versus the Culture of Love." The goal was to say that the institution of marriage allows you to have certain principles, rituals, and rules that people adhere to, but it's the culture of love that helps to sustain the spark, the excitement, etc. And I think that what relationships have to be able to do is to not get so wrapped up in the institutions of relationship, the ritual of relationship, or the mechanisms of relationship, that they forget how to [be in the relationship and love one another].

What specific advice would you have for non-Black clinicians working with Black couples? Specific advice for Black clinicians?

The first advice I would give would be to study. Study, study, study. Become culturally competent around Black culture and lifestyle. Second, I would help them understand that culture is not a surface structure understanding. But rather is a complex constellation of mores and values and customs and traditions, that define an individual's design for living and a pattern for interpreting reality.

Thirdly, I would recommend that they learn how to understand the residual baggage that both men and women carry within the context of their relationships. You have lots of Black folks with wounded souls and they play that wound out within the context of their relationships because typically we impact the people who are closest to us and those that we love. So part of what a clinician has to do is to be able to recognize where a person has been either cracked or broken. But also you have got to figure out how to help them heal in the broken places.

Specific advice for African American clinicians?

Some of my advice would parallel because what I am very clear about is that there is a difference between skin color and consciousness. So the fact that you are an African American clinician does not make you culturally competent. It does give you an edge. But if, for example, you are a Black clinician who grew up in the White suburbs of America and have no clue about Black culture, being Black does not necessarily equip you with the skills to understand and manage your own people and circumstance. They have to develop a level of cultural competence too, even though life experience and training can give them a little bit of a leg up. But life experience is not enough—you need to have clinical training and cultural competence as well for working with Black folk.

Secondly, I would let Black couples know that clinicians have to be aware of their own biases and assumptions they bring with them into a clinical space. One must be aware of those particular pieces. The other thing that Black clinicians need to have is credibility [which often comes with life experience]. It is hard to teach a couple how to navigate the space between them, their children, and taking care of parents/elders. If you are a 28-year-old clinician who is single and have never had a child before, this may impact your credibility with couples.

So trying to talk to couples about how to navigate that space becomes a bit more difficult if [you] don't have not only the worldview but the experiential base to be able to bring a level of credibility to the table.

What are the advantages of marriage/long-term committed relationships for Black couples and the Black community?

I think that the longest enduring institution in the black community is family so the family is one of those places that provides for nurturance of its young people, it stimulates intellectual creativity in its young; it provides a point of grounding and anchoring for the adults that are committed to try to build something that is bigger than them as single people. In Black communities, it is important to not only build strong families for individuals, for the development of the children, for the grounding of the adults in something bigger than themselves, but also it is the most salient element in building strong communities. One of the reasons why our communities are not as strong as they could be is because of the deterioration of the black family.

Is there anything else you think we should include in the book?

There ought to be a chapter in the book on discovering or uncovering your residual baggage. Everybody has it, not everyone is aware of it and not everyone has the insight to know how it impacts them in their current relationship. The developmental perspective is so important.

9

CULTURALLY SENSITIVE GUIDELINES FOR NON-BLACK THERAPISTS WORKING WITH AFRICAN AMERICAN COUPLES

Khyana K. Pumphrey

As stated throughout this book, African American couples may struggle with cultural mistrust when seeking counseling (Boyd-Franklin, 1989). This is especially true if the clinician is not African American. Most African Americans are familiar with society's perception of them as "problem people." Marginalization for Blacks comes in many forms such as police profiling, routinely getting followed in stores (because of the assumption that Black people steal), being seen as a threat when walking down the street (e.g. many people cross the street when confronted with a Black male passing them), and not having a positive media presence (e.g. popular news stories consistently report incidences of Black violence and crime). These are daily painful reminders of the many racial microaggressions African Americans face simply by virtue of being Black in a society that rejects Blackness and Black people. Sue et al. (2008) defines racial microaggressions as those subtle, as well as hidden, racialized slights common in the workplace (and society) that often denigrate and invalidate the culture and experience of people of color. When an African American couple present for therapy to a non-Black clinician, the couple may automatically be on guard for racial microaggressions. They may keep secrets from the therapist (Boyd-Franklin, 1989) to minimize negative judgment. Thus, it is especially important for non-Black clinicians to be culturally sensitive and understand how to build an effective rapport with Black couples so that counseling can be successful.

The American Psychological Association (APA) has developed and published two documents to address the necessity for multicultural competence in mental health care. They are the "Guidelines on multicultural education, training, research, practice, and organizational psychology" (2003) and the "Guidelines for providers of psychological services to ethnic, linguistic, and culturally diverse populations" (1990). Together these documents outline the APA's principles for providing culturally sensitive treatment. In sum, they suggest counselors do the following: remain current in the multicultural literature regarding culturally competent practice; recognize the role culture/ethnicity plays in their own lives, as well as the lives (and identities) of their clients; respect diverse family structures/roles and understand the adverse social, environmental, and political factors impacting their clients lives; work to eliminate their own biases and stereotypes of oppressed groups; and develop the knowledge, skills, and awareness necessary to work sensitively with diverse populations.

To this end, the purpose of this chapter is two-fold: first, it seeks to identify the client/therapist dynamics that can challenge the therapeutic process and the necessity for cultural competence with African American couples and, second, to elucidate strategies for non-Black therapists in the treatment of Black couples. One challenge experienced by many non-Black clinicians is a lack of awareness and knowledge of the historical context of the African American experience and perspective that influences their daily decisions/choices. Non-Black therapists may be unaware or may significantly minimize (or even overestimate) the impact of the contextual factors discussed in Chapter 2. As repeatedly stated throughout this book, there can be no culturally sensitive treatment without an adequate understanding of these factors. This chapter will provide specific strategies for non-Black therapists to increase cultural sensitivity in their work with African American couples. As discussed throughout the book, specific contextual factors faced by African American couples include: socio-historical issues (painful legacy of slavery, stereotypes of Black masculinity and femininity); disparate Black male incarceration, unemployment/underemployment, poverty within the Black community, decreased multigenerational wealth (even amongst the Black middle class), declining marriage rates; imbalanced sex ratio; the purported "gender war" between Black men and women; societal constrictions on Black men's inability to achieve "primary breadwinner" status and resultant role strain (i.e. couples may desire this but reality prevents black men from achieving it); and racism, oppression, and daily discrimination. Strengths of Black couples include a strong spiritual focus for many, the importance of family, a positive racial identity, kinship networks, and a collectivistic identity (Boyd-Franklin, 2003; Carolan & Allen, 1999; Chapman, 1995; Cowdery, Scarborough, Knudson-Martin, Seshadri, Lewis, & Mahoney, 2009; Dunham & Ellis, 2010; Glick, 1997; Pinderhughes, 2002).

Resistance and Cultural Mistrust

If therapy is not a common experience Black couples may feel a sense of vulnerability in the presence of the therapist whom they may see as intrusive or part of a system/institution that seeks to oppress them (Boyd-Franklin, 2003). For example, many African Americans see therapy as labeling and believe that others will think of them as "crazy." Additionally, there is often pressure amongst family to keep relational problems within the family. If the couple is mandated to therapy by the court system, this further stresses the ability to establish rapport and thus they may resist the experience. A sensitive approach for mandated couples is for the clinician to make clear the relationship between the facility, the therapist, and the referring agency, so that couples understand the limits of confidentiality. Grier and Cobbs (1968) discuss resistance with Black clients as a "healthy cultural paranoia." They describe it as a protective factor African Americans use in response to racism and discrimination. Non-Black clinicians should know that African Americans place a high value on privacy and keeping family secrets within the family unit; therefore, there may be a fear of exposing them in therapy and being negatively judged by the therapist. This often presents as "resistance." Boyd-Franklin (2003) suggests that a sensitive approach to deal with mistrust is for clinicians to examine the specific timing of their interventions. For example, instead of doing an initial intake assessment the same way for all couples (e.g. asking questions in which some couples might find intrusive), concentrate on building rapport and personalizing the assessment and therapy process specific to the couple with which one is working. This may go a long way in providing sensitive treatment. Oftentimes assessment and therapy happen together and should not be considered separate processes. Because African Americans are more likely to utilize their extended social network (family, friends, church, etc.), by the time they present for therapy, they are in crisis mode. This may heighten their sense of vulnerability and mistrust. Boyd-Franklin (2003) believes the goal of couple therapy ought to be to empower couples and diminish the history of powerlessness. She defines the empowerment as the "process whereby the therapist restructures the couple to facilitate the appropriate designation and use of power within the couple's relationship and to mobilize the couple's ability to successfully interact with each other and external systems" (p. 86).

Black Couples Presentation in Counseling

According to Boyd-Franklin (2003) she finds that most African Americans presenting for counseling fit into six categories: 1) traditional marriage counseling; 2) unmarried couple in long-term, live-in, or "common law" relationship; 3) premarital therapy—considering marriage but concerned about their relationship; 4) couples in crisis—appear after a fight and then disappear for long periods of time; 5) a couple seeking divorce mediation; and 6) a couple who presents with a child as the presenting issue. These categories are more distinct in the types of issues they bring to the therapeutic relationship especially with non-Black clinicians. Couples in category two tend to be the most common client; they are older, of low income demographically and their presenting issues include not having married because of finances, and one partner is now pressuring the other to legalize their relationship. Additionally, category two couples may seek treatment because one member has become dysfunctional (AODA [alcohol and other drug abuse], medical, psychiatric problems, etc.). Couples in category three tend to be younger African American professionals, living together considering marriage, and are taking a preventative approach to therapy and are much more sophisticated about couples' therapy. Couples in category three tend to present after a fight/confrontation and may have a series of crisis interventions. Divorcing couples are often referred by their legal representative or the court to help families work through problems. The last category of couple appear with their child as the presenting issue (often times school referred) but find it a safer approach to address their own interpersonal struggles through discussing their child's issues, instead of directly focusing on their issues as a couple.

Couples in general seek marital therapy for interpersonal difficulties related to intimacy and lack of emotional affection, economic issues, generational issues, power dynamics, and communication problems (Boyd-Franklin, 2003; Doss, Simpson, & Christensen, 2004; Whisman, Dixon, & Johnson, 1997). The issue of intimacy often suggests a lack of sexual or emotional connection but, as Sperry (2010) identifies, the loss of intimacy is complex and complicated especially for African American couples. Common intimacy issues of presenting couples may involve physical and emotional violence, Internet pornography and cyber-sex, work/career demands, health problems, financial issues, and unrealistic expectations (Sperry, 2010). Specific barriers to intimacy for Black couples have been explored throughout this book (e.g. gender and power dynamics, trust issues because of internalized stereotypes, etc.). Non-Black clinicians need to be aware of the unique barriers to intimacy African American couples face, as well as common intimacy issues influencing most couples' relationships.

Additionally, Black couples may be more likely than their white counterparts to present with generational issues. Generation issues often have to do with unresolved family of origin issues. Communication issues between African American couples often revolve around not knowing how to talk to one another given that many Black men limit expression of feelings because they are often seen as a sign of weakness. Black women frequently present with this as an issue of focus in couples' therapy (Boyd-Franklin, 2003). As DeLoach suggests in Chapter 8, clinicians should attempt to join the couple and become part of their couple system. Exploring their experiences (e.g. family of origin, past romantic relationships, etc.) will help illuminate the couple's communication issues. Clarifying couples' relational expectations is also important in understanding the couple's presenting issues. It is also useful for clinicians to provide psychoeducation around positive communication patterns which include both positive and negative feelings as well as suggestions regarding how each can listen and hear what the other is saying and feeling. Clinicians should also explain the process of therapy with couples. Boyd-Franklin (2003) recognizes that this may be a new experience for some African American couples but sees it as the clinician's duty to prepare the couple for the discomfort in communicating their feelings in and out of therapy which will lead to new meaning in how they communicate.

Therapist–Couple Matches

The previous chapter provides an extensive review of traditional and non-traditional therapeutic approaches as well as specific ways to make these approaches more culturally sensitive for work with African American couples, thus they will not be reviewed here. Instead, the rest of this chapter will provide non-Black therapists with specific strategies for working with Black couples and highlight important areas of awareness not previously covered. African American couples' selection of therapist may be voluntary, by referral, word of mouth, or involuntary (e.g. mandated); chosen for them either by an employee assistance program or based on accessibility provided by an insurance carrier. Even if couples request an African American therapist they may only have access to a non-Black therapist. Therefore, clinicians ought to be aware of some of the challenges and barriers they may face in cross-cultural and/or cross-racial therapeutic relationships. Helms (1980) introduced to clinicians and researchers alike the idea that there is a developmental process to racial consciousness/identity for both Blacks and whites. This theoretical explanation of the effects of race on counseling is extensive (Atkinson, 1983; Atkinson, Morten, & Sue, 1998; Banks, 1975; Brown, 1950; Butler, 1975; Cross, 1971, 1978, 1995; Gardner, 1971; Harrison, 1975; Helms & Cook, 1999; Jackson, 1973: Jones, 1978; Sattler, 1977; Smith, 1991; Sue & Sue, 1999; Sue, Arredondo, & McDavis, 1992; Vontress, 1971).

To summarize, it is first important to understand the stages of racial consciousness, the behavioral dispositions clients and counselors may enter with into the therapeutic relationship, and the effects of the counselor's and client's stage on the counseling process. Racial identity development models have been used to conceptualize how important race is to African American clients in terms of who they are. In other words, is racial/ethnic background an important variable or not (for clients)? These models are typically stage models but here they will simply be used as a conceptualization tool for culturally sensitive treatment. Understanding how important race is to African American clients' identity and sense of self will go a long way in a counselor's ability to provide culturally sensitive treatment. The therapist should not assume that racial identity is or is not an important identity variable for all African American clients. Instead, therapists should assess this in the first session. The foundational model of Black Racial Identity Development (BRID) is Cross's (1971, 1995) stage model. Stages include: pre-encounter, encounter, immersion/emersion, and internalization. Within these stages are the attitudes toward Blackness, whiteness, and attitudinal correlates. In the *pre-encounter* stage Blacks may be in denial or denigrate themselves but idealize and identify with whites. This can produce high anxiety, low self-actualization, low self-regard, preference for white counselors and low self-esteem. In the *encounter* stage Blacks have a sense of euphoria and an uncritical eye about being Black; however, they are confused and critical about their attitudes toward whites. This produces low anxiety, high self-actualization, high self-regard, and preference for Black counselors. In the *immersion/emersion* stage Blacks have an idealization about self but reject or denigrate whites, thus producing high anxiety, low self-actualization, low self-regard, hostility, and see whites as having an evil orientation. In the *internalization* stage Blacks emerge from immersion/emersion with a sense of security about their racial identity and translate that security into activism around concerns of their racial group (Helms, 1980). This model is useful given the complexity of race and how much it may influence individuals as well as couples and their psychological processes. It may also provide clinicians with a window into the couple's attitudes, acceptance, or rejection related to counseling and the issues that arise, and may assist the clinician in assessing the comfort level of the couple with the therapist and quite possibly with one another.

Helms' conceptualizes white racial identity as a stage process, similar to that of the original BRID (Cross, 1971, 1995). This model provides a framework for understanding how race relates to individuals' and couples' identity. Other racial and ethnic identity models, also useful conceptualization tools, include Sellers, Rowley, Chavous, Shelton, and Smith's (1997) Multidimensional Inventory of Black Identity (MIBI) and Phinney's (1992) ethnic identity model. Helms' White Racial Identity Development (WRID) model statuses are: contact, disintegration, reintegration, pseudo-independence, and autonomy. This model is important for non-Black therapists to understand in their self-assessment of meeting multicultural guidelines (American Psychologist Association, 2003) which suggests clinicians be encouraged to recognize that, as cultural beings, they may hold attitudes and beliefs that can detrimentally influence their perceptions of and interactions with individuals who are ethnically and racially different from themselves. In the *contact* stage whites can choose situations or circumstances that will keep them separate and apart from acknowledging their racial consciousness. In *disintegration* the person has to acknowledge their racial consciousness which is usually connected to guilt and/or depression as it relates to the idea of racism and one's part in perpetuating racism. It is in this stage a person can choose to over-identify with Blacks in the use of language, behaviors, and/or attitudes and whites may seek to become protective of Blacks and their experience or they regress back to their comfort zone of their whiteness. In the *reintegration* stage whites feel a strong pressure to conform to the norms of the society. Acting against racism may have costs. There is a tendency to slip backwards, often blaming the victims of racism or their life circumstances. Whites will also attempt to distance themselves from the white collective saying, "But I am an individual." Or "I don't do those things!" They may choose to identify with some other marginalized group. In the *pseudo-independence* stage whites begin to understand institutional and cultural racism, but are not yet sure about what to do about it or how to be an effective ally to people of color in the struggle for racial justice. Finally, in *autonomy* whites accept the racial similarities and differences, recognize that norms exist but seek out ways to involve the self with diverse cultural opportunities (Helms, 1980). Having knowledge and understanding of these stages will assist the clinician in respecting and assessing not only the client's but their own worldview, psychosocial functioning, and expressions of distress. However, a cautionary note, these models may not always be appropriate nor should they be applied to all African American clients and/or all white counselors.

These models can be useful predictors of the relationship between a Black couple and a white therapist as they can help predict how differences in racial awareness on the part of both the couple and therapist become operationalized in therapy. For example, there is the *parallel* relationship where the counselor and client are in the same stage. In the *crossed* relationship, the counselor and client are in opposite stages, and, in the *progressive* relationship, the counselor's stage is one stage further along in the continuum than the client's. Finally, in the *regressive* relationship the client is at least one stage more advanced than the counselor (Helms, 1980) which may not bode well for treatment. Counselors should be sensitive to these pairings and their potential implications for the success of treatment. These models have more often been applied to individuals than couples; however, they still serve as an important conceptual framework in couples' treatment.

In considering how racial consciousness and the relationship between clinician and client may develop, it is necessary to examine how Helms (1980) predicts outcomes in Black dyads, white dyads, and mixed dyads. In Black dyads if the relationship is *parallel* in the pre-encounter stage both will use strategies designed to deny and avoid racial issues and to reinterpret whatever happens in a manner consistent with perceived negative stereotypes. As a result clients often terminate with little symptom remission and the client frequently leaves counselling before it is completed. If the relationship is *crossed* there may be a general non-acceptance of one another; the counselor may be low in empathy, use advice giving, and the client may be passive and may not engage in the process. If the counselor is a positive role model the client may develop feelings of Blackness and self-esteem may be enhanced. If the relationship is *regressive* the client may attempt to reform the counselor and the counselor attempts to avoid racial issues. These may be short relationships because the client's anger is enhanced thereby increasing the counselor's anxiety. If the relationship is *progressive* there may be discussion around each trying to prove they are Black enough. These may be longer relationships but may only increase enthusiasm to engage the client. This does not mean therapy is getting done. This competitive triad then may become superimposed on the couple's dyad bringing about another complication when couples may not match one another in their racial identity awareness. When this occurs the client–therapist relationship may become ineffective and may begin to parallel the couple's relationship. Therefore, therapists should provide psychoeducation to the couple in order to process the possible psychological processes, interventions, goals, and expectations. In mixed-raced dyads if the relationship is *parallel* the client may test and manipulate and the counselor may be unassertive and task oriented. The relationship may be long-lasting but only because it reinforces stereotypes. In the *crossed* relationship there may be refusal to become involved with one another and these relationships are short-lived. In the *progressive* relationship the counselor attempts to model positive adjustment and to elicit denied feelings. The potential for client cross-racial skill development is enhanced. In the *regressive* relationship the counselor interacts in a reserved manner, with uneasiness, and incongruence is evident. These relationships often have premature termination and the client will seek out a counselor more in line with their attitudes, values, and beliefs. Again, although these models have predictive utility non-Black clinicians should also use their own clinical judgment in forming relationships with Black couples. Most seasoned clinicians know that relationships with couples are not always predictable—sometimes we form strong bonds with clients we least expect to, yet have difficulty establishing rapport with clients we'd assume easily formed relationships.

In couples counseling with African Americans, non-Black therapists may not have had many experiences with African Americans (Knox, Burkard, Johnson, Suzuki, & Ponterotta, 2003) and may find themselves being overly cautious about making mistakes, so much so that they behave in a meek and mild manner which does not show the couple the expertise and credibility clients are looking for in the therapeutic relationship (Boyd-Franklin, 2003). Second, non-Black therapists may engage in inappropriate use of slang in an effort to join the couple; however, this can be seen as condescending (Sue & Sue, 2003) and disrespectful. Third, non-Black therapists may feel the need to be perfect in their work with African American couples but clinicians need to have patience and allow the therapeutic relationship to develop (Boyd-Franklin, 2003). To develop this therapeutic alliance Sue & Sue (2003) suggest clinicians be willing to extend themselves in an authentic way and establish a connection with their clients. Clinicians should allow couples to express their feelings of anger and rejection, and appreciate their right to reject therapy, in that the expressions may have little or nothing to do with the therapist but be more about the cultural paranoia described earlier. In addition, clinicians often have difficulty deciding if and when to raise the issue of race with their clients. When clinicians do not raise the issue Boyd-Franklin (2003) suggests they are colluding with the couple to deny race. The issue of race is too important to ignore and Sue & Sue (2003) recommend that asking couples how they experience being seen by a non-Black therapist may elicit a response that expresses anger and/or rejection but clinicians should not personalize the couples' response. Giving the couple permission to discuss race will suggest they can discuss anything in the therapeutic context (Boyd-Franklin, 2003). Bringing up race early in the therapeutic encounter (first session) demonstrates the cultural sensitivity of the therapist and could make non-African American therapists appear more credible. Arguably, this is a critical skill non-Black clinicians should have in working with Black clients and other clients of color. It typically works well when therapists bring up race, social class, gender issues, values, and other areas of difference that could impact therapeutic rapport in the first session when therapists review the rights and responsibilities of counselors and clients in therapy. Bringing up racial differences as an area that could impact the trust in the relationship may encourage clients to openly express their concerns if the therapist is not African American. For therapists who share a minority group status with clients, caution is required so as not to assume an automatic connection to African American couples as cultural paranoia may extend to them as well as white therapists (Sue & Sue, 2003).

Counselor Cultural Awareness and Knowledge: A Therapeutic Necessity

Counselor cultural awareness and knowledge is paramount for the therapeutic relationship with African American couples. As such, this interaction process should encourage therapists and therapists-in-training to consider questions to assess their own racial and cultural biases along with the knowledge and skills necessary to enhance the therapeutic relationship (Kwan, 2001). It is the clinicians' responsibility to regularly explore these issues within themselves as this demonstrates a willingness, openness, and capacity for genuineness that is easily transferable to work with African American couples. To assess racial and cultural biases clinicians should ask themselves the following questions as proposed by Helms and Cook, 1999 (as cited in Kwan, 2001):

> 1. What do you consider to be normal therapist and client behavior during therapy? (Normal Behavior); 2. If group goals are in conflict with the client's individual needs or desires, how do you resolve the conflicts? (Individualistic orientation); 3. At what age do you believe that a "child" should leave his or her parents and make a life independent of them? (Overemphasis on Independence); 4. What strategies do you use to include client's support systems as allies? (Client Support System); 5. Can you describe an instance in which you intervened to change a system to fit the client's need rather than requiring him or her to change to fit the system? (Discomfort with System Change).
>
> (p.165)

Likewise, Arredondo et al. 1996 (as cited in Kwan, 2001) provide guidelines for multicultural competency, attitudes, and beliefs: culturally skilled counselors believe that cultural self-awareness and sensitivity to one's own cultural heritage is essential; are aware of how their own background and experiences have influenced attitudes, values, and biases about psychological processes; are able to recognize the limits of their multicultural competency and expertise; and can recognize their sources of discomfort with differences that exist between themselves and clients in terms of race, ethnicity, and culture. Arredondo et al.'s knowledge guidelines of culturally competent clinicians include:

> having specific knowledge about their own racial and cultural heritage and how it personally and professionally affect their definitions of and biases about normality/abnormality and the process of counseling; knowledge

and understanding about how oppression, racism, and discrimination, and stereotyping affect them personally and in their work; knowledge about their social impact on others and knowledge about communication style differences, how their style may clash with or foster the counseling process with persons of color or others different from themselves and how to anticipate the impact it may have on others.

(as cited in Kwan, 2001, p. 3)

Arredondo et al. (as cited in Kwan, 2001) believe that culturally skilled counselors will take action in several ways: "seek out educational, consultative, and training experiences to improve their understanding and effectiveness in working with culturally different populations and will seek to understand themselves as racial and cultural beings and are actively seeking a nonracist identity" (pp. 3–4). One imperative for non-Black therapists is to acknowledge that race matters in both the lives of African American couples and in the therapeutic process.

Additionally, Jones (1985) and Wilson & Stith (1991) formalize four and five components, respectively, that are critical issues for non-Black clinicians working with Black couples. Jones' (1985) four factors that must be considered in working with Black clients/couples are: 1) the couple's reactions to racial oppression; 2) the influence of African American culture on the client's behavior; 3) the degree of adoption of majority cultural values; and 4) a focus on the personal experiences of the individual couple. Similarly, Wilson & Stith's (1991) components include understanding: 1) the historical perspectives of the experiences; 2) the historical social support system of the community; 3) the value systems of the couple; 4) the communication barriers that may interfere with the development of trust between couple and clinician; and (5) the development of strategies for providing effective therapy outcomes. All of these recommendations should serve as valuable guidelines to increase the cultural sensitivity of non-Black clinicians working with Black couples.

Contemporary values of Blacks can be represented as African, American, and Victim. The experience of living under oppression has led to victimization, making it hard for African Americans to trust in institutions, communities, families, and even other individuals. These values vary from one African American to another and from one couple to another and clinicians should allow for heterogeneity amongst African American couples. Class and values refer to how those in poverty focus on day to day survival rather than long-term goals of middle class Blacks. From the clinician's perspective values should be seen as strengths rather than deficits (Wilson & Stith, 1991). Communication refers to how miscommunication can cause alienation or premature termination during the therapeutic process. Under the component of communication Standard English vs. Black English may also play a role in how non-Black therapists perceive their clients. Nancy Boyd-Franklin (1989) states the above in the following way:

243

Black people, because of the often extremely subtle ways in which racism manifests itself socially, are particularly attuned to very fine distinctions among variables in all interactions...Because of this, many Black people have been socialized to pay attention to all of the nuances of behavior and not just to the verbal message. The term most often applied to this multilevel perception on Black culture is "vibes."

(p. 97)

Boyd-Franklin (1989) suggests that "clinicians should be aware that Black clients are 'checking them out' in terms of appearance, race, skin color, clothing, perceived social class, language, and a range of other clues like warmth, genuineness, sincerity, respect for client, willingness to hear the client's side, patronizing attitudes, condescension, judgments, and human connectedness" (p. 96). Being sensitive to the multitude of ways racism and discrimination play out in the lives of African American couples goes a long way to providing culturally sensitive treatment and building a trusting relationship between counselors and couples.

Differences in Addressing Race in Therapy

A study conducted by Knox, Burkard, Johnson, Suzuki, & Ponterotta (2003) found that African American therapists were engaged in cross-racial encounters throughout their lives, reported more years of experience as therapists, and more work with racially different clients.

African American therapists addressed race due to perceived discomfort in their clients and were perhaps more attuned to discomfort in their clients because of their experience being the minority in society. African American therapists were found not to report discomfort in working with people of different ethnic backgrounds, engaged in the topic of race, and most addressed it directly.

In comparison, Knox, Burkard, Johnson, Suzuki, & Ponterotta (2003) found European American therapists had more of a distant point of reference for racial differences in that what learning they received about how to work with those of different races came not from actual experience but instead via coursework in their academic training. European American therapists indicated that later in their career they brought up race with clients early on in the therapy session despite their lack of contact/exposure to training or supervision. Some indicated that they brought the issue of race up because they wanted their clients to believe they were open to the discussion of race only if the client wanted to discuss it but they reported discomfort while engaging in the topic of race. White therapists working with a Black couple may be so concerned with how the couple will perceive them that they deviate from their normal interaction style so as to be perceived as non-prejudicial (Wyatt, Strayer, & Lobitz, 1976). Knox, Burkard, Johnson, Suzuki, & Ponterotta (2003) suggest that non-Black therapists use "post-session consultation with a Black co-therapist and be willing to accept the couples' experience which might be expressions in forms of behavior different from their own" (p. 478). Thus, because most African American therapists have interactions across racial lines on a daily basis, bringing up race with Black and non-Black couples may be easier for them than for non-Black therapists who may not be as practiced in dealing with racial issues. In some ways, it is far more important for non-Black therapists to bring up racial issues than for Black therapists simply because it opens the door for Black couples to talk about racial issues and the impact these issues may be having on their relationship. Black couples seeking treatment with Black therapists may automatically do this without being invited to do so or simply may assume that the Black therapist already implicitly understands this without being told.

Obviously, "ethical practice requires therapists to understand their own reactions to clients whether clients are members of diverse groups or not" (Kelly & Green, 2010, p. 196). They must also understand what they and their racial/ ethnic background may conjure up in clients and how it may affect the therapy process, as well as how to comfortably explore that material in treatment. Since the characteristics of both the client and the therapist contribute to the establishment of rapport and subsequent development of the therapeutic relationship, cultural competence is imperative (LaTaillade, 2006). The counselor–couple relationship is as affected by the clients' perceptions of the therapist as it is by the therapist's perception of the clients and the perceptions of the couple can lead to the development of transference. "It is the transference that is an important ingredient in the therapy process that can facilitate insight and behavioral change" (LaTaillade, 2006, p. 348). "The therapist's expression of her or his underlying racial identity statuses, influences his or her interaction to the client, and the client's underlying statuses, in turn, influence his or her reactions to the therapists…each complementary response to the other person's observable expressions of his or her racial identity…constitutes a relationship" (Helms & Cook, 1999, pp. 180–181). In order to address the so called elephant in the room—race, ethnicity, gender, and/or class differences between clients and therapists—invite couples to discuss their feelings about being seen by a therapist whom they experience as different from them. Kelly & Green (2010) advise clinicians "to address with each couple underlying assumptions about the implication of racial and ethnic matching for therapist trustworthiness, knowledge, expertise, understanding and credibility" (p. 195). Sanders-Thompson & Alexander (2006) believe practitioner training needs to extend beyond the dominant culture. They suggest that therapists must help African American clients feel comfortable using mental health services and gain their trust. Cardemil and Battle (2003) suggest a need to examine when and how race is discussed and managed as a part of the therapeutic relationship.

Culturally Sensitive Considerations for Non-Black Clinicians

Sue & Sue (2003) developed specific guidelines for clinical practice with African Americans. These are appropriate considerations for individuals, couples, and families:

- During first session, address the issues of race. Even though African Americans have a same race preference, being culturally competent has been shown to be more important.
- If clients are referred from another agency or mandated to therapy explain to them the relationship between the client and the third party and set limits of confidentiality.
- Identify the expectations of and worldviews of the client. Explore feelings about counseling and how they see the problem and possible solutions.
- Establish an egalitarian relationship. African Americans tend to establish a personal commonality and thus this can be accomplished through self-disclosure.
- Determine if and how the client has been impacted by discrimination and racism and their response to these experiences. Also, examine issues around racial identity.
- Assess the positive assets of the client, such as family, community resources, and the church.
- Determine the external factors that might be related to the presenting problem.
- Help the client develop alternative means for dealing with the problem. Help the client define goals and means for attaining those goals.
- After the therapeutic alliance has been formed, apply problem-solving and time-limited approaches (pp. 307–308).

Finally, because most African Americans are aware of the "angry Black man/woman" stereotype, non-Black therapists should be prepared to accept clients' strong emotions without pathologizing them or automatically assuming that strong reactions are based in anger. Wilson and Stith's (1991) writings are useful in addressing clinician's attempts to become more culturally sensitive. They recommend the following strategies specifically in working with Black families but these can also be useful tools with Black couples (p. 40):

- Be aware of the historical and current experience of being Black in America.
- Consider value and cultural differences between Black Americans and other American ethnic groups and how your own personal values influence the way you conduct therapy.
- Consider the way your personal values influence the way you view both the presenting problem and the goals of therapy.

- Include the value system of the client in the goal setting process.
- Be sensitive to variations in Black couple norms due to normal adaptations to stress, and be flexible enough to accept these variations and be aware of how ineffective verbal and nonverbal communication due to cultural variation in communication can lead to premature termination of therapy.
- Become familiar with nonstandard or Black English, and accept its use by clients.
- Consider the client's problem in the larger context. Include the extended family, other significant individuals, and larger systems in your thinking, if not in the therapy session.
- Be aware of your client's cultural identification with his or her own race and learn to acknowledge and to be comfortable with your client's cultural differences.
- Consider the appropriateness of specific therapeutic models or interventions to specific Black couples. Do not apply interventions without considering unique aspects of each couple.
- Finally, consider each Black couple as unique and do not generalize the findings of any study or group of studies on Black couples to all Black couples. Use the studies to help find your way, not to categorize individuals.

Treatment Implications

So what does doing all of "these things" do for the outcomes of treatment? Clients may gain respect for the therapist because of his/her willingness to engage in the discussion of race and its impact on the therapeutic process and on the relationship. Discussions of race might increase couples' willingness to remain in therapy even though they have some reluctance about cross-racial interaction with the non-Black therapist. There may also be an increased sense of connectedness with the therapist and security in the therapeutic relationship.

Even though results on ethnicity pairings are mixed or inconclusive, researchers suspect ethnic similarity may increase client retention, willingness to return, and facilitate treatment effectiveness (Sanders-Thompson & Alexander, 2006). In all actuality, what may be seen as most important for counselor/client ethnicity matching is similarity in attitudes and beliefs between therapist and couples. Ethnic matching between client and counselor may be an issue for some but not all or every Black couple (Sanders-Thompson & Alexander, 2006). Increased respect for the therapist may also be gained if he/she is willing to discuss race early on and an increased connectedness and security with the therapist (Sanders-Thompson & Alexander, 2006).

When non-Black therapists utilize the recommendations addressed earlier in this chapter Doherty (2002) sees clients being more open to ask questions of the therapist related to background, training, and theoretical orientations. Also, couples may be more likely to appropriately inform the therapist about their culture/race/ethnicity that is misunderstood by the therapist. Non-Black therapists can look forward to increased intimacy, increased modeling for couples, and increased therapeutic relationship maintenance (Carolan & Allen, 1999).

Therapists do not have to feel as though traditional techniques and strategies are thrown out with the bath water but if the listed strategies and approaches are used those same strategies and techniques can be incorporated with culturally compatible traditions. Just as couples learn to collaborate for the benefit of their relationship, the non-Black therapist can be included in the collaborative relationship (Durodoye & Coker, 2007). Subsequently, depending on the therapeutic issues the enhanced relationship between the African American couple and the non-Black therapist may lead to the couple selecting either individual or family counseling to address those issues with the same therapist or less hesitation with another ethnically different therapist.

The use of the strengths perspective offered by Bell-Tolliver, Burgess, & Brock in their 2009 study of African American therapists working with African American families found that a focus on strengths brings about increased problem solving/coping skills; and increased dignity, self-worth, and validation for the couple. Their results also showed acceptance of the therapy process by the couples, improved communication skills, and confidence building.

In conclusion, the non-Black therapist who is successful in developing and maximizing the culturally competent techniques/strategies may find themselves as conduits of long-term relationships and/or successfully married African American couples. As that conduit therapists will be able to inform the understanding of how all couples negotiate their roles, manage stressors and conflicts, and maintain healthy, flexible, and vigilant relationships (Pinderhughes, 2002). Ultimately,

> A good therapist, a brave therapist, will help us to cling together as a couple, warming each other against the cold of winter, and to seek out whatever sunlight is still available while we wrestle with our pain and disillusionment. A good therapist, a brave therapist, will be the last one in the room to give up on our marriage, not the first one, knowing that the next springtime…is all the more glorious for the winter that we endured together.
>
> (Doherty, 2002, p. 16)

Case Study

The following case study will provide the reader with a brief summary of a couple in therapy with a non-African American therapist and the counselor's process in establishing a culturally appropriate model in working with this couple. Vanessa (36) and David (40) present together at a community mental health clinic via a referral of Vanessa's employee assistance program (EAP). The EAP has confirmed two sessions for assessment and an additional six sessions for brief couple's counseling. The couple presents for relationship issues related to poor communication, anger, and financial concerns. They are not married but have been together for 10 years and lived together for 5 years. They have no children together but David has a 10-year-old daughter from a previous relationship who lives with them. Vanessa is a high school English teacher and David works in construction and supplements his income with part-time employment at a home improvement retail store. Based on intake interview information, Vanessa was raised by her widowed mother along with her two siblings; David is from a two-parent family of blue-collar parents and has a younger sister. Recently Vanessa has been experiencing a great deal of work stress and anxiety around decision making to pursue graduate studies in school counseling. Vanessa indicates that she has been experiencing sleepless nights and constant worry about her career and how her decision making or lack thereof around pursuing more education will impact her romantic relationship. David reports that he has noticed that Vanessa has been more tense than usual and short/abrupt in her communication with himself and his daughter. He describes their relationship as pretty stable but over the last year things have been a bit distant and very tense. They are financially strained due to David's seasonal work. Vanessa hopes to marry David in the near future but there seems to be some hesitation on David's part because of his seasonal and sometimes unstable work opportunities. They describe their current concern as lack of communication regarding Vanessa's decision to go back to school and the financial strain which is causing emotional distance between them.

The Therapist

The couple is assigned to a Caucasian therapist, Candice, who is a 10-year professional. As part of her introduction to the therapy process Candice educates the couple on the process of counseling, expectations, scope, confidentiality, and orientation. She shares information about her educational and professional background to establish a connection with the couple and evidence her professional credibility and tells the couple that she was raised in the same community as they were. Candice has worked in the public school system as a counselor and in community case management, with families and children of diverse ethnic and economic backgrounds, and is thus experienced in working with diverse populations. Kwan (2001) cites Arredondo et al.'s 1996 work regarding guidelines for multicultural competency, attitudes, and beliefs: culturally skilled counselors believe that cultural self-awareness and sensitivity to one's own cultural heritage and identity is essential along with how one's own background and experiences have influenced attitudes, values, and biases. Candice is quite proud of her Polish American heritage but recognizes that in the urban community Polish immigrants, although the majority in this community, were the working poor and had many economic and familial hardships related to employment, family dysfunction, and achieving the "American Dream." Candice discloses to the couple that she comes from a lower middle class Polish family of blue-collar workers and is married to a Caucasian man 10 years her senior who has two adult daughters. This disclosure may in fact bring the couple and the therapist closer in regards to issues of class, values, and doing things outside of expectations.

The Process

With this summary information Candice pursues the following process in working with Vanessa and David and their presenting concerns: establishing a culturally appropriate relationship; identification of relationship issues; assessing the impact of cultural variables on their relationship; setting culturally appropriate processes and goals; implementing culturally appropriate interventions; and decision making and implementation (Swanson & Fouad, 2010).

Candice sets the context by exhibiting warmth, empathy, and positive regard. Candice asks the couple for both of their responses to the question, "What do you expect of counseling and of me as your counselor?" She also asks the couples if they foresee any barriers or challenges in working with a white female counselor and her ability to understand their worldview. Candice provides the couple with some background on her training, experience in the field, and work with culturally diverse clients, having worked in both the public school system as a school counselor and with the local county in case management with children and families of varying backgrounds.

Candice asks the couple to share their "couple story" and the way they see the problem/s they are most concerned about as Boyd-Franklin (2003) and Bell-Tolliver, Burgess, & Brock (2009) suggest a narrative approach externalizes the problem. It also suggests finding ways for the couple to unite and become stronger together to overpower the problem. Candice suggests that they approach their brief work together as a couple and therapist with structure, strategy development, a solution focus, and address stressors and resources (Boyd-Franklin, 2003). Candice also asks the couple to identify their strength as a unit so that she can build upon them in therapy, thus utilizing a strengths-based approach from the very beginning of treatment.

Candice approaches the couple's concerns by asking how important family expectations, values, and beliefs are to the both of them which demonstrates her respect for the role of family in both of their lives. She also considers with the couple how the social and environmental factors of Vanessa's and David's careers/work are impacting their relationship (narrative therapy intervention). She asks the couple to consider: "In a perfect world without all of the barriers and challenges you are facing now what would the relationship look and feel like?" David admits he would like to be spending more time together as a couple and as a family. He states he misses talking to Vanessa because she holds everything in like she's "every woman." Candice inquires about the "every woman" reference. David explains it's a take-off of a popular 1970's R& B song about Black women's independence and being able to do it all. Candice expresses her appreciation of the education and the three of them smile/laugh at this. Vanessa admits that as a couple they would be more financially secure and be able to live a lifestyle they could both enjoy. Candice illuminates that the couple already has skills to work together to resolve issues around finances but questions where they see themselves in relation to gender expectations. They both express that their relationship is not conventional by "American" standards but they have couple role models in their lives that have provided examples for how to work together and pick up the slack when it's needed. Candice asks the couple to discuss how they can create alternative meanings for their "couple norm" and couple identity. Candice then works with the couple to establish treatment goals for working together.

Examining Candice's Approach

An examination of Candice's approach demonstrates that she is consistent with Sue & Sue's (2003) guidelines for clinical practice with African Americans. In the first session, she addresses the issues of race as a Caucasian therapist and the perspective of her clients who are African Americans and builds a relationship with the couple based on their similarities (e.g. growing up in the same community), while attending to and respecting their differences. She inquires about the couple's expectations of counseling and their respective worldviews by asking them to tell their couple story. She uses language that evidences that they are working together as a triad to address the issues the couple presented. In addition, she also assessed and brought to light for the couple the strengths they already have related to their individual "couple model," family, and shared power skills. Candice helps to externalize the factors that are related to the presenting problems so that the couple can develop alternative means for dealing with the problem.

Lastly, she assisted the clients in defining goals, means for attaining those goals, and applying problem-solving skills to the presenting issues.

Similarly, Candice utilized Dunham & Ellis' (2010) suggestions for restoring intimacy with the African American couple. She oriented the couple to the therapy process, she did not assume familiarity with the couple, joined the couple, maintained a broad definition of family, used a problem-solving focus, and acknowledged strengths, resources, and successes the couple already possessed.

Candice's approach also mimics Dunham & Ellis's (2010) reinterpretation of Chapman's work around intimacy. She attempts to show the couple that they are valued by one another, they are sacrificing for one another, they are committed to interdependence, and unconditional acts of love are seen as support, respect, equality, and companionship. As Pinderhughes (2002) suggests the success of a non-Black therapist in developing and utilizing culturally competent techniques may become an extension of the relationship of African American couples. They may also assist in a better understanding of how all couples negotiate their roles, manage stressors and conflicts, and maintain healthy, flexible, and vigilant relationships.

References

American Psychological Association (1990). Guidelines for providers of psychological services to ethnic, linguistic, and culturally diverse populations. *American Psychologist*, 48, 45–48.

American Psychological Association (2003). Guidelines on multicultural education, training, research, practice, and organizational change for psychologists. *American Psychologist*, 58, 377–402.

Atkinson, D. E. (1983). Ethnic similarity in counseling psychology: A review of research. *The Counseling Psychologist*, 11 (3), 79–92.

Atkinson, D. E., Morten, C., & Sue, D. W. (1998). *Counseling American minorities* (5th Ed.). Boston, MA: McGraw Hill.

Banks, H. C. (1975). The Black person as client and as therapist. *Professional Psychology*, 8, 470–475.

Bell-Tolliver, L. B., Burgess, R., & Brock, L. (2009). African American therapists working with African American families: An exploration of the strengths perspective in treatment. *Journal of Marital and Family Therapy*. 35 (3), 293–307.

Boyd-Franklin, N. (1989). *Black families in therapy: A multisystems approach*. New York: Guilford.

Boyd-Franklin, N. (2003). African American men and women: Socialization and relationships. In *Black families in therapy: Understanding the African American experience* (pp. 86–111). New York: Guilford.

Brown, L. B. (1950). Race as a factor in establishing a casework relationship. *Social Casework*, 31, 91–97.

Butler, R. O. (1975). Psychotherapy: Implications of a Black-consciousness process model. *Psychotherapy: Theory, Research, and Practice*, 12, 407–411.

Cardemil, E. V., & Battle, C. L. (2003). Guess who's coming to therapy? Getting comfortable with conversations about race and ethnicity in psychotherapy. *Professional Psychology: Research and Practice*, 34, 278–286.

Carolan, M. T., & Allen, K. R. (1999). Commitments and constraints to intimacy for African American couples at midlife. *Journal of Family Issues*, 2 (1), 3–24.

Chapman, A. B. (1995). *Entitled to good loving: Black men and women and the battle for love and power.* New York: Henry Holt & Company.

Cowdery, R. S., Scarborough, N., Knudson-Martin, C., Seshadri, G., Lewis, M. E., & Mahoney, A. R. (2009). Gendered power in cultural contexts: Part II. Middle class African American heterosexual couples with young children. *Family Process*, 48 (1), 25–39.

Cross, W. E., Jr. (1971). The Negro-to-Black conversion experience. *Black World,* July 13–27.

Cross, W. E., Jr. (1978). The Cross and Thomas models of psychological nigrescence. *Journal of Black Psychology*, 5, 13–19.

Cross, W. E., Jr. (1995). The psychology of nigrescence: Revising the Cross model. In J. G. Ponterotto, J. M. Casas, L. A. Suzuki, & C. M. Alexander (Eds.), *Handbook of multicultural counseling* (pp. 93–122). Thousand Oaks, CA: Sage Publications.

Doherty, W. J. (2002). How therapists harm marriages and what we can do about it. *Journal of Couple & Relationship Therapy*, 1 (2), 1–17.

Doss, B. D., Simpson, L. E., & Christensen, A. (2004). Why do couples seek marital therapy? *Professional Psychology Research and Practice*, 35 (6), 608–614.

Dunham, S., & Ellis, C. M. (2010). Restoring intimacy with African American couples. In Jon Carlson and Len Sperry (Eds.), *Recovering intimacy in love relationships: A clinician's guide* (pp. 295–316). New York: Routledge Taylor and Francis Group.

Durodoye, B. A., & Coker, A. D. (2007). Crossing cultures in marriage: Implications for counseling African American/African couples. *International Journal of Advanced Counseling*, 30, 25–37.

Gardner, L. H. (1971) The therapeutic relationship under varying conditions of race. *Psychotherapy: Theory, Research and Practice*, 8, 78–87.

Glick, P. C. (1997). Demographic pictures of African American families. In H. P. McAdoo (Ed.), *Black Families* (pp. 118–138). Thousand Oaks, CA: Sage Publications.

Grier, W., & Cobbs, P. (1968). *Black rage.* New York: Basic Books.

Harrison, D. K. (1975). Race as a counselor/client variable in counseling and psychotherapy: A review of the research. *The Counseling Psychologist*, 5, 124–133.

Helms, J. (1980). Toward a theoretical explanation of the effects of race on counseling. *The Counseling Psychologist*, 12 (4), 153–165.

Helms, J. E., & Cook, D. A. (1999). *Using race and culture in counseling and psychotherapy: Theory and practice.* Needham Heights, MA: Allyn & Bacon.

Jackson, A. M. (1973). Factors associated with the race of the therapist. *Psychotherapy: Theory, Research, and Practice*, 10, 273–277.

Jones, A. C. (1985). Psychological functioning in Black Americans: A conceptual guide for use in psychotherapy. *Psychotherapy*, 22, 363–369.

Jones, E. E. (1978). Effects of race on psychotherapy process and outcome. An exploratory investigation. *Psychotherapy: Theory, Research, and Practice*, 15, 226–236.

Kelly, J. F., & Green, B. (2010). Diversity within African American female therapists: Variability in clients' expectations and assumptions about the therapist. *Psychotherapy Theory, Research, Practice, and Training*, 47 (2), 186–197.

Knox, S., Burkard, A. W., Johnson, A. J., Suzuki, L. A., & Ponterotta, J. G. (2003). African American and European American therapists' experiences of addressing race in cross-racial psychotherapy dyads. *Journal of Counseling Psychology*, 50 (4), 466–481.

Kwan, K. K. (2001). Models of racial and ethnic identity development: Delineation of practice implications. *Journal of Mental Health Counseling*, 23 (3), 269–277.

LaTaillade, J. J. (2006). Considerations for treatment of African American couple relationships. *Journal of Cognitive Psychotherapy: An International Quarterly*, 20 (4), 341–358.

Phinney, J. S. (1992). The Multigroup Ethnic Identity Measure: A new scale for use with diverse groups. *Journal of Adolescent Research*, 7, 156–176.

Pinderhughes, E. B. (2002). African American marriage in the 20th century. *Family Process*, 41 (2), 269–282.

Sanders-Thompson, V. L., & Alexander, H. (2006). Therapists' race and African American clients' reactions to therapy. *Psychotherapy Theory, Research, Practice, and Training*, 43 (1), 99–110.

Sattler, J. M. (1977). The effects of therapist-client similarity. In A. S. Gurman & A. M. Razin (Eds.), *Effective psychotherapy: A handbook of research* (pp. 252–290). New York: Pergamon Press

Sellers, R. M., Rowley, S., Chavous, T. M., Shelton, J. N., & Smith, M. A. (1997). Multidimensional inventory of Black identity: A preliminary investigation of reliability and construct validity. *Journal of Personality and Social Psychology*, 73 (4), 805–815.

Smith, E. J. (1991). Ethnic identity development: Toward the development of a theory within the context of majority/minority status. *Journal of Counseling and Development*, 70, 181–188.

Sperry, L. (2010). Intimacy: Definition, contexts, and models for understanding its development and diminishment. In J. Carlson and L. Sperry (Eds.), *Recovering intimacy in love relationships: A clinician's guide* (pp. 3–14). New York: Routledge.

Sue, D. W., & Sue, D. (1999). *Counseling the culturally different: Theory and practice*. 3rd Ed. New York: John Wiley & Sons, Inc.

Sue, D. W., & Sue, D. (2003). *Counseling the culturally diverse: Theory and practice*. 4th Ed. New York: John Wiley & Sons, Inc.

Sue, D. W., Arredondo, P., & McDavis, R. J. (1992). Multicultural competencies/standards: A call to the profession. *Journal of Counseling and Development*, 70, 477–486.

Sue, D. W., Capodilupo, C. M., & Holder, A. M. B. (2008). Racial Microaggressions in the life experience of Black Americans. *Professional Psychology: Research, Methods, and Practice*, 39 (3), 329–336.

Swanson, J. L., & Fouad, N. A. (2010). *Career theory and practice: Learning through case studies*. 2nd Ed. Thousand Oaks, CA: Sage Publications.

Vontress, C. E. (1971). Racial differences: Impediments to rapport. *Journal of Counseling Psychology*, 18, 7–13.

Whisman, M. A., Dixon, A. E., & Johnson, B. (1997). Therapists' perspectives of couples problems and treatment issues in couple therapy. *Journal of Family Psychology*, 113, 361–366.

Wilson, L. L., & Stith, S. M. (1991). Culturally sensitive therapy with Black clients. *Journal of Multicultural Counseling and Development*, 19, 32–43.

Wyatt, G. E., Strayer, R. G., & Lobitz, W. C. (1976). Issues in the treatment of sexually dysfunctioning couples of Afro-American descent. *Psychotherapy: Theory, Research, and Practice*, 13 (1), 44–50.

10

AFRICAN AMERICAN COUPLES AND PASTORAL COUNSELING

Byron Waller

Ninety percent of Americans and 96 percent of African Americans reported that they believe in God (Gallup, 2001). Sixty-five percent of Americans reported in recent surveys that religion is important (Crabtree & Pelham, 2009). At the same time, 79 percent of Americans acknowledge that faith can help people recover from illness (*USA Today*, 1996, as cited in https://aapc.org/node/3). For African American adults, 92 percent belong to a church and 68 percent attend church (Taylor & Chatters, 1991). Most African Americans are very religious people (Jackson, McCullough, Gurin, & Broman, 1991) and have been found to demonstrate higher levels of religious involvement and participation than other groups (Chatters, Taylor, Bullard, & Jackson, 2008). Knox (1985) stated that "spirituality is deeply embedded in the Black psyche" (p. 31), "religion permeated every aspect of the African's life" and is an "integral part of man's existence" (Nobles, 1980, p. 25). Historically and currently, spirituality and religion have been vital in helping African Americans/African American couples cope with many of life's challenges in America, from slavery to racism to poverty. Although the words are often used interchangeably, religion and spirituality are different concepts.

Religion is a belief in a metaphysical and supernatural reality and the external expression of spirituality, usually connected to a religious organization or group of people who share similar beliefs, values, and rituals (Shafranske & Maloney, 1990). Religion also has a structure, roles, and a hierarchy established to follow the practices, rituals, and values of the group. With African Americans, the Black church represents the place for this external expression through various practices and denominations. Spirituality, on the other hand, is the external expression of internal beliefs and values and may not have an established structure or connection with people. It is a personal meaningful experience that is individualistic and could include various forms of religion (Taylor & Chatters, 2010), but does not necessarily involve religion (Shafranske & Gorsuch, 1984). This inner expression emphasizes the belief in a higher God/power being/presence and a search for love, forgiveness, patience, meaning, and purpose in one's life. Spirituality and religion have been found to influence how one relates to oneself and to others. For a large group of African Americans, they view themselves as both spiritual and religious (Taylor & Chatters, 2010).

Spirituality, religion, and mental health for African Americans have always been connected. However, mental health training has ignored the impact of spirituality and religion in the life of Black individuals, couples, and families (Boyd-Franklin, 1989). Recently the counseling profession has recognized the importance of spirituality in the lives of Americans and African Americans alike. The counseling and psychological literature has been more attentive to the influence of spirituality and religion in the lives of their clients, and with the rise of multiculturalism and the Association for Spiritual, Ethical, and Religious Values in Counseling (ASERVIC), spirituality and religion have received additional focus (Powers, 2005). These concepts have begun to be integrated into practice and training (Walker, Gorsch, Siang-Yang, 2004). Since so many clients have reported that their beliefs have helped them to deal with their life issues (*USA Today*, 1996, as cited in https://aapc.org/node/3), professionals had no choice but to use them as resources. In fact, the counseling and psychological literature reports that religious couples experienced higher levels of marital satisfaction (Allen, & Olson, 2001; Brown, Orbuch, & Bauermeister, 2008). For Americans in general, their religious affiliation has been important in dealing with their personal problems (Taylor, Ellison, Chatters, Levin, & Lincoln, 2000). In fact, 39 percent of Americans seek the help of their religious leader/clergy with their life issues, and more than half consult their clergy for marital concerns (Veroff, Douvan, & Kulka, 1981). For Americans and African American couples, long before seeking the help of a professional counselor (if they ever do) they seek counseling services through their churches. Taylor et al. (2000) suggested an increase and even resurgence in interest in religion and how it affects the help-seeking behaviors of African Americans. It is, therefore, important to examine how religious and spiritual factors and the church influence the choices of African Americans and African American couples. Some professional counselors work in tandem with pastors because this is a comfortable treatment modality for many African American couples. Thus, understanding the role of the Black church, religiosity and spirituality, and the relationships and support systems religious African Americans form through their church communities, is critical to doing effective treatment with African American couples. This chapter will discuss pastoral counseling and how it is understood and used by African Americans, specifically African American couples.

African Americans and the Influence of the Black Church

The Black church has always been a place of refuge and support for Black people. It has been a significant part of the Black experience in America by helping to develop the religious and spiritual foundation for Blacks in America (Lincoln & Mamiya, 1990). Historically, the Black church has been central for African Americans in dealing with life circumstances and conditions that have negatively impacted the health and well-being of African Americans (Taylor & Chatters, 2010). There is evidence that the Black church began as far back as 1774 when African slaves began to question the conflict between the teachings of Christianity and slavery. The Black church was a place where African slaves could go in secret and safety to express aspects of their African heritage, their unexpressed emotions from the oppression of slavery and achieve distinction and status, and locate meaning in their lives (Frazier, 1996). It also provided a sense of solidarity and a social bond as they worshipped openly with each other (Love, 2011). Only on Sunday did slave owners allow slaves to engage in Christian worship without supervision. The Black church became a place where Black slaves could find a source of connection and peace in a place and time where there was none. Additionally, church was the one place slaves were allowed positions of leadership, education about the bible, and a place to congregate with one another without being watched by the slave master.

By the 1800s both the free and enslaved sought places where they could worship their God and fight for inclusion in a society who did not want them (Pinn & Pinn, 2002). By 1936, there were more than 5 million members in Black churches (Guzman, 1946 as cited in Love, 2011) with seven different denominations and 30,000 churches (Love, 2011). In the 1950s and 1960s, the Black church was the birth place of the Civil Rights Movement (Taylor, Ellison, Chatters, Levin, & Lincoln, 2000). Church was the organizational structure that gave rise to national Black leadership (e.g. Dr. Martin Luther King, Jr. was a minister), the Montgomery Bus Boycott, Brown v Board of Education, and other significant events that changed the way Blacks were viewed and treated in the United States (Taylor, Ellison, Chatters, Levin, & Lincoln, 2000).

Presently, the Black church is one of the primary resources that attend to the psychological, social, and spiritual needs of religious African Americans (Richardson & June, 2006). It continues to be a place in which Black people depend for educational, political, social, economical, and emotional support as well as pastoral counseling (Lincoln & Mamiya, 1990). The Black church—and, most especially, the preacher—became the most influential person by providing comforting and inspirational words that expressed the emotions and experiences of Black people at a time when Blacks were not allowed to speak freely for themselves, lest they bear the consequences (e.g. lynching, Ku Klux Klan (KKK), and intimidation from the police, etc.). The church served as a resource for encouragement to live on and to live together. Although slaves were not legally able to wed, preachers often conducted ceremonies to validate romantic connections between male and female slaves, formally recognizing the Black couple amongst the group. Even then, the minister or pastor was a strong force and resource for the Black community, including the Black couple. Currently, the place of the Black church in the African American community is significant and many African Americans continue to look to the church (or other organized religious places, e.g. mosques) for spiritual and personal guidance. The church's historical and current significance continues to be an important part of how many African Americans choose to identify themselves, as many identify strongly with church teachings, activities, and social groups. Thus, the church is located central to the daily lives of many African Americans.

Pastoral Counseling

The pastor/minister is seen as the most significant person in church leadership (Brown et al., 2008). This statement is more true in the Black church (Taylor & Chatters, 2010). The pastor is recognized as the key leader and organizer, the gatekeeper to mental health services, the professional present in the church, and the deliverer of the crucial needs to the congregation, even the counseling. The pastor is the most consulted professional an individual seeks when faced with a serious personal problem, even higher than psychologists/counselors, and doctors or psychiatrists (Veroff et al., 1981). Therefore, counseling from the pastor is a vital service offered by the church. At the same time, the definition of pastoral and spiritual counseling is not widely understood as it is currently integrated into the counseling profession. Pastoral counseling has both a general and professional view. Generally, pastoral counseling has been understood by relating its meaning to the activities and services of the pastor in local churches. Thus, the various counseling duties performed by the pastor defined pastoral counseling. For example, in many churches when couples wish to get married, they are required to come in for a few sessions of counseling with the pastor. Sometimes individual church members may seek the pastor's guidance on personal issues. Pastors do not require specific training in psychological theory/interventions to do this type of counseling. Professionally, however, pastoral counseling is a branch of counseling in which psychologically trained ministers, rabbis, priests, and other persons provide counseling and support services both professionally and personally to people requesting help with life issues (American Association of Pastoral Counseling, 2011). Rather than just the pastor providing services, this definition of pastoral counseling utilizes the clergy as the professionals performing duties, often going beyond the service provided to a particular church. Pastoral counselors often integrate psychological thought with traditional religious training in an effort to address psycho-spiritual issues in addition to traditional counseling services.

> What distinguishes pastoral counseling from other forms of counseling and psychotherapy is the role and accountability of the counselor and his or her understanding and expression of the pastoral relationship. Pastoral counselors are representatives of the central images of life and its meaning affirmed by their religious communities. Thus pastoral counseling offers a relationship to a spiritual understanding of life and faith. It uses both psychological and theological resources to deepen its understanding of the pastoral relationship.
> (Paul, 2005)

Some pastoral counselors have developed special training programs to encourage cooperation between religious professionals and non-religious professionals on treatment of issues, since spirituality is an important part of recovery for many clients. Many states have license requirements for pastoral counseling. The American Association of Pastoral Counseling (2011) indicates that:

- Pastoral Counselors are able to work with a state license in most states today.
- Only six states actually license the title Pastoral Counselor. They are: Arkansas, Kentucky, Maine, New Hampshire, North Carolina, and Tennessee. In many other states Pastoral Counselors may qualify for licensure as Marriage and Family Therapists or as Professional Counselors. They may have to take supplemental courses to match a model curriculum, or take a certified Post-graduate program.

Many African American couples reported that "God" is the center of their relationship (Love, 2011). Counseling that does not recognize the importance of God, prayer, and religious beliefs and practices may miss a significant part of African Americans' relationships. In fact, African American and white couples reported that religion and attending church services increased their martial stability (Brown et al., 2008). Clinicians who ignore this major factor may alienate the couple and may not nurture a significant coping mechanism for the couple to overcome marital/relational challenges while in treatment.

The professional definition of pastoral counseling is very different than what is accepted generally. *Pastoral counseling* is conducted by clergy who have received graduate training in both religion and therapeutic concepts. Thus, professional pastoral counseling requires specific formal training in both pastoral and psychological approaches. Many pastors are not formally trained in pastoral counseling. The goal of professional pastoral counseling is to integrate both psychological and theological disciplines (American Association of Pastoral Counseling, 2011). Wimberly (1997) stated that pastoral counseling takes into account three sources: 1) the human condition revealed by the social and behavioral sciences; 2) theological disciplines and its wisdom; and 3) information learned from pastoral ministry and the interaction of these components over the years. Professional pastoral counselors believe that there is a God or Higher power in whose image and likeness human being are created. Professional pastoral counselors believe that people are looking for a transforming connection with the Divine and that psychotherapy can help in that process and mediate the healing that comes along with the connection as it assists in dealing with life's stressors and problems (Neighbors, Musick, & Williams, 1998). Pastoral counselors also make therapeutic use of traditional religious resources such as prayer, scripture reading, mediation, and participation in the worship and community life of a congregation. They pay special attention to the religious history of the client and his or her family, noting how it may contribute to the suffering or resources needed for coping

(Williams, Griffith, Young, Collins, & Dodson, 1999; http://pastoralcounseling. tripod.com). African Americans and African American couples experience the use of pastoral counseling often through the Black church and their pastors. Again, some of these pastors are formally trained pastoral counselors and some are not.

Pastor Counseling and African Americans

The Black church has shaped social attitudes and values in the Black community for several hundred years. The preacher/minister held (and continues to hold) a special position in the Black community and in gatherings by adapting Christian beliefs to meet the psychological, social and spiritual needs of the people (Frazier, 1996). In today's Black church, the minister/pastor continues to help the congregation with their personal, family, and community needs. However, today, pastors can openly aid the community with their needs (Love, 2011). Only recently have African American's seen pastors having received training to integrate the psychological and the spiritual.

Little is known about how Black pastors and congregations use professional pastoral counseling in the Black church. Presently, many African Americans may not see the difference between professional pastoral counseling and counseling with their pastor at the church. Counseling from the pastor is a service sought out by members as it does not bring the same stigma as going to see a professional for counseling for several reasons. Seeing the pastor at the church is usually free and the person is often someone they have known for a period of time. Traditional pastoral counseling with Black persons incorporates some cultural adaptations that take into consideration the unique experiences African Americans have had in this country like poverty, racism, discrimination, family practices, and religious traditions. Wimberly (1997) believes that successful professional pastoral counseling integrates an understanding of the positive contributions of Black persons, Black people's collective identity, their family life, and work and religious orientation and how each component shapes their lives. Professional pastoral counseling for Blacks demands a commitment to understanding and sharing the struggles of individuals within the context of their culture and community.

For African Americans pastoral counseling implies meeting with the pastor to discuss personal issues and relational struggles. In the African American community, the pastor was, and still is for many, the person to call when many of life's challenges visited the family or couple. Many of life's negative issues seemed to disproportionally impact the lives of Black people and couples. Issues such as poverty, unemployment, the criminal justice system, unexpected death, health problems, and relationship challenges seem to more significantly impact Black people than society in general (Taylor, Ellison, Chatters, Levin, & Lincoln, 2000). The "go to" person in these situations is the pastor, who provides pre-marital counseling, bereavement and loss counseling, performs weddings, conducts spiritual discipleship classes, organizes funerals and burials, helps with financial issues, and counsels couples who are having a difficult time. As such, pastors and other clergy are present for church members best (e.g. the birth of a child) and worst (e.g. the death of a parent) life moments. Most pastors are well-integrated into their constituents' daily lives thus trust is built with the couple over years. These services are usually provided free of charge, especially to church members or members' families. For African Americans, pastoral counseling includes many services, but is seen as a service provided by the church as a service from God, not a professional. The pastor is a spiritual and religious leader provided by God to aid his or her people in dealing with life's challenges. Modifying this view of pastoral counseling for African Americans may be very difficult and may even be seen to go against the grain of the culture. Seeking a pastor's guidance is a tradition that is several hundred years old. For many African Americans, pastoral counseling holds a deeply personal value. Many may not see the professional nature of the counseling services because of the long tradition of seeking supportive counseling from a pastor as a service from God (Neighbors et al., 1998). Thus, many religious African American couples understand the need for counseling services when they struggle with issues within their relationships; however, they may be loath to pay a professional counselor (or even recognize the value of professional counseling) when, in their worldview, this is a service provided by the church, inspired by their relationship with God, free of charge (Campbell, 2010).

For African Americans religion and spirituality are used often as significant coping mechanisms and are identified as significant to their life issues, so, although stress and unhealthy family relationships are accepted as causes for mental health distress, problems with one's relationship with God, not confessed sin, and stunted spiritual growth are viewed just as significant. In fact for religious African American couples, a presenting issue could be that one partner doubts the other's faith or commitment to the church community because he or she stops attending church or praying with their partner.

African American ministers functioning as pastoral counselors constitute an engaging and useful group with experiences and skills that can be tapped by interested secular counseling professionals. Their work represents a significant mental health resource for persons who lack sufficient access to needed care. They often address serious problems similar to those seen by secular mental health professionals, with whom they reported not exchanging referrals. In fact, many saw pastoral counselors as more qualified than mental health professionals because pastoral counselors did not ignore spiritual issues and treated the "whole" person (Neighbors et al., 1998). African American pastors believe that use of the Western bio-social-medical model is inappropriate, ineffective, or limited for African Americans and therefore do not refer members of their congregation to the mental health professionals who use it for treatment (Neighbors et al., 1998). Pastors are now treating and seeking to more competently treat these individuals. Professional pastoral counselors have begun to recognize this dynamic and have increased their training to work with mental health issues. Many pastors are now seeking specialized education for their counseling work—including both spiritual and psychological dimensions.

A Note about African Americans and Specific Religions

The spiritual and psychological dimensions of counseling are significant factors for pastors and counselors to understand when working with African American couples. In order for pastors and counselors to be culturally competent, they must develop an awareness of their personal and client's cultural viewpoints, have a cultural knowledge base, and a set of intervention skills that focuses on understanding the client's worldview (Sue & Sue, 2008). Spirituality and religious beliefs influence how African American couples view themselves and the world (Pew Forum, 2009; Wimberly, 1997). African Americans have unique cultural and spiritual beliefs that emanate from African culture and their early life in America, which many pastors may recognize. However, clinicians must also develop a knowledge base of African American religious backgrounds to better understand the various spiritual and psychological dimensions. An understanding of these areas could aid in helping counselors and pastors alike to become culturally competent. For example, culturally sensitive clinicians should not assume that all African Americans are Christian, or that all Christian sects practice Christianity in the same way. An exhaustive review of specific religions and practices are beyond the scope of this chapter; however, a brief overview of African Americans and specific religions will be provided.

Seventy-eight percent of all African Americans are Protestant. These Protestants are divided into three distinct traditions: Evangelical Protestants, Mainline Protestants, and historically Black Protestants. The Black church consists of eight major denominations: the African Methodist Episcopal (AME) Church; the African Methodist Episcopal Zionist (AMEZ) Church; the Christian Methodist Episcopal (CME) Church; the National Baptist Convention of America (NBCA); Unincorporated NBCA; the National Baptist Convention, USA; the Progressive National Baptist Convention (PNBC); and the Church of God in Christ (COGIC) (Lincoln & Mamiya, 1990). Some suggest that two new black denominations (organizations) have been developed recently: the National Missionary Baptist Convention (NMBC) and the Full Gospel Baptist Church Fellowship (FGBCF) (Wardell, 1995). Fifteen percent of African Americans belong to evangelical denominations (Southern Baptist or Assemblies of God) and 4 percent are mainline Protestants (Disciples of Christ). The remaining African Americans identify with various religious groups: Catholic (5 percent), Jehovah's Witnesses (1 percent), Muslims (1 percent), several groups with 0.5 percent (Mormon, Orthodox, Jewish, Buddhist, and Hindu), and 12 percent are unaffiliated (Pew Forum, 2009). Religious African Americans in the United States typically practice some form of Christianity;

262

however, the Civil Rights Movement and immigration gave rise to the presence of other religious ideas (i.e. the Nation of Islam) in the Black community.

These additional religious ideologies have diversified some religious thought in the Black community, especially as they are related to the progression of individuals and couples. Islam has always been a part of the African American culture as it was brought over by slaves. The first generation of slaves practiced their religion but it was lost as many slaves were forced to convert to Christianity and thus generations lost contact with this religious heritage. During the depression era, many of the Islamic teachings re-emerged in the African American community in the Moorish Science Temple of America founded by Noble Drew Ali and promoted by Wallace Fard who later founded the Nation of Islam. The Nation of Islam was led by the Honorable Elijah Muhammad and promoted by Malcolm X. Today, the Nation of Islam continues under the leadership of the Honorable Minister Louis Farrakan. Some other African American Muslims followed Warith Deen Mohammed, the son of Elijah Muhammad, and converted to Sunni Islam. Yet other African Americans chose religions like mainstream Judaism, and others again non-mainstream branches of Judaism such as the Hebrew Israelites. A small number of African Americans practice traditional African religions such as West African Vodun, Santeria, Ifa, and Rastafari (Pew Forum, 2009), while other African Americans choose other religious traditions, some mainstream and others non-mainstream (Catholic, Jehovah's Witnesses, Muslims, Mormon, Orthodox, Jewish, Buddhist, and Hindu).

Pastoral counselors and counselors must be aware of the African American couple's specific religious tradition. They should know the basics about each religion and seek the couple's guidance on how this tradition shapes their lives as a couple and their worldview. Without such knowledge, it would be very difficult to effectively work with a couple who held their religious beliefs at the center of their relationship. A counselor's familiarity with these religious differences and language can help them bond with African American couples by joining with them in their religious understanding and worldview. Understanding terms such as first lady, deacon, usher, or being "saved, sanctified and filled with the Holy Ghost," speaking in tongues, being baptized, and praise dancing are important vocabulary that African American couples might use to explain their worldview. This may be more complicated if each member of the couple has differing religious traditions. Therefore, the counselors must find out from the couple their religious activities, values, beliefs, and traditions that shape their worldview and understanding of their relationship.

African American Couples and Pastoral Counseling

Historically, African American couples do not seek counseling from tradition counseling professionals (Taylor & Chatters, 1991). There are various reasons why African Americans do not use traditional counseling, including availability, quality, and under-representation of services provided by African Americans, cost, stigma, perception of therapy, cultural differences, and lack of knowledge of what professional couples' counseling can provide (Brown, Ojeda, Wyn, & Levan, 2000; Snowden & Cheung, 1990), using prayer to cope, or just believing in their own ability to overcome obstacles (Love, 2011). It is estimated that less than 2 per cent of mental health professionals are African American and African Americans are more likely to seek counseling from other African American professionals (Harley & Dillard, 2005). As stated previously, African American couples are more apt to seek couples' counseling from a clergy or pastoral counselor than a traditional counselor because the clergy often has known the family for a long time and has developed the necessary relationship with the family over time that would allow for the couples to approach the pastor for counseling (Campbell, 2010).

Thus, the Black church could be instrumental in influencing church members' attitudes about seeking counseling both within and outside of the church. When mental health professionals and clergy collaborate in providing counseling services, these partnerships could have the potential to change African American's attitudes about seeking professional counseling services. Professional pastoral counseling is new to many African American couples, although many of them may have received pre-marital counseling from their pastor. Pastors are trusted professionals in the Black community. At the same time, many African Americans seem to be more comfortable with counselors that have therapeutic skills like pastor counselors than with those who do not (Love, 2011). Professional pastoral counselors and counselors operate very similarly with couples, but with some differences. Both professionals complete an assessment of the presenting problem to determine how the couple is functioning individually and together. Pastoral counselors assess the relationship by examining the presenting problem in a religious and theological context first, while the counselor or mental health professional would start with the psychological and most would not incorporate a religious worldview. A pastoral counselor may consider other factors that contribute to the presenting problems and may use the scriptures as a principle of behavior or mediation or prayer as a method in coping with personal or relationship issues (Love, 2011). Pastoral counseling includes examining the presenting problem by understanding the spiritual worldview of the couple and family members. This is the key for spiritual and religious African Americans couples. The religious context helps many African American couples see beyond personal fault and the blame process to recognize the principles they look toward to guide an understanding of their marital issues. Specifics in how to do this with African American couples will be addressed.

A common theme when working with religious and/or Christian African American couples is the issue of headship and roles in relationships. For many African Americans, traditional ideas define this issue according to a conservative biblical interpretation where the husband is the head of the wife, and they both operate along pre-determined gender roles promoted by mainstream society and traditional religious values. Christian African American couples tend to follow a more conservative biblical interpretation, and follow more traditional gender roles even though they have different view on social and racial issues (Wimberly, 1997). However, Campbell (2010) suggested that contemporary Christian African American couples are questioning traditional beliefs about marriage, redefining gender roles, and re-examining the "male-centric" interpretations of verses where women are told to "submit" to their husbands, while failing to emphasize that men should love their wives as Christ loved the church and be willing to die for her (Ephesians 5:22). Wimberly believes that the aforementioned conservative viewpoint is based on religious patriarchy that is racist and sexist, and based on a history of discrimination and oppression. He promotes a more liberal viewpoint and writes that:

> Given the history of racism and discrimination and some experts talking about the emasculation of African American men, it does seem that male leadership in the home is very important. However, this male leadership is expressed through utilizing stereotypical images of masculinity and femininity that permeate all society. Drawing on these stereotypical images, many African American men have sought the sanction of religion to support a particular domineering leadership style in the home that is oppressive rather than liberating to the growth potential of their spouses and children.
>
> (1997, p. 2)

Couples try to find space to express themselves within their relationships and express a desire to follow what they believe God wants them to do. Each may be struggling to have a positive self and couple identity. This demonstrates the dilemma faced by many African American couples, and the issues that pastoral and traditional counselors must take into consideration when working with these couples. African American couples tend to respond to a problem-solving approach (Campbell, 2010; Love, 2011). The key, then, for each person is to respond to racism and other struggles in ways that facilitate the growth of each person (Wimberly, 1997). In promoting growth, African Americans have particular challenges that pastoral counselors must be aware of in counseling.

African American Men and Pastoral Counseling

For many African American males, religion and spirituality have been the vehicles used to deal with their life problems and to provide spiritual cleansing (Gayles, Alston, & Staten, 2005). Although the government and court system are the primary referral sources of African American men to counseling services, African American men tend not to use the services they recommend (Carter, 1995) because they do not trust them (Gayles et al., 2005). In fact, many African American males bypass traditional counseling services and go to their friend groups and the church for assistance (Chatters et al., 2008). The church and the pastor has been found to be one of the most trusted places for African American men to go for support (Gayles et al., 2005). The minister/pastor is often the first and sometimes only professional an African American person encounters (Love, 2011; Taylor et al., 2000). For many African Americans, the pastor and minister is also an African American male, although many Black men still hesitate to go to male pastors for help in personal/relational issues.

Black men who do seek the pastor's guidance believe that they can talk to him because of their shared experience of being African American men (American Counseling Association, 1998). Whether seeking pastoral or traditional counseling, African American men do not easily seek help. Boyd-Franklin (1989) addressed how many African American males are taught not to show weakness from an early age, to avoid being ostracized from the group— going to someone for help might be seen as weakness for African American males. Boyd-Franklin used the example of a young boy falling down and the mother wanting to go soothe him, his father and other men of the family would stop her and tell him to get up, he's OK or to "act bad even if you're scared." African American men who show vulnerability or weakness in not being able to deal with problems themselves are ridiculed by other Black men and sometimes by Black women (Campbell, 2010; Dueck & Reimer, 2009). African American men tend to be socialized not to ask or seek help or they might be seen as weak or not strong enough to handle their life challenges.

Sanders-Thompson and Alexander (2006) suggested that many African Americans may believe that seeking traditional counseling may be counter-indicative to solving their problem. The American Counseling Association (1998) has identified several barriers African American men encounter when seeking counseling in their report *Counseling African Americans: Counseling African American Men*. These barriers are: problems of aggression and control, cultural alienation, self-esteem, dependency issues, and reluctance to ask for help. Each of these issues ought to be taken into consideration when working with African American males.

Boyd-Franklin (1989) discussed Black men and counseling and has identified several factors that socialize Black men and their beliefs regarding relationships. She suggested that two primary and complicated dynamics shape Black male attitudes. They are sexual prowess and power. Sexual prowess provides opportunity for Black men to exercise that "macho role" and exert their influence and strength on the world. This flexing is in reaction to the impact of racial discrimination, fear of showing weakness, and the need to use their power and leadership in the environment. These ideas are in direct conflict with most spiritual and religious values presented in pastoral counseling which would want them to behave in love. In fact, Wimberly (1997) addressed the notion that many African American men enter pastoral counseling focusing on promoting the traditional male leadership role in their marriage that allows for an expression of power and control, but find that this style is helping each spouse attain their goals within the relationship. He stated that couples engaged in power struggles when husbands attempt to dominate their wives and they fight the effort; this process promotes constant conflict within the relationship. He found that many African American men struggle to find areas in their lives in which they can express their power and control. This action in the relationship may be in reaction to a Black man's lack of power and control outside of the home because of discrimination and racism (e.g. education, employment, etc.). Along the same line, Campbell (2010) discussed the impact of oppression, racism, and discrimination on the psyche of African American men. He also discussed how it impacts how the African American Christian males might view relationships as a result of these factors. He asserts that African American males embrace the "conflict theory of human relation" and see racism as the determining factor in social interactions. In other words, the African American male stresses the importance of providing and being successful even knowing that the problems of racism, oppression, and discrimination frequently prevent him from doing so to his fullest potential. Thus, when he encounters a problem with success, he often looks at the environment as the source of his issues.

An example of how this process works is if a Black man does not receive a promotion he believes he deserves, he may see racism as the reason, especially when he has done everything possible to attain that success. He tends to look toward the conflict issue and what he believes is hindering him, and he may look toward racism, oppression, and discrimination as the social and environment factors that are stopping him from achieving success. This becomes more complicated when he goes home, looks for support and comfort from his wife and partner, and perceives that he is not being supported. This can become a major inhibitor of the relationship and may profoundly influence the communication with and within the couple's relationship and expression of gender roles. Some African American men will often express their power and dominance at this point. These issues can affect the overall relationship, whether the African American man is religious or not. Some African American men use a traditional view of scripture to support their view of dominance, while ignoring the biblical call to live and to relate in love and mutual respect (Campbell, 2010; Wimberly, 1997). Post-modern, Black liberation, and womanist approaches encourage African American men to "'look beyond the surface' and allow the scripture to bear witness to their desire for wholeness and freedom from oppressive structures of all types" (Campbell, 2010, p. 16). At the same time, this calls for giving up the power and sharing that feeds many African American males' ambivalence in seeing the value of marriage. This kind of decision challenges them to redefine gender roles and challenges their traditional religious beliefs as they deal with racism, discrimination, and oppression externally (Campbell, 2010). As a result of many of the economic, social, religious, and financial challenges African American males are encountering in marriage in the United States, many African American males are avoiding marriage and over time their desire to marry has been declining (Allen & Olsen, 2001; Pinderhughes, 2002). Pastoral counselors should recognize these specific challenges faced by Black men. On the one hand, religious Black men are taught to suppress their sexual needs and aggressive impulses, on the other, society routinely denies them masculine-specific outlets for being successful in societal terms (e.g. high earning potential).

African American Women and Pastoral Counseling

African American women have a long history in interacting with the pastor and the Black church and are more likely than Black men to use the church's support services (Love, 2011) and seek help from ministers (Neighbors et al., 1998). Similarly, African American women tend to be more involved in religious practices than African American men (Levin, Taylor, & Chatters, 1995). In fact, according to the 1995 National Survey of Black Americans, 68 percent of Black men pray nearly every day in contrast to 84 percent of Black women (Levin et al., 1995). This appears to show that Black women are even more religious than Black men and have higher levels of religiosity when compared to Black men (Love, 2011). African American women often seek to discuss bereavement, loss, family challenges, and relationship issues, especially their marital relationships (Love, 2011). Consequently, African American women have become more involved in the church leadership and are now becoming the pastors, providing support and services to other African American women as pastoral counselors. This is a recent shift, as traditionally men were pastors and women did not enter this domain. Although most pastors continue to be men, there are a significant number of women now seeking this role.

Although the church has been a place of support and refuge for African American women, even in the church African American women are faced with social challenges and blamed for the problems in the African American community (Townes, 1999). Some of these social challenges include dealing with stereotypes, socialized role confusion, the pressure to marry within their race, and familial and relational stress. The lives of African American women have been affected by racism, sexism, classism, and colorization (Collins, 1991; hooks, 1981). African American women juggle a host of responsibilities. They manage careers, raise children, contribute to society, and take care of extended family members. Religious Black women are often taught to practice "selflessness" and put taking care of themselves last, if at all. As a result, some African American women experience the "Superwoman" syndrome (Wallace, 1978), a cultural legacy that is both a positive and a negative coping strategy, where she does not pay attention to her own mental health needs. As a result of managing these challenges, African American women continue to deal and work with managing negative stereotypes of themselves (e.g. the "angry Black woman") and are identified as being controlling, confrontational, and angry (Campbell, 2010). Many times, African American women then overcompensate and become passive in their relationships.

Another area of challenge for African American women is their use of socialized roles. African American women are taught to take care of the children, get an education, work hard to provide for themselves and the children, and to develop management and leadership qualities that allow them to overcome their personal issues. For many women, the Black church also socializes the value that women should be married to fulfill their spiritual potential as women and their role as members of the Black community. This can be problematic because many Black women struggle to find stable partnerships with Black men; thus, they can sometimes blame themselves and feel spiritually deficient if they remain single for long periods of time—a dynamic that may be seen in both individuals' and couples' counseling. Black women who hold this value may hold onto dysfunctional romantic relationships to fulfill this ideal. It should be noted, however, that marriage as a value is not just socialized within the Black church, but is a traditional value of most Christian churches.

Although many African American women have made an advancement in their personal lives, their relationships with African American men continue to face challenges within and outside of the church. African American women, many of whom are traditional Christians, want to be accommodating to the religious values that they feel are important. However, some women are in conflict because they feel that what they are expected to do, does not lead to their personal growth and development. Consequently, many of them are in a "spiritual quandary" (Wimberly, 1997). How do they develop to their fullest potential while being obedient to what God wants them to do within their romantic relationships? This conflict in perceiving and dealing with their life problems often promotes a lack of trust and suspicion within their relationships, making it full of conflict and mistrust (Campbell, 2010). This dilemma often becomes the conflict with the African American relationship that unsettles the foundation of the relationship and causes continued debate within and outside of the church, and in their religious lives. This is an area that can be explored in pastoral counseling.

Campbell suggested that Black women embrace the moral, religious, and kinship parts of the Black culture in order to cope with their life challenges, while Black men often choose to provide and seek material success and rely on this success to cope with their relationship and personal challenges. For African American women, this connection to kinship makes their struggles and ways of dealing with them very different from African American men. For example, Black women tend to use the support of other women in sharing their feelings and life issues with one another. This is not the typical male coping style. Men are more likely to internalize problems and not seek help from others. These differences in coping may cause a lack of understanding within the couple and can be easily incorporated into counseling with a spiritual focus, as it influences how the couple deals with their problems together.

When couples share a spiritual life together it strengthens their relationship— especially if they hold similar religious/spiritual values. It is not uncommon for men to have been involved with church as young children, depart from the church, and then come back to church when they are involved with a religious woman who attends church regularly. Thus, men who were once disconnected from their religious/spiritual lives often become reconnected through their romantic relationships with their partner.

269

Problematic relational issues within the African American couple are often incentives for African American women to attend church or to get involved in the Black church in an effort to cope with these challenges. African American women are exposed to higher levels of dual-role stress and therefore may use religious coping strategies to assist them in moderating the stress and regulating their mood (Ellison & Taylor, 1996). El-Khoury, Dutton, Goodman, Engel, Belamaric, & Murphy (2004) suggested that prayer helps African American women better cope with racism, discrimination, oppression, relationship, and other personal issues. Many religious women participate in prayer groups or prayer circles in which they call one another each morning and pray together, further illustrating how these women use prayer consistently in their everyday lives. According to El-Khoury et al. (2004, p.389) religion and spirituality help African American women in many ways to:

1 Interrogate and accept their reality
2 Gain the insight and courage to engage in spiritual surrender
3 Confront and transcend limitations
4 Identify and grapple with existential questions and life lessons
5 Recognize purpose and destiny
6 Define character and act within subjectively meaningful moral principles
7 Achieve growth
8 Trust in the viability of transcendent sources of knowledge and communication.

These eight spiritual and religious coping mechanisms help African American women realize that "God is capable of accomplishing great things despite opposing obstacles" (Campbell, 2010, p. 59). This coping and overcoming strategy has helped many religious African American women deal with problematic relationships. This ability to rely on God is a significant strength for African American women. Many religious individuals strongly believe that faith and prayer changes things. However, at the same time, this strength could interfere with the women seeking help from others, especially when problems are severe. This could hinder women from pursuing help from the pastor or from a professional counselor. Mattis (2002) explained that for many African American women, their religious and spiritual beliefs challenges them to create new meanings out of circumstances, and to reflect the idea that God is capable of helping them to overcome all of these life challenges. In fact, their spiritual commitment to intercessory prayer, and reliance on God's and ancestors' direction and support promotes coping and self-reliance. Although seeking help from a pastor with whom one already has a relationship in pastoral counseling would be acceptable, there still remains a stigma in seeking assistance from other professionals (Love, 2011). Decreasing the stigma of attending counseling, and pastoral counseling specifically, for all African American couples could be the key to increased marital satisfaction, decreased divorce, and to helping the couple and individual within the couple to reach their fullest potential.

Implications for Pastoral Counseling and African American Couples

As stated previously, when couples who value religion and/or a spiritual focus share this together, it serves as a protective function in their relationship as they face problems. For these couples, prayer and spiritual guidance from a pastoral counselor are frequent, effective coping tools in times of crisis.

Pastoral counseling, in the forms of pastoral help and support, has always been integrated in the lives of African American couples and the Black church will continue to be important to those couples seeking to deal with their relationship issues and to overcoming the effects of oppression, racism, sexism, and many of life's challenges in their relationships. In order to assist African American couples in managing and resolving issues, pastoral counselors and counselors must also consider the joint impact of external factors along with the religious and spiritual views and involvement of African American couples when counseling them. When working with African American couples, pastors and counselors should be aware of certain treatment issues and most especially the worldview of the couple. Pastoral counselors find that several factors shape the couple's spiritual worldview and suggest exploring the following:

- Family background and influences (of racism, oppression, and discrimination) in the marital context.
- The bi-cultural state of the couple (i.e. involvement with the church) and in the marketplace including the world of work, and any poverty issues that may exist.
- The impact of racial discrimination as a stressor (Wimberly, 1997). Assessing these factors is pivotal in helping the counselor understand the couple's worldview and should allow the counselor to join with the couple in helping them make adjustments (if necessary) that will help them address the problems in their relationship.
- The role religion and spirituality play in the life of the couple, individually and jointly.

Another area in which pastoral counselors and professional counselors can assist African American couples adjust is in how they view themselves in relationships. Many African Americans tend to follow traditional Christian viewpoints of the married relationship and therefore attempt to live within traditional roles even when they may not be satisfying or healthy. As stated previously, a strict adherence to gender roles or the idea that the only socially acceptable romantic relationship is the marital relationship represent such traditional values. When individuals' or couples' life choices differ from these traditional values, they often punish themselves or feel guilt and shame or struggle trying to make adjustments. They may even withdraw from attending religious services while struggling with these issues. While integrating spiritual and religious principles within African American couples, Eurocentric values and romantic relational models (e.g. man as the provider) often directly impact male and female relationships and reinforce feelings of inferiority for both African American males and females. A primary challenge for the counselor is to assist the couple in figuring out how to form balanced relationships and values, which allow for each individual to experience satisfaction and fulfillment. Such a balance might include negotiating and dealing with stereotypes, redefining gender roles, living out their spiritual values, and managing racism, social pressure, financial crises, child(ren), and household duties within their relationship.

Pastoral counseling with a spiritual focus can help couples examine the impact of the value structure on their relationship. Both members can then make the necessary adjustments, take responsibility for their relationship, and become interdependent. This interdependence for couples tends to be at the heart of most religious teachings that view the couple as a unit. Through pastoral counseling both men and women might be encouraged to make necessary changes such as expressing their love and care of their partner within their relationship, as well as negotiating responsibility for the relationship and roles within the family. Pastoral counseling would also include other ways of helping couples adjust (e.g. prayer). Wimberly (1997) states that pastoral counseling for the African American couple is to help create an environment where each family member could find a way in "God's unfolding drama of salvation" by attending to issues that hinder and attending to the external factors that produce stress in the marital relationship. Coles (2010) suggested that pastoral care and counseling can help by doing "soul care" by spiritually healing, sustaining, guiding, and reconciling for the care and cure of the soul of the individual and the community by using biblical narratives and theological principals.

Most Black churches have "couples' ministries" led by married couples, focusing on group support for the congregation's married couples. Black couples typically find this support helpful and safe, as both partners get a chance to bond with other couples.

Clearly, pastoral counseling can help couples focus on their spiritual connectedness as a unit and mutual support system, thereby allowing more role flexibility and still upholding the couple's religious value system by allowing couples the ability to mutually honor one another through the core values of respect and care, understanding and empathy necessary for successful romantic partnerships.

Finally, pastoral counseling has traditionally sought ways to help others in difficulty. Encouraging struggling African American couples to attend counseling has been and will continue to be a supportive service. The guidance and support that can aid African American couples in overcoming their challenges and improving the ways in which they manage their issues can help them strengthen their relationships.

Case Study: Mr. and Mrs. M

Married for 25 years, Mr. M (age 52) and Mrs. M (age 48) were referred to pastoral couples' counseling by a church minister who met with Mrs. M regarding her marriage issues. Mr. M would not go to the church for marriage counseling, as he stopped attending services several years ago. Mr. and Mrs. M are a religious couple who had been experiencing several major life and marital challenges. They have two grown children. When asked about his relationship with his kids, Mr. M reported that he often felt "like a third wheel" in his family, as Mrs. M and the children are very close. He believes that Mrs. M. and the children keep secrets from him. Mrs. M. spends a good deal of her time with their grown children. Mr. M. has always felt excluded and is resentful of this but felt that their religious beliefs kept them together. At one time, Mr. M was a deacon and Mrs. M was a respected member at their church. Their family was very involved in the church.

They report that their problems began when Mr. M wanted to invest in additional properties and consulted Mrs. M. They discussed the decision and came to a mutual agreement; however, Mrs. M. later reneged on her financial contribution to the properties, leaving the family in a financial bind. Instead, she took her contribution and decided to go back to college. Mr. M was upset but dealt with this reality, as he saw his family role as the primary provider. He struggled through the financial burden until he lost his job and became emotionally distant from Mrs. M and God. He soon resigned his deaconship and left the church, although he stayed in the marriage and at home. Two years later, he began an extramarital relationship and began to stay away from their home. Mrs. M. went back to college and Mr. M. continued his affair, staying away from the home for long periods of time. When Mrs. M graduated, four years later, she realized that her husband was not available to her. She turned to God, the pastor, and her friends for support. Recently, Mr. and Mrs. M's house went into foreclosure and she wanted him to make a decision about their relationship so they could decide to separate or move together into an apartment. Mrs. M called for a counselor who was African American and Christian, and who understood Christian values and traditions. Mr. M was willing to come in for counseling if these requirements were met. He reports ending the affair last year.

Assessment of Presenting Problem and Relationship History

For the first session, the couple came to the office separately. The counselor purposed to *join* with the couple, especially with Mr. M, as he was more reluctant to engage in counseling. The counselor wanted to collaborate with Mr. M so he could become fully engaged in counseling, to get full cooperation. Mr. M discussed the presenting problem in the relationship and some of his personal challenges with his career, children, and marriage. Also, having a counselor who was willing to hear his side of the situation was vital as Mrs. M called to schedule the appointment. Mr. M slowly addressed his understanding of the events. He reported he had been unemployed for two years, but had been relying on his rental properties to pay his bills and to support the family. Recently he had not brought in enough money to pay all of the expenses, and turned off the "luxuries" in the home (cable, extra phone line, Internet, etc.). He also maintained a relationship with his children at a distance by talking to them on the phone. He felt that Mrs. M was unsupportive and only focused on her own needs, especially since the children left home. Mrs. M was also asked about the presenting problem. She primarily discussed her feelings of loneliness and her disappointment in not having her husband around to interact with during the evenings and weekends. She admitted that she had made mistakes in the past, including the ones Mr. M discussed in session, with the children and finances, but she was ready to work through the issues and make a decision about their future with God's help. She believed that the problems could be solved if Mr. M "reconnects" with God. She is aware of his past affair.

The counselor began to assess where the couple was in their relationship with God and their religious values and principles, along with the functioning related to the presenting problem. Mr. M reported that he was doing his own thing and he believed that he could not make a decision about his relationship with his wife because he knew that he was not in a good place spiritually. He is not attending church nor praying because he does not believe that God would hear him. He feels spiritually adrift. Mrs. M stated that she was attending church and was meeting periodically with her minister to talk. She has several girlfriends at work and at church to support her. She prays everyday but is feeling alienated from church because her husband and family is not with her. Mrs. M did not want to make a decision about her relationship because she was waiting on her husband, as the Bible directs, to make the decision for the family. She was willing to discuss her viewpoint and feelings about the issues, but would not make a unilateral decision without her husband. She stated that she has learned from her past mistakes. The couple cannot focus on their marital and religious context because Mr. M is in conflict within himself. Spiritually, on the other hand, Mrs. M uses her social and religious support system to cope with her life stressors. She has "submitted" to her husband and has accepted the patriarchic and traditional role in the relationship.

Conceptualization

Mr. M was struggling to redefine himself as he transitioned to another life stage. He defined himself as a "man of God" but felt he'd lost his way spiritually. Mr. M felt more alienated and disconnected from his family, and then, when he lost his job, he believed that he lost all support, even with God. He also lost his role as his family's provider, so he left the church, and detached from everyone and everything for a time to try to cope with these events. He felt that Ms. M was self-absorbed and did not notice him for years. He was invisible (Franklin, 2004), so Mr. M chose to move on emotionally and figure everything out on his own. He seemed to exercise some form of power, influence, and connection by getting into the extramarital relationship but realized that continuing to engage in an affair further distracted him from God and his own values, so he stopped.

Mrs. M reported attempting to manage her transition to a stronger and more decision-making position of growth in her life and marriage. This transition came from dealing with role confusion within her marriage, and personal life stressors. Mrs. M had apparently been socialized to balance her self-reliance with her role as a wife within a traditional Christian marriage when their children were small. She focused on taking care of the children, working hard, and getting an education while being married in a traditional relationship. She felt she deferred to her husband during the early years of their marriage and it was "her turn" to finally focus on herself when the children left home. Mrs. M acknowledged that she may have overcompensated and lost focus in her marriage. While seeking her own growth, she embraced her moral and religious values by staying connected to the church, her prayers and religious values, and sought the support of her friends to help her cope throughout her pursuit of her personal goals. She now fears being alone without the support of her husband, and it is this which is fueling her willingness to forgive and move forward. She wants to be more attentive to her marriage but believes that Mr. M has to make the decision to return or leave the relationship. She has been praying and doing what she can to heal their relationship and is seeking further support from the church.

Specific interventions will focus on problem-solving by determining whether the couple want to separate, divorce, or stay together by addressing their decision-making and the extramarital affair. If they decide to separate or divorce, the counselor will help them through the transition of breaking up and help them resolve some of their relationship conflicts. The couple will have to decide whether to separate or divorce, as well as cope with some of their own personal challenges moving forward. One of the recommendations would be to reconnect with the church and the pastor who referred them to counseling. However, if they want to try to work through their issues, the counselor will help them to form a more balanced relationship and values that allow them to grow into their fullest potential by negotiating decision-making, gender roles to meet their needs, and anticipating the impact of external forces, so they can build trust again. Another area of concentration will be to help them improve their communication and understand the differences in how each of them communicate within their relationship. Finally, the counselor will address, if they desire, how to re-integrate God and the church back into their lives and relationship to reconnect spiritually.

Conclusion

Religion and spirituality have always been important parts of the lives of African Americans and have been the foundational resource that has aided African Americans to overcome and cope with many of life's challenges. For African American couples, religion and spirituality have assisted them to persist through their relationship problems (Brown et al., 2008). The pastor, for African Americans couples, has been the most consulted person when faced with personal or marital problems. However, all pastors have not been trained to treat some of these issues. Pastoral counselors integrate the psychological, spiritual, and religious principles to nurture relationships and help others to cope with their life or marital challenges (Frazier, 1996; Neighbors et al., 1998). Pastoral counselors and professional counselors are competent in helping individuals and couples manage their psychological, spiritual, and relationship issues. For African American couples, these new competencies for pastoral counselors provide the opportunity to seek counseling services and address some of their unique and complicated relationship issues.

By helping African American couples consider their religious and spiritual viewpoints, as it relates to their individual and couple identity, pastoral counseling can help strengthen couples' relationships through their faith. Spiritually focused counseling incorporates an important identity variable (religion) and coping strategy (prayer) in helping them resolve their conflicts. Finally, pastoral counseling provides an untapped resource that could help to redefine how African American relationships are defined, and make the necessary changes to grow in a fast changing and evolving world.

References

Allen, W., & Olson, D. (2001). Five types of African American marriages. *Journal of Marital and Family Therapy*, 27, 3 (July), 301–314.

American Association of Pastoral Counseling (2011). *What is Pastoral counseling.* Retrieved from http://www.pastoral-counseling.org/asp/page.asp?ID=1003.

American Counseling Association (1998). *Counseling African Americans: Counseling African American men.* Retrieved September 20, 2003, from http//aca.convio.net/site/News2?page=NewsArticle&id=7164&news_ctrl=1023.

Boyd-Franklin, N. (1989). *Black families in therapy; A multisystems approach.* New York. The Guilford Press.

Brown, E., Orbuch, T., & Bauermeister, J. (2008). Religiosity and marital stability among Black American and White American couples. *Family Relations*, 57, 2 (April), 186–197.

Brown, E. R., Ojeda, V. D., Wyn, R., & Levan, R. (2000). *Racial and ethnic disparities in access to health insurance and health care.* Los Angles: UCLA Center for Health Policy Research and the Henry J. Kaiser Family Foundation.

Campbell, J. W. (2010). *Assessing the views of African-American men and women on the impact of racism on African-American marriages: A communications model that promotes mutuality.* Dissertation Abstract. UMI Microform. Drew University.

Carter, R. T. (1995). *The influence of race and racial identity in psychotherapy: Toward a racially inclusive model.* New York: Wiley.

Chatters, L. M., Taylor, R. J., Bullard, K. M., & Jackson, J. S. (2008). Spirituality and subjective religiosity among African American, Black Caribbeans, and Whites. *Journal for Scientific Study of Religion*, 47, 725–737.

Coles, A. H. (2010). What makes care Pastoral? *Pastoral Psychology*, 59, 711–723. Springer Science Business. Published online: July 9, 2010.

Collins, P. H. (1991). *Black feminist thought.* Boston, MA: Unwin Hyman.

Crabtree, S., & Pelham, B. (2009). *What Alabamians and Iranians have in common: A global perspective on Americans' religiosity offers a few surprises.* Retrieved from http://www.gallup.com/poll/114211/Alabamians-Iranians-Common.aspx.

Dueck, A., & Reimer, K. (2009). *A peaceable psychology: Christian therapy in a world of many cultures.* Grand Rapids, MI: Brazos.

El-Khoury, M. Y., Dutton, M. A., Goodman, L. A., Engel, L., Belamaric, R. J., & Murphy, M. (2004). Ethnic differences in battered women's formal help-seeking strategies: A focus on health, mental health, and spirituality. *Cultural Diversity and Ethnic Minority Psychology*, 10 (4), 383–393.

Ellison, C. G., & Taylor, R. J. (1996). Turning to prayer: Social and situational antecedents of religious coping among African Americans. *Review of Religious Research*, 38(2), 111–131.

Franklin, A. J. (2004). *From brotherhood to manhood: How Black men rescue their relationships and dreams from the invisibility syndrome.* New York: John Wiley and Son.

Frazier, F. (1996). *Negro church in America.* New York: Schocken.

Gallup, G. J. (2001). Americans more religious now than ten years ago, but less so than in 1950s and 1960s. *Gallup News Service*, March 29, 2001. Retrieved October 17, 2001, from http://www.gallup.com/poll/releases/pr010329.asp.

Gayles, T.A., Alston, R. J., & Staten, D. (2005). *Understanding mental illness among African American males: Risk factors and treatment parameters.* In D. A. Harley & J. M. Dillard (Eds.),

WALLER

Contemporary mental health issues among African American (pp. 49–59). Alexandria, VA: American Counseling Association.

Guzman ,J. P. (1946). *Negro year book: A review of events affecting Negro life, 1941-1946.* Tuskegee, AL: Department of Records and Research of the Tuskegee Institute.

Harley, D. A., & Dillard, J. M. (2005). *Contemporary mental health among African Americans.* Alexandria, VA: American Counseling Association.

hooks, b. (1981). *Ain't I a woman: Black women and feminism.* Boston, MA: South End Press.

Jackson, J. S., McCullough, W. R., Gurin, G., & Broman, C. L. (1991). Race identity. In J. S. Jackson (Ed.), *Life in Black America* (pp. 238–253). Thousand Oaks, CA: Sage.

Knox, D. H. (1985). Spirituality: A tool in the assessment and treatment of black alcoholics and their families. *Alcoholism Treatment Quarterly,* 2 (3/4), 31–44.

Levin, J. S., Taylor, R. J., & Chatters, L. M. (1995). A multidimensional measure of religious involvement for African Americans. *The Sociological Quarterly,* 36, 157–173.

Lincoln, C.E., & Mamiya, L.H. (1990). *The Black church in the African American experience.* Durham, NC: Duke University Press.

Love, D. R. (2011). *The role of the black church in fulfilling the therapeutic needs of the African American population: A review of the literature.* Dissertation Abstracts, 143 pages.

Mattis, J. (2002). Religion and spirituality in the meaning-making and coping experiences of African American women: A qualitative analysis. *Psychology of Women Quarterly,* 26, 309–321.

Neighbors, H. W., Musick, M. A., & Williams, D. R. (1998). The African American minister as the source of help for serious personal crises: Bridge or barriers to mental health care? *Health Education and Behavior,* 25, 759–777.

Nobles, W. W. (1980). African philosophy: Foundations for Black psychology. In R. L. Jones (Ed.), *Black psychology* (2nd ed.) (pp. 23–36). New York: Harper & Row.

Paul, P. (2005). "With God as my shrink". *Psychology Today.* Retrieved September 9, 2010, http://www.psychologytoday.com/articles/200505/god-my-shrink.

Pew Forum (2009). A religious portrait of African Americans. Retrieved January 30, 2009, from http://pewforum.org/A-Religious-Portrait-of –African-Americans.aspx.

Pinderhughes, E. (2002). African American marriage in the 20th century. *Family Process,* 41, 2 (Summer), 269–282.

Pinn, A. H., & Pinn, A. B. (2002). *Fortress introduction to Black church history.* Minneapolis, MN: Fortress.

Powers, R. (2005). Counseling and spirituality: A historical review. *Counseling and Values,* April, 217–225.

Richardson, B., & June, L. (2006). Developing effective partnership in order to utilize and maximize the resources of the African American church: Strategies and tools for counseling professionals. In C. C. Lee (Ed.), *Multicultural issues in counseling: New approaches to diversity* (pp. 113–123). Alexandria, VA: American Counseling Association.

Sanders-Thompson, V., & Alexander, H. (2006). Therapists' race and African American clients' reactions to therapy. *Psychotherapy: Theory, Research, Practice, Training,* 43 (1), 99–110.

Shafranske, E., & Maloney, H. (1990). Clinical psychologists' religious and spiritual orientations and their practice of psychotherapy. *Psychotherapy,* 27, 72–78.

Shafranske, E. P., & Gorsuch, R. L. (1984). Factors associated with the perception of spirituality in psychotherapy. *Journal of Transpersonal Psychology,* 16, 231–241.

Snowden, L., & Cheung, F. (1990). Use of inpatient mental health services by members of ethnic minority groups. *American Psychologist*, 45 (3), 347–355. Berkeley, CA: School of Social Welfare, University of California.

Sue, D. W., & Sue, D. (2008). *Counseling the culturally diverse: Theory and practice*. New York: Wiley.

Taylor, R. J., & Chatters, L. M. (1991). Importance of religion and spirituality in lives of African Americans, Caribbean Blacks and non-Hispanics Whites. *The Journal of Negro Education*, 79, 3 (Summer), 280.

Taylor, R. J., & Chatters, L. M. (2010). Importance of religion and spirituality in the lives of African Americans, Caribbean blacks and non-Hispanic whites: Findings from the National Survey of American Life. *Journal of African American Studies*, 79 (3), 280–294.

Taylor, R. J., Ellison, C. G., Chatters, L. M., Levin, J. S., & Lincoln, K. D. (2000). Mental health services in faith communities: The role of clergy in black churches. *Social Work*, 45, 1 (January), 73–87.

Townes, E. M. (1999). *Troubling in my soul: Womenist perspectives on evil and suffering*. New York: Ordis Books.

Veroff, J., Douvan, B., & Kulka, R. (1981). *The inner American: A self portrait from 1957 to 1976*. New York: Basic.

Walker, D., Gorsch, R. L., & Siang-Yang, T. (2004). Therapists' integration of religion and spirituality in counseling: A meta-analysis. *Counseling and Values*, 49, 1 (October), 69–80.

Wallace, M. (1978). *Black macho and the myth of superwoman*. New York: Dial.

Wardell, J. P. (1995). *Directory of African American religious bodies: A compendium by the Howard University School of Divinity*. Washington, DC: Howard University Press.

Williams, D., Griffith, E., Young, J., Collins, C., & Dodson, J. (1999). Structure and provision of services in Black churches in New Haven. *Cultural Diversity and Ethnic Minority Psychology*, 5 (2), 118–133.

Wimberly, E. (1997). *Counseling African American marriage and family*. Louisville, KY: Westminster John Knox Press.

11

CONCLUSION

Katherine M. Helm, Anton M. Lewis, and Jon Carlson

As a Black married couple in the United States both my wife and I (Lewis & Helm) have become increasingly aware of what an endangered species we seem to have become. We perhaps know of two other married Black couples with children in our immediate social circle. This in itself is an assault on Black marriage and relationships. This is a quandary, as we live in a large Black metropolis and have myriad Black professional friends, a number of which are in committed relationships but are not married. I ask individuals reading this book to ask themselves "how many Black couples do you know?" and implore them to seek an answer in their own experience.

This book has extensively reviewed many of the contextual factors specific to African Americans that stress their romantic unions. Strong romantic relationships, perhaps marriage, perhaps other types of committed partnerships, strengthen Black families. Parham (see expert interview, p. 229) emphasizes that the Black family is the most enduring institution in the Black community and Rowe and Lyons-Rowe (see expert interview, p. 193) state that Black marriage (couple-ships) are larger than the two individuals in them, and represents African values of community and collectivism—the "we" over the "I." This view of marriage is specific to people of African descent and should be incorporated into counseling with these couples.

We make an impassioned plea for all readers to recognize the structural fissure currently taking place in Black marriage/committed partnerships and understand that modern society has transformed Black marriage into an atypical phenomenon, as it is now not a commonplace experience. We also argue that Black marriage is not the only type of successful family structure. Healthy couples' unions—married or not—are what strengthen Black families and communities. Clinicians doing counseling with Black couples should, as we have suggested throughout this book, understand the myriad contextual stressors constantly facing these couples but also understand their significant strengths. With such little representation of successful, happy Black couples in the popular media (except the Obamas and other limited examples), the authenticity of Black marriage and Black unions are consistently undermined. This lends credence to racialized tropes underlining the pathos of Black relationships. At a hidden level a tacit acceptance exists in society of maladjusted Black couples, as Black families are systemically locked out of wedlock; a situation now considered the norm. Creating, supporting, and understanding the strengths of

Black couples, while understanding the multiple contextual factors impacting these unions, is paramount in being able to provide culturally sensitive counseling.

We provide the following suggestions to augment what has already been discussed.

1   As Parham suggested in his interview, our current training models are not providing counselors-in-training with the knowledge and skills necessary to treat Black couples. He notes that continuing education for professional counselors presents culturally sterile training models. This is simply unacceptable. Even though all students take a class in multicultural issues, rarely if ever does this class extend to providing adequate knowledge regarding culturally sensitive treatment to specific populations, given that each oppressed group exists differently in the United States, based on culture, length of time in the United States, history, and cultural stressors (e.g. racism).

2   There is clearly not enough literature and research specific to clinical work with Black couples. Much more is needed so the diverse experiences of Black couples are represented in the couples' discourse (e.g. the impact of geographic region, education, cultural background [African American, Haitian American, etc.], SES, years together [married for 30 versus cohabitating for 5], and the impact of children and multi-fertility/step-parents on couples' relationships).

3   All culturally competent work requires that clinicians honestly and consistently introspect about their own values, biases, judgments, and internalized stereotypes. This is true regardless of clinicians' racial/ethnic backgrounds. Too often we fail to do this after our graduate multicultural course ends. The ability to acknowledge and work on our own biases carries over into the sensitive treatment of those struggling couples who come to us in crisis seeking our assistance in healing their relationships.

4   Finally, as Bethea and Allen discuss in Chapter 2, counseling for African descent couples is an act of healing. The role of the healer is to become a part of the couple's relationship and the greater community, as problems are centered at the community level, not at the level of the individual. Healers work in collaboration with couples. They are not experts above the process— they are active participants within the process. True healing cannot occur if the healer does not understand the pain or its genesis.

This book illuminates the many challenges Black couples face, when they present for counseling. Understanding contextual factors, strengths-based approaches, kinship networks, spiritually focused counseling, cultural competencies, and healing interventions have all been discussed as critical parts of successful counseling for African American couples. As our expert interviewees have highlighted, strong Black couples' beget strong Black families; therefore effective therapy is larger than the couple themselves—in essence, effective therapy is a community-strengthening intervention. Sensitive counseling can be a powerful tool in fortifying couples. This book is an important tool in helping clinicians understand how to provide such treatment.

COUPLES INTERVIEWS

Twelve married Black couples were interviewed for this book. Due to space limitations, we are unable to include all of the interviews; however, the interview data is summarized. Couples were between the ages of 30 and 76. They had been married between 1 and 40 years. For most couples (but not all), this is their first marriage. Most have children (most within their marital relationship; three within blended families; three had none at all). Almost all couples had college degrees or higher levels of education. We know that these couples are not necessarily representative of all or even most Black couples.

Each couple gave brief biographies of how they met and how long they had been married. Sincere thanks to all couples who gave us their time and thoughtful window into their relationship. Clearly, the voice of strength comes through these couples regarding their relationships.

- *If married, how did you decide to marry?*

    - We were in love
    - We wanted children
    - We always wanted to be married
    - We dated for years, so this was the next logical step
    - We wanted a stable future together
    - Compatible goals
    - Just decided to "do it"
    - Our friendship turned very deep—marriage was the next level
    - God sent me my partner
    - Didn't want to "just play house"
    - It seemed the perfect time

- *If you have children, how did children change your relationship? If you have a blended relationship (one in which you have children from a previous relationship, how did this impact your relationship?).*

    - We don't have children but are close to our nieces and nephews

– Our children grounded us and brought us closer together
– We have a blended family; sometimes my spouse wanted to "re-parent" my 13-year-old daughter. This caused problems early on, but we were able to work through them
– We struggled with differences in parenting styles
– When you have children, they become focus of everything
– Made us work together
– Our sense of family was magnified
– Made our relationship stronger but also made things more complicated
– Changed our roles and responsibilities as our kids become our focus
– Taught us about selflessness
– Children enhanced our relationship
– We had some early feelings of inadequacy regarding our parenting but worked together through them
– Changes the way you relate to one another, as they come first
– Keeps us on our toes and makes our lives more fulfilling

• *Talk about some of your developmental milestones as a couple and how it impacted your relationship (e.g. birth of a child; death of a parent; marriage, etc.).*

– Purchasing a home together and starting a business together—very stressful because we had different ways of doing things. Had to learn to accept each other's preferences and needs. Taught us a lot and taught us how to work together and trust each other
– Aging (mid-life crisis)—my wife supported me through this. I felt, like many Black men do, suppressed by society and unable to progress. My wife supported my dreams which made all the difference
– The death of my husband's father and my father's illness. It strained our relationship and emotional resources, making us less able to be there for one another and take care of our family's needs
– Getting married, as it was tough to learn to negotiate/compromise
– The death of our parents (as we were so close to them and relied upon their support); the birth of our children— because we had to put them first
– Career promotions and geographical distance between us—we learned to trust one another
– Several familial deaths (aunts, older brother, etc.). Becoming grandparents restored our joy
– The birth of our children forced us to learn to play to each other's strengths. We experienced a role-reversal in that my husband had to give up his full-time job to stay with the kids which taught us a lot
– The death of our parents, having jobs in different states, miscarriage and fertility problems, birth of our grandchildren, retirement, and seeking

couples' counseling due to my husband's problems with alcohol—we nearly divorced at this point. All of these milestones taught us how to "tough it out" and stay together but also that we were capable of change and loving one another through very difficult times

- Preparing ourselves for marriage as we needed to learn to compromise and consider one another's needs
- The differences in our ages (14 years) is sometimes difficult to deal with as my husband has been single for so long. Our work with this is ongoing but it has taught us the power of negotiation
- We are still working our way through developmental milestones (e.g. learning to do things together as opposed to acting as two single people. We are learning how to make joint decisions. Also, the birth of our child one year after we married and the death of my husband's mother two years after we were married. Together these were overwhelming experiences, although because we worked together, we now have a closer bond
- Graduating from college, as we were at two different universities. Because much of our 10-year relationship has been long distance, it has forced us to have good communication skills, develop a sense of independence, and to trust one another and our relationship

- *What specific coping strategies do you use to get through tough times?*

  - Couples counseling and talking to family members
  - Learning how to "let stuff go" and that you don't always have to have the last word; learning how to listen and that we won't always agree but to respect each other's opinions
  - Having couples' counseling before we got married to clarify things
  - Talking to family members, leaning on scriptures and prayer
  - Working together to find solutions to problems
  - Using our faith in God, patience, and understanding; talking to each other and not at each other
  - Learning not to take ourselves too seriously and recognize that most disagreements are minor; utilizing a Christian framework to reconcile and understand our challenges and disappointments; never going to bed angry at one another
  - Communication is key; we try to talk about everything and give one another an opportunity to deal with what the issue might be; we also do not "think" for the other person. We let one another speak, even if what they are saying hurts
  - We went back to church together; premarital counseling through the church helped us identify our similarities/differences; we give each other space; we find the things we love to do together (e.g. traveling)
  - We try to stay positive and not stress too much

- *How involved are your extended families in your lives?*

  - We are very close to my sisters and brothers
  - Both of our extended families are supportive of our relationship; they bring us love and support: we both understand the importance of extended family
  - We talk to members of our extended family every day
  - Very. We also take care of my elderly mother and include her in family activities
  - We have a very close-knit family and attend annual family reunions
  - Somewhat involved; at one point they were too involved so now we limit it
  - Mostly just around holidays, not in our everyday lives
  - They are not involved in our relationship; some members are deceased and others live far away
  - We spend time with both sides but don't let them impact our judgment or decisions for our family. We keep our issues between ourselves and God
  - Mine is more involved than my husband's but he has a good relationship with my extended family. They accept each other
  - They are very involved but we are careful not to share too much, lest they negatively judge our spouse long after whatever fight we had vented to them about is over

- *What specific advice would you have for other African American couples contemplating marriage or a long-term commitment to one another?*

  - First you have to decide if what you have is worth fighting for; the grass will always be greener on the other side but you have to remember the reasons you married this person in the first place, only then does it get easier. They day you realize it's forever, you can mellow out and live your better life. Trust is critical.
  - It's great to have both families' support—but not necessary. Don't let negativity from others divide you. Make your relationship first in your lives and enjoy one another; live your life with family in mind at all times
  - Get counseling before and during marriage; each partner should have a mentor; recognize one another's value systems and discuss real expectations for long-term commitment and success of your relationship
  - Get to know one another well first. Talk often and learn to compromise but also say what you believe in; be friends before you are lovers; don't try to change anyone, love them for who they are
  - Make sure that you share the same values and are equally yoked (similar levels of education, an appreciation of family); make sure that your love is beyond attraction

- Communication and faithfulness are key; stick to one topic during disagreements and know you can table the topic if it becomes too emotional; reserve a date night
- Communicate with one another and keep your partner's well-being as your first priority. Understand the different stages of marriage and always remember that you are in the relationship with that one person, so only he/she knows his/her needs/wants; also know that not everyone is excited about your relationship—so steer clear of those haters; surround your relationship with likeminded couples
- Keep God and church at the center of your lives; get involved with your church's couples' ministry; give your husband a "man cave"
- Have perseverance and keep checking in with your partner; keep communicating and showing them you love them; know that it's a process; be open to one another's feelings; know that it's hard work but so worth the effort; trust one another and be open and honest

• *Does religion or spirituality play a role in your relationship? Explain what this means to you as a couple and how important it is to you both.*

- We are both spiritual but she is more religious; don't force religion onto anyone. She goes to church, and I go when I want—this works for us
- It helps us deal with our issues and find our unique purpose [as a couple] as we believe that our relationship was created in heaven; we keep a spiritual focus at the center of our lives
- Helps us serve as an example to others as we see our marriage as having a community purpose as well as an individual one
- We are strong believers in God, although we do not attend church every week; we keep Christ in our hearts and everyday lives; Christ is there in good times and bad
- Christianity is the overarching bond that unites us; it's the framework that we utilize in all aspects of our lives
- It's the guide to everything we do
- We try to live by "the word" and our Christian faith gives us the strength to keep trying
- We put God first, and everything else follows. It's very, very important. We also pray together a lot
- We use our spirituality to serve as our guide. It allows us to forgive one another; it allows us to reap the rewards of good living as you reap what you sow. Good comes back to you; spirituality helps us through the hard times—knowing this too shall pass
- It is at the core of all our values; she attends church regularly and I do inconsistently
- We are not very religious but we are spiritual and believe in God. We try to follow some values and be moral and honest

- *What do you see as the advantages/disadvantages of marriage?*

  – Having a partner for life; having someone to lean on; you can't always have your way and compromise is miserable and not easy. Nobody likes it
  – Being able to share life's experiences with someone you love; having a trusting bond with someone is very special; can't always get what you want or buy what you want
  – Friendship, companionship, someone I can show myself to fully; not always having what you want
  – Being with your soul mate and sharing a wonderful life with that person— if you pick the right one; having someone there who understands your moods and what you are going through; having someone to grow old with; hurts when you grow apart; always a risk of divorce
  – A sense of oneness
  – Growing as a couple, improving each other, and combining finances; agreements, compromise, and combining finances are disadvantages
  – Security, having someone who has your best interests in mind; it's never just about you
  – Learning to share with someone you love makes you less self-centered; planning the future with a significant other; learning how to trust; you can't have all your personal wants, you must commit to one person and can't always grow individually at the rate you did prior to your relationship; involves some self-sacrifice
  – Marriage builds character
  – Means you're not lonely anymore; you can share good times and bad with them and memories; get to gain extended family through your spouse; you take this person literally "for better or for worse"

- *What challenges have you had as a couple? How did you face them and what kept you together?*

  – We are both strong willed and want our way—we struggled with this over the years. We work on this through compromise and communication; financial challenges were tough and we learned not to take it out on each other; loving each other keeps us together
  – Both of our families have required our financial assistance which was hard on us. We have experienced intimacy, financial, and communication issues; counseling and re-evaluating our relationship has kept us together; using couples' counseling and prayer has helped
  – Our challenges have been dealing with our adult children and grandchildren; we worked this out by talking with one another and presenting a united front; we help our children but don't enable them; caring for my elderly mom has also been a challenge

– Extensive travel early in our relationship was a challenge, especially after we had a baby; we worked to balance our responsibilities and made it a point to spend quality time together as a family and relied upon our Christian faith

– Having arguments in disrespectful ways—we learned to change our behavior

– Managing career and family demands—we stopped spending time together which caused relational strain; we learned to communicate better and reserve a date night and developed other ways of spending time together that worked for us in new phases of our lives

– My wife's breast cancer challenged us—I learned to be supportive and she to accept my support; she had to deal with feeling comfortable with herself and changing body image; we are able to laugh and talk to each other and not take everything so seriously when talking about personal issues

• *What are the strengths of your relationship?*

– We have always been best friends and share a drive for success and travel; we always take care of one another

– [we have] true love and sacrifice for this union; we are open to looking at the other person's side of things but also recognize one another's weaknesses; we have a willingness to step in and step up without question which strengthens the partnership as a whole

– [Mutual] spiritual commitment to our faith; common morals, values, and a willingness to compromise; believing that our marriage has a purpose to others; long-term love and commitment

– Patience, commitment, understanding the fact that we love one another

– Love and respect for one another; sharing ideas and pursuing common/ compatible goals; raising a family together

– Doing things together

– We have minimum expectations for our relationship including: love God and love me; we play off each other's strengths and weaknesses—my weaknesses are his strengths and vice versa; our desire to continuously learn from one another

– After 40 years, we still love and want one another very much; we support each other's goals and strengths: our strong belief in God and faith are strengths; despite all we've been through, we still have each other's back

– Appreciation for who we are as individuals and accepting one another's differences

- *How open would you be to couples' counseling? Would the counselor's racial background matter? Do you have a preference for a Black therapist? Specific gender?*

  – We've been to couples' counseling; racial background is not important but my wife would prefer a female since our last counselor was male, she thinks there may have been some bias
  – Got to be Black to understand Black!
  – We are open to couples' counseling; what would matter to us the most is someone who agreed with us spiritually and shares our faith; [male partner]—gender doesn't matter but there are certain things a woman wouldn't understand such as the roles, goals, and direction for a man
  – The gender or racial background isn't important but we would prefer an African American counselor
  – Experience and competence is the main criteria although a Black therapist might have better insight into the struggles of African American life. Gender doesn't matter
  – We have a slight preference for a Black counselor. Gender doesn't matter
  – We have been; we would strongly prefer a Black therapist
  – Be experienced, knowledgeable, sincere, and honest—not opinionated and judgmental
  – They should themselves have experienced marriage—either now or in the past; we'd prefer a Black therapist but we would go to a non-Black therapist
  – We would be hesitant as we aren't comfortable sharing our personal business; we would want a Black therapist
  – We'd be open to it after trying to work through things ourselves; gender doesn't matter to my wife, but it does to me [husband] I think that an African American therapist would have more insight and understand the way we were brought up; we would want someone we are comfortable with—someone who does not judge you and can really help

- *What qualities would be important to you in a couples' counselor?*

  – Someone with personal relationship experience themselves
  – To listen attentively and effectively; someone who could help us regain our balance
  – Objective, professional, experienced
  – Someone not so quick to solve the problem or offer solutions
  – Mature, competent, sincere, empathetic, experience, knowledgeable
  – Argument management, effective communicator
  – Someone who is/was married themselves
  – Educated, openness
  – A Christian therapist

- Have several years of experience in the field
- Be warm and provide a comfortable environment
- A smart person with a sense of humor, someone who really understands, someone who doesn't just butt in but helps you express your feelings better; someone who helps you negotiate

- *What have you each learned about being in a relationship that makes your relationship successful? What have you learned as a couple?*

  - Compromise is key to a successful relationship; learn to choose your battles; respect one another's opinions even if you don't agree
  - Respect one another for who they are and what's important to them; know that your choices determine the success/failure of your relationship; be open to listening to what's really being said
  - That marriage is a partnership; learn what "speaks" to one another; understand your roles
  - Love each other no matter what; understand one another's personal needs and give each person space when needed; like one another; have a mutual investment of your lives together; fight for the relationship; we believe that all things are possible through God
  - Share ideas and pursue goals together; spend quality time together; share joys and successes with family which keeps you closely bonded together
  - Keep the lines of communication open; we learned that we can't go into business together but can support one another's individual businesses
  - Selflessness; we continually learn from one another how to be productive spouses, parents, and well-rounded people as it relates to our personal/ professional lives
  - You must give and take! It's the two of you against the world
  - Put each other first; be able to talk about anything and everything
  - Patience and the ability to share feelings is important; be agreeable and learn how to adjust to the changes marriage brings; accept your partner's input
  - Don't take each other for granted; it takes hard work and commitment; have weekly family time which allows us to stay connected to each other
  - I have learned to be more giving and compromising towards my spouse; respect one another's feelings; understand that marriage is always a work in progress; have common interests but interests outside of one another; learn to be caring with one another

- *What specific advice do you have for counselors working with Black couples?*

  - We don't see that being a Black couple is any different than being a White couple

- Find a way to show couples how important it is to work together to be successful
- Recognize preconceptions exist and address them up front
- Allow the couple to talk; be patient and understanding
- Remain cognizant of the impact of the Black experience on Black individuals and couples; be knowledgeable of the reasons for the predominance of single Black female heads of households; know the main causes of divorce amongst Black couples; counselors cannot overlook the issue of race when seeking therapeutic interventions for Black couples
- Understand the couple's background and provide the pros/cons of counseling
- Don't treat them as a "Black couple" treat them as a couple first, because no two Black or any other couples are the same
- It's important to be honest and use both your experience and book knowledge to evaluate and treat the couple
- Understand a lot of Black people's issues still stems from slavery days. So many African American people try so hard to break the cycle of discrimination and oppression but yet somewhere it creeps back up. It's deeper than we think and may not ever go away, so any counselor needs to know/understand where we as Black people come from
- Be sensitive to family values, respect each partner's opinion, get the male involved; be sensitive to the fact that men see things differently; there isn't a right/wrong way to do things; emphasize that the partner is not the enemy; know that there is a lot of pressure in Black families—not just in couples themselves (e.g. situations with other family members) [impacting the couple]; technology has changed the Black family as now we have to work to stay together and connected
- Within Black couples, each person may have been raised differently and blending values take time
- Be patient and listen—don't judge us by the societal stereotypes of Black men and women; counselors should not give up on couples; need to understand what African Americans go through, as this influences their problems.

INDEX

Campbell, J.W. 265, 267, 268, 269, 270
Caribbean immigrants 124–5
case studies: couples therapy 222–5;
culturally sensitive guidelines
248–52; intimacy threats 106–9;
intercultural couples 142–5; lesbians
and gay men 164–6; male–female
romantic relationships 78–81; NTU
47–50; pastoral counseling 273–6
Cazenave, N.A. 34, 37
Cerbone, A. 152
challenges for couples 18, 117, 193,
194, 230, 287–8
Chapman, A. B. 10, 182; expert
interview 117–19
children 282–3
church, Black 256–8
clinical issues: communication 133–5;
cultural values 129–30; familial
roles 130–3; gender roles 130–3;
intercultural couples 129–34
Cobia, D.C. 69, 89
cognitive-behavioral couple therapies
201–3
collectivistic cultures 133–4
Collins, P.H. 25, 33, 98, 106
Combs, G. 211
communication issues 133–5
community-based educational programs
218–21
*The Consequences of Marriage for African
Americans: A Comprehensive Literature
Review* (Blackman) 5–6
control issues 75–6
Conversations in Marriage (CIM)
219–20
Cook, D.A. 242, 245
cool pose 69, 72, 92
coping strategies 74, 132–3, 269, 270,
284
counseling paradigms 44–6
counselor–couple matches 238–42
counselors: couples interviews 289–91;
cultural awareness 242–4; expert
interview 19, 194, 229;
couple relationships: pastoral counseling
263–5; sexual stereotypes 31–2;
therapy 289 *see also* treatment
strategies and techniques
couple–therapist relationship 238–42
couples' clinicians 8–9
couples interviews 282–91

Cowdery, R.S. 73, 74
Crockett, L.J. 66
Crohn, J. 138
Crook, T.M. 69, 89
cross-cultural communication skills
139–41
cultural assessments 138
cultural characteristics 39
cultural continuity 126–7
cultural differences 128, 137–9
cultural healing systems 39
cultural mistrust 235–6
The Cultural Mistrust Inventory (CMI)
(Terrell, Terrell, and Nickerson)
186
cultural traditions 21–3
cultural values 129–30
culturally centered therapy 216–18
culturally competent assessment
177–84; children 183–4; clinical
interview 180–2; personal baggage
182
culturally consistent paradigm 41–2
culturally sensitive assessment 173–
91; assessment process 174–5;
presenting issues 175–7; strategies
177–84
culturally sensitive guidelines 234–52;
assessment 173–91; case study
248–52; counselors 242–4; cultural
mistrust 235–6; presenting issues
236–7; race 244–5; resistance
235–6; specific strategies 246–7;
therapist–couple matches 238–42;
treatment implications 247–8

Davis, A. D. 23
Davis, J.E. 35, 99
de Shazer, S. 213
definitions: Black/African American
124; intercultural Black couples
124–8
Dickson, L. 36, 51, 71, 72
discrimination 37–8
distrust in relationships 100–1, 157
Dixon, P. 63, 64
Doherty, W.J. 247, 248
Dominicans 135
Dressler 186
Dunham, S. 137, 141, 218, 252
Dunn, S. 29
Dzobo 220

INDEX

White Racial Identity Development
  (WRLD) 239
Whitfield, K.E. 77
Willis, J. T. 30–1, 32
Wilson, L.L. 243, 246–7
Wilson, W.J. 28, 34
Wimberly, E. 259, 260, 265, 266, 268
Wolfe, D.A. 64, 65, 70

women 28–30, 272; education 34–5,
  77; modeling 71–2; and pastoral
  counseling 268–70; sexuality
  68–9, 98–100; stereotypes 158;
  Strong Black Woman Syndrome (SBW)
  30, 91–2

Zalaquett, C.P. 180–1

298

Made in the USA
Las Vegas, NV
19 September 2021